ARDENT SPIRITS

REYNOLDS PRICE

ARDENT SPIRITS

LEAVING HOME, COMING BACK

SCRIBNER

NEW YORK   LONDON   TORONTO   SYDNEY

SCRIBNER
A Division of Simon & Schuster, Inc.
1230 Avenue of the Americas
New York, NY 10020

First Scribner hardcover edition May 2009

SCRIBNER and design are registered trademarks of The Gale Group, Inc.,
used under license by Simon & Schuster, Inc., the publisher of this work.

For information about special discounts for bulk purchases,
please contact Simon & Schuster Special Sales at 1-866-506-1949
or business@simonandschuster.com.

The Simon & Schuster Speakers Bureau can bring authors to your live event. For
more information or to book an event contact the Simon & Schuster Speakers Bureau
at 1-866-248-3049 or visit our website at www.simonspeakers.com.

Manufactured in the United States of America

1   3   5   7   9   10   8   6   4   2

Library of Congress Control Number: 2009002376

ISBN-13: 978-0-7432-9189-7
ISBN-10: 0-7432-9189-1

PHOTO CREDITS

p. 50: Photograph by Betmann, courtesy of Corbis; p. 96: Photograph by
Walter Stoneman, courtesy of National Portrait Gallery, London; p. 136:
Photograph by Erich Auerbach, courtesy of Getty Images Houston Archive; p. 156:
Photograph by John Menapace, courtesy of Duke University Press; p. 265: Photograph
by Jeremy Grayson, courtesy of Spectrum Color Library/ HIP/ The Image Works;
p. 284: Photograph by Terence Spencer, courtesy of Getty Collection, Time & Life
Pictures; p. 344: Photograph by Imogen Cunningham,
courtesy of The Imogen Cunningham Trust

FOR

PAUL FLESCHNER

ARDENT SPIRITS

A FOREWORD

T WO YEARS AFTER I became paraplegic in the wake of
spinal cancer, I was living with severe pain down my back and legs—
the steady result of surgical scarring and radiation burns. When drugs
proved all but useless, I underwent training in self-hypnosis at Duke
Medical Center in the hope of some degree of relief. Soon after I
completed that eventually unsuccessful training, my mind began to
yield (as if in reward for the difficulties of the past) great stretches of
memory.

It was memory that returned to me an array of figures from my early
life—parents, aunts, cousins, and teachers who'd guided me into
manhood with selfless care. The reality of the memories soon compelled me to begin recording them, and that work gave me more pleasure than any of my prior efforts. So in 1989 I published the resulting
volume, *Clear Pictures.* It spans the years from my birth, as the Great
Depression sank to its nadir, through my father's death in 1954 when
I was twenty-one. Once I'd launched those memories, I was free to
write a stretch of fiction, poetry, and plays.

But when I'd advanced a considerable distance into the inevitable
wheelchair life, I began to feel that an account of my experiences in
the brutality of cancer treatment might be of interest to others moving
through such a maze. In 1994 then, I published a second memoir
called *A Whole New Life.* It covered three years—from the discovery
of a spinal-cord malignancy in 1984 to the failed first attempt to
remove that tumor, a disastrous resort to radiation, then further surgeries and a slow return to rewarding life, though a life that left my

legs paralyzed and my days dependent on live-in assistants. The writing of *A Whole New Life* was hardly a pleasure; but like most forms of narrative, it brought its own relief. Better perhaps, it found me able to describe an ongoing life that—oddly—was often enjoyable and certainly more productive than before.

This third volume—*Ardent Spirits*—recalls an especially rich time, from the autumn of 1955 till the early summer of 1961. Comprised in that era were three years of study at Oxford—a stretch that included my first chance at both sustained writing and rewarding love. And that time was followed by three years of financially strapped teaching back at Duke and the completion of my first novel, *A Long and Happy Life*, to substantial benefits.

Ardent Spirits is the most detailed of the three memoirs, likely because the first is built from the distant memories of childhood and the second recalls a chasm of pain and fear, one which could only be crossed on a narrow bridge with few handholds. By contrast, *Ardent Spirits* means to convey a succession of moments which combined, through six years, in producing intense stretches of the rarest human privilege—prolonged joy. That privilege came from a series of outright gifts, given me by a line of friends and lovers whose generosity is honored in both the title of this book and the substance of these memories.

It's usually with the arrival of a fitting title that I begin to know what I'm writing about and how to proceed. The phrase *ardent spirits* arrived one evening in October 2004 when I'd been in a group of lucky writers who were guided through Thomas Jefferson's home, Monticello, after the paying tourists were gone. As we were led through the surprisingly few rooms in that sensible dwelling, we'd reached Jefferson's bedroom and were hearing of him and his slave Sally Hemings when full dark waylaid us. In an instant we learned how little modern light that most famous American home has to offer; and I promptly sensed Monticello as a human dwelling, not a tourist site. Our well-informed guide suggested that members of the group join hands for safety as he led us through other pitch-black rooms out onto one of the pavilions that Jefferson extended from the front side of the house.

There, under a clear autumn sky, he concluded our visit by telling us of Jefferson's near-bankrupting love of French wines. Finally the guide said that, over and above the Burgundies and Bordeaux which stocked the retired president's cellar, "Mr. Jefferson kept very few ardent spirits, only for those few friends who required them." As we scattered, I paused to ask the guide what he meant by *ardent spirits*. Despite my Southern childhood, the phrase had eluded me. On the spot, I learned that they were, simply, hard liquor—homemade spirits for those Virginia and Carolina squires who declined (or scorned) Mr. Jefferson's fancifications from the grand French vineyards.

Back home a few days later, the phrase rang on in my head as I continued thinking of a book I meant to begin soon—this memoir of high adult happiness. Soon I knew that *Ardent Spirits* would be my title. By the word *spirits*, I'd intend the intimates who'd lent such usable heat to the years I'd describe—years which would seldom again be matched for such gifts in my life.

As I began the writing, I knew that I meant to preserve above all the most striking of those impressions. But I'd kept no journals of the first three years in England. So I moved on through a first draft of Part One by relying entirely on unwritten memories that were five decades old. It was only when I'd finished a draft that it occurred to me to ask the Duke Library for copies of the letters I'd written home in those years— a typed page-and-a-half every Sunday. Mother had saved them all; and when I discovered them at her death in 1965, I added them to the papers the university had requested and then barely thought of them again.

There are, to be sure, events and feelings you don't include in letters to your mother. Yet apart from what I'd already recorded in Part One, there was little in those letters by way of fresh news from the past—a couple of dates I'd misremembered and a steady reminder (in the midst of so much pleasure) of how homesick I'd often been for the remains of my inmost family. The details of Part One then are owing almost entirely to the enduring goodness of those three years in my memory. Only long after thinking I'd completed it did I discover, buried in a drawer, a fragmentary calendar of my first term at Oxford. I've used it to supply a few minor details—the name of the college physician, for instance.

Part Two begins with three years of apprentice teaching back at Duke, by a very raw apprentice indeed; and it proceeds more rapidly than Part One—first, because my memories were less complex; and second, because my life at the time was a great deal less eventful than my time in Europe. Generally I was either in the classroom, teaching my students to write brief essays and conferring with them in my office about their results; or I was at home alone, slowly teaching myself to write a first novel, one set in a landscape much like the country woods where I was living in a small house-trailer. My personal memories of the time are surprisingly few—I was doing so little that proved memorable.

The reader may be glad to know that the realities of wheelchair life have made a deep plowing through my voluminous papers impossible; and with the exception of a very few investigations undertaken by a helpful friend, I didn't want to rely on research assistance. What's here then, throughout, is literally a memoir. And despite the recent scientific assaults on our faith in the accuracy of memory, I can say that if I didn't feel that what's recorded is reliable, I wouldn't have offered it. I'm now past seventy-five, and I share with my contemporaries a loss of short-term memory that's forest-fire in its sweep, but the distant memories grow even more crystalline in their clarity and depth. Only yesterday, as my young dentist picked sharply at my teeth, I was flooded by a sudden wash of visually precise memories of my dentist's tragically gifted father—a man whom I'd known well forty years ago, whose impressive efforts at fiction writing were swamped by alcohol. Trapped in the dentist's chair, I could still have given a police detective the details from which an accurate portrait could have been drawn, years after my friend's early death.

As a writer, I'm even more grateful than others might be for such a change in the quality of memory in the face of age. In fact, though I was a vain enough man in my early and midmanhood, I've long since ceased to regret the downward pull of years. That glacial action has proved literally painless; and now if I pause at the mirror for anything more than a shave or a combing, I answer my frequent *Who's that?* with a settled *Well, it's me*. And *me* is who I've been since about the age of four or five, the earliest time of sustained self-consciousness.

If I roll away, discard my momentary visual confusion, and ask myself *How old do I feel?*, the answer is seventeen or eighteen (however comic such an answer may seem for anyone but my calendar contemporaries). Most days, despite the pain that goes on serving me loyally after numerous gougings and burnings, I sense myself as a mainly cheerful young man poised on the edge of independence and increasingly aware of the strengths, weaknesses, and secrets that I hope will follow me as faithfully as any good dog to the end of my life.

But does my sense of continuity mean that I remember in reliable detail the events, thoughts, and emotions of the man I actually was in North Carolina, the British Isles, continental Europe, and elsewhere some five decades ago? Anyone who's known me for most of my life can confirm that I've been essentially the same mind in a sequence of bodies as separate as those on any extended strip of movie film (and no one is alive who's known me all my life). However, recent studies of human recollection suggest to some scholars that what we mean by memory may frequently be fresh creation.

To simplify drastically what I know of their work, a number of scholars assert that, in an effort to recover the past, we take a few strands of accurate memory, then interweave them with imagined strands into a detailed visual narrative—a good part of which (if we could check that narrative against a film of our entire lives) would never have occurred in the exterior world. In light of such a theory, we are as much artists in the production of "memory" as when we shut our eyes in sleep and produce the poems which our species has long called dreams.

Such a theory of memory has some occasional groundings in fact, groundings that should make us profoundly suspicious of potentially accusatory memories. If we're the creators of our memories, then those inventions have often been a calamitous source of tragic consequences. Any sworn testimony from a witness in a court case may well be at the mercy of creative memory. And many appalling results of the recovered-memory movement of the 1970s and '80s arose from such unexamined views of memory—occurrences like the false accusations of employees in children's care centers or adult children's "recovered," but often inhumanly false, memories of sexual abuse at the hands of close relations. Such fantasies have often been encouraged as reliable memories by doctrinaire therapists and have sometimes resulted in prison sentences and ruined lives for innocent fathers, mothers, kin, teachers, and devoted caretakers. The documentary films made by Ofra Bikel, several of which have aired on PBS's *Frontline*, are meticulous and frightening accounts of such fantasies and their overwhelming power in the hands of the cruelest, most self-deluded, and most easily panicked among us.

My two parental families, though, are proof that what we call memories may often be astonishingly faithful to history—and accurate through the length of long lives, even in kinsmen who've never transcribed so much as a single memory. It's easy enough to believe that a family may preserve group memories that it's shared, in identical form through decades of family reunions, say. But kinsmen have occasionally saddened or delighted me with detailed accounts of awful or hilarious events to which we've each been witnesses, though we may have kept those details from one another for many years.

For that reason then, and many more, I'm not inclined to agree with anyone's claim that memory is largely re-creation. Most friends with whom I share an experience in the distant past tend to affirm that my recall of the experience matches their own, give or take a small point. And a surprised affirmation occurs so often that I'm compelled to wonder whether the chief distinguishing trait of a serious writer of narrative may not be a brain wired with unusual powers of faithful memory. It's by no means a distinction imagined solely by me, as I'll detail below.

My insistence in this matter comes at a time when several of the most successful memoirs of recent years have been exposed as outright inventions. In the light of ensuing public concern, while I can hardly claim that all the memories recorded here are unerring, I can assert my confidence that they bear a high resemblance to actual happenings in my life and in many lives near me. And that achievement is by no means a personal virtue—only a phenomenon of birth like the color of my eyes and a craftsman's skill, honed by long polishing.

Three final details are worth noting—when I've attributed remarks to friends or others, I've attempted to preserve the content and characteristic rhythm of their speech; but the presence of quotation marks is not a guarantee of verbatim record. And in the case of a few friends and others, I've changed names. To the best of my knowledge, nonetheless, no lies have been told; surely none was intended—especially in matters involving sex.

R.P.

O N E

THE UNITED STATES, BRITAIN, AND THE CONTINENT
1955–1958

1

O N THE AFTERNOON of September 30, 1955 an elegantly trim and all-but-new ocean liner slid from its berth on the Hudson River in New York City and headed for England. With its other passengers in tourist class, I was among a group of some thirty American men bound northeast for Oxford University. Our ship was the S.S. *United States* which, on its maiden voyage three years earlier, had shaved ten hours off the prior record for transatlantic voyages. We'd be five days on the early-autumn sea and, with any luck, could dodge the great storms that had roiled the Atlantic in recent years.

Only a few months earlier, I'd met the distinguished historian Bernard De Voto when he came to lecture at Duke, my undergraduate alma mater. I'd heard that De Voto was famous for his strong pro-American tilt; so a chill lifted the roots of my black hair when the young woman who was backstage beside me suddenly told De Voto that I was now a Rhodes Scholar. He looked up into my sudden pallor, chuckled a little sardonically, and said "Mr. Price, I'm glad to have met you while you're still a bearable man." Startled though I was, I managed to ask what he meant; and he said "I've never met a Rhodes Scholar, of whatever age, who didn't inform me of that fact within two minutes of shaking my hand." So here, more than fifty years later, I've fulfilled De Voto's prophecy and started this book with such a declaration. I hope it proves relevant at least.

On the pier, to wave me off with decidedly mixed emotions on both sides of the gesture, were my mother and my only other near kinsman, a brother. They'd driven me up from our home in North Carolina two days before. We'd stayed in the now-defunct Taft Hotel (lamented Times Square home of the world's best club sandwich and inexpensive clean rooms for businessmen and tourists). And we'd eased our lengthy parting with a visit to the Metropolitan Museum and a Times Square showing of *On the Waterfront* with Marlon Brando at his early sympathetic best and Eva Marie Saint in her own serenely luminous youth.

Transatlantic crossings in those days of the great liners—so different from present-day slummy cruise ships—were famously preceded by departure parties complete with champagne, flowers, and last-minute bon-voyage telegrams from friends. I had a few telegrams from my aunts and teachers; but despite the family's native buoyancy, we were finding it hard to provide genuine cheer that day. Though none of us mentioned it, separately we knew that this latest parting marked the ritual definition of a painful fact—once more, our close and likable family was drastically changing.

My father, Will Price, had died of lung cancer only nineteen months before. A brilliant comedian, he was a man perennially strapped by money woes; and his horizons had been lowered early by the fact that—like Mother—he'd concluded his education with high school. Through the hard years of the Great Depression, he'd struggled to support us with salesman jobs while contending with the demon of alcoholism (he managed to quit for good when he was thirty-six and I was three—thus I never saw him drunk). When he died at fifty-four, he was holding down the best job of his life; but he was still a high-class traveling salesman, often away from home three nights a week. And alongside his first-rate comic talents, he had the melancholic tendencies of many more famous clowns.

At middle age, he was a tired man who was worrying—and smoking—himself to death. A hypochondriac, convinced of heart troubles he never had, he'd foreseen an early end from his mid-forties on. So in addition to meeting the monthly bills, he'd strained to set aside enough life insurance to guard us at his parting. Yet in those days of minimal health insurance, his brief hospitalization—and the hopeless surgery to remove a lung—gutted his financial leavings. Within a few days of his funeral, my mother had been forced to take a job selling boys' clothing at a local retail store.

She was forty-nine when he died and had never worked outside our home. I was a college junior then, age twenty-one, who stepped up my own money-raising effort—the painting of suspicious coats-of-arms for relatives and friends. And my brother, at thirteen, took on a summer job for the Department of Agriculture—measuring our home county's lush and lethal tobacco fields. Till then, we'd been unusually close; and our grief had brought us closer. Now we were breaking our bond.

Yet while I'm a shameless weeper, I don't recall tears as I stood on deck among my new friends and looked down at my mother and brother—Elizabeth and Bill (who'd later assume my father's name, Will). Like most Americans of my Depression and World War II generation, I'd traveled very little till then. There'd been an early boyhood trip through the historical sites of eastern Virginia and the city of Washington, a few trips to New York to sample the riches of a Broadway that still produced frequent real plays (often brilliantly cast), family trips to Virginia Beach and Myrtle, more nearby historic-site touring, and a summer-long job in 1953 as the counselor to a cabin of boys at Camp Sequoyah in the Great Smoky Mountains. Since early adolescence, I'd all but tasted the strong desire to visit Europe; but as the son of a father who had no money to spare, and as a boy too young to fight in Europe or the Pacific, my chance of such a visit had been near impossible.

Now, incredibly, I was off. In another half-hour the tugs turned back, though the Statue of Liberty would be visible behind us for a while longer, more radiant with emotion than I'd have guessed likely. Then I turned in earnest to meeting my Rhodester colleagues and attending to a passenger's duties. I signed on for a second seating at all meals in the third-class dining room—thereby gaining the chance of a later breakfast—and I stowed my good wool trousers and a Harris-tweed sport coat in the tiny closet in my shared cabin so the wrinkles would hang out (another lesson from a traveling father). That way, I'd be as well turned out as a serious young man of my time and place was expected to be.

After dinner on the first night at sea—pleasant-enough food but served with the usual American big-city absence of grace or human connection—I celebrated with my new friends at one of the ship's several bars. In early childhood I'd learned from a wicked uncle about my father's problem with drink and had developed an early fear of its presence in our home (though my parents never stocked it, they had no problem when friends turned up with their own bottles, a practice that scared me nonetheless—wouldn't Dad be tempted to start all over?).

That fear had lasted, well disguised, right through my membership in a swinging college fraternity. Since the possession of alcohol was then strictly forbidden on the Duke campus, my friends only drank at weekend parties in town or in stark concrete-block party spaces available for rent in the local woods. So it had been easy enough for me to rely on Cokes. Maybe oddly, my father had never asked me not to drink. He'd only said, when he and I were alone in his car on the afternoon of my fraternity initiation, "Son, there's just one thing to remember—the men in your family have never been very good around liquor." And so they hadn't—the men on both sides of my family—as by then I well knew.

I never tasted ardent spirits then until he was dead, though hardly a year before this first voyage, I'd gone out with some of my fraternity brothers to an illegal Durham saloon and ordered a drink I'd heard of in a movie—Sauternes and soda: a semi-tolerable mix of sweet dessert wine and soda water. It was not only illegal; it confirmed even more indelibly my brothers' delighted sense of me as an intellectual fop who was nonetheless their bemusing fool of a mascot. My grades were helping keep the fraternity off social probation after all, and I enjoyed their fond kidding. My fraternity name, for instance, was Misterfofelees after an essay I'd published in the campus literary magazine concerning the evil Mephistopheles in Christopher Marlowe's Elizabethan tragedy *Dr. Faustus*. I continued to drink the same syrup once or twice a month for the remainder of my college years, nursing a tall glass as slowly as possible despite my brothers' tendency to force frequent complimentary refills on me.

Still unaccustomed to saloon life, however upscale, on my first night at sea—surely no more than a hundred miles from New York—I relaxed,

drank another Sauternes and soda, and received no jesting comments from my friends. It was maybe one o'clock in the morning then
before I turned in with a new sense of mature independence, to my
three-man cabin—all three of us were Rhodesters. We had no port-
hole, no natural light to wake us; but at six I was wakened by the whisk
of something slid under our door. I was in a lower berth, so I got up
quietly and fetched the brief mimeographed shipboard newspaper. At
the top of the front page, among announcements for dance contests
and badminton tournaments, a headline said "Actor James Dean
Killed in Car Crash." I was still more affected than I'd realized by the
death of my father, even here well beyond the three-mile limit; and at
once that piece of the news struck deep.

I'd never met Dean, I knew almost nothing about his life—except
that he was two years minus three days older than I—and I'd had no
forewarning of the power of his acting when I went alone to see his
first film *East of Eden* just a few months earlier and had been deeply
moved. On my first trip to New York five years before, I'd seen young
Julie Harris in her Broadway triumph in *The Member of the Wedding*;
and she'd been Dean's co-star in the film. The scene with their kiss on
a small-town Ferris wheel remains one of the great romantic moments
in film; but the final scene, with Dean and Harris determined to stand
watch at the bedside of Dean's father, who'd suffered a stroke, chimed
with my own recent family sadness. (For more than two weeks, I'd
slept in a chair in my father's hospital room at his request—a request
that honored me more than any other I'd got. After the surgery that
removed a lung, I was there in his room when something awful broke
loose in his chest; he panicked, a too-young doctor came, did something I couldn't see; and Dad was never truly conscious again. But my
finger was on his thready pulse when his heart ceased to beat some
three days later.)

Stronger still, though, was the plain perfection of James Dean's
meticulous portrait—from start to finish—of a man my age, externally
very different from me but internally a near twin in his need for a
father's love and respect. I'd got more of both from my own good father,
yet the sudden news that James Byron Dean had died in the mangled

wreck of a car on the day when I was gladly parting from a mother who suffered still from the death of a man whom I'd tended through his last awful days seemed more than uncanny. (Another young man had died almost exactly a month earlier—Emmett Till, age fourteen, murdered at the hands of Mississippi white men for allegedly whistling at a white woman. I'd followed that story with a sense of awful omen, an oncoming tide of unstoppable violence from my part of the world.)

But neither death marred for long the five days of pleasure at sea. Despite our tourist-class tickets, the captain gave us privileged bright boys access to numerous cabin-class privileges—their swimming pool, their masseurs, plus evening music and dancing in their lounge, plus a last-night-at-sea dinner in first class, complete with my introduction to baked Alaska (a dessert which had yet to reach the upper South except as a treat for the idle rich in MGM movies). Chiefly, though, I relished two things.

First among the pleasures were the nighttime hours I could spend alone on deck submerged in plutonian darkness with almost alarmingly bright star-shine above. In my contented eight years as an only child before my brother's birth, solitude had been my natural condition; and despite a shipload of some two thousand other passengers, I was generally free to walk the decks and feel the rhythmic but enormous surge of the ocean beneath a ship that, however large, was the merest cork to the gorgeous giant that heaved to all sides and beneath us and could, no doubt, turn this gentle week into something appalling if not deadly (in five later crossings, I experienced days of bad winter storms and high turbulence; but the fall of '55 was far more peaceful).

Among the numerous matters I considered in those dark nights on deck was the basic young man's question of the Fifties and Sixties— *Who am I?* I was no doubt too confident, by a wide margin, of most of the answers. I was the son of upper-middle-class Southern parents, each of them born within forty years of the end of the Civil War and the African slavery which precipitated that war's slaughter of 620,000 men (if we destroyed that many men, proportionally, from today's population we'd kill six million). Years later Dad's sister Lulie Price Gay said to me of my great-grandmother McCraw, "Ma-Mammy lost five first cousins in one battle." More than I liked to think still, I continued to share—generally in silence—a small percentage of their trust in the inevitability of the Southern racial arrangement—the benign separation, as they saw it, of two races who (in an inexplicably close bond) had built an immensely complex agrarian civilization across a huge stretch of land. The old South, after all, was geographically larger than Western Europe and almost as prolific in the production of distinguished art—specifically music, poetry, drama, and fiction (if we extend its history from the work of Mark Twain, a short-term Confederate soldier, on through the time of my early manhood).

Owing to the Great Depression and the Second War, as I've said, I'd never left the nation till now. My passionate absorption in the arts—first, painting; then serious reading, then writing—began in that order when I was still an only child and we lived in a wooded suburb that nonetheless, to me, seemed like the deep forest. Those piney acres, with occasional snakes and a stream that was rich in lizards and crawfish, were the source of early answers to mysteries that could have balked my life if I'd met them first in the crowded streets of concrete cities—*Who put me here? And why?*

Helpful as they were, those solitary country years, though, had kept me from serious out-of-school connection with my age-mates. When I joined them, back in town, in the fourth grade, I took to their interests with excited pleasure; and despite a period of hostile rejection from a pair of other boys, I'd ultimately reached high school with no memorable sexual connections with anyone but myself. My memories of the start of an erotic life center on a room of my own when I was eleven. It had a floor-length mirror, left behind by a prior renter; and I launched into the early outskirts of puberty with long reflected games at that mirror—me and my own bare skin in fantastic stories and games that erupted before long in outright sexual elation.

From there I moved onward through the years before high school in minor fascination with a dark-haired girl who seemed to me the summit of human beauty. She was in fact lovely and kind; but in the rare times we were alone together, I felt none of the intense magnetism of physical attraction. That magnetism, which our deepest needs eventually assign to one of the genders—an assignment which is still entirely mysterious—would wait awhile longer. It came in my first year of high school. When I was fourteen we'd moved to Raleigh, a small Carolina city luckily rich in its artistic resources; and it was there that I quickly sensed a new excitement in the presence of a few boys my age. Soon a neighbor boy, now long-dead, was laboring strenuously to join me in frequent early expeditions into the delights of intimate— and laughing—physical contact; and for years he remained a cheerful resource.

But from the time I entered high school, I fixed—at a distance—on one tall classmate as my Apollonian ideal. For that whole year I literally never met him. When we chanced, though, to sit beside one another in second-year Latin, a friendship formed that survives even today in class reunions but has never shed the quality of good-natured distance that only deepened my sense of genuine awe at what seemed to me male grandeur—especially the gold-haired variety that excels in sports and courteously sheds from its shoulders, like an insignificant warm rain, the admiration of other boys and—till one of them captures him—the nervous pursuit of girls.

Though I'd had intimations from, say, age seven that men were the world's magnetic core for me, I was fifteen before I'd begun to know enough about a person's sexual destiny to suspect that I was more than half likely to be bound in that direction (we didn't, in those days, speak of genetic tendencies; but I can think of no other explanation for the leaning that became a full commitment). Though I felt pleasantly drawn to several other girls, right on through college, I date the irreversible proof of my course to the year in which I mail-ordered André Gide's book *Corydon*.

One of the pioneering modern European texts on the subject of homosexuality, it was written in high-toned French neoclassical dialogue by a then still-living novelist and winner of the Nobel Prize for literature. It was published in the States only in 1950, and by then I was seventeen. What I didn't quite know, in the last year of high school, was how fiercely most Americans were then opposed to the whole reality of male homosexuality, if they knew of it at all. It was a life which was then called *queer* (lesbianism was more nearly the subject of comedy than of outright rejection). Nonetheless, I kept my strong suspicion undercover — and rather enjoyably so. I was after all at the I-love-a-mystery stage.

It would have been interesting had I known, so early, that my father's closest friend, from early childhood till well past the time of Dad's marriage at age twenty-seven, was a man who'd later be distinguished in politics and who I learned, on very credible evidence after Dad's death, was almost surely queer. He and Dad had been close, right through the days of Dad's worst drinking. The friend could never quit the habit; and he served as best man at my parents' wedding — a fact that led Mother frequently to joke that she'd never been sure she was married: "Your dad's best man cried so loudly at the wedding, I couldn't hear the vows."

I have many reasons to affirm that my father was strongly heterosexual; but I wouldn't be at all surprised to learn that, like so many men, he'd had other outlets in earlier life. In any case, the last hospital visit Dad received on the night before he underwent a lung removal that caused his death seven days later was from that best man; and I was present through the entire visit. Amazing to think that, in adult life, I might have discussed such a secret with my father. The English memoirist J. R. Ackerley — a discreet homosexual whom I'd meet in London — writes in his own brilliant memoir *My Father and Myself* of discovering just such a possible mysterious bond with his own father, well after the father's death. As a young man Ackerley's father had lived for some years with a queer Swiss nobleman.

At first I suffered almost no pain on the subject of my own sexual longing; and despite a considerable adolescent involvement with institutional Christianity, I certainly never felt condemned by God. I'd read the four gospels since childhood and noted that Jesus — who almost surely lived and died a single man, one who traveled and lived in a small group of other men, one of whom was called (in the Gospel of John) "the disciple whom Jesus loved" — was never recorded as having spoken a word against the love of men for men. On the other hand, he denounced fornication, adultery, divorce, wealth, and family loyalty (among other realities that most churches, obsessed as they currently are with homosexuality, seldom condemn). That silence of Jesus in the matter of same-sex relations is all the more remarkable, considering that his early followers could easily have invented a denunciation from Jesus if they had no recorded statement on hand.

Sexual pain came to me only in my freshman year in college, when the object of my first infatuation rejected me. Yet in April 1952—the spring of my freshman year at Duke—when that first rejection left me feeling desolate, I wrote a poem that was my one early attempt to write about private loneliness. The poem is sadly typical of a million adolescent plaints. I was nineteen, the age at which Rimbaud wrote the greatest adolescent poems in any Western language. At least mine is brief, and I set it down here—without the slightest claim for literary value—as an honest glimpse of a mainly buoyant young man's confrontation with a possibly daunting future.

> *Because I am,*
> *Because I am what I am,*
> *I have been always alone.*
> *Always hoping that someday*
> *I would round some corner of my heart*
> *And see and smile and say at last*
> *That this is that for which I cry.*
> *And so in each new face and always*
> *In the old, in each new love or day*
> *Or song, I wait to see if here*
> *The world has broken through the colored glass to me.*
> *And then I know, as ever over I must know,*
> *That I am here and it is there*
> *And between us, wide and deep, is a*
> *Dark and winter sea.*

Way more than fifty years after writing the poem, I'm not at all sure what I meant by the word *it*, three lines from the end. Most likely, I meant "contentment"; or more specifically, at the time I wrote the poem, "reciprocated love" must have been central to my desires. And love in those days of my early manhood surely meant "contiguous flesh" as much as anything more spiritual. Looking so far back I can see that, from my own point of view, what was truest in the poem was my realization that the force dividing my love from other human beings—or theirs from me—was deeply enigmatic, an external force. The mystery threaded its constant way through my shipboard thoughts, but I have no memory whatever of thinking I'd marry and go my father's way with the children he loved yet who left him supremely anxious many days of our lives. I likewise don't recall feeling guilt or any sense of omen.

Looking back from a long way, I do think my deep involvement in Dad's death was, oddly, an unexpected means of sexual liberation. Now I'd never have to worry about what he thought of my sexual life (I still suspect he'd have been amazingly tolerant). And deeper still, our final three weeks together reminded me strongly of the nonsexual forms of physical contact he and I had in my early childhood—how he'd wake me for breakfast on Sunday mornings by lying atop my covered sleeping body and calling to me: "Preacher, Preacher, way past breakfast time. Haul yourself up."

Whether my eventual erotic life bore any strong relation to such memories, I won't attempt to guess; but I do know how much I honored his body and made every effort to steal into the bathroom whenever he might be drying from the shower and study his strength and amplitude. I assume that most boys, with resident fathers, have shared some early form of the same fascination with their dad's anatomy. I suspect I was one who took that fascination further than most—and with a prevailing sense of tenderness that prevented any later interest in sex that had no substantial affectionate component. To a very large extent, I was stuck with love.

Still, another realization was rapidly overtaking love as a crucial fact of my oncoming life. At the age of sixteen, encouraged by a superb English teacher, I'd declared to myself and then to my family that I meant to become a writer of fiction and poetry who also taught English in a university. The announcement met with no objection from any of them, and I proceeded through four years at Duke with the same banner flown from my mast. I found a good many classmates to like, I enjoyed almost all my studies (mainly English, history, and world religions); for all my romantic rejections, I managed a fair amount of nonwoeful poetry and fiction above and beyond my class assignments; and in the fall of my senior year, I won this scholarship that was then given to thirty-two men nationwide for graduate study at Oxford (women only became eligible years later). So here now I stood in mid-Atlantic on my way toward a life that—despite the appalling scenes of my father's recent agony—seemed under my control, some small degree of control. The ocean itself and this lean, fast ship—a toy on the surface—were a joint vehicle bearing me onward.

The summary seems fair enough. Does it imply a self-important narcissistic bastard? One or two friends had implied as much. At times, I believed them and backpedaled for a while. I was no doubt self-important for my age and achievements; but my sizable band of friends seemed a validation of my ability to make myself an original and useful acquaintance. What was more complicated for me was the fact that, like many other human beings, I'd often been told from early childhood that I was good to look at—thick black hair, wide brown eyes, eyelashes "big as mink hearth-rugs" (according to an aunt), and an eager smile above a pointed chin that I always deplored. I can honestly recall deciding—when I saw my grinning sixth-grade school photo—that I'd try to use any degree of physical pleasantness as a means of entertaining my friends, long before I knew I had words to do the same work. I was still far from thinking of looks as a tool in the oncoming seduction events of adolescence and thereafter. *Who I was* seemed to me then, alone aboard the *United States*, not radically different from the men I was traveling with. The size of my error was bearing down on me, wider and faster than I knew.

Meanwhile, second among my seaborne pleasures was the chance to begin knowing a few of my Rhodester colleagues. I recall my quiet cabin-mate Del Kolve, who would become a distinguished scholar of medieval literature and a man who'd live his adult life with a male partner. To the best of my subsequent knowledge, Del was one of the four scholars of our class who were queer, more than confirming Kinsey's controversial 1948 claim that ten percent of all men were homosexual for at least three years between sixteen and fifty-five. Among the most glamorous straight men of our Rhodes generation was Ham Richardson, a wealthy Southerner who was already established as a world-class tennis player and one who might well have won the Wimbledon singles title if he hadn't been troubled by the hard demands of diabetes.

I was with Ham once—we were driving to Stratford for a play—when he began to react to an overdose of insulin. Two more Rhodesters were with us; and after a useless stop for chocolate bars and the sugar they'd provide at a roadside shop, on Ham's directions we got him to a teashop a few yards from Shakespeare's birthplace, ordered warm sugary water, and watched uneasily while he drank it fast. By then he'd begun to seem to us, and our sedate nearby tea drinkers, more than a little drunk; but the sugar water brought him back to sane strength in under ten minutes, and we made the play on time. Amazingly Ham made it through a busy life as a New York investor—and frequent tennis player—to the age of seventy-three. Another memorable companion on the voyage was Rex Jamison, an Iowan with an unvarnished Plains accent, an ever-ready wit, and the steady dark eyes of a man intent upon dispelling as many mysteries as the world would yield to his intense focus. Rex would become a famous renal specialist and a lifelong friend.

Jim Griffin, a recent Yale graduate who would immerse himself in the new brand of linguistic philosophy at Oxford, became the most genial of my American companions in the next three years; and of all things for such a dyed-in-the-wool Connecticut Yankee, he'd prove to be the only member of our class who eventually chose to spend his life in Oxford, teaching philosophy, marrying a British wife, and raising a family. Jim was, by the way, a welcome confirmation that all Rhodes Scholars didn't have to fulfill—as I surely didn't—Cecil Rhodes's specific stipulation that his Scholars must demonstrate "a fondness for and success in manly sports." Once at Oxford, my own sport would become—very quickly—vigorous walking. On average, even in heavy rain, I'd circumnavigate the perimeter of Christ Church Meadow at least once daily, well over a mile's walk.

There was one night at sea when Jim and I sat beside one another in deck chairs and spoke, first of our reading and then of our futures. Jim was likewise set on the plan for a university teaching life; and he displayed, with no hint of ostentation, the chief external signs of the breed—a calm but magnetic diffidence plus a willingness to make a firm assertion and then laugh at his own solemnity (Jim's large pipe, then firmly clamped in his teeth, is no longer a mark of the teaching clan, may time be praised).

I told him of my own intention to teach—in college or a good prep school—and to write poems, short stories, and eventually novels. As we talked on late in the mid-Atlantic dark, my hope felt realistic at least—almost in reach, if only I could close my hands around it. What I hadn't yet learned was the ultimate charm of the sea for all eternal sailors; if you never touch land, the oceans themselves will nurture any dream you choose to harbor and spin out for any listener's ears. There were personal qualities, of which I was then insufficiently aware, that might make my own intentions difficult if not impossible. But three years at Oxford would uncover those, even to my own presently blind gaze.

Still I knew that I must wait for any firm seizure of the way of life toward which I yearned. If I meant to teach in a good American university, surely I'd need the Ph.D. degree; and that would require at least another three years of study beyond the two years I'd already committed to Oxford. And how could I write my poems and fiction in the face of such demands? Was it merely my too self-confident nature, or the low-key air of a boy of the Fifties, that kept me moving onward with no paralyzing fears? Well, somehow I gambled on believing I'd do all I had to do, most of what I meant and wanted to do with my life. I'd just completed a crowded senior year at Duke—five courses each semester, editing the literary magazine, and writing an honors thesis on John Milton's entry into contentious public life. So if hard work was the worst that lay before me, then stand aside. I'd somehow plow through it.

Other nights, alone, I'd think with considerable guilt of my mother and her ongoing plight. In the wake of Dad's death and its financial devastations, she now had herself, my brother, the remaining years of a substantial home mortgage, and bits of my own life to help with. An endlessly warm and haplessly generous woman, she came to enjoy the store-time contact with old friends and new customers. But her salary was modest; and she experienced the standard exhaustions of retail sales—long hours upright on her feet, selling little boys' blue jeans, plus the two nights a week when she was required to work till nine. And now she was fifty, lightly overweight, and a pack-a-day smoker. With her lack of higher education, her opportunities for a better-paying job seemed nonexistent. My brother had just entered high school and was aiming at college, but his summer job could do little to improve his hopes or to improve Mother's outlook as she faced the relentless bills of middle-class life.

Despite the early deaths of her parents and growing up in a sister's crowded home, no one was ever less selfish than Elizabeth Price; and she'd never once hinted that I could pass up graduate study and stay behind to help her. In my eventual three years away, I recall no occasion when she wrote to me of financial woes. In the nine months since receiving the scholarship, I'd improvidently assumed that the Rhodes Trust would cover my expenses abroad. I'd soon discover how wrong I was. The grant was generous but it mainly covered tuition, room and board. The rest was expected to come from my own resources, and I'd shortly be leaning hard upon that limited backing (which consisted of three thousand dollars from a now-dead bachelor cousin and a few hundred dollars in graduation gifts). In retrospect it's hardly a mistake to say that all those concerns gathered round me in the nights at sea as I left North Carolina farther behind by the slow and rolling moment.

2

T HEN LATE on the sixth afternoon—October 5—we reached our English port, Southampton. By the time we cleared customs with our old-time steamer trunks—mine was literally the size of a cabaret piano—we discovered that the Warden of Rhodes House had troubled to make the three-hour trip down from Oxford in a coach or charabanc (what we'd have called a middle-size bus). Edgar Williams was a middle-aged man of considerable eminence. The son of a nonconformist minister, he was almost forty-three when we met him—by then the equivalent of a calm and bemused college dean. But his early manhood had been far more exciting. He'd been among the architects of the North African campaign at El Alamein, a critical confrontation in which the British all but destroyed the Nazi desert tank corps under General Rommel. Accompanied now on the darkening pier by his eternal tobacco pipe, he grinned pleasantly and saw us safely boarded for the drive north. We stopped only once on the trip, for an unceremonious pee as all thirty of us stood by the roadside draining our bladders in the chilly drizzle as small cars whizzed past (a common-enough sight in the Britain of those days, devoid as it was of roadside facilities).

When we reached Oxford around nine, the sky was inky black; and the rain was pouring precisely as—since boyhood, in a thousand films—we'd all heard it should be. The coach proceeded through narrow streets, past a few miserable-looking students huddled on bikes, to deliver each of us to his assigned college (Michaelmas, or autumn, term wouldn't begin for another week). Rex Jamison and one other fledgling got off with me at Merton, in all important ways the oldest of Oxford colleges.

Founded in 1264 by Walter de Merton, bishop of Rochester, it had distinguished itself in the Middle Ages as the home of numerous important philosophers and theologians. And within the past century, it had been the college of Winston Churchill's father, Lord Randolph Churchill; the great Edwardian satirist and caricaturist Max Beerbohm, who'd also written one of the most famous Oxford novels *Zuleika Dobson*; and T. S. Eliot, who'd spent a brief year as a graduate student during World War I (surely an eerie and shame-inducing time for a noncombatant like Eliot, when the college was virtually bereft of healthy young Englishmen, many of whom would have their lives flung away beyond the trenches by their generals).

To increase my surprise that the Warden of Rhodes House had come all the way to meet us in Southampton, I discovered in the Porter's Lodge at Merton that my scout stood waiting to lead me to my rooms. In those days your scout was your personal attendant. Mine's name was Bill Jackson, an affable and immensely lean man in his early forties whose duties included waking me (by opening my bedside curtains and saying "Morning, sir" at seven each morning); then making my bed, giving my rooms a light cleaning, and washing my tea things in late afternoon.

I was delighted to learn that I had a pair of rooms all to myself in Mob Quad, just off Front Quad. First, there was a long sitting room with a wide bay window that looked out, past a tall chestnut tree, over the lush Christ Church Meadow, replete with actual cows (however much they resembled movie-prop cows); and equally prop schoolboys at their afternoon sports—the river Thames ran unseen beyond (as it flows through Oxford, it's called the Isis). And second, I had a cubicular bedroom with a freestanding wardrobe and—crucially—a just-installed washbasin with running hot and cold water, the importance of which I'll clarify later.

The rooms, not at all incidentally, were Mob Quad staircase 2, set 1; and to increase the enviable nature of my lodgings, I quickly learned that Mob Quad was not only the oldest quadrangle in Oxford, it was almost surely the oldest academic quad in Britain. Its immensely thick limestone walls had gone up from about 1306 on; and it had housed not only some seven and a half centuries of students but also (on two sides) the college library, the oldest portions of which were among the finest examples of early English libraries. A few of the most ancient volumes were still chained, as they'd always been, to the shelves.

Once Bill Jackson had showed me the toilets, which were called the Mob Quad bogs quite accurately—a mere line of commodes in a lean-to against the south side of the chapel—he departed, leaving me a plate of warm dinner which he'd saved from the dining hall. With no reading matter, TV, radio, telephone, or phonograph as yet, I had little to do but open my trunk and begin to skim its many layers of clothes, books, framed pictures and other memorabilia which I'd brought with an eye toward at least an unbroken two-year absence from home.

In those days airfare across the Atlantic was exorbitant and boats were slow. Barring extreme emergency I couldn't consider returning till I'd finished the work for my degree. So in typical American college-boy fashion, I was unpacking in my underwear briefs and a T-shirt; and when there was a knock on my door—past ten o'clock—I answered it, in acceptable dormitory attire (for another two decades Merton would continue to be an all-male college; and women were not allowed, even as guests, after nine).

There before me stood my actual living introduction to the Oxford undergraduate population—a short dark-haired man in thick glasses with sizable ears and a pleasantly troll-like face. He declined to extend a hand to be shaken, but he compensated by offering his name in what I'd long hoped to hear in person—the true Oxbridge accent. He was Henry Mayr-Harting; and he suggested that since he and I were to share the same staircase landing for the coming year, I might like to come to his rooms for a cup of bedtime cocoa and a little talk. He gave no signs of alarm at the impropriety of my dress.

I did, however, fish what I'd have called a bathrobe from my trunk; and soon I crossed the ten feet of landing to Henry's rooms. They were roughly the same ample size as my own; and in addition to the college's supplied old desk, couch, and chairs, there was a true cabaret-sized piano which Henry had rented from a shop in town. All the next year, filtered through our dense stone walls, Henry's skillful performances of Bach and Mozart would be my main access to music. For now he poured our cups of cocoa; and we launched ourselves upon the chief occupation, gift, and reward of Oxford life—conversation. We spoke about an astonishingly broad array of subjects—my recent voyage, recent movies (still called *cinemas* here), forthcoming performances of music and drama at various nearby public halls, and the peculiar behavior of American airmen who came to Oxford on weekends—it appeared—for drink and women, in that order apparently.

Finally we turned to discussing our work. Henry was beginning the second year of his three-year study of history (undergraduate history at Oxford then was mostly British history); and like virtually all Mertonians, except a sizable number who'd already done their required national military service, he was three years younger than I. I recall his giving me, first, a brisk and nimble introduction to the long and noble history of our college and then a rundown on the particular topics he'd be studying in the autumn term.

When he politely asked about my plans for study, I told him that I hoped to write a thesis on John Milton for the Bachelor of Letters degree (then the Oxford equivalent of an American-earned M.A.). Henry gave his first enormous grin—"Oh *Milton*"—and then embarked upon well-informed remarks and questions about Milton, a fund of knowledge which I could imagine almost no American undergraduate's possessing. Soon I'd be accustomed to the fact that, in the 1950s in any case, almost every undergraduate had arrived at Oxford with the equivalent of at least two years of American college education. It would prove—as Henry's did, so promisingly that first night—a fund that would not only be firmly possessed and eager to engage itself with the knowledge won by others, it was also almost invariably worn lightly and with much salty laughter in the midst of a normal young man's life. (Though I didn't know it for years, it may be relevant now to note that Henry indeed had been born in Prague to Viennese parents, and would eventually become the first Roman Catholic to hold the eminent position of Regius Professor of Ecclesiastical History at Oxford.)

By midnight I was back in my narrow scholar's bed, lying atop—

I swear—a mattress stuffed with rough straw (could any medieval scholar in this same room have retired to sleep on worse?). I slept nonetheless like the saint I surely wasn't, even then, and woke only when Bill Jackson opened my thick blue curtains as the chapel tower—only fifty yards away—rang its quarter-hourly chime to announce the arrival of day. Since the college lacked showers, and the huge Edwardian bathtubs were a good walk's distance from my rooms (out of doors, past the library entrance and around a corner), I gave myself what my father might have called a whore's bath—face, pits, and fundament—in my new basin, then entered the first gray and mildly chilly English morning and walked to the adjacent hall for breakfast.

The hall covered more than half the south side of Front Quad. First built in the late thirteenth century to feed the gathering band of scholars, it was one of the college's oldest buildings, though largely reconstructed in the nineteenth. Still it bore its enormous old door with the fanciful black ironwork (sufficient to hold off any monster from the river or any posse of enraged townsmen—there'd likely been a few in the early centuries' war between town and gown), and its tall interior was roofed with dark wood beams in the usual inverted-boat fashion of Gothic ceilings. At the east end, a slightly raised platform bore the high table, where dons and distinguished guests dined (*don* was the colloquial name for a senior member of a college at Oxford or Cambridge, a title transferred from the Spanish title for a gentleman). Above them, among other portraits, hung imaginary pictures of the founder and the medieval scholar Duns Scotus who may or may not have had a connection with the college. At right angles to the high table, the students' tables and backless benches filled the remainder of the space.

To the left as I entered, I faced a large tray of kippered herrings (one of my father's favorite dishes—he called them salt herring) and a huge pot of glutinous oatmeal. I dodged those grim offerings and served myself scrambled eggs, cold toast, and coffee. There were few other students in sight, only those who'd come up early for various reasons. Not wishing to force my company upon three men who were talking with more energy than I possessed that early in the day, I chose their table but sat a good distance from them and began to eat.

In a matter of minutes, one of them—David Gilchrist, another historian who'd later be a boon acquaintance—turned my way and said "Good morning."

I returned the welcome greeting and stood to offer my hand.

David kept his seat and regarded the hand as though it were the herring I'd recently declined. I'd still to learn that Britons of that era shook hands as seldom as they employed one another's actual name in conversation—first names were then called Christian names and were almost never used in conversation (nor were surnames).

I sat back and thought I could at least offer my name.

When he heard my accent, David said "Ah, you must be the chap who called on Mayr-Harting last night in your dressing gown." His breakfast partners chuckled and turned their square Anglo-Saxon faces and huge blue eyes toward me.

A child might have run for cover; and I felt a childish chill but reminded myself of my official maturity. More and more I was silently recalling that anyone who'd managed a loved one's awful death as I'd done could face a few strangers who were at least guaranteed to avoid physical mayhem. So I managed a bleak smile and acknowledged that I'd indeed drunk cocoa with Mayr-Harting last evening. And that, for then, was that. The three men showed no need for a further exchange with this new Yank who owned a fancy dressing gown, and I downed my cold eggs in silence and returned to my rooms.

Bill Jackson had just finished making my bed—pajamas folded under the pillow—and was ready to talk. I'd be needing tea things, he said—a pot and sufficient cups and saucers for a few friends, a pitcher for milk and a sugar bowl. He recommended Elliston's for those items, the main department store in town. And he couldn't help observing that he'd noted the socks and underwear I'd rinsed out last night and left on the towel rack to dry. "I think you'll find, sir, that in this climate, you'll never get them dry like that." When I told him how I hoped to save a little money by washing my own smalls, he countered promptly—having heard that line from more than one American—

"You might save a very few shillings, sir, but at the expense of rheumatism in you feet and hips, not to mention *piles*. I'll be quite glad to take anything to an honest laundry and bring them back by the end of each week."

I agreed on the spot, and only later learned that Bill's second job was at the identical laundry. It proved an honest business, all the same; and though I'd soon sustain more than one ailment, rheumatism in any organ was never among them, not to mention piles (which had tormented my mother after she'd borne two large male babies and a stillborn daughter).

I shaved, unpacked a few more layers of my trunk, and awarded myself a quick unguided tour of the college—first, a few yards away, the building in St. Alban's Quad in which Eliot had lived. I'd spent a lot of time at Duke on a lengthy paper about Eliot's connection with the Spanish mystic poet St. John of the Cross; and the Anglo-American writer's work remained important for me (he was still much alive, in London, though I'd never have the good sense to ask for a meeting—he was famously approachable, if cool). Above all I was impressed by the college's spacious garden—private for the dons and students—with its tall lines of resplendent lime trees (lindens). I'd spend many of the rare forthcoming warm hours reading here on the semi-circular bench and table that rode atop the college's south wall, a remnant of the old city wall (the lower walk that ran along this stretch was called Dead Man's Walk, owing to the execution here of a soldier during the civil war of the seventeenth century or—alternately—because it was the path from the medieval synagogue to the nearby Jewish burial ground, long since covered by the university's botanical garden). The lime trees, by the way, succumbed to age and were recently felled, alas.

My years at Duke had been spent on a main campus built, near the time of my birth, with James. B. Duke's opulent millions and designed in the then popular American taste for a form of architecture called collegiate Gothic. Though Duke's neo-Gothic buildings were subject to occasional wit and scorn at their structural pretensions, for me they'd been a handsome place to live during my four undergraduate years (as they've been for some fifty years of a later teaching career). But it took me very few minutes to realize, with mounting expectation, that at Merton I'd be enclosed in an entire walled village whose oldest buildings — including my own quad — were Gothic in the pure original forms and were patently haunted by the lives of some seven centuries of students and fellows, though the soft limestone of many college walls was in a scabrous state as a result of the ruinous atmospheric acid created by a combination of rainwater and auto exhaust.

If at Duke I could sometimes permit myself fanciful moments, imagining life in small medieval quads, here at Merton I could see not only T. S. Eliot's windows but also — facing Front Quad — the windows of the Queen's Rooms, which had entertained Henry VIII's hapless first wife Catherine of Aragon in 1518; Elizabeth I in 1592; and the doomed Charles I's wife Henrietta Maria for a winter or more when Oxford was the royal headquarters late in the Civil War. She was succeeded in the rooms by William Harvey, Merton's most illustrious warden, who first described the principle of blood circulation in the human body. Well, so much for collegiate Gothic, handsome as it might be with the backing of enough tobacco dollars.

Then with no more urgent duties, I headed up Magpie Lane to the High Street in search of my tea things and a little knowledge of the town. Despite the university's total then of some twenty-nine constituent undergraduate colleges, most of them with their serene interior quads and gardens, all mostly walled and closed to the public, the town itself was a noisy small city with a dire traffic problem (the Morris Motor Works, a giant automobile factory, was on the outskirts — to which extent Oxford was the Detroit of England). I concentrated on recalling that British drivers kept to the left-hand side of the street and managed my first chores with no broken bones.

The lorry-crammed streets were unavoidable, as were the plump red-cheeked housewives with even plumper babies in old-fashioned wicker carriages. The city was then so safe that the babies were frequently parked outside grocery shops and left alone, apparently content behind their own startling red cheeks, while their mothers picked through a limited array of foods. So far as I could see, the array offered mostly cabbage, brussels sprouts, turnips, potatoes, lamb, mutton, and the ever-popular pork items—chops, sausages, and pies (the strict food rationing introduced at the start of the Second War had ended only a year ago, in 1954). Apart from the housewives and the clerks in the shops, there were numerous men my age, up early for the Michaelmas term.

They were all dressed in neckties and wool jackets, most of which broadcast the distinct odor of infrequent baths. And I'd soon hear a maybe apocryphal tale of a recent meeting of Merton dons to discuss the wisdom of installing showers for the students. After considerable talk, at last one elderly don lurched to his feet and said "Shower *baths*? But *why*? The young gentlemen are only here for two months at a time." End of debate. Showers would be installed at Merton only several years after my departure when the college was approaching the 700th year of its founding (the actual date was 1264).

Finally I noted a marked visual class distinction, similar to the one I'd have seen at home between whites and blacks. Apart from the obvious students, there were small huddles of working-class men, all of whom were white and many of whom seemed to be named Alf or Bert. They might be digging up a mysteriously ailing spot in the midst of the High (students knew that it was distinctly uncool to call it High Street) or scrubbing a moldy stone wall with stiff wire brushes; and they always seemed oblivious to their social superiors—and frequently, I thought, to their jobs. The making of endless pots of tea often seemed more urgent than their assigned tasks, and their bodies often seemed stunted—was it a genetic trait in the working class or the simple result of poor nutrition in childhood?

Invigorated by my brief exploration and the gradually unfolding vast difference between this place and the one I'd left in America, I was back in college for a revealing hall-lunch of shepherd's pie and bread, then my usual half-hour's afternoon nap; then off to the adjacent college—Corpus Christi—for my first Oxford tea. Corpus was even smaller than Merton and was nearly as venerable, a college visited and praised by Erasmus, that beacon of the northern Renaissance—and a man who, in his portrait by Holbein, resembles nothing so much as "the direct descendant of a long line of maiden aunts," as one of my Duke professors had said.

My shipboard friend from Yale, Jim Griffin, had acquired a tasty small cake—dark brown with raisins—at a baker's shop in the Cornmarket (which intersects the High); and as we lingered by Jim's hearth to share our first-day's discoveries, we managed to wash the entire cake down with numerous cups of strong tea. I didn't quite tell Jim; but I was a little chastened to learn that he'd already met—that morning, while I was wandering open-eyed and buying crockery—with his forthcoming tutor and had acquired a detailed sense of what would be expected of him as a graduate student in philosophy.

In those postwar days Oxford was still entering the world of graduate study with some misgivings. Its undergraduate degree—laid atop the superb fullness of British secondary education—was so thorough in the required mastery of a given field that postgraduate study was still considered by many to be one more regrettable case of surrender to American excess. Wouldn't anyone who'd won his Oxford B.A. or B.Sc. spend the rest of his life in continued self-education? So Rhodes Scholars of our generation were faced with a choice. Given that all of us had American undergraduate degrees of varying qualities, should we opt for a further and perhaps finer (certainly more demanding) undergraduate degree; or should we sign on for one of the few graduate degrees—a Bachelor of Letters, say, or the more demanding D.Phil.?

Jim and I had already gathered, in reading our way through an indispensable handbook called *The Oxford University Examination Statutes*, that graduate students were very much on their own. Sooner or later each of us would be assigned a tutor or thesis director with whom we'd meet, say, four times in an eight-week term. We'd be free to attend any of the university's hundreds of public courses of lectures, many of them from world-renowned scholars; and likely we'd participate in a handful of small seminars to prepare us for our work. Then we'd undergo a rigorous written test followed by a nerve-racking oral. If we succeeded in that test, we'd be certified to begin the real work of graduate study—deep reading, thinking, and writing on whatever subject: again, very much on our own, with our thesis director standing ready to give our arms an occasional nudge to left or right but, generally speaking, little more. Thus Oxford avoided a grave and continuing danger of American graduate study—the possibility that a thesis or dissertation director might prove so controlling as virtually to write the student's thesis.

Had I, for instance, chosen the B.A. degree, I'd have had to learn Anglo-Saxon and—in a packed two years of work—read my way through virtually the entirety of then-canonical English literature from *Beowulf* to the great poets, novelists, and essayists of the late nineteenth century. Anything more recent had yet to prove itself durable and was thus not studied. At least once a week, during term time, I'd have written an essay assigned by my tutor and then read it to him in his room while he listened (or occasionally dozed) and then offered his comments. At the end of my two or three years of reading, I'd have sat for the final examinations—called *schools*—some five days of papers and an eventual face-to-face questioning by other dons who'd award me my degree, First Class, Second Class, Pass, or Fail—to *fail* was called to *plough*, and there were sufficient suicides by schools failures to constitute an imposing warning. By now, though, I'd firmly decided to try for the graduate B.Litt. with a thesis on Milton. I wasn't eager to restudy many texts I'd only just finished reading. I also sensed that a B.Litt.—with its freedoms—would give me far more time to spend on my own fiction, a hope that had, in the past year, been cut deeper in my mind than before.

As I walked the two hundred yards back from Jim's rooms to Mob Quad, I underwent my first immersion in an English evening. It was only six clock, and I was stationed not that far from the south coast of Britain, yet it was already dark; and while it wasn't raining, the air was all but drenched with the damp that Bill Jackson had so darkly warned against—*Aargh, piles!* Suddenly, and for the first time, I felt a dull grind from the tooth of loneliness—and worse: a maybe misguided separation from the roots of my emotions and thus my writing. What the hell was I doing here?

I'd effectively abandoned the only house that anchored me for the past eight years, the Raleigh home of my much-loved mother and brother, the actual ground of my whole past life (the rolling pine-dense landscape of eastern and central North Carolina), not to mention the numerous other kin and friends of my childhood and youth. Now they were all four thousand miles to my west, my *southwest*— Britain is after all on a virtual parallel with Newfoundland, whereas my home is parallel with Algeria.

A vast ocean now lay between me and mine, an ocean strewn with the ruins of millennia of human hope at least as passionate as my own. I'm not attempting to exaggerate—or elevate—a boyish emotion, only to re-create a wave of long-distant feeling. And here I was, alone as a stone, in a city and country as different from my home as, say, Germany or Poland—and I wasn't wrong about this, not in 1955 before American economic and cultural influence radically transformed so much of British culture.

I had no proof—beyond the language I shared, in part, with the half-dozen kindly Britons I'd met—that I could manage to live on here, live and work, for at least two more years. I'd meant for six years now to be a fiction writer and poet, one who taught literature to good students. Did I have the faintest chance of being both or either, essentially sidetracked here as I feared I might be—in the country of Shakespeare, Milton, Wordsworth, and Keats—so far from everything I knew? An artist as uncannily gifted as James Dean had got only two more years of life than I and had died a week ago through an error at the wheel of a speeding Porsche. What good was likely to come to me here?

3

WITHIN THE NEXT WEEK, other than several other social events with my fellow Yanks and endless knockings on my door by people trying to sell me memberships in everything from the Film Society to the Communist Club, there were two important meetings. The first occurred when an undergraduate tapped on my door, advanced a step, took one look at me at my desk as late afternoon light crept through my Meadow window, and with no particular scorn in his voice (though with a slightly wry smile) said "I don't suppose you'd be interested in soccer." It was not a question. At that point his smile became a grin as he stood on in my doorway, in case I chose to surprise him. Did I look that hopelessly unathletic; and after my first Oxford haircut, was I still that ineradicably American looking (he'd said *soccer*, not the more British *football*)?

I said I probably wasn't interested, though in high-school gym I'd played it without the shame I earned in baseball and basketball. By then I'd turned my chair to face him. His was, again, another unmistakably English face but a markedly well-shaped one, topped with blond hair in unarranged rings as in one of Leonardo's late drawings of floodwater. So I repeated that he probably didn't want me on the college team—it was the Merton team he was promoting. Then I stood and invited him in for coffee—powdered coffee but still a beverage that seemed to connote manly vigor more nearly than the tea for which I was only just equipped.

The Hon. Secretary of the Football Club accepted, took a seat; and before we finished our first cups, we were further along toward a mutual liking than I'd so far anticipated with an Englishman. His name was Michael Jordan (not a relation of the later basketball star). Like Mayr-Harting and Gilchrist, Michael was also in the second year of history. He'd lived in Canada with his mother's sister for a year in early adolescence, and he was "very keen indeed for classic jazz." With his likable baritone speaking-voice (which became a bass when he laughed) and an accent that, while not supremely Oxonian, was clear and mildly upper-class, he had the poised cool I'd expected of my college friends.

My trunk contained no record player and I owned few jazz records—though I'd already liked both Louis Armstrong and Duke Ellington in concerts at Duke—but I tried to wing my way here with Michael, pretending to more jazz expertise than I possessed. He lightly corrected my errors, knowing the details right back to King Oliver and beyond. We talked our way on in to glasses of sherry; and then he trotted off to his room in Rose Lane, beyond the college garden, to don his gown and meet me at the steps of the hall for seven o'clock dinner. We sat amid a cluster of his history and football friends, and much welcome laughter consumed us as they consumed rapidly (to my amazement) a monumentally awful dinner of tasteless fish, brutally roasted potatoes, and sodden gray cabbage. I ate enough to insure survival, then went to Michael's smaller but unusually orderly rooms for after-dinner coffee and more talk—this time about movies, I think—on into late evening when I found my way through the towering dark trees, and the mumbling spirits, back toward my straw bed.

The second important early meeting soon followed the first when I received a crabbed handwritten note from my potential thesis director, a man named J. B. Leishman (he had presumably been assigned by some member of the English faculty, as it was then called). He was inviting me to call upon him, very soon, in his home in the Victorian awfulness of nineteenth-century north Oxford. I'd hoped to work with the famed C. S. Lewis, a distinguished Miltonist—among other things. But though Lewis had spent virtually his whole life at Oxford, he'd only just accepted a post at Cambridge. Though Leishman was not a member of Merton—he was a lecturer at St. John's—he'd published numerous essays and books in the field of what was then called Elizabethan and Jacobean literature. I'd heard of him in yet another of his connections. For a year I'd owned and attempted to comprehend the translation of Rilke's exciting but obscure *Duino Elegies* which he'd made with the poet Stephen Spender.

When he answered my diffident knock then, I expected a scholar in the picturesque Oxford mold—a tangled mane of rusty white hair, Benjamin-Franklin-style half-glasses, and dandruff-dusted clothes. Not at all. With virtually no pause for introduction, Mr. Leishman led me toward a large sitting room on the ground floor, motioned me toward a chair, then stepped to his mantel and continued standing as he proceeded—before anything else—to note my origins at Duke and then commence deploring a book on *Paradise Lost* by one of my professors there. That was Allan Gilbert, an admired American Miltonist with whom I'd studied in my senior year; his enthusiasm had proved especially contagious. Young as I was, in under two minutes Leishman's continued and inexplicable attack had begun to rile me. In another few minutes it became clear that Leishman had reviewed Gilbert's book in a professional journal and had satisfied himself that the volume was therefore buried forever (along with any enduring Gilbertian allegiance which I might be nursing).

Later years have let me see that Gilbert's book is a little dotty but is also usefully provocative and never boring—considerably more than can be said for a great deal of the work of J. B. Leishman (an immensely learned scholar, in six languages, his work is almost uninterruptedly dull; and his Rilke translations are astonishingly poor). As an introduction to me, however, Mr. Leishman had—pompous as it may sound in the mind of a scholar as young as I—stepped off on a very wrong foot (eight years later he would die by stepping off a mountain in Switzerland). And as I continued to sit beneath his tirade, which included further deplorings of "you Americans," I had ample time to take him in.

Far from the dusty geezer I'd expected, he was a man in his early fifties, dressed entirely in shades of brown—a thorn-proof brown tweed jacket with a brown pocket handkerchief, brown knickerbockers (our men's knickers) with brown stockings, and a brown silk scarf (what Americans call an ascot). I wondered if he'd somehow devised this costume for my visit, but *The Oxford Dictionary of National Biography* says that this was his "inevitable" dress, and *The Oxford Magazine* described his appearance as that of "a genial and benevolent witch." On first encounter, those adjectives failed to occur to me, though his get-up did strike me as entirely original, winningly comic, and no doubt memorable. I'd soon deduce that he was a bachelor gentleman who kept open house on Thursday evenings for his male students.

At the time I was too impressed by the consistency of his attire and the fervor of his tirade to release the laughter that rose in me in increasingly powerful waves. I kept my seat and, given a chance at last, I told him a little about my intent to write a thesis on Milton's play *Samson Agonistes*. He grumbled for a while longer about the unlikelihood of my being prepared for such an effort, especially if this Professor Gilbert had taught me; but we somehow got to near-dusk without an untoward external incident.

Then he showed me back to the door with a final insistence that I begin to attend his "Thursday evenings" for "wine and good talk." I never did. In fact, I saw him only once more in the course of that whole term—a second meeting when he went on cranking his hurdy-gurdy's repetitive "you Americans," as though a twenty-two-year-old Yank was too simpleminded to realize that his own lower standing in the hierarchy of this till now infallibly courteous institution was being justified by this brown-knickered witch.

Strangely enough, my first meeting with Mr. Leishman failed to depress me. In all my years of formal education in America, I'd encountered only one really bad teacher, a woman in the fourth grade. Too many arresting British novelties were breaking round me by the hour for a single bizarre academic to cause grave discouragement—not yet. Furthermore in the first two or three weeks of the eight-week term, I was discovering that—far from living up to their reputation as icily reserved and culturally superior pricks—the Brits I'd met (with the exception of J. B. Leishman) were generally proving to be no more chilly or superior than the run of Americans in any sizable town.

They were helpful and pleasantly curious about me and my needs (young Americans were far scarcer at Oxford than now, and even Mr. Leishman had his evenings). From my student colleagues, their teach-

ers, and their world, I was learning a dozen facts and skills per day—
not to mention the acquisition of a virtually new language and accent,
or a dialect of English that amounted to a far more distinct language
than I'd anticipated from the courtly but emotionally resourceful
language of the upper American South that I'd spoken for two decades
and in which I'd begun my written fiction, poetry, and critical essays.

At least half my conscious mind, then, was beginning to be
rewarded by thought of my oncoming work, by most of my new
teachers, and several promising friends. So my bout of uncertainty as
to the wisdom of being here had retreated for now. And soon I'd
learn that the elastic rules of the English faculty would yield up a welcome access to someone other than Mr. Leishman.

In the first full week of term, after all, I'd attended the lectures of
the famous Helen Gardner on the metaphysical poets of the seventeenth century (John Donne and George Herbert prime among
them). I'd also joined a highly informal seminar—Lord David Cecil's
in practical criticism. And I'd begun, with my twenty-odd fellow
B.Litt. aspirants, to attend the small classes designed to prepare us for
our eventual research. Professor F. P. Wilson, a kind bulky rabbit of a
man, instructed us in methods and sources of research for work in the
literature of the English Renaissance (he was then at work on the volume covering a portion of that period in *The Oxford History of English
Literature*). Helen Gardner was not yet Dame Helen and was thus a
good deal less formidable than she'd eventually be. In addition to her
huge lecture course, she led us B.Litt. aspirants through a meticulous
class on the textual editing of poems of the same period. She was then
involved in editing the poems of Donne, and we used her photostats
of earlier editions and manuscripts—Xerox was a decade down the
road—to make the difficult choices among numerous verbal candidates which would lead us to the poet's intentions (the detective in me
was steadily aroused).

Herbert Davis, an English scholar of eighteenth-century literature
who'd also been president of Smith College, taught us how Renaissance books and broadsides were printed; and he eventually supervised our printing, on the Bodleian Library's large old handpress, a

small gathering of the poems we'd edited for Miss Gardner. Finally a likable man in Hertford College taught us to read, and even to write, many of the otherwise illegible handwritten scripts of the time (see Shakespeare's signature on his will, for an instance of seventeenth-century illegibility).

Each of the classes was continuously interesting; and they offered the chance to begin an acquaintance with the few other students who hoped to pass a one-day exam, plus an oral, at the end of our second term. Success would either certify us to begin work on our theses or forbid our proceeding. Both Miss Gardner's lectures on the Metaphysicals, in one of the booming lecture rooms of the enormous and icy Examination Schools, and Lord David's small class in criticism—some fifteen students—which met in his slightly warmer rooms in New College were superb in almost startlingly different ways. I could see, when Lord David sat and raised his trouser legs a little, that he was the only Briton of my time whom I discovered as a wearer of men's long underwear. Later I'd be wearing the same in the grimmer months.

Helen Gardner knew her subjects exhaustively and conveyed her mastery in lucid, but never condescending, lectures—one of the rarest of academic skills. She'd nonetheless been subjected to many of the disappointments of a brilliant woman in what was then distinctly a man's world. Stephen Spender would eventually tell me that he'd heard from W. H. Auden that, when she held a job at the University of Birmingham, Gardner fell in love with the poet Henry Reed. Reed, however, was queer; and Gardner's encounter with that reality led to a psychotic breakdown. In the absence of a good biography, I can't vouch for Auden's story; but it has a likely sound, especially since I slowly became aware of her reservations about many of her male colleagues at Oxford, and more than once I heard her cast strong aspersions at Auden and his friends. As her pupil, of course I was fascinated to hear of those possible early troubles in her life.

In any case her ferocious conviction of the rightness of her opinions and her thrusting ambition in a time when women were still not expected to possess such aims left her unpopular with many of her fellows in the English faculty. And I later learned from one of her more

Lord David Cecil, photographed by my friend Thomas Victor when David visited the States in 1979. I flew to New York to see him, and spent a memorably bibulous and affectionate evening with him and his wife Rachel in the otherwise empty but opulent apartment of Mrs. Brooke Astor (she'd lent it to the Cecils for their New York stay). The next morning I phoned Tom Victor—than whom there's been no better photographer of writers—and asked him to photograph David and, if possible, to catch his lordship in the unself-conscious midst of one of his most famous Oxford-lecture gestures—both hands upright in the air near his face, with the long fingers extended on the verge of stroking one another nervously. Luckily, Tom succeeded. Here David is seventy-seven years old, yet the picture clearly summons back the splendid talker who never treated me with anything less than unbroken kindness. Tom died of AIDS at far too young an age, and his best photographs have never been collected in a book.

sympathetic colleagues—David Cecil—that "Helen is the only person I've known who went barking mad and then came back—partway at least." Luckily I collided with none of her unlikable traits. On the contrary—after a well-earned knuckle-rapping, she always treated me warmly.

It's worth noting here that she then had no earned doctoral degree; but that was true of virtually all the best teachers with whom I worked at Oxford—again, British academics would generally receive an initial bachelor's degree; then proceed to educate themselves thereafter, and brilliantly so in a good many cases. F. P. Wilson, David Cecil, Helen Gardner, and Nevill Coghill (among my early teachers) possessed a depth of knowledge and reflection which they wore with a grace, wit, and often elastic readiness to learn that was new to me. It's been disturbing to learn, however (from the last book published by my eventual digs-mate Anthony Nuttall), that "when Dame Helen Gardner, famous for her academic ferocity, lay dying, she too was visited [as Richard III was in Shakespeare's play] by the figures of those whose theses she had failed, whose careers she had marred; they stood round her bed." Tony didn't say where he'd learned of her deathbed trials (and now he too is dead); but he himself had been a student refused by Gardner, though his superbly successful career was hardly marred by her.

David Cecil, the critic and biographer of Lord Melbourne and Max Beerbohm (among numerous others), was the object of more affectionate and unskilled mimicry than any other member of the English faculty, of which he was now the most internationally noted member. The grandson of Lord Salisbury, Queen Victoria's long-serving prime minister, and a descendant of William and Robert Cecil, who had served Elizabeth I and James I in similar offices, Lord David had more than a few justifications for self-confident oddities. And in fact he was notorious—in his well-attended lectures—for eccentricities of performance which may or may not have been intentional or neurologically required.

For example, he tended, in his frequent moments of genuine aesthetic excitement, to spray his nearby auditors with tiny drops of spittle. In even more powerful moments, he'd clamp his eyes shut and rise to his toes in an *O altitudo!* of appreciative ecstasy. Simultaneously the mile-long fingers of either hand might extend and wave round before him with what his delighted students called "Lord David's porridge-stirring." Even in calmer moments, his thumbs executed a ceaseless stroking rhythm on his second fingers—a habit which I sometimes find myself unconsciously imitating, even today.

However if a student troubled to approach him with a serious question—or to attend a term's worth of one of his small classes and immerse in the texts he set for his weekly meetings—that student could come to know a senior scholar-critic of unfailingly keen intelligence, warmed with a generous admixture of kindness and an utterly personal humor. But lest I've suggested an excessive softness, I'll add that he suffered no fool gladly, even the then-notorious Dr. F. R. Leavis of Cambridge, who'd often employed David Cecil as a foppish straw-man representative of all that was wrong in British literary studies. Yet if an apparent student-fool proved to be psychically disturbed, he'd find real compassion from Lord David. In the first term's class, I saw him deal helpfully over several weeks with a genuine madman in our midst, one who seriously imagined that Princess Margaret was about to visit him.

Sad to say, a friend's wit in conversation is the most fleeting of gifts. When the friend is gone, so is the humor, since it's invariably a function of that person's entire body in action (especially in so peculiar a body as Lord David's and in however small a room). But in a lifetime's acquaintance with several world-class talkers, I've known no other conversationalist who equaled David Cecil. And I stress the word *conversationalist*. He was most definitely not a monologist, and he took watchful care to avoid boring his company. He even once told me that his uncle Hugh Cecil had encountered a man who was famed as "the greatest bore in England." After a long prologue the great bore paused and said "I *hope* I'm not boring you, Lord Hugh"; and the kindly Lord Hugh replied "Not *yet*." The fact that David Cecil gradually became one of the greatly treasured friends of my life continues to be a source of real thanks for me.

As I've written these lines about him, I've returned to a fascinating volume of recollections—*David Cecil* edited by Hannah Cranborne, his great-niece by marriage. Reading the memories of such friends as Isaiah Berlin, John Bayley, Anthony Powell, and the old family retainer (third footman at one of the Cecil estates) who said of David "He wasn't sporty and he didn't like shooting," I've found myself sad again to have lost such a man. In fact I can think of no adult friend— and almost no kin of my own, however beloved—whose physical presence and voice I miss more than David Cecil's; thus hereafter I'll mostly refer to him as David, which (early on) he asked me to do. In any case, his lordly status was a courtesy title, received as a son of the Marquess of Salisbury; and in those pre-Thatcher days, most of us enjoyed our work with an affable lord.

But in the midst of so many pleasures—such a rush of gladness—an unexpected darkness began to consume me. First, as October accumulated its shorter and shorter days, I was growing aware of my position on the planet. I was after all on a latitude with the start of unoccupied Labrador. By early November, full day wasn't dawning on Merton College till about well past eight o'clock; a blue dusk was descending by four as the river mists rolled across the Meadow toward my window, and I had nearly two months to go before we reached the winter solstice—the year's shortest day. That long ago very few of us knew anything about a now-familiar condition called SAD—seasonal affective disorder, a possibly severe psychic response triggered by hormonal change, to sunlight deprivation. Symptoms might range from mild depression to more serious derangements.

Among my many pleasures then, I was somehow growing sadder by the day. Something told me that I was responding—almost two years later—to my active role in Dad's last weeks, the awful days after the removal of a lung in the hopes of surviving—for a few months or, at most, two years longer—the cancer he'd earned (at age fifty-four) for the smoking he'd joked about beginning in pre-adolescence. Mostly I'd served him as an efficient manager in critical situations; and as an elder son who'd never been called on for significant help, I took way too much pride in my final role. So it was months before I'd begun to feel at all troubled. I knew that I'd yet to undergo a full acknowledgment of Dad's death; and I didn't realize the inevitability of some such recognition. Was that what was gripping me now?

Whatever, one evening I returned to my rooms from a musical outing with a friend from New Zealand, Jeremy Commons; and as I stripped before donning my pajamas, I felt a small uneasiness in my left side, some five inches west of my navel. I explored the spot and soon discovered a firm lump, no bigger than a boy's agate marble. The skin around it was not numb, but the shallow-buried lump seemed to lack all feeling. Was that a bad sign? Whatever, in an instant I was drenched in a downpour of certainty—*cancer*. My father had died of it twenty months ago, and now I'd join him.

Through the next two weeks, my mind increasingly sickened me; but I told no one. Who was there to tell? Among my new friends, no one yet seemed near enough to burden with the news. They were all my own age or younger; and if I needed anything just now—short of healing—it was wisdom. In those days only the wealthy could afford phone calls to the States (in the three years to come, I'd phone home one single time); and I wouldn't want to alarm my mother with unconfirmed news.

After maybe ten days, during which I walked through my duties and a round of modest entertainments in near-zombie fashion, I went to Dr. Kirkham, the college physician whose office was a good distance across the city—near the almost disturbingly hideous Keble College, built (as it was) from an array of Victorian colored bricks, almost like some child's entertainment. Kirkham patiently heard my complaint, examined me briskly, and told me that I had no cause for concern. This was plainly a small fatty tumor, he said, a lipoma—a collection of fat cells—and it might be reabsorbed as rapidly as it had formed. It would hardly grow further. I should ignore it and go about my life.

I recall telling myself a dumb joke as I walked back to Merton. *Ignore it and go about my life*—fat *chance!* The joke of course was no help at all. In the coming days—in an effort to calm myself (and with little thought that sheer work might serve me best of all)—I'd begin to indulge in one of the fine sidebars of Oxford life: plays and other theatrical events. My Rhodester friend Frank Sieverts organized at Balliol College a public reading of Tennessee Williams's brand-new play, the deeply felt—and for those days, startlingly candid—*Cat on a Hot Tin Roof*; and I read the leading male role: the sexually and psychically tormented Brick. I didn't feel then (and never would) a special affinity with Brick's passive agonies, but Frank's gentle demand for extensive rehearsals—and the large and enthusiastic audience who turned out for our single performance—gave me some relief.

The other immediate possibilities for diversion included productions available in the town itself. There were two professional venues—the New Theatre and the Oxford Playhouse—plus numerous college productions of all sorts. In London, only forty miles southeast and reachable by numerous trains per day, there were endless inexpensive shows. And at the end of a brief hitch-hike ride some forty miles northwest, there was Stratford-upon-Avon with its Shakespeare Memorial Theatre which—just a stone's throw from either his birthplace or his tomb—provided a rich variety of first-rate actors in mostly fine productions of the work of the world's ultimate Hometown Boy. In my first term I also went to what seemed a thousand films. Apart from the numerous cinemas in town, the Oxford Film Society offered screenings of classic films that had been past my reach in Raleigh or Durham, and Michael and I attended at least one such offering each week.

Then with Michael and another friend or two, I saw—at the New Theatre—an uncut pre-London production of *Hamlet* with Paul Scofield as the Prince and Diana Wynyard as his mother. After Laurence Olivier's filmed *Hamlet* of the late 1940s, Scofield's seemed excessively dry and monotone—a hard young man to care for, certainly not for the very long hours of an uncut performance; and though Wynyard was a glamorous Gertrude, Mary Ure's Ophelia was a howling embarrassment. In Stratford I saw Anthony Quayle and Joyce Redman in a rollicking, if obvious *Merry Wives of Windsor* and then John Gielgud and Claire Bloom in *King Lear*. Though the

Vivien Leigh and Laurence Olivier as the murderous Macbeths in a production at the Shakespeare Memorial Theatre in Stratford-upon-Avon in 1955. I saw a performance with several Rhodester friends, and afterward we proceeded back-stage for a meeting with Miss Leigh (Lady Olivier) who told us in amusing detail about a recent and loudly ballistic Guy Fawkes Night at the Oliviers' home in the countryside. The two of them—near the end of their long and famous marriage—were appearing in a full season at Stratford—*Macbeth*, *Twelfth Night*, and *Titus Andronicus*. I'd eventually see their astonishing *Titus* three times but each of the other plays only once. It was a decade in which some critics felt that Leigh was exposing a smaller classical talent to dangerous comparisons by appearing with her titanic husband, whom she far surpassed as a film actor. Before the Stratford *Macbeth*, I'd seen the two of them together in New York in a superb *Antony and Cleopatra* where her Cleopatra was plainly superior to his underheated Antony (the same week, I saw their *Caesar and Cleopatra*). At Stratford, Olivier's Macbeth was incomparable in its detailed portrait of a man slowly consumed by evil; but then Leigh's smaller-scaled Lady Macbeth was a gorgeous viper who adored her husband and lured him into his murders by her sexual power over him. I've never seen better Shakespearean performances than the two of them delivered that fall at Stratford.

sets and costumes for *Lear* by the Japanese-American artist Isamu Noguchi were too independent an attraction, the acting was unforgettably potent. Most impressive of all, in the midst of my descent into cancer fear, I saw the three most imposing Shakespeare productions of my life: Vivien Leigh and Laurence Olivier in *Twelfth Night*, *Macbeth*, and *Titus Andronicus*.

But with all the attempted distractions, my cancer worry continued till it had deepened into a real phobia, even the beginnings of a psychic breakdown. As the lump in my side seemed—to my probing fingers— to grow, I seriously thought of going to the one midtown travel agency and inquiring about the costs of shipping a corpse from Oxford to the States. As easily as I can imagine any reader's laughing at the revelation, to me it still doesn't seem a comic idea. The fact that I held off my inquiry was some sort of dawning realization that I was almost in deeper water than I could return from. I went back to the college doctor, and by then he perceived the gravity of my mental condition and sent me to a surgeon.

British surgeons are called *Mister* not *Doctor,* and I seem to recall that the fine man I visited in his offices in north Oxford was called Mr. Till. In any case, he patiently sat and heard me describe my recent history, then examined me, then sent me to the Radcliffe Infirmary for full X-ray studies. When he had the images in hand, he called me back to confirm what I'd already been told more than once—the X-rays had revealed a harmless fatty tumor. Since I'd told him of my accompanying stomach upsets, Mr. Till added a further interesting detail (in words to this effect)—"Mr. Price, I suspect that your gastric health may be complicated by your recent immersion in an English college diet. At the end of the war, we encountered a number of released prisoners of the Nazis who were suffering what we came to call carbohydrate shock. After months of sadly deprived rations, the sudden flood of potatoes, turnips, swedes, and bread swamped many of them with excess starch; and we had to warn them to limit their consumption, especially of potatoes" (at least two of those items were major components of virtually every Merton meal, and turnips had begun showing up only days

before—swedes are what Americans call rutabagas). Having consoled me to that extent, Mr. Till then said that he'd like me to see a
physician in Longwall Street—"Dr. Mallam, just a good internist to be
sure everything else is in working order."

I saw that elderly gentleman who examined me, stem to stern;
then said that Mr. Till had mentioned my father's recent death—
would I tell him more about it? I recounted my role in those events,
Dr. Mallam nodded and said "Well, of *course* you've been concerned." Then he repeated the harmlessness of my tumor but said
that, if I'd feel better about it, he could arrange with Mr. Till to have
it removed—a simple procedure. With a kindly upraised hand,
though, he stalled a prompt agreement from me and said that I
should take a few days to think through the prospect, then let him
know my decision. When he stood to see me out, he actually touched
my shoulder—something no one had yet done in England—and he
said "Mr. Price, if you have a cancer, I'm about to have a litter of pup-
pies." His rosy plump face grinned enormously, I suddenly burst out
laughing, and my weeks'-long fear was dispelled on the spot.

On my way back to college, I stopped in at Corpus to see Jim
Griffin. He and I had discussed the possibility of a joint trip to Italy during the upcoming Christmas holiday or vac, as it was called—each of
us would be expected to clear out of our college rooms for most of the
time—and I'd held him off while I contemplated my imminent
death, though of course I didn't give him that excuse for my delay.
(The Oxford academic year basically consisted of three eight-week
terms—Michaelmas, Hilary, and Trinity—interspersed by vacs of
some six weeks, with a longer summer vac.) Now I could tell Jim about
my misplaced worry and confirm that I hoped we could move ahead
with Italian plans—the fact that we had no erotic interest whatever in
one another was one of the firmest grounds of our friendship.

Our original interest in such a trip had been encouraged by one of the
unique Britons whom I'd encountered—a woman named Pamela
Redmayne. I'd first met her when she'd visited friends during my final
semester at Duke and had taken me to lunch in Durham. At the time

she seemed to be in her mid- to late fifties and was the epitome of what I took to be a certain kind of English maiden lady—tall, not quite handsome but physically imposing, given to a steady stream of talk about herself and her famous friends. The years would sadly prove that—despite the hospitality of her home in the Cotswold village of Burford—Pamela was given to mythomania, a form of narrative invention in which she placed herself at the center of many important events, often political events which she couldn't have witnessed, much less engendered.

For a single example, she once told me (in words to this effect) "Yes, I well remember when I was in Russia midway through the war, Joe Stalin called me in, showed me a long ward of starving boys and girls and said 'Miss Redmayne, I only have food for ten of these children. You alone can make the choice; which ones shall we save?' " I honestly don't believe that I've misrepresented her story—or more precisely, my memory of her story. Whether the stories proceeded from a walled-off set of delusions about her past or a simple desire to entertain guests or to make her own quiet life seem more dramatic, I can't say.

Still, she had many forms of thoughtfulness, none of which I've forgot. Operating from her narrow two-story cottage attached to a large farmhouse called Bartholomews on the high hill at the end of the Burford High Street beyond the church and the Windrush River—and surely with a small minimum of funds—she'd often invite six or eight Rhodes Scholars to board a bus early on an Oxford Sunday morning and make the fifteen-mile trip to Burford (with the usual young man's lack of curiosity about his elders, I never asked her how she acquired her interest in Rhodesters). There by her omnipresent sitting-room fire, we'd toast ourselves with sherry and then eat an ample lunch of well-cooked and blessedly seasoned chicken with copious amounts of rice. Though not a subtle cook, Pamela claimed time at the Cordon Bleu school in Paris; and while most of her recipes seemed more nearly Spanish than French, they produced unfailingly likable results.

After lunch she was likely to produce a walking stick for each of us and lead us off on a thoroughly brisk two-mile walk down the hill to

Burford's superb church or along the line of the slender Windrush, barely more than a creek, where Queen Elizabeth I had been welcomed by the villagers nearly four centuries earlier. And for this hospitality, she asked nothing more from us than, perhaps, "Four of the best lettuces from the Open Market in Oxford" or that we up-end the full rain barrel by the front corner of her house. As dusk began to close in, she'd give us a quick cup of tea with one of her fresh scones and homemade quince jam; then imperiously shoo us on our way downhill for the last bus back to Oxford (we'd flag it down, in the dark, with our white handkerchiefs).

One of the favors she'd done for me and Jim Griffin was to provide the name and address of a pensione in Florence, almost every Englishman's favorite Italian city. It was the Pensione Quisisana, right on the Arno, only a few yards from the Uffizi Gallery and the city's central piazza. But our first term still had a couple of weeks to run; and freed as I now was from cancer, I was still oppressed by the darkness and the indoor chill as winter drew near. Each Mertonian had a single electric-coil heater to warm his two rooms; but given the size of my rooms and the river damp, switching on the heater was about as effective as lighting a match in a chilled gymnasium. My return to health was completed, though, by an increasing number of friends—from England, New Zealand, Holland, and the States. Michael Jordan, with his keen interest in American culture and his readiness to go with me to films, plays, and concerts had soon become what David Gilchrist (he of the "dressing gown" breakfast) called my sparring partner.

And I managed to do a good deal of the reading called for by Miss Gardner's lectures, Lord David's class, my several prep courses for the B.Litt. exam, and my ongoing love of Milton. During my freshman year at Duke, in a major's introductory course, I'd come to love *Paradise Lost* for the Baroque complexity of language which it managed to combine with an ultimately paradoxical tenderness toward its hapless and all-too-fallible human stars, Adam and Eve in their perfect home—Eden. And here four years later in a dark and freezing Oxford, I had a just-sufficient supply of scholarly genes to power me through the necessary hours of reading in an underheated Bodleian Library and my own ancient rooms (though Milton attended Cambridge, he was known to have visited the university library in which I studied; his father was a native of Oxfordshire, and the poet married his teenaged first wife some three miles away).

Stronger still, however, and growing steadily was the hope to write my own fiction and poetry. Late in the first term, I conceived a story called "The Warrior Princess Ozimba." If I could find time to write it, it would be my second attempt to enclose—and partially defuse—some of the lingering intensities of Dad's dying in a well-controlled and compelling narrative. Less than a year before, I'd written—in the single writing class I ever took—a story called "A Chain of Love." It dealt with a death like my father's and the family ordeal which surrounded it, and it still needed work.

Nonetheless it seemed firm enough to stand alone—a story that centered on an imagined girl named Rosacoke Mustian (my first use of a character who'd appear in three later novels) and on Rosa's sympathetic fascination with a family who accompany a dying husband and father across the hospital hallway from her own dying grandfather—such a country family were encamped with an old kinsman in a room near Dad's, though I never spoke with them. In contrast, "The Warrior Princess Ozimba" would center on a young man's assuming a duty of his father's soon after that older man's death—the delivery of a promised pair of tennis shoes to an old black woman who had worked for their family through many decades. Even while I read for hours in the work on which I might soon be examined by the English faculty, I thought obsessively about both my stories. The two—one nearly finished, the other not yet begun—had all but convinced me that I was not wholly wrong to head for a writer's future.

Less than a year earlier, Eudora Welty had been invited to Duke by a committee from the Woman's College. She delivered a lecture that would become her much-admired later essay "Place in Fiction"; and at the request of my teacher William Blackburn, she met with a small group of students and commented on their manuscript stories.

Eudora Welty on her first trip to Italy, probably in the fall of 1949. Not long after we met in 1955, at my request she sent me this picture and called it, in her accompanying letter, "Eudora of the Boboli." She's in the Boboli Gardens in Florence, and the picture is by Anthony Bower. Taken years before osteoporosis began to produce a slowly painful spinal curvature that stole seven inches off her height, she's clearly a tall woman here, as she still was some five years later when I met her. Never a natural beauty, Eudora had nonetheless an overwhelming attentiveness and concern that left most people who met her with the sense of a beautiful nature. Uncoached, many—on their first meeting—remarked how much she was like Eleanor Roosevelt: devoid of surface attractions yet powerfully magnetic. Though I'd see her hereafter, time and again till near her death, I almost never saw her otherwise than elegant and lovely. She signed a picture of the two of us, taken in the mid-1980s, with these few words that move me deeply still—"Ours the best of friendships."

At that point in my dreamy notion of a writer's career, I'd finished a single very short story which I was prepared to show a writer of Welty's distinction. It was called "Michael Egerton," was no more than three thousand words long, and again it dealt with an emotional and ethical quandary I myself had experienced at the age of twelve in my only time as a summer camper.

At the end of her impromptu class—and in the presence of other students—Miss Welty told me that my story was thoroughly professional; might she show it to her agent? I was semi-pulverized with surprise, knowing that she'd actually published a handful of stories as good as the best of Chekhov. So I accepted her offer at once; and very shortly thereafter her agent—the superb Diarmuid Russell (pronounced *DUR-mid*)—contacted me, said that he thought "Michael Egerton" was "good," and offered to circulate the story and any others that might be ready. At the time I was completing the first draft of the Rosacoke story, and I sent that on to him not long before heading to England.

He and I stayed in regular touch thereafter. Diarmuid's extremely prompt letters had the quality of the e-mail whose invention was still decades off—a near-telegraphic speed, brevity, and pith. A cradle Irishman and the son of the mystic poet Æ (George Russell), Diarmuid had come to America as a young man but had maintained an ironic Irish view of Britain. One of his first letters to me at Oxford previewed his characteristic brand of brisk sympathy. He responded to my early complaint of insufficient indoor heating by informing me that the young Charles Darwin had encountered on Tierra del Fuego, while voyaging on the *Beagle,* indigenous folk sleeping naked (with no apparent discomfort) in the snow.

For all his salty attention, however, Diarmuid could not place any of my first finished stories—not quickly—and like so many apprentice writers, I spent more time in balked yearning than was good for my academic duties. *When would my work reach even a small public of readers?* I can even recall experiencing, on my straw bed, more than one dream in which I went to my pigeonhole in the Merton lodge and found—Yes! Letters of acceptance and actual checks.

So my first term's work was more than a little compromised by all the uncertainties that surrounded my prime ambition to write and by the physical and psychic complexities that had surfaced in the wake of Dad's death. I did, as I noted, see Mr. Leishman a second time in the term, though I recall nothing about the meeting. But the remainder of my degree work was accomplished in the B.Litt. classes and other public lectures. My chief memory of those weeks of work would have to be a partly delicious, partly melancholy sense of solitude as I'd walk the few hundred yards back to college from a long afternoon of reading in the Bodleian.

Once I dodged my way through the murderous traffic of the High, I'd duck down the narrow lane that led to Merton Street. Its modern name is Magpie Lane; but in medieval documents it's a little startlingly but charmingly—and no doubt truthfully—called Gropecunt Lane (even in my time I'd occasionally come down the lane late on a weekend night and pass American airmen and English girls embracing upright against the old walls).

Apart from my two kinds of work then, and my growing friendship with Michael, I immersed increasingly in Merton's distinctive social life. I've noted that there were a few other Americans in college; but I'd decided—on the voyage—that it would be absurd to stick with a group of American contemporaries when I had the chance, in what I assumed would be a two-year stay, to learn as much as possible about another country and its culture (one of my compatriots made it clear that he thought I'd made a wrong choice in adhering to the Brits— "none of whom will follow you home," he said—but I ignored the warning, thank God).

I was soon joining, then, a small circle of English undergraduates in someone's rooms to have coffee (weak powdered Nescafé) for forty-five minutes after a hall-lunch. I might then return from the library around 4:30 for a copious tea in the Junior Common Room bar with a few dozen student colleagues—most of us seated at minuscule tables, eating tomato or Marmite sandwiches while a skilled few of us threw darts with fierce concentration at a dartboard hung on a wall some eight feet away. At six I'd likely offer sherry to one or more friends in my rooms, or go to theirs for the same varieties of mostly South African sherry—a decent inexpensive version called Dry Fly was a frequent label. Then I'd put on my hip-length black gown (required for attendance at all lectures, college dinners, and other official events) and sit on a tightly packed wood bench to hear one of us read the college Latin (Christian) grace and then to bolt down in typical young-male fashion the dinner served over our shoulders by white-coated scouts.

As ever with institutional food, there was a fair amount of howling about its quality, though both the available British foodstuffs and the ambition of British cooks were still—as I've noted—overshadowed darkly by the Second War; the college meals were, I suspect, not a good deal worse than what many of my friends endured in their homes. First, there'd be a lumpy cream soup; then lamb, mutton, or sausage accompanied invariably by potatoes (fried, roasted, or mashed) and brussels sprouts, turnips, or cabbage; with a final pudding drowned under custard—all overcooked to stringy toughness or sodden tastelessness. Still, our vigorous table-talk proceeded, despite the fact that anyone could be sconced (compelled to drink a large tankard of beer without pausing to breathe) for talking "shop"—that is, discussing our studies. Our talk was, in fact, about little else.

Other dinner subjects were politics, sports, cinema, the telly, and Oxford characters (of whom there was always an ample supply). Oddly, in all my three years at Merton, I had no real friendship with another student in the entire university who was anticipating life as a novelist, poet, or dramatist; and I never felt the lack. In my second year, I met Willie Morris, a new Rhodester from Mississippi who'd eventually become a distinguished autobiographer. I enjoyed occasional meetings with him and his friends in New College, an all-American group that included the very bright and amusing Neil Rudenstine—a future president of Harvard—but Willie and I never grew close. His sense of rivalry was surprisingly strong; and it only relaxed in later years when (against his will) he left the editor's chair at *Harper's* magazine.

What I'd of course read about—but was finding it hard to judge this early, except as I developed an ear for accents—was the social revolution under way at Oxford and Cambridge (and to some degree in the "redbrick" provincial universities): the nation-altering results of the postwar Labour government's decision to subsidize virtually any young man or woman who could succeed in passing through the strenuous obstacle courses set in their secondary-school educations. The colleges now—with a few exceptions, say, Christ Church and Trinity at Oxford—were no longer primarily haunts of the rich or the upper middle class; and what I was getting to know, for better or worse, was a whole new Britain.

The 1920s Oxford of, for instance, Evelyn Waugh's novel *Brideshead Revisited* was meant to be dead. I say *meant to be* because, despite the presence of many "grammar school boys" at Merton—the sons of fathers who could never have afforded to send them on from secondary state schools to the university—many of my college friends came from well-to-do homes and spoke some version of upper-middle or upper-class British English (always the surest class identification test). At Merton there was even a small clutch of "Old Etonians" who spoke in the plummy tones that one seldom hears now, even in British plays and films.

In fact, I've now sat through numerous such performances in which native-born actors were *supposed* to be speaking in Oxbridge accents but could no longer produce a flawless simulacrum of those rounded vowels, produced at the very front of the upper row of teeth and then fed through the nose. There are even small errors in the accents of several otherwise fine performers in the brilliant televised production of *Brideshead.* I did occasionally reflect on the surviving chasm involved in our being served, both in our rooms and in hall, by men who were often as old as our fathers—many of them had defended the Empire in the recent war. As a native of the American South of course, being served by my elders was no strange phenomenon; but all those servants were black and the descendants of slaves, whereas in the Merton of the 1950s all the college servants were white.

In the face of such intentionally benign social engineering, I was still more than mildly concerned to encounter—more than once during my first year at Oxford, and a few more times in my British years—sudden outbursts of anti-Americanism from some otherwise friendly acquaintance. I've noted that Mr. Leishman was much given to commencing his cultural ventings with "Oh, you *Americans.*" Coming from his parodistic tweed-knickered frame, such moments came as no surprise and were the subjects of whatever comedy I could rouse on my return to college.

But from acquaintances of my own age and educational background, anti-Americanism came as more nearly a shock. In retrospect it's also surprised me to recall that I was never challenged to explain or defend the particular evils of racial repression—and worse—in my own native province, the old Confederacy where, in those very years, the civil-rights movement was gathering speed and force. The complaints were always about American foreign policy, the continued extensive American military presence in Britain, and the bad taste in civilian clothing of American airmen on their boozy weekends in Oxford (possessed, as they seemed to be, of endless ready cash).

I was ready—perhaps too ready—to agree that the United States had plenty to be ashamed of, on the grounds of its own past (in the present world of George W. Bush we're deplored, even hated, as never before in my lifetime). But to meet with such virulent expressions from a very few highly educated young Britons was to be amazed at their own refusal to acknowledge at least a pair of realities—both the long and oppressive imperialist history of their own country and a failure to consider that their resentment of the States might derive in part from their blindness to the fact that the quite incredible hegemony of their own small island nation in two and a half centuries of imperial world power had ended quite decisively, only a few years before my arrival in Oxford. A piece of real estate no larger than, say, that American region called New England had managed, through intelligence and luck, to rule a very large portion of the planet since the beginnings of the eighteenth century. Now it no longer did so.

The young protestors, however passionate and sincere (and some of them had only recently completed their required two years' service in the British military), had a grave problem for their own personal futures. And it was a problem which they often seemed peculiarly unaware of. Since the old Britannia was effectively dead, there was no empire left to go out to, or to profit from, with the abstract skills for which their brilliant educations were preparing them. The thousands of jobs available to their forefathers were gone — and apparently forever.

I knew only one Mertonian from my three years who, on graduation, assumed an old-time Empire job — he went to Fiji to work in the postal system, I believe. What did these young men propose to do on the small and already crowded landmass of the United Kingdom? In all the hours of lively talk I heard at Merton, I literally never heard a word on the subject (but then I've never heard a word from a young American on the subject of our own inevitably shrinking empire). In any case, that first term ended at a peak of good cheer.

The crowning social event of the term was also its last — the college's commemoration ball (what were we commemorating?). It was scheduled for the last night before we were due to scatter for the six-week Christmas vac. While spending an earlier weekend with Redmayne in Burford, I'd met an attractive young woman called Jill. She and her mother had taken me, on my first visit to Stratford, to see *The Merry Wives*. And eventually I invited Jill to be my date for the ball. She wrote back, accepted gracefully, and concluded by asking (in effect) "Shall I bring the Rolls? It might be fun for us." I'm not sure I'd known that her family possessed a Rolls; but of course I said "By all means" (on my one visit to Jill's home village, Swinbrook, Jill had driven me to see the Mitford family graves in the local churchyard — I had a curiosity then about the three remarkable Mitford sisters, primarily Unity who involved herself, perhaps romantically, with Hitler; then attempted suicide).

On the night in question, Jill drove herself from her Cotswold village into Merton Street where she parked an astonishingly well-tended antique Rolls by the college gate. *What larks!* as Joe Gargery says in Dickens's *Great Expectations*. I can't recall where we went for dinner—likely to the Café de Paris off the High or the Café Royale, two eateries by no means as grand as their names implied but as good as there was in the city then—or as good as Michael, our friend Garry Garrard, and I could afford for ourselves and our dates. Neither restaurant was more than a few blocks from college; but I'm sure we all packed into the Rolls and let Jill drive us there (none of us men yet possessed a British driver's license).

Then back to college for dancing in the garlanded hall. Restored though it was, the medieval space retained its original lines and its noble volumes of timbered air overhead. Who provided the music, I don't recall, nor precisely how we danced. Early in the evening there was a Scottish line dance, to bagpipe music, for the few Merton Scots, dashing in their kilts and sporrans. Afterward, it was mainly close dancing, with serious attention to proper footwork for the foxtrot, the waltz, or whatever else. By the time I'd left America, almost no one of my generation had mastered such steps; but stumbling though I was, I enjoyed myself.

The only small mishap was when, at our prior dinner—in the midst of inquiring about English dancing—I asked our assembled table "And do you also shag?" I was referring of course to the modified jitterbug which had originated in the Forties at Myrtle Beach, South Carolina and then spread through the South. My friends took a gap-mouthed moment of silence, staring at their plates in a textbook illustration of the British idiom for sudden embarrassment, *I didn't know where to look.* Then at last Michael said "Well, seldom on the actual dance *floor.*" It would later prove that *shag* was a British verb for "copulate"—only one of a number of idioms that divided our versions of the language in those days. The other great favorites were "What time shall I knock you up in the morning?" (meaning "wake you") and "Keep your pecker up" (*pecker* meant "chin" in England).

We promptly recovered ourselves in gales of laughter. Though busily social, Merton was not especially famed for decadence; so I can't recall that we drank ourselves into real inebriation. I do remember our taking pauses from the ball itself for quiet resorts to my nearby rooms where the six of us could talk awhile, but I think we stayed in possession of our wits. And at literal sunrise I saw Jill out to Merton Street and the Rolls which she'd drive back to her village.

4

I'D ALREADY PACKED to leave for London with Jim Griffin, Michael and his hometown date Anne, and Garry for the midmorning train. I'm an inveterate early arriver at depots and airports; but as I'd learn that day, to travel with Michael was to be required to leap onto already-moving vehicles. He firmly believed that any minute spent in waiting for transport was a minute lost. So a moving vehicle it was at the Oxford station—the train for Paddington. Once there, Michael and Anne got themselves to Victoria Station by tube for their train to Brighton. Garry lived in London, and Jim and I checked into our room at the Regent Palace Hotel smack off Piccadilly.

The hotel had opened for business late in 1915; and a recent biography of the great poet Wilfred Owen tells me that he stayed there, forty years earlier, in October 1915—at the age of twenty-two, the same age as I. He registered at the hotel some three weeks before enlisting in the British army, a fatal choice which would kill him exactly seven days before the Armistice in November 1918. Still in business as I write this, and looking very much like its old self in the Internet pictures—the Regent Palace even now offers rooms "with shared facilities"—this bustling but modest hostelry was comfortable enough for the few days we paused there. By that time both Jim and I were accustomed to shared facilities; and I at least had been taught long ago to avoid long walks down hotel corridors by peeing in my own room's sink (followed by a careful flood of hot tap water of course). The same brand of peeing prevailed at Merton, with no coaching from me. Any male visitor to your room might well rise in the midst of tea and ask to employ your newly installed sink for a private moment.

I never quite got used to long walks down corridors to bathe in tubs available to miscellaneous strangers. Again, though, youth and penury bolstered us; and in our London pause, Jim and I were seldom in our room while awake. We were out to see the irresistible high spots—the National Gallery (unmatched, I think, for overall quality of the collection), the Tate, the Victoria and Albert, the British Museum, and Westminster Abbey. More than half-empty of tourists as the great sites were so near to Christmas, none of them failed us—though Jim was less an on-the-spot enthusiast than I, a difference imposed at birth no doubt by our geographical origins: his chilly New England, my balmy South.

We began, as well, to taste the all but endless resources of London theatre. First, we saw a peculiar play called *The Strong Are Lonely*. Concerned with Jesuits in colonial Latin America, it starred Donald Wolfit—notorious for his stagy silent-film lurches. I'd never see his famously powerful King Lear; yet I noted that his Jesuit elder was monumental, though trapped in a boring play. Far more impressive was the first London production of Beckett's *Waiting for Godot*, his first stage fame in the English-speaking world.

Like most other Anglo-American theatregoers, I'd never heard of the Irish-French writer till we bought our tickets; and I came out into the cold December air more than two hours later, near overwhelmed by the indescribable power of what we'd experienced. For all the Shakespeare I'd seen in recent weeks at Stratford, the towering richness and variety of Beckett's language, wit, and architectural wisdom, the absence from a long play of any dead wood (a thing one can seldom claim for even the supreme Shakespeare plays) put new coals under my own determination to write as much as possible through the upcoming weeks in Italy. Jim had declared his intention to reread all the Platonic dialogues in the time; I'd begin a new short story—but what about?

*   *   *

No further fiction had suggested itself from the recent subject of my father's death (I'd sketched out "The Warrior Princess Ozimba" but had decided to wait awhile before finishing it). Nothing from my own recent life seemed sufficiently digested to produce controlled fiction, despite the fact that I seemed on the verge of the first worthy love of my life and the further reality that I'd apparently abandoned organized religion. Till leaving home, I'd been a fairly regular churchgoing Protestant; and at Oxford—in problematic times—I'd make solitary visits for prayer and meditation to the stark beauty of Merton's thirteenth-century chapel, but I'd abandoned ordinary services. Here I was, though, on the doorsill of Italy with just enough money from the ill-gotten gains of Cecil Rhodes to enjoy myself. Surely some good notion would come in the calm of a shared room in Florence.

Jim had London friends whom he planned to see before we departed, so Michael took a quick train back to town, and he and I went out by tube to Twickenham stadium for the annual varsity rugby match between Oxford and Cambridge. I'd gone with Michael to watch several prior rugger matches up Iffley Road in Oxford and had liked the game at once—the unpadded roughhouse and the breathless uninterrupted nature of the play appealed to my old childhood liking for neighborhood touch football. The Twickenham match (I've forgot who won) was played in the usual amount of London mist and mud, but being there with Michael was fun enough.

Meanwhile the only real rock in my shoe was a chiding note from Mr. Leishman, received just before my departure from college. Why had I not called on him again toward the end of term? Well, I folded the letter and buried it in my desk; I'd think about that in a warmer place. He'd certainly given me no assignments, papers to write or assigned readings. Still, why hadn't I attended at least one of his at-home evenings? Partly because I disliked him as intensely as I've noted above—and with good reason, I still think. Partly because I considered myself sufficiently employed in my work for David Cecil, Helen Gardner, and the teachers of my four B.Litt. preparatory classes. And again, partly because of the full circle of pleasures and fears that had swarmed so thickly around me in the previous two months. Then of course, like many Americans I was more unprepared than I realized for an educational system that left me almost entirely in control of my studies with no older sympathetic watchdog to rein me in or lead me on. Nonetheless, I was badly at fault; and I'd ultimately pay for my negligence.

And inserting here an almost simultaneous event in a still warmer place—a place from which I was very much absent but an event which would profoundly affect not only my homeland but all the work I'd eventually do there—I note that, while I had no immediate awareness of it, on December 1, 1956 in Montgomery, Alabama a black seamstress named Rosa Parks had refused to surrender her seat on a city bus to a white passenger. Parks's subsequent impeccable fame, the bus boycott which began among local black riders— warmed by the nonviolent rhetoric of a previously unheralded black minister named Martin Luther King—and the renewal of racial violence among many white Southerners were matters I'd learn of only when I returned to my Oxford fastness in January (my mail from home gave no reason to think that a major revolt had been triggered among us at last, yet the changes in my old world were hastening toward us, and I was far gone).

Since the spring of 1954—immediately after Dad's death, the Supreme Court issued its *Brown v. Board of Education* ruling—I'd of course known that the social order of my home and all my kinsmen would gradually undergo a mammoth upending. I was uneasily glad to know as much. One of my first published prose sketches had appeared in my high-school newspaper in 1951 and reflected an early puzzlement at the often decorous cruelty of my white world; and my gradual withdrawal from involvement in organized religion was largely fueled by a sense of bafflement at the general silence of white Protestantism on so huge a subject. But I'd never been, and would never become, a social activist—not with my actual body on any physical rampart—yet almost all the manuscript short stories I was taking to Italy involved black characters in important actions: important and admirable, or at least virtuous, acts. Still, as the civil-rights movement got initial fire in its bones with Mrs. Parks's slender refusal to move from a bus seat in Alabama, I was a long distance off, in more ways than planetary miles. And I'd remain so, in characteristic ways, for years to come.

On December 9—John Milton's birthday and exactly one year since Jim and I had won our scholarships—he and I flew south out of London on a British European Airways prop-jet to Milan (in those days apparently Florence had no landing strip for full-size commercial planes). My first flight over the Alps was silently and vastly beautiful, and a single image I gathered as we passed the massive Mont Blanc imprinted itself deep in me and became the final sentence of a story I'd eventually call "The Anniversary." We reached Milan in late afternoon, a bus drove us straight to the cavernous railway station, and Jim stood aside as I went to a ticket window and made my first attempt at spoken modern Italian.

I'd never studied the language formally, but one of my history teachers at Duke had offered an evening class for six or eight students who were interested in further investigation of Renaissance literature and history. The group proceeded, oddly but effectively, by beginning on the first night to read Dante's *Commedia*. Despite his archaic Italian, Dante writes with a relatively easy syntax and vocabulary (he virtually invented the language as we know it); and I made considerable headway in his *Inferno* before I left Duke. Then once I'd known that Jim and I were set on a visit to Florence and Rome, I all but memorized an Italian grammar that I bought at Blackwell's.

So I felt a certain new power unfolding in my hands as I asked the ticket seller when the next train departed for Firenze. He pondered my exotic grammar and accent, then nodded, kindly took a pencil, wrote the time on a small notepad, and extended it toward me with a bleak north-Italian smile. Good—we had barely an hour to wait. We managed a snack in a coffee stand in the station and went to the platform. It was still being said of Mussolini—then only a decade after his lynching by a mob not far from where we stood—that at least he'd made the trains run on time. They still did, to the veritable moment. We climbed aboard a carriage much like the British railcars I already knew, then sped on southward into gathering night.

*   *   *

The Pensione Quisisana was just as Redmayne had described it—a clean, smoothly run, and almost phenomenally quiet establishment, presided over by a likable older woman who spoke reasonable English, way more reasonable than my Italian. And well she might have—her premises could have arrived intact from an E. M. Forster novel about the British in Florence more than fifty years before (in fact, the Quisisana was actually used in the Merchant-Ivory version of Forster's *Room with a View* in 1985). And while the place was by no means swamped with British guests—it seemed half-empty in the midwinter lull—there were several English couples. Two or three were plainly heterosexual, though a little old for hijinks; one was unmistakably lesbian, complete with severely bobbed hair and neckties straight out of *The Well of Loneliness*. All gave us friendly nods in the elevator or in the dining room, where we could choose to eat only breakfast or all three meals—good pasta, lamb, fish, and a good Chianti.

Jim and I took most of our meals there, chiefly for economy's sake; but occasionally we'd choose a more imaginative place in the city—there was even one near the central piazza that served first-class beefsteaks. After two months of no decent beef, I treated myself on at least one evening to a full-sized steak, broiled rare, and languished in the pleasure (the restaurant priced it by the gram; and I hardly ate again for the rest of the week, though I never regretted my splurge). We thought we knew no one in midtown, though I'd hear soon that my old Milton teacher, Allan Gilbert, was there—the scholar so scorned by Mr. Leishman.

I wrote him a note, and he promptly phoned the Quisisana to invite us to dinner at his own small hotel. When we went there on the appointed evening, we discovered that he was experiencing an indisposition (he'd just retired from Duke at, I think, the age of seventy); but he received us cheerfully in the room he shared with his second wife, and she led us downstairs for dinner. Only then did she explain, in a whisper, that the trouble was constipation and that he'd been greatly pleased when his local physician gave him a laxative pill described as an *archibusiere* (I believe)—an arquebus. Since Allan had spent much time in studying Renaissance weapons—and an arquebus was an early matchlock gun—he took the pill with relish, and it was indeed working ballistically.

Still, a chance to see Professor Gilbert—with his almost alarmingly amused bright eyes and his snow-white short beard (one of the only two beards at Duke in that clean-shaven era; a colleague once described him to me as resembling Santa Claus's grandfather)—reminded me of the frequently preservative effects of a genuine love of scholarly pursuits; how I wished I could somehow arrange for him to supervise my thesis. Failing that, however, my Florentine hour with him—and our glass of wine—did a good deal to restore my sense of why I was at Oxford after all: to burrow a little deeper into a mind as enormous and useful as Milton's. Like so many distinguished scholars whom I've since known, Allan Gilbert's ceaseless intellectual curiosity had kept him brilliantly alive and sympathetic to such interests in others.

Blessedly quieted as Jim and I were then, we made serious headway with our original intentions for the trip. He'd spend the mornings and late afternoons in our spacious room, reading Plato in an armchair beside our window on the Arno. I'd sit at a small desk and continue revising "A Chain of Love" and attempting to build a story backward from my airborne impression of Mont Blanc. As we passed it, I'd noted on the back of my ticket stub the following simile—"like some proud mountain, yielding to the sun its flanks of snow." And now I heard the fragment as the end of a longish story that was entirely invented but that was rising on the visible givens of several visits I'd made to the rural North Carolina residence of my beloved seventh-grade teacher, Miss Jennie Alston.

She'd retired by then and was living in her family's ancestral home—Cherry Hill, a tall and spacious antebellum plantation house which has since been superbly restored—with her elder sister Carrie and her elder brother Ed Falc. It was that setting and especially Miss Carrie's physical appearance that underlay what I hoped to build into a story. Though I'd bought a handsome Olivetti Lettera 22 portable typewriter a few days after arriving in Florence, I was still writing all my work by hand, then typing it up a few days later (that practice would continue for thirty more years until word processors entered my life). And the early pages of the story were coming slowly.

There in another country, surrounded by generally friendly people who were nonetheless barely comprehensible to me—and accompanied by only one American acquaintance whom I'd known for little more than two months—I found myself immured, for the first time in my life, in a new and weighty kind of silence, almost a bathysphere of the sort that in childhood I'd seen exploring the ocean floor in my library books. And in that silence—punctuated by daily afternoon visits to the Uffizi Gallery, barely a block away—I could study such incomparable human achievements as Leonardo's large sketch for a *Visit of the Magi to the Christ Child*, his *Annunciation to the Virgin*, and Botticelli's prime masterpieces (the *Venus* and the *Primavera*). Then I could wander a little farther toward the north, to the Accademia with Michelangelo's *David* and his late *Pietà* which was then in the cathedral with the face of the sculptor himself on one of the figures supporting the corpus. And in those richly loaded days, I was slowly—and very usefully—forced to accept a new fact about myself.

In sixteen years of formal education in public school and at Duke, I'd seldom heard a discouraging word about myself and my work (from arithmetic to drawing). A bright boy, I was generally recognized as such and, in one of the poorest American states, I was praised way more steadily than I deserved. Now after two months at Oxford and a few days in Florence, I was coming to realize that a career in prep school or college teaching should present me with no insurmountable problems.

But as for the second half of my aim since the age of sixteen, the joint intention to be a good writer as well as an inspiring teacher—well, though in the past year I'd completed two short stories which even Eudora Welty liked, I was realizing that (despite my excellent high-school teachers and the one undergraduate class I'd taken in imaginative writing) *I truly didn't know how to write.* That's by no means to say that I should have gone on, after Duke, to study advanced writing at what were then the only two widely respected such programs in America—at the University of Iowa and Stanford. I'm not at all sure I even knew about them.

And even now, after decades of teaching various sorts of undergraduate writing back at Duke, I never urge advanced writing-study on talented students. I'm more than convinced that the best writing of fiction, poetry, and drama is the result of intense independent work by a naturally gifted man or woman who finds the time—while working at whatever other job is necessary to pay the bills—to deepen those skills in the act of probing further down into what will prove to be his or her best subject matter, matter to which only he or she has guided him or herself, not a teacher nor a group of workshop colleagues. In long retrospect I feel that what I didn't know, as I sat alone in Oxford or Florence, was the nature of my own creative metabolism.

What needs did my body have—of sleep, food, drink, sex, and love for instance—before it could write steadily? How fast should I expect to write well? What daily quotas should I set for myself? And what should I do if I failed to meet my quota? How best could I warm a brain that cooled or quit in the midst of some effort—or worse, at the start? And where would I go if I failed entirely? It would be another decade before I acquired reliable answers to most of those questions—and I've yet to meet a student who acquired them in graduate school—but at least I'd begun the process.

The story I was hoping to construct (in reverse, from my sight of Mont Blanc) was sitting, in my notes, at an upper corner of my desk in the Quisisana. I already knew that *this* would happen, followed by *this* and *this* and *this*, all the way to an ending; but when it came to managing the machine that would write that story down—the machine of my body and mind—those notes were poised in grinning refusal to enter me and move ahead.

Young and elastic as I was, I consoled myself with the thought that I was, after all, on vacation. American students are notorious for taking a hundredweight of books home for Christmas and never opening a single one. Oxford students were expected to do the majority of work for their degrees during vac time, and most of my young English friends told me how seldom that dream proved a reality. Why should

I have thought that I could come to the cradle of the Renaissance and sit in a dim room, contentedly writing? Out to the streets then—and Jim often joined me—for further roaming.

The Ponte Vecchio with its tiny gold shops and the Pitti Palace, with its own great pictures and the surrounding Boboli Gardens, were nearby and unavoidable. The alarmingly green and white cathedral, with its revolutionary dome, retained not only Michelangelo's *Pietà* but also the blood-smirched memory of the conspiracy of 1478 when the Pazzi family, in an attempted power seizure, succeeded in murdering Giuliano De' Medici and wounding his brother Lorenzo near the altar. The adjacent Baptistery detained me for the better part of a morning.

Its astonishing bronze doors, with their gilded panels of biblical scenes, had not yet been replaced by the replicas that stand there now. The interior space, in its gloom, was a reminder that the infant Dante was baptized there; and the most distinguished of its adornments then was Donatello's carved-wood statue of the penitent and toothless Mary Magdalen in rags. The nearby Medici Palace was the grim and long-dead hive of so much honey in the life of the city and of Western civilization. As boys—for instance—Leonardo, Botticelli, and Michelangelo were welcomed there for instruction and high-class dining.

The Medici Chapel, however, struck both Jim and me—and our tastes were, again, far from identical—as the city's most imposing offering (even more so than the David, though he—even with his unhistorical uncircumcised penis—is as fine as his world-fame augurs). Like several of Michelangelo's other gigantesque projects, the chapel—within the church of San Lorenzo—was never completed. Its austerity of space and color, an almost exclusive white and gray, may be far from his ultimate intention but is nonetheless memorably arresting in clarity and dignity. And its numerous sculptures—of Medici princes, of Day and Night, and the shyly tender Virgin and Child—have more than earned their canonical standing. The entirety may not generate a traditionally sacred air; but given the ruthless power of the family enshrined here, the chill space and its statues of such somber genius are merely characteristic.

So the two weeks rolled on toward our next destination. Looking back through more than fifty years, there's a strange fact I can't explain. Why did we meet no Italians, in Florence, whom we might later have wished to go on knowing? The Florentines are hardly the open-armed, big-bosomed movie stereotypes of southern *bas Italia* (a component, no doubt, of the city's popularity with the English). But I was a talkative and genial-enough man, and Jim was far from forbidding. I encountered numbers of friendly-enough men and women in our pensione and in various museums, shops, and restaurants. Maybe that's one more old-fashioned Yank tourist's regret; but let it stand as a partial explanation of why I've returned only once to Florence, and then very briefly.

From the start of our trip, we'd planned to push on to Rome very near to Christmas Eve. Redmayne had given us the name of another reliable pensione, reasonably priced (though again located on a superb site only two blocks from the Via Veneto with its mischievous movie stars). Further, Redmayne's recommendation boasted a name especially winning for me—the Bellavista Milton. Yet shortly before we departed Florence, our otherwise sedate landlady learned of our choice and urged us to switch our reservation to what she insisted was a far better place—a pensione very near the railway station in central Rome (she warned that the Milton was "distant from things"). We were so inexperienced, we'd liked her at the Quisisana, and her urging seemed so authoritative—she even said she'd phone and make the change for us—that we surrendered with no foreboding.

On December 22 then we left Florence by train. Even the third-class carriages were near empty; and all the way south, I sat by the window and read from my copy of Dante's *Inferno* in the invitingly small bilingual edition published in London by Dent but purchased by me in Florence as a farewell souvenir (I have it still, much used in the interim but in good strong shape—Hell apparently resists destruction). Jim was still deep in his Plato in the old but eloquent Jowett translation, and we reached Rome almost sooner than expected—midafternoon.

5

W<small>ITH A CITY MAP</small> in hand, we found our way on foot easily down the Via Nazionale—a busy commercial street—rode the elevator up to our pensione, and checked in. Immediately I was struck by an initially indescribable hint in the air of something peculiar. There was no offensive odor or (at that point) noise; but this was not the Quisisana, clearly. What was it though? After brief naps we found our way to the dining room in the hopes of a more or less decorous semi-British tea like the ones we'd enjoyed in the dim indoor Florentine light.

Wrong. The dining room had several tables occupied by our compatriots—boys roughly our age, dressed much like the off-duty American airmen we'd seen on weekends in Oxford, drinking beer or red wine and accompanied by Italian girls who appeared to be both waitresses at the Nazionale and something more (when they fetched the refills of beer and wine, they'd sit down briefly and laugh with the boys). *Where had we landed?* We were hardly alarmed. But Jim gave me more than one quizzically amused look; and since there seemed no chance for afternoon food here, we went outside.

Back toward the station we'd passed a place which advertised itself as "American Bar." We turned in there. I know that I ordered two grilled-cheese sandwiches—a childhood comfort snack—and at length I was served two fairly convincing replicas of that American classic. When we returned to the street, I was struck by a local phenomenon which may long since have vanished—numerous pairs of young Italian men, many of them in army uniform, were walking arm in arm—and soon we encountered a small clutch of American acquaintances from Oxford.

With them, we exchanged a little mutual information—mainly useful local addresses. Their parked car had been robbed the previous night of all their ski equipment—they were ultimately headed for

Switzerland—but on the advice of the police, had located it this morning at the central Roman flea market. Then one of them said he was sure he'd see us at the week's oncoming big event, which he then previewed for us—two evenings hence there'd be a Christmas Eve mass at the ancient basilica of Santa Maria Maggiore. Jim had been reared Catholic but had left the church, I've mentioned my own withdrawal from formal worship, but the sound of the words *Christmas Eve mass* proved potent.

Back to the pensione for dinner—and an even more relaxed display of our fly-boy countrymen and their pensione-employee girlfriends. Neither Jim nor I was remotely censorious about healthy sex; but how much was desirable, here in the midst of the pensione's only dining room? There were no overt displays, but there was a good deal of pinching, squealing, and occasional bear hugs and smacking kisses. For a very few minutes, it was likably amusing; but then it was unlikably odd, especially since we were paying for two meals per day but apparently had no choice in the matter of atmosphere.

Nonetheless, we got through a filling but disappointingly prepared dinner—a distinct letdown from Florence. Our landlady at the Quisisana was plainly misinformed; had the pensione changed hands without her knowledge? Our compatriots and their girlfriends were nothing less than cheerfully friendly, though. We had no fear of late-night black eyes or a burglarized room. While the Nazionale hardly promised to be the resort for writing and reading that we'd had in Florence, Jim and I kept our thoughts mostly to ourselves (apart from Jim's amused looks and my occasional observations on the accents of the airmen, many of them Southern). So we spent the better part of the next day in the beginnings of an exploration of the literally endless fascinations of Rome. The weather was damp and chilly; so most of our explorations were indoors—the museums of the Capitoline Hill and then, in a brief patch of sun, a preliminary walk through the Forum itself and the adjacent forums of a few later emperors.

Two sights are still deeply printed in memory. On the streets there were frequent young women with as many as three snotty children and a babe at the breast, extending their hands for money in a smiling attempt at beggary. And actual shepherds from the hills beyond Rome, with lambs tied beside them, were playing their handmade pipes in what (for local ears) may have been recognizable Christmas tunes. I'm sorry to say that, in suspicious American-abroad fashion— were these *real* shepherds?—I failed to give even one of them a tiny gift from my already heavy pocketful of the featherweight aluminum coins of that era.

On Christmas Eve itself, by the time full dark had fallen, we were on the Avenue of the Imperial Fora; and without knowing our exact whereabouts, we walked ahead till we wound up gazing at the flood-lit Colosseum just ahead of us—the real proto-Roman Colosseum, the sink of centuries of mayhem and blood, one of the magnets of my boyhood imagination. Films like DeMille's rousing *Sign of the Cross* and my two years in high-school Latin classes, where our textbooks were crammed with nineteenth-century photographs of the remains of the ancient city, had given me a powerful appetite for walking through the originals (spruced up by Mussolini) and touching a stone that Augustus or even Nero might have touched, not to mention mad Caligula. In the ninth grade I'd even assembled, from pasted-together sheets of typing paper, a ten-foot-long scroll to which I attached every photograph I could find of the places I was now on the verge of touching. Near as I was to my twenty-third birthday, I'd never been this elated since seeing my first live elephant at maybe age five.

Here tonight, traffic was winding around the great arena as though this were the end of any business day. I kept reminding myself that Christmas was only a couple of hours ahead. Despite the appropriate live shepherds and begging young mothers, Italy had not yet adopted the visual Germanic components of American Christmas—the lights, the trees, and Santa. And my Christmas emotions were still off-stride. We dodged our way safely through a hundred honking Fiats and the ear-splitting Vespas and Lambrettas that were recent additions to the cacophony of Italian city life. Safe so far, we moved forward past no barricades or guards whatever and spent the better part of a black hour in winding through the arches till we paused on the lip of the vast oblong arena and tried to glimpse what was barely visible there below us.

It was probably a risky thing to do, at any hour, much less in the night (we'd asked for no guidance on coming here). Once or twice I thought I saw a faceless shadow moving beyond us—a homeless tramp or a silent cutthroat? But no one came near, no knife-wielding contemporary, no gladiatorial or Christian-martyr ghost. Maybe it was now too cold to be outdoors. Any Roman mugger or madman would have to be as inured to cold as Jim and I after two months in Oxford colleges and that seemed unlikely.

Eventually we made our way back uphill and asked the way toward the midnight mass we'd heard of at Santa Maria Maggiore. So it must have been well past ten when we entered the basilica—one of Rome's most beautiful, dating in its earliest stages to the fifth century (seven centuries before Mob Quad). Already the long space was jam-packed—no benches or chairs, everyone standing. If our American friends were there, we never found them, locked as we were in the fervent mob. The most we could see of the altar suggested that priests and their acolytes were at work in the complex Latin rituals of pre–Vatican II, far more beckoning than the later vernacular substitutes. Incense filled the air with its mystifying smoke and the lavish odor that seemed a promise at least of the sweetness of the child to be born as midnight struck. Several processions were winding their difficult ways through our midst, and a choir was chanting in the vault above us.

Though reared a Protestant I'd long been mesmerized by Catholic worship; and I was riveted now, despite a mild tendency to claustrophobia. For all that Jim had fallen away from the church, he held his ground too; and as huge deep bells began to toll midnight, yet another procession sought a path among us, slowed by the many who sought to touch its burden. Many young men were bearing on their shoulders an immense baroque reliquary with a crystal-sided central container holding what appeared to be worm-eaten boards. I overheard an American near me tell his female partner "It's the actual manger from Bethlehem." And so it claimed to be, brought here from Palestine some twelve hundred years ago.

As it passed, Jim declined his chance at touching it. I touched for us both and could think of no Christmas, among my twenty-two, that equaled this in its nearness to the actual cause of the celebration—a child's arrival, that simple ineluctable core of the faith I was born in. Unchurched as I'd been in the year behind me, those wormy boards (whose crystal box I touched in the mob) reignited my absolute certainty that the babe they'd borne was, in some incomprehensible sense, God himself—a God designed to die in agony three decades later, then rise from the dead, and save us all: Platonic Jim and even me. I'd never truly doubted the fact; now its bedrock depth was uncovered for good.

When we reached the pensione again near two o'clock, the premises were fairly quiet. But by the time we'd shut our books and turned out the lamp between our beds, the nocturnal games were just cranking up beyond our door. We made a jocular remark or two about what the next hours might hold. We were each almost entirely exhausted; but all night long I'd be roused long enough to hear what seemed to be touch football played along our hallway, cheered on by squealing girls and bystanding drunks (the sudden shouts were all in American English). I'd seen no sign of other paying guests for our military comrades; and since Jim and I were more or less unconscious, there were no complaints.

Certainly no one from the all but invisible management requested any reduction in boisterousness. Still, just when I'd think I might as well dress and head back out to walk till dawn, the din would go completely silent as though all the players and cheerleaders had retired to their own beds for whatever after-game sleep or alternate entertainment was pursued. But then occasional shouts and grunts would revive in the hall till maybe an hour before real dawn, when silence slowly descended; and I must have then got two hours of sleep.

More church bells woke us in broad daylight. Jim and I wished each other Merry Christmas, brushed our teeth, and staggered toward breakfast (could food be offered after such a night?). The dining room bore signs of the recent capers; but none of our countrymen had stirred, not upright at least. Two or three of the dark-haired girls I recalled from yesterday wished us *"Buon Natale,"* brought us coffee, rolls, butter, and apricot jam; then—a little shamefacedly—withdrew to the kitchen. No sooner were they tucked out of sight when Jim and I met one another's whey-faced grins, confessing our first big continental folly, and burst out laughing.

All but in unison we mouthed in stage whispers what even a baby boy might have guessed two days ago—"We're staying in a *whorehouse!*" I may have been a little more temporarily pleased by the fact than Jim. In his calm but firm voice, he reminded me of his intention to complete a reading of all the Platonic dialogues in the next three weeks. Could Socrates continue his explorations of virtue, truth, and beauty here? Jim didn't quite ask me, but I was a little chastened by his gravity; and in another few sentences, we'd devised a plan. We'd find the Pensione Bellavista Milton and go on our knees if necessary in the hope of reclaiming the reservation (canceled by our Tuscan friend). If all else failed, we could claim she was dotty and had made a big mistake. Well, she had. But why? We'd never know.

The Milton's address was indeed perfect—the morning was bright and the pensione sat literally across the street from the vast and green Borghese Gardens. But the tiny clerk at the ground-floor reception desk took an endless moment to open a ledger and stare down his truly Ciceronian Roman nose at the fact that we'd canceled a perfectly good reservation and had now turned up—and on Christmas morning? *Where had we been?* I was too flummoxed to tell him. Jim, with Socratic candor, gave a simple explanation. "Ah," the clerk nodded, "the Nazionale." Then he looked up, knowingly. "You enjoy your night?" We both said "No." At last the clerk managed to release a thin-lipped smile from the depths of his heart. Then more gazing down his nose at the giant ledger before, with agonizing slowness, he entered our names.

Back we raced to the Nazionale and closed our bags. The clerk there expressed mild regret at our proposed departure; but with the now-welcome laissez-faire attitude of the establishment, he wished us well and even exchanged a few of our dollars at a favorable rate. So we splurged on a taxi for the trip back up to the peak of the Pincian Hill. All the way, we were subject to further laughing at what our eminently respectable Florentine landlady had parked us in. Could she, after all, have co-owned a brothel, well south of Florence? We almost hoped so. And of course we hadn't departed in any sense of dudgeon, only in the hope of undisturbed sleep, good food, and a slightly less louche atmosphere than the Nazionale was offering under present management.

I noticed, the moment we entered our room, that there was no soap at the basin; and I asked about it. The bellman seemed initially surprised that we hadn't brought our own but said cheerfully that he could walk down the street and buy it for us. We handed over the small sum and off he went. Only as we were unpacking at the Milton—in our sizable room with shared facilities down the hall—did I realize that neither Jim nor I had thought to buy even the smallest Christmas gift for one another, and a modest wave of nostalgia rose and swamped me.

This was my first Christmas absence, ever, from home. In Florence I'd bought presents for my mother and brother—an antique gold cross for Mother from the Ponte Vecchio, a leather box for Bill. In time I'd pay American Express, here by the Spanish Steps, to pack and ship them. I felt a longing to phone home and at least hear the family voices. But again the cost of transatlantic calls was huge, and in any case I'd heard nightmare stories of Italian phone service. So when Jim took a seat by our tall wide window and opened his Plato, I said I believed I'd take a long walk. We'd meet at dinnertime.

I still had no guidebook, but I set off downhill in what I thought was the general direction of the Colosseum. I've never known why but—on that one day, at many crossroads—there were orderly piles of pristine foodstuffs (cans, boxes, bags, even unopened boxes of panettone). I assumed they were set out for the poor, but no one seemed to be collecting them. Auto traffic was remarkably sparse. Instead, on foot, there were frequent middle-class Italian families, focused round their youngest child, invariably clothed (like their parents) in holiday splendor—new cap and coat, new shoes but above all the brand of adoration that Italians seemed always to reserve for the youngest.

As I reached what was plainly the center of the ancient city—I didn't yet know it, but the Palatine Hill was rising beside me—I came on a long narrow empty piece of muddy ground with a single strand of rope on waist-high poles around the perimeter. Maybe it was meant to exclude human beings; but since there was no one in sight, I stepped across it easily and strode to the midst before I realized where I must be. This had to be the Circus Maximus; and while there were no signs of excavations in progress, the ground was strewn with smallish fragments of marble. The largest were, say, the size of a man's head; the smallest, egg-size. Of course I was tempted to pocket a reminder—anyone could bring a bag, step over or under that one strand of rope, and take home twenty pounds of fragments uncaught. I took one piece, smaller than a pack of cigarettes, with only the most rudimentary signs of human shaping. Then I fumbled my way into a left turn and, lo, the Colosseum was there just ahead.

Even now in midafternoon, warm sunlight was bathing the city. *Golden* sun would be a cliché; but the light was near golden, both in color and in its value to my sun-starved mind. Yet there was almost no one else, not even a guard, in this enormous construct—one of the world's most famous tourist magnets. The family-centered Romans were surely at their ancestral homes, and again the tourist trade had still not reached its present suffocating heights. There was even no ticket seller, no policeman to block me. With last night's knowledge of the basic structure, I walked straight to the upper rim of the arena, went a few steps downward, and sat on a seat occupied no doubt by the butts of many generations of bloodthirsty Romans on holiday.

A few years earlier I'd developed a susceptibility to sunlight; I'd break out in hives if I spent more than an hour or so in direct exposure. But now I unbuttoned my white nylon shirt, lay well back; and what I thought of through my long Yule light-bath was not gladiators or psychopathic Caesars or my allergy to sunlight but my Carolina home—how far off I was from the roots of my life and intended work, not to mention a bereft only parent and my only near kinsman, a younger brother with whom I'd never had the least grave disagreement in our years together. I was not homesick but, if a mind can truly transport a body through space—and of course it can—I was back with all my maternal family in the rambling house in its tall oak grove in the village of Macon where I'd been born. And soon I was seated at the bountiful table of my aunt Ida, one of the very few human beings whom I loved without a trace of reservation—a secular saint, much given to both deep-diving depression and guarded laughter.

By the time I was back uphill at the Milton, it was likewise dinnertime in Rome. I can't remember what we were served; but since it was our first chance at a good local meal, I'm glad to recall that it tastes good in memory—surely some form of domestic bird preceded by fish and followed by a complex Christmas cake and first-rate coffee—our English coffee had been so weak that, as my father said of such brews, "It needed a crutch to get out of the cup."

Maybe all these years later, when so many young people travel early and roam far afield, it's hard for some to imagine the unprecedented mixture of joy and sorrow I felt that single day and most of that night—joy that I was *working* (or at least worrying about the slowness of my work) and living on my own in entirely new territory; joy that I'd fallen in love again and sorry at all I'd left far off: family, old friends, and a landscape and culture whose urgency to me I couldn't yet fathom. The pleasurable compound was so immensely powerful, it drove me on through many days to come—days, months, even the better part of three years—and here I'd first sensed its force in a city which, with Jerusalem and Athens, had witnessed more of the crucial thought and work of the human race than any of its newer and larger successors. No wonder I'd seek every later chance to return to Rome.

The remaining weeks there coincided with a season of early winter rain—not downpours but drizzles in the midst of fairly warm air and frequent stretches of sunlight—yet Jim and I, together and apart, availed ourselves of as much of what Rome had to offer as we could digest. The day after Christmas, when I bought the encyclopedic and very scholarly Club Italiano Tourismo guide to the city (a thick handful in easy Italian and bound in bright red cloth), I realized that this city, which was then by no means enormous, offered endless wonders. But I did my share of visits. And again we wandered on our own—nothing so corn-fed as an organized tour for us. I never left the room without my CIT guide. The fact that it was in Italian quickly improved my comfort in the language, and its thoroughness contributed greatly to our decisions on what to see and what we were seeing when we got there. The obvious first visits were imposing. We took a whole day, almost by ourselves, to roam the plentiful remains of the Forum and the (then) little-visited Palatine Hill, the cradle of the city with its memories of the twins Romulus and Remus, legendary founders of the city.

Beyond legend, the long plateau at the present summit of the hill bore its still tangible remains of good and evil, sane and insane, and merely brilliant or incompetent emperors. Among so many sites that astonish with their survival, I retain especially deep-cut memories of my first visit to the House of Livia (the wily wife of Augustus and the malign female star of Robert Graves's novel *I, Claudius*) and the nearby Temple of Cybele with its memories of self-castrated priests and the reputed site of the Lupercal, the cave where the twins were nurtured by a she-wolf.

After my first climb up the hill with Jim, I returned more than once—and many times in later years—in an effort to begin imagining the sheer quantity of power once contained in, and dispensed from, this single place—supremely peaceful as it is now and crowned only with Rome's towering umbrella pines. In 1955 we'd only recently come through the now little-remembered Korean War, and the worst of Vietnam lay more than a decade ahead. What stared all American young men in the face during my draft-eligible years was Moscow and the Cold War threat of mutually assured nuclear destruction—or MAD as it was called. Nonetheless there amid the defiant survivals of imperial Rome, I harbored no thoughts of the eventual and inevitable decline of the empire which America was so half-consciously but gorily building for itself. Was that a symptom, in me, of the famous political oblivion of 1950s America or merely of my own monumental unawareness of the present dire state of world power? (the big majority of my present students, five decades later, seem at least as oblivious).

God knew, I'd been intensely conscious—for the nearly five years since I turned eighteen—that my country meant to draft me for service if I met its none-too-rigorous standards for induction; and I'd picked my way through the eggshells of the Selective Service System (never considering that my sexual tilt might disqualify me). Yet in Europe, while I never once thought of permanent exile, I felt a blind safety. Since my father's death and given my absence from Mother's widowed life, I wanted to feel my separation from everything meant by *home*; and I know that I read no American paper or magazine with anything resembling steadiness.

Another day we moved on—a few years forward in history—to the basilica of San Pietro which stands on the site of the Circus of Nero (where tradition says St. Peter was crucified) and above the foundations of the first great church completed by the emperor Constantine in A.D. 326. With my tendency to give Roman Catholics a bye in a good many matters, it's hard for me to see a way that a sane visitor would not be impressed, if not deeply moved, by St. Peter's with the calm spatial volumes of its vast central aisle climaxing under Michelangelo's dome where Bernini's spiraling bronze canopy soars above the main altar with St. Peter's skeletal remains beneath. And against the back wall of the apse, Bernini's towering shrine for the Chair of Peter is supported on the bronze fingertips of the prime doctors of the church—Augustine and Ambrose, Athanasius and John Chrysostom. The crowded side aisles—which begin, on the right, with Michelangelo's exquisite first triumph, his elegant *Pietà*, and proceed on both sides to offer their sometimes dignified, occasionally bizarre tombs—may prove another matter for almost any visitor, especially Protestants accustomed to much less adornment of their shrines.

At the time of my first visits during that Christmas season, the adjacent Vatican palace was occupied by the austere and endlessly controversial Pius XII — was he pro-Nazi or not; did he help the Jews or not? But I never saw him, though when I walked round the roof of the basilica, I glimpsed a moving shadow at what I'd heard was his window. His skull, which was then almost all one could see of his gaunt face; his circular steel-rimmed spectacles, his unsmiling mouth — if the shadow was Pius, it never came nearer than a hundred yards' distance.

There were plentiful other indelible sights. First was the church of San Pietro in Vincoli which displays not only the chains St. Peter wore to his upside-down crucifixion but also — in a dim side aisle as almost an afterthought — Michelangelo's potent statue of Moses, larger than life with an unnerving resemblance to the actor Charlton Heston. When Jim and I were there, a professional photographer suddenly lit the statue for pictures; and we had the luck of seeing Moses in a way that even Michelangelo can never have seen him — almost blindingly revealed in every detail of the surface. That brilliance only served to increase the threat inherent in the biblical moment which the sculptor intended — Moses returned from Mount Sinai, with the newly revealed tables of the Law, only to find his people engaged in the worship of a golden calf.

Third was the emperor Hadrian's enormous round tomb, Castel Sant'Angelo, gutted within by centuries of looting invaders who even disposed of Hadrian's ashes but were powerless to destroy so enormous a monument to his virtue as a ruler. Then came Ostia, the seaport of ancient Rome which Jim and I, for some reason, were so determined to see that we actually took a train to the literally deserted site, long since beached by a gradual silting up, only to find little to see but the roofless unadorned walls of many undistinguished buildings; ruins without interesting stories attached are as lifeless as mummified dogs by the road. The short train trip however, on another gray day, was a welcome relief from the hours we'd been spending in our room — Jim with his increasingly incredible fidelity to Plato, me with *Samson Agonistes* and my attempt to push on with a few more paragraphs on the story which I'd commenced in Florence.

Next was the by-then-underground, the huge and almost never visited Golden House, built by the emperor Nero after the fire which destroyed much of Rome in A.D. 64. Most of the original structure, intended to cover some 125 acres, was destroyed or buried by later emperors. Still I could wander—entirely alone (no guards were present, not one other visitor and Jim was elsewhere)—through high vaulted spaces whose walls bore dozens of barely visible frescoes that had proved so enriching to painters who first saw them when the house was rediscovered late in the fifteenth century. I could linger in enormous state rooms—and briefly in the cubicles in which unimaginable crimes or lunacies at least might have occurred. Since early boyhood I'd had a revolted fascination with Nero—his bull-necked head and the history of his progression from his beginnings as a reasonably benign ruler to a ludicrous madman and eventual suicide. And here in his megalomanic palace, he began to seem so uncannily near me that, after a gloom-burdened hour, I hurried out into welcome sunlight.

Among so many other sites, those that would prove useful in later memory, there were the Borghese Gardens and groves, so serene by day, and poised just opposite our pensione. They surrounded the Galleria Borghese with—among a horde of objects too beautiful to digest—I recall most clearly (for its awfulness) Canova's Ivory-soap vapid statue of Napoleon's sister Pauline, Bernini's painfully imaginative Apollo and Daphne, his truculent David, and the many sinister but beckoning Caravaggio boys. The same wooded throughways and bushes also converted, almost instantly at sundown, into the central pick-up spot for whores of all gender. In the mid-1950s, as Jim and I tested the periphery by night, the arrangements seemed more orderly—and safer—than those in a number of other Roman street fairs. You stopped your tiny Fiat or opulent Ferrari by the curb, a particular girl or boy (mostly well-dressed) approached your open passenger door; you leaned over to discuss your needs and the fee to be charged for their satisfaction; then you beckoned your hooker into the car or drove ahead to the next eager provider. Only an ancient city, surely, could have organized its sex life so relatively painlessly (for its men, of course—the darlings of all southern cultures).

The fact that I've postponed the Sistine Chapel till this late in my list of wonders says nothing about the extent of my response to Michelangelo's ceiling and altarpiece. I visited the chapel more than once on that first trip; and though it had not yet undergone the highly dubious cleaning of the 1980s, I understood plainly that it was the only man-made thing I'd yet seen which was past belief in the extent of the sheer brain- and hand-power involved in the achievement of such grandeur, such witnessing to a human desire to come before God with a power dangerously comparable to God's own.

Supremely for me, though, the site that struck and moved me most powerfully—and has gone on doing so through every subsequent visit—was the Pantheon. Not only is it the best preserved of all ancient Roman buildings (its broad dome is inexplicably intact), there can never have been a structure built here—or elsewhere in all the succeeding centuries—which equals the immensity of its majesty, its passionate intent to honor its native city and the gods who sustain her, and the genius of whomever conceived its glory.

And speaking of glory and its decline, on my first visit to the Pantheon, ex-king Umberto II of Italy was there, visiting the tomb of his father. Though Umberto of Savoy had served as king for only a month, after World War II, he had continued to inspire considerable loyalty in numerous Italians. And as I stood apart and watched him at the family tomb, a woman approached him, knelt, and tried to kiss his shoes. Umberto quickly drew her upright and spoke briefly with her. The encounter left me thinking of the realities of another vanished power in such a place. Had Hadrian himself, on this spot, ever experienced such an awed tribute? And speaking of Roman mysteries, the Italian constitution of 1947 had forbidden Umberto to return to Italian soil in his lifetime. Yet several bystanders whispered to me, that morning on the spot, that the man with the wreath was Umberto; and my own acquaintance with photographs of the ex-king confirmed the fact. Had he simply come incognito to his father's grave?

By evening our long walks up and down the city's hills left us more than ready for the good dinner that the Milton always provided— mostly plain but delicious and served with mute elegance by men who seemed Roman to the core, dark and dignified but ready to respond to any word of thanks with a smile that was either genuine or was one more tribute to the Roman gift for perfect simulation. After the cheese and fruit, Jim and I mostly took our books back to the room or to the small lounge and read there, unless a certain pair of old women who seemed to be permanent residents were seated with their knitting and their endless low-pitched stream of complaint against life in general. I could stand about three minutes of their cranky duet; then I'd go to our room, though if I'd lingered with more patience I might have improved my Italian markedly, as well as my list of warnings against a grudging old age.

In retrospect it seems to me a remarkable fact that two healthy young men, neither of them possessed of extraordinary needs or demonic pressures, could have spent more than a month of evenings as quietly and compatibly as Jim Griffin and I. When I think of the students I've taught in the past five decades, I suspect that most of them would find our behavior weird or, at the least, incredible in its calm dedication to what's now called the "academics" of university life. Where was the other half—our *social* life? I think I'm fair to the majority of my present-day students in saying that they'd read the above pages and wonder why we weren't seeking the Florentine and Roman bars and clubs, meeting our Italian contemporaries, and getting on with the dancing and talking, drinking and hooking up (that latest name for no-fault sexual events)—those involvements that now seem not only desirable but a kind of life's blood to so many American middle-class "kids" (Jim and I would have been kids by current definition).

Any explanation of the contrast that's overtaken contemporary American youth is almost sure to sound more like the old ladies in the Milton lounge than useful good sense, so I won't engage in guessing— except to say that Jim and I were the offspring of parents who'd survived the deprivations of the Depression and the steady demands of the Second War. We had no genetic connection with the lively sociopolitical generation of the 1960s and early '70s, and some of our innate quiet was likely a product of that difference. To go further, as I've said, would involve me in deploring a great deal of what I see now. In any case, I can't recall either Jim or me expressing, or feeling, any lack of excitement in our Italian weeks.

Before we headed back to Oxford, though, we made one attempt to compensate for the fact that we'd failed to seek any real acquaintance with live Italians. An older English friend had given us the name of a young brother and sister—Vieri and Nicoletta Traxler—and we made postal contact with them in our final days. They replied with an immediate phone message at the Milton. Could we come to dinner a few nights later at Vieri's home? We accepted gladly and, with a certain amount of fumbling, we found his house in the silent dark of the Via del Velabro near the Arch of Janus, between the Palatine Hill and the Tiber. In memory it seems a small house, but the dining room had a handsome large fragment of old mosaic on the wall, and an excellent dinner was served. The talk, in impeccable English, was pleasant; so in all, we spent a warm and jocular evening with the two Traxlers.

They apparently enjoyed it as well; and with no coaching from us, they suggested another evening with the chance to meet a few of their friends. On that second occasion, we met Vieri and Nicoletta—with three or four friends of roughly our age—in a loud and cheerful restaurant in the funky cross-the-river district of Trastevere and had an even finer time. *Fine* with a single strange moment of exception. When I noted that several of our wineglasses were empty, I took the neck of the huge flask of Chianti in hand to repair the lack.

But before I could proceed to fill the glasses overhandedly (as wine is normally poured in America), the most beautiful of us—the gorgeous Olga Millo—seized my wrist and said "You are holding the bottle wrong." She made me set the flask down and showed me the proper method. With a certain male American stubbornness—and in hopes of a mild, maybe slightly inebriated, joke—I took up the flask again, just as I'd held it before. Olga then flung a fiery gaze at my eyes—"In Sicily they would *kill* you for this." Ah, *right*. I repaired my mysterious gaffe, the evening recommenced happily; and afterward several of the party took us on to what they said was the only English-language film theatre in Rome.

There was in fact such a place—very small but elegantly fitted—and the film was *Doctor at Sea,* a brand-new entry in a series of stories about the life of a young English physician. Only just recently, fifty years later, I found a videotape and reminded myself of its innocuous details. The doctor was played, as ever, by a young Dirk Bogarde who was serving as a ship's doctor on a luxury voyage in the Mediterranean. The female flirtation on board was played by a new French actress called Brigitte Bardot. This was before Bardot glittered to the top of international fame as an outrageous sex kitten, and none of us had seen her on screen before now.

When we eventually entered the theatre, the lights were already out, a newsreel was playing loudly, and we groped our way into seats on a row toward the back. When my eyes adjusted, I could see that—apart from the four or five of us—the theatre was entirely empty except for a couple who sat literally just ahead of me and slightly to my right. The film proceeded on its feather-light and easily forgettable way. The one really striking component was the *chanteuse* aboard ship—played by, surprisingly, Bardot—and the difficulty with which, in a 1955 English movie, she managed to damp down to acceptable levels her naturally high rate of physical smolder.

When the film ended and the house lights rose, I looked at the well-behaved young couple just ahead of me. It consisted, without question, of Brigitte Bardot and a young male companion. I can see her clearly still—in a French version of the standard tan British duffle coat and a slim modicum of makeup. She may have felt my recognizing gaze just behind her; and when she and her friend stood, she turned a full-face smile back toward me. She was after all nearly two years younger than I. I said *"Merci, Mademoiselle Bardot"* in my best French accent. I'd never been to France but had studied the language for two years at Duke. She gave me a charming bow, the others then recognized her, and we all shook hands (natives of the Romance-language world then shook hands as inevitably as the British fled the practice).

Had we been prepared for such an encounter—and I'm surprised that Vieri the diplomat wasn't—we could at least have invited her and her companion for an espresso nearby; there was surely a caffe in reach. They were plainly our age and apparently at rather loose ends in Rome, Bardot was not yet (even in France) a raging celebrity, they might have joined us. But no. We parted in the lobby; and my chance at talking with one of the genuine film sensations of our time—and exercising my almost never tried French—vanished as she walked away, hand in hand with her friend in the chill, just-after-New-Year's night.

Recalling those two good evenings, and a further dinner with Nicoletta and Olga, I'd say that our new Roman friends differed from our Oxford and American contemporaries most obviously in being a good deal more fashionably and expensively dressed, with an unspectacular self-dignifying elegance. Yet their warmth was unmistakably southern, and their curiosity about Jim and me—who we were, where we came from, what we intended to do with our lives—was very different from the then basic English tendency to go with what they could *see* about a stranger and ask him nothing more. Again their command of our language was embarrassingly excellent; and their appetite for pleasure seemed virtually identical to ours. The fact that Vieri Traxler was a few years older, and as I've only discovered in consulting Google while writing this page, he would ultimately become the Italian permanent representative to the United Nations (1989–1993) was not then visible to me or to Jim; and I hoped to see them again in time—as I hoped to see Rome, through the rest of my life.

After only a few months in England and a few weeks in Italy, I could say that these new Roman friends showed far fewer signs of World War II than my young Oxford colleagues and Britain in general—an entire country still in the grip of what might have been called advanced melancholia. Admittedly the Traxlers and their friends were financially secure; and their homes had surely not been bombed by Allied planes. Yet I sensed far fewer notes of depression from these technically *defeated* Italians than from the victorious British. The Brits of course were compelled to fight for their lives; but had they, in the end, been forced to pay too much for their survival? Well, Italy after all had been a unified nation for less than a century, whereas Great Britain had not only been unified since the reign of James I in the seventeenth century, it had ruled—and greatly benefited from—increasingly large portions of the planet for nearly two hundred years. Now that rule was rapidly ending.

6

A FEW DAYS LATER Jim and I flew north in sunlight, and that was very nearly the last sun I recall through the next two months. I was sorry to leave a city that I'd only begun to plumb. No lifetime could plumb it, especially given two enormous facts about the place—the fact that, in contrast to Florence, say, or London, so many of Rome's fascinations lie out of doors, and in the further fact that so much of the present-day city exists in easily seen layers, from the oldest recovered prehistoric sites right on through republican and imperial times, through the Dark Ages of barbarian havoc on into the Renaissance, modern Fascism, and the ever-growing fringe of a contemporary metropolis. As our plane lifted off, I know I told myself I could live here, something I've never felt (before or since) about another large city.

Simultaneously, though, I was especially glad to return to England and my growing friendship with Michael Jordan. I'd thought about him a great deal in the past five weeks and had even received a letter from him—he'd delivered post-office packages in Brighton for a while before Christmas, then gone skiing in Austria. As far as the prospect of even colder rooms and a drastic shortage of daylight, I could tell myself that at least I'd been in Italy for the year's shortest day. But January and February—even in the south side of England—were wet, dark, and cold. In those days of no central heating in Oxford (I literally knew no one who possessed it), my ancient rooms were heated only by the previously lamented single-bar electric heater. I've also noted that Merton provided us with a certain number of kilowatt-hours without extra charge (British electricity, being coal-produced, was phenomenally expensive then); but in the hope of something like an indoor fifty-degree level in the midwinter daytime, I employed my heater so relentlessly that my extra charges came, by the end of term, to a scandalous total.

My English student friends were indifferent to the problem. They thought nothing of warming the rooms to, say, forty degrees; then flinging their door wide open as they left for an errand and leaving it agape. My younger friend Anthony Nuttall, who'd later became a distinguished critic and teacher, used to tell our colleagues that "Reynolds is growing orchids over there in Mob Quad—orchids and iguanas." He was rather proud of my Yankee extravagance. I seemed to be his tame billionaire. My prodigality kept me at least from perishing of cold, and I took a certain pleasure in being something of an outrageous college pet—the Man Who Craves Heat.

What any partial solution to my heating problem couldn't help, of course, was my difficulty with darkness; and lamps which provided the required spectrum of daylight were decades off. So I battled a steady case of the blues—low-grade most of the time but by no means all. I was reaching an age, in my two parental families at least, where a man was expected to have a decent job and be carrying his own weight in the world, if not a wife's and children's also. And while I don't recall seeing myself in that particular way, in retrospect I think that I did feel a considerable degree of shame.

The large amount of sheer pleasure I was taking in my life, the satisfactions of a lively reciprocated friendship with a Briton who had strong American interests, the enormous amount of dangerous spare time I had at my disposal, and the fact that a substantial gift of money from the Rhodes Trust was deposited in my name at Barclay's Bank at the start of each term—all those things combined to cast an intermittent regretful air around me. I was doing fine—I made that clear in my letters home—but I did so with a troubling degree of wondering: were my letters to some degree sadistic, rubbing my pleasures into whatever wounds my mother and brother might still carry from Dad's death?

Rereading my every-Sunday letters home after five decades, I can see that she and Bill were far from socketed in abject misery in Upper Dixie, awaiting me and my first paycheck. Mother had her consuming job, Bill had his high-school duties; but they had more friends than even I had, they had loving family, they were not—to my knowledge—in deep financial difficulties, and I thought I'd be home in eighteen months to widen any straits through which they might be moving (I'd eventually discover that Mother was concealing a few serious money troubles). To some extent then my guilt was excessive, but the degree of self-punishment was a gauge of the genuine care I felt for them.

Meanwhile I slogged on with my B.Litt.-prep classes, my choice of university lectures, and the patch of serious worry that bedeviled me when I thought of Mr. Leishman (if I visited him in January, I don't recall the circumstances). But that one problem was soon dispelled. At the end of one of Helen Gardner's lectures early in the term, I went forward to ask her a question about the day's poetry. We talked for three minutes; then she glanced at her watch and said "Could we step across the street to the Eastgate and have a glass of sherry?" It was near lunchtime and the small Eastgate Hotel, with its pub, was only a few yards away.

In those days Miss Gardner was in her late forties; but her prematurely white hair and her bright, often smiling, eyes lent her head and face a real distinction. That, and the fact that she was already a renowned scholar in the small world of transatlantic literary studies, gave me an immediate sense of promotion to have this moment with her—a slight step-up in the then-minuscule world of the Oxford English faculty which, nonetheless, had my local fate in its hands. By the time our sherries arrived, we were launched on a discussion of the portrayal of evil in seventeenth-century English poetry—from the Macbeths to Milton's Satan—and a mention of my unhappiness with Mr. Leishman had surfaced (not that I thought he was evil). Miss Gardner asked me a few slyly amused questions about his procedures. Then she sipped from her small glass—I'd soon learn that we

Helen Gardner, only a few years after she supervised my thesis on Milton. For a commercial photograph, it's very much like the woman I knew, through so many hours of pleasant, yet probing—and surprisingly revealing—one-on-one conversation in two and a half years of work. Note the guarded reserve of the smile and the absence of vanity in her refusal to remove her glasses for the picture. The head is extraordinarily packed with information—facts combined with intense feeling. And that huge quantity is held by her with no false modesty; in fact, she'll fight with all the strength of her small body for the rightness of her knowledge (her books and essays and the correspondence columns of *The Times Literary Supplement* sometimes scorchingly attest to the trait). As was often observed, she was not much loved by her colleagues; and many of her students approached her with fear, though my own experience was more enjoyable. Yet our relations never resulted in a lasting friendship. Apart from a two-minute encounter in our mutual bank on the High Street, soon after my return in 1961 for a fourth year in Oxford, I don't recall that we ever met or corresponded again. As a man who's now taught longer than she at our final meeting, I can well understand her subsequent silence toward me—I'd been one of her hundreds of students—but I regret my own silence toward a teacher who rescued me from early academic trouble and then bore patiently with my initial failures of academic focus. It seems that she died in misery. As a rigorous Christian, did she feel she was paying on debts she owed in a long life's work? She owed me nothing whatever.

were having what was called *elevenses*, a short drink and perhaps a bis-
cuit (a dry cookie)—and she said "Would you like me to take you on?"

I'd been a mainly lucky man; but this degree of kindness from a distinguished teacher was surprising, though I'd revered most of my
teachers. I'd attended Miss Gardner's lectures for two terms and was
a member of her seminar in textual editing, but this was the first
time I'd sat down alone with her, so I leapt to say Yes. She made the
arrangements promptly with no further requirement that I see Mr.
Leishman, on whom I never laid eyes again. And soon I began to visit
Miss Gardner in her almost unnaturally uncluttered rooms in St.
Hilda's to discuss a thesis subject (an old guilt at abandoning work
with Leishman led me to include him, twenty-five years later, as a
sympathetic minor character called Fleishman in my novel *The
Source of Light*).

Since my sophomore year at Duke, Milton's late verse play about
the tragic Hebrew champion Samson had been my pick of all his
work. The poet's genius in the sheer manipulation of English (which
he virtually reinvented for his purposes) had been the characteristic
that first drew me to him, and in no other work is that genius more
amply on view than in *Samson*. As Miss Gardner and I talked through
our first meetings, it began to seem that my own interests and what she
knew about prior work on the play—it was not then much studied—
suggested a subject that might be most helpful to the world of scholarship: an exploration of Milton's use of the Chorus in *Samson*. The
play is far the most successful English-language attempt to write on
the ancient Greek tragic model, and the Athenian dependence on a
centrally important character called the Chorus (portrayed by fifteen men in the theatre) offers perhaps the greatest challenge to anyone working in the form, in whatever language.

We agreed on the nature of my early reading. It was going to be
voluminous; and Miss Gardner was especially pleased with my suggestion of reading Italian Renaissance critics in their discussions of the
Greek plays which were only beginning, in their time, to be published
in anything resembling reliable editions (I felt ready to explore both
Italian and Latin texts, with dictionaries handy). Soon I was keeping

regular hours in both the upper reading room of the Bodleian and in its oldest wing, the fifteenth-century Duke Humfrey Library (built to house a donation of books from Humfrey, the brother of Henry V).

Otherwise I was continuing to prepare for the qualifying exam and went on attending lectures by Miss Gardner and David Cecil. I don't recall in which order I heard them, but eventually I attended all David's superb lectures on the early English novel and his full set of lectures on Shakespeare. I've never known another scholar with his particular gift for making a given work of fiction or poetry seem irresistible. Who would have thought anyone could take Samuel Richardson's early seven-volume *Clarissa* and make it seem as riveting as a first-class film? More than once I'd left Lord David's lecture, gone straight to Blackwell's, and purchased a work he'd discussed that morning—in which process I discovered that *Clarissa*, for instance, is a very great, though extremely strange and lengthy, tragic novel.

My social life continued apace—considerably faster than was wise— and the numerous acquaintances I'd made in my first term had begun to winnow to a smaller group of close friends with whom I spent many good hours. Among my core of English friends was Ronald Tamplin, whose poetry and wit I much admired, and Tony Nuttall whom I've already noted. Tony's own interest in exotic drama shone out one morning when he burst into my sitting room, fully attired in a suit of Japanese samurai armor which he'd suddenly discovered, inexplicably concealed in a cupboard in his rooms. For two minutes he gave me a hilarious imitation of samurai-movie grunts and lurches; then left as fast as he'd arrived (samurai films had only lately reached the West).

My close American college friend was the droll Iowan, Rex Jamison, with whom I made several more hitching trips to Stratford. Assorted others included Jeremy Commons, the New Zealander of what seemed invincible cheer and enthusiasm. He'd eventually return to his home country to teach and write about nineteenth-century Italian opera. Of younger vintages, I eventually located John Speaight, a textbook example of an English eccentric (though in his case the eccentricity was genuine, not manufactured for public entertain-

John Speaight, caught by me on the edge of the Merton garden in the winter of 1958. The odd black streamers down his shoulders are the draped remains of his Oxford Commoner's gown, the gown that most of us were required to wear for any academic exercise—a tutorial, an exam, attendance at a university lecture, a college dinner, etc. Perhaps he was four or five years younger than I, but our shared interest in opera and drama gave us a good deal to talk about over tea in the afternoon or coffee after college lunch or dinner. John welcomed most chances to laugh and elicited much fun from his friends. Especially good were his long narratives of vacation trips to Soviet-era Bulgaria, where his father was British ambassador. Shortly after my return home in the summer of '58, John turned up in Durham for a visit that took us as far south as Charleston. His unself-conscious eccentricity strengthened my liking for him as he returned to Britain to teach in several prep schools, and I much regret that I haven't seen him for fifty years.

ment). John's immensely thin body, his high nasal voice, his returns to college from exploratory visits to the secondhand shops of the city with a string bag full of peculiar small attractions, and his fervent love of the voice of Maria Callas on early 78 records left an unshaken memory with me. And Peter Heap, though a different sort of man— a bass-voiced veteran of two years in the British Army—would likewise survive the years as an ongoing friend (he'd ultimately enter the British foreign service and conclude his career as ambassador to Brazil, prior to knighthood).

Michael Jordan remained the friend whose company I sought most often. Though he was deeply buried in his history studies, he seemed to find all my own interests welcome; and we continued meeting often for Indian meals in town (cheap and tasty, though one of our restaurants—the Cobra—got indicted for serving cat meat in one of the curries on its menu). After dinner we'd often go on to films, plays, concerts, and occasional train trips to London. Again, Michael was in the second year of his undergraduate work; but like most Mertonians he seemed to invest as much time as I in our eminently respectable, yet busy, nightlife. I've noted several other events that held our attention. Almost nothing, though, surpassed two of our London ventures—the Leicester Square premiere of James Dean's *Rebel Without a Cause* (the least good of his three films but still the most famous) and a single winter evening at Covent Garden. That would prove my only chance to see one of the supreme ballerinas as Margot Fonteyn and Michael Soames danced Prokofiev and Ashton's full-length *Cinderella*. Ballet has never been a great pursuit of mine; but on this night, Fonteyn's body performed unending miracles of grace that I've never seen matched by another human creature.

Despite Michael's being two years younger, by the deep midst of the winter of '56 he'd become a strong magnet for the loneliness that—in the face of so much pleasure—had steadily increased in my absence from home. One evening we were sitting up late in my rooms when I was overcome by nausea from a wretched college dinner—bitter calf's liver and onions. Suddenly I was forced to race off to the equally awful Mob Quad bogs for the first of numerous attempts to empty my stomach. When I returned from the second attempt, I told Michael that my flashlight showed that I'd also retched up blood; and he quietly said that, with my permission, he'd like to sleep on my sofa just to be sure I made it satisfactorily through the night.

I was astonished at the offer, coming from so self-possessed and beautiful a man. I accepted gladly and again Michael's value rose a long notch in my mind. I've noted my earlier sense of suspecting I loved him. More than any other man I'd known, he seemed to warrant such commitment—so long as my own offer could shape itself to the fact of his straightness; and his concern for my well-being on that one night almost surely is the fact that prevented my reviving the prior round of fatty-tumor cancer scare.

The memory of my bad-liver night reminds me of my favorite example of donnish undergraduate wit. Quite mysteriously one morning in my first year, white porcelain holders for toilet tissue appeared in the bogs, firmly screwed to the dark brown walls. Previously our "bog paper" had been flung about on the filthy floors—and good luck for finding usable pieces. British toilet paper of those years was frequently of an inexplicably dreadful quality—tiny sheets, slick as wax paper—and one wag was heard to say "Did you hear that old Westrate has broken his arm? Ah yes, slipped off the bog paper and hit the floor hard." In any case, to memorialize the appearance of paper dispensers in the Mob Quad, the incomparable Henry Mayr-Harting wrote the following in the Junior Common Room suggestion book (and I quote from memory), "Let me record with surprise and gratitude the appearance this morning of porcelain tissue dispensers in the Mob Quad bogs. Let it not be forgot, however, that the French Revolution was, in part, hastened by a *slight* alleviation of the misery of the Fourth Estate" (that is, the commoners).

In the midst of the winter gloom, one of my efforts at lifting the horizon was the beginnings of an effort to purchase a car. When I was a freshman at Duke, my bachelor cousin Macon Thornton had given me $3,000 shortly before his death (the equivalent of some $22,600 in current funds). I'd banked it for long-term needs, and a car now seemed an urgent need. With Michael's enthusiastic help then, I investigated the conceivable options. They quickly boiled down to two possibilities—first, a Morris Mini (manufactured in the Oxford suburb of Cowley but gimcrack in many details) and second, a Volkswagen. At that point in world history, I was still loath to invest in a German product—Hitler's famous "People's Car"—but the small VW Beetle seemed an affordable yet elegantly stubborn road hugger.

The price was initially daunting. At the Oxford dealership on the Plain in St. Clement's Street, it would cost me $1,192—some $8,500 today. That would constitute a major bargain in new cars but a mammoth hole in my savings. In March of 1956, all the same—late in my second term—I ordered a new black Volkswagen with steering wheel on the left, American style (I intended to export it to the States at the end of my second year). I wouldn't receive delivery till sometime in May—VWs were still scarce in Britain and imports were slow. However unpleasant the delay, it was just as well that I'd be firmly grounded in Oxford awhile longer—only four days after ordering the car, I sat for the B.Litt. qualifying exam.

Having studied ferociously in recent weeks, reading through the greater parts of most days in the Bodleian, I sat down in full academic regalia—cap, gown, and white bow tie—in one of the smaller rooms of the Exam Schools and endured the three-hour written portion of the exam (all questions centered on the period I'd chosen, the English Renaissance). That was soon followed by an oral conducted by four or five members of the English faculty. Both halves of the ordeal were based on the preparatory courses we'd taken in the past two terms, and they proved to be the most rigorous intellectual workout I'd experienced till then.

As I recall, seventeen of my fellow B.Litt. hopefuls stood for the testing. A letter to my mother reports that thirteen of us passed and could now proceed to the writing of a thesis, four of us failed. Two of the failures were non-Rhodester American acquaintances, and the sight of their collapsed faces as we clustered round the just-posted list of passes and fails was sad to say the least (no second chance would be offered them; the Oxford of those days was remorselessly realistic, and my friends' single remaining chance was to leave the university). God knows what I'd have done had I failed.

7

PASS OR FAIL, throughout the second term, Michael and I had been planning to visit Italy during the Easter vac. He'd been there once before, though not to Rome. In any case the chance to go on the road with any close friend had always been high on my ladder of hopes, and this trip began only some two weeks after I passed the exam. Garry Garrard, our Merton friend from London, and a Brighton schoolmate of Michael's named Ashley Basel were to join us for part of the trip. I'd only met Ashley briefly at a London party but I liked him. And Garry had been a cheerful friend in college, reading Arabic at the time and regaling us with his findings of the apparently endless sexual vocabulary of that language.

Before our departure, though, I had a week on my hands, unnecessarily idle. Instead of remaining in college and working away, I decided that—after the ordeal of my exam—I could hardly expect myself to continue to work uninterruptedly (clearly the remains of my American sense that college vacations were precisely that, vacations). In Britain then a Scottish noblewoman called Miss MacDonald of Sleat ran an organization that found vacation lodging for foreign students with no place to go. I applied for a week of such lodging; and Miss MacDonald found me an aged couple in rural Sussex who took me in. They were Mr. and Mrs. A. W. Street, and they lived near the town of Crowborough in Sussex.

Rather like tiny snow-haired dolls, both the Streets were well on in their late seventies, maybe older; Mr. Street had (I believe) once been chairman of the board at Lloyd's of London, and their home was a large, calmly luxurious house surrounded by spacious gardens. There was no other guest but me, and I had a great deal of time in their silent house for reading and naps. Mrs. Street was still her own (rather scary) driver, and she took me off one day for a good view of the great house at Knole, the enormous ancient home of the Sackville family.

Otherwise we listened to a great many recordings of Mozart operas, and we ate especially well—they had a German cook. When I sat down for my first lunch, Mr. Street—a cheerful senior—asked what I'd drink with my meal. I asked for a glass of water; and he looked at me with amazement—"*Water*, Mr. Price?" I confirmed my request—"Haven't you ever been thirsty, Mr. Street?" His face cleared slightly and he said "Well, I suppose I have, yes, frequently; but it never occurred to me to quench it with *water*." So I drank water and he drank ale; in the evenings we all drank excellent wine. Brighton was not far away; and at the Streets' urging, I invited Michael for lunch one day. He came by bus and assisted in cheering our willing hosts. At the end of the week, I left them with considerable affection for their kindness, took a bus into Brighton, and joined up with Michael for our journey.

Our budgets allowed us an only partial airborne trip. Before our early-morning flight to Geneva then, Michael and I spent the night in London in the digs of a Duke fraternity brother of mine who was then stationed at an American air-force base nearby. We arrived shortly before our friend and his fellow airmen were about to depart for their base; and the atmosphere of the flat, in its jollity, resembled that in the Pensione Nazionale on Christmas Eve—a likable mix of away-from-home Yanks (some of whom flew the bombers that were then in perpetual patrol, with their hydrogen bombs, above Cold War Europe) and their English girlfriends.

When the airmen and the girls finally left, Michael and I found some pub food down the road; then returned for an early night. When I turned back the covers on the bed I was to occupy, I was reminded again of the bed-linen realities of male college life in the States—the sheets were almost indescribably filthy—but my other choice was the chilly floor. Well, I was a mere child after all; so I took a deep breath, crawled into bed, and fell asleep in two minutes. Michael chose the sofa and the clock woke us well before dawn. We were due to meet Garry and Ashley at Heathrow at an ungodly hour.

We made our flight with Michael's usual minimum of waiting time, then flew one more arc above the dazzling Alps and were in Geneva in time for a long walk round to acquaint the three of us with this odd combination of Calvinist grimness, international-organization world-optimism, and Swiss smugness (and that was before we knew the extent to which this scrubbed-clean country had financed a considerable portion of Hitler's Holocaust). Then we found an inexpensive restaurant with superb fried potatoes and settled in for a clean night's sleep at a pensione which Garry had found for us.

For some reason Garry and Ashley took an earlier train to Milan next morning, with the understanding that they'd find two cheap rooms to contain the four of us, get gallery tickets to whatever opera was scheduled for La Scala that night, then meet us on the steps of the cathedral at an assigned hour in the early evening. Michael and I rose in good time to find our way to the station and board a midmorning express train. Continental trains then always seemed considerably more crowded than the English; and finding seats in the packed compartments was one more challenge (everywhere, I was accompanied by my new but weighty leather luggage, a graduation present).

Still, Michael and I were standing on the steps of the cathedral at the promised dark hour. We waited a long while, long enough to watch a mysterious man box the perimeter of the large piazza at least a dozen times (could he have been fulfilling a religious vow?). He'd commenced another round when our friends appeared, breathlessly explaining their lateness, and rushed us to the highest balcony of La Scala just as the glamorous Herbert von Karajan, less than a decade from his denazification procedures, raised his baton and poised his famous profile for a performance of Richard Strauss's *Salome* (Strauss's own relations with the Nazis were hardly impeccable, but he did at least have a Jewish daughter-in-law whom he struggled to protect).

The greatest exponent of the outrageous leading role—the flame-haired Bulgarian Ljuba Welitsch—had sung her soprano to ribbons by then, and her successor Christel Goltz was no match for Welitsch's demonic teenager with the ice-razor voice; but Karajan led a potent performance all the same, though the doings were rendered a little bizarre when it came time for Princess Salome to deliver the dance for her besotted stepfather King Herod. At that moment Goltz (who was neither unsightly nor obese) inexplicably slipped offstage as unobtrusively as she could manage; and the beautiful Russian ballerina Tamara Toumanova slid memorably into view to dance Salome's crucial, and ultimately murderous, Dance of the Seven Veils to Strauss's eminently and intentionally sleazy music.

A cheap supper followed the opera (all four of us had laser vision—before the invention of lasers—for good cheap food), then back to the hotel our friends had found. It proved considerably more expensive than I'd hoped, but the rooms were handsomely simple and clean. Tired as we should have been, Michael and I had the leftover energy to sit for hours more in our room and talk our friendship into a higher orbit; then a deep-drowned sleep. The room, incidentally, offered the only bidet I'd yet seen. I was embarrassed to reveal yet another layer of American naïveté; so I didn't ask Michael for its purpose. I assumed it was a footbath.

Next morning we visited the remnant of the monastery where the shadows of Leonardo's *Last Supper* were tantalizingly visible on the refectory wall above us. Leonardo's almost pathologic ability to damage his paintings by radical experimentation with his pigments, and the fact that Napoleon's soldiers would later cut a door through the foot of the mural, had severely damaged the dramatic focus—that moment when Jesus says to his twelve chosen companions "One of you will betray me." Though I'd read Freud's fascinating essay on Leonardo, as I stood near his ruined masterpiece I failed to reflect on the fact that a queer painter like Leonardo settled on such a potentially personal moment (a few years earlier, he'd been charged with homosexuality to the authorities in Florence and almost certainly arrested before he was finally, and inexplicably, released).

For all the ruinous state of the wall however, just being in the same room which Leonardo occupied for the long months he took to complete his work was exciting to a young man with my Romantic-era sense of human heroism—a sense I've never lost. I might never rise to such an enduring height, but I knew a precipitous peak when I saw one, and here was an unquestionable summit on a not-so-large wall just above me. Its richness was thus more comprehensible and usable as a goad to my own ambitions than Michelangelo's titanic ceiling in Rome.

Then we headed for the station and off to Venice, arriving at dusk in the light rain that was to mark almost a whole Easter week in the Western world's strangest city (Robert Benchley, on arrival, cabled his editor at *The New Yorker*, "Streets flooded. Please advise"). By water-bus we made our way to the university center whose existence I'd discovered in the Bodleian and were directed onward to a private home in which the center had reserved a spartan but clean room for the four of us with a toilet just down the hall, past the narrow cot on which a never-explained but friendly old woman slept. If any one of us stumbled past her in the night, she'd raise her head in the dark, grin, and say *"Buona notte, signore."*

My memory of the next few days—my only visit to Venice—is discolored by the fact that I'd brought only my pair of leather loafers with me, and their soles began to separate from the uppers as I slogged through the cold early spring rain. With my tight budget I lacked sufficient funds to purchase a new pair of Italian shoes; and while a friendly cobbler made emergency repairs as I stood in his shop, they lasted no more than a day. I was back to the misery of sodden socks. Still, I recall the tedious grandeur of numerous Tintoretto walls, the riches of the Accademia (especially Giorgione's ominous *Tempest*); and above all the golden dim interior of St. Mark's cathedral.

On our first visit there, I encountered an unexpected presence. At the time I didn't know what had brought him to Venice—I'd later learn that Stephen Spender was there for one more of his endless gatherings of writers from both sides of the Iron Curtain—but his shambling height and his striking large face were unmistakable. I'd seen him for an earlier moment in Oxford when a group of students brought him to the Café de Paris where I was eating. Spender's repute is now undergoing an inevitable postmortem deflation, but in those days he was a much-respected figure in European and American literary circles and a powerful force in the literary cold war. Here in St. Mark's he was wandering alone; and when he saw me and Michael across the incense fog of the cathedral—in our unmistakable Anglo-American attire—he nodded pleasantly.

That night we saw him again, coming toward us on a bridge and accompanied only by the frog-eyed, near-dwarf body of Jean-Paul Sartre. I recognized Sartre from the famous Cartier-Bresson photograph of his phenomenal ugliness, an ugliness that proved sexually irresistible to troops of women. Spender seemed two heads taller than Sartre, and his prematurely snow-white hair was unmistakable. They were chattering on in French; but by then Spender recognized us and paused for a second nodding instant as we passed. Even Sartre removed the pipe clutched in his teeth and gave a curt bow in our direction—the first and last time I'd ever see him, the most famous philosopher of the twentieth century looked to me like nothing so much as a Cyclops. His thick glasses gave his cocked eyes the quality of a single huge eye.

Again on a faster schedule than ours, Garry and Ashley departed Venice after two days. Ash was another man I'd never see again; a few years later, he was briefly imprisoned for manslaughter in a traffic death. Michael and I stayed on in the rain, largely because I'd invited one of my best friends from Raleigh to join us for Easter. While we waited, we saw a poster for a jazz concert that evening, to be given by the Jazz Club di Venezia. Given our mutual interest, and the seduction of the group's name, we bought tickets and turned up in a small-ish hall at the announced time—8:00 p.m. Silly lads. What we might have known by then was that announced times in Italian entertainment circles were highly approximate.

So we sat, patiently enough, as a young and well-dressed audience filtered in. Then the band materialized, man by man, on a brightly lit stage and indulged in a good deal of leisurely handshaking, embracing, and private but clearly enjoyable conversation among themselves. Finally, past 10:30 the music began—a likable and mostly original blend of Dixieland and more modern jazz. Eventually we realized that the main truth of the announcing poster was the word *concert*. There would be no dancing, no drinking, no cheering from the audience—pure music. So we listened till far past midnight, then quietly left as the band seemed ready to play till dawn. Tired as we were by then, we were young enough to remark before bed that we could at least return to college with a no-doubt-safe distinction—the only Mertonians who were likewise dues-paying members of the Jazz Club di Venezia (our ticket fee had enrolled us).

The Raleigh friend I'd invited to join us had a striking name—Jane Savage (Milton had written one of his college poems on the death of Jane Savage, the Marchioness of Winchester)—and as my friend's father never ceased to tell me, their first direct Virginia forebear was Thomas Savage, a teenaged member of the original Jamestown colony of 1607, one who was given as a long-term hostage to Chief Powhatan (the father of Pocahontas) and who spent the remainder of his life in being an English settler, a fluent Algonquian-speaking friend of the local Indians, and the recipient of some nine thousand acres of Virginia land from one of his Indian friends.

Jane and I had shared a high-school romance that rapidly resolved into permanent friendship (we'd never repeated the soft-core petting of our early dates). At present she was working for Radio Free Europe in Munich and was rooming with a cheerful American named Liz McNelly. Driving an antique car, they were to reach us a day or so before Easter; and at last the sun broke out on Venice, just as I'd begun to start howling for light. Exactly as scheduled we met them under an unmarred sky in the main piazza; and once we'd exchanged introductions and embraces, the girls had a piece of news that couldn't wait.

Through their job they'd just learned that Premier Khrushchev of the Soviet Union had delivered a secret speech—little more than a month ago—to the Twentieth Congress of the Communist Party in Moscow. Jane and Liz could tell us only the barest facts; but the

Liz McNelly, Michael Jordan, and I picnicking beside Duino Castle between Venice and Trieste during the Easter weekend of 1956. It had been a generally rain-soaked week, but the skies cleared beautifully for this day and the next (Liz and her roommate had driven down from their jobs in Munich for three days). When we began the day's trip to Trieste in Liz's rattletrap car, I had no idea we'd pause so near the birthplace of Rilke's great *Duino Elegies*, among my favorite modern poems; but my poetic excitement in no way reduced my interest in our mortadella sandwiches and wine. My high-school friend Jane Savage—Liz's roommate—is concealed behind my camera.

CIA seemed to know that, in its usual enormous Soviet length, Khrushchev's speech detailed in awful specificity the crimes of Stalin and his henchmen—it was as revolutionary a statement as anything ever said by Lenin. Standing there, cooed at by pigeons and pelted by sunlight, the four of us could barely begin to weigh the effects of such a revelation. So no doubt Michael and I nodded sagely, then suggested a coffee nearby. But the girls were staying at a slightly more upscale place across town and felt the need to unpack and wash.

We gave them a generous hour and were then determined to share a few of our own discoveries while the sunlight lasted—a few of the potentially sinister corners of a tortuously complex town. Mainly though we sat over coffee at Florian's in the piazza and then over drinks at Harry's Bar, made bafflingly famous by Hemingway despite its cramped charmlessness. Throughout, Jane and Liz regaled us with hilarious stories of their lives as low-level employees of the small clannish group in Munich who appeared to run Radio Free Europe. They were convinced, years before the secret was public, that their network—which broadcast "the best of America in news, music, and the arts" to Iron Curtain countries—was a CIA-front organization and was by no means entirely supported by the donations which it sought in TV commercials back home.

On Easter Saturday we decided, for lack of a better plan, to drive east to Trieste. For insurance reasons the women did the driving; and the trip was my introduction to the hair-raising reality of Italian highways, even then. The distance was not more than a hundred miles, but it seemed to take forever (the engine emitted desperate noises at disturbing intervals). Shortly before our destination I saw a sign—DUINO. I'd known that the poet Rilke had received his first inspiration for the *Duino Elegies* when he was staying there in the winter of 1911–12 in a castle owned by the Princess Marie von Thurn und Taxis-Hohenlohe. This had to be the spot.

In any case it was lunchtime, and with considerable relief I called for a detour. Jane took the right turn, we found a grocery, bought the makings of mortadella-and-cheese sandwiches and a liter of local wine, and paused by the Adriatic to eat our lunch in sight of Rilke's castle—a heavyset fortress on cliffs that plunged to the Adriatic not more than a few hundred yards from our picnic. It had apparently started life as a Roman watchtower (that portion was in ruins); and Dante was supposed to have written parts of the *Commedia* in the early days there. We could see no signs of present movement, and no hope of entrance in those days; the castle is still owned by the Thurn und Taxis family. But the memory of that proximity only some forty years after Rilke's great beginning—*Who if I cried would hear me among the angelic orders?* (and the snapshots I still have as proof)— remain mysteriously more potent for me than my visit to, say, Shakespeare's tomb or the altar of Milton's first marriage.

Trieste left almost nothing with me in the way of recollection, only the thought of a jubilantly manic guard at yet another sunlit castle in the city—a man who kept flapping his arms for us, crowing like a rooster, and calling Liz *"una bomba atomica"* with apparent reference to her striking good looks. We could only laugh and beat a slow retreat in late afternoon, back to our sick-sounding car and the hope of reaching Venice somehow before Easter dawn.

We made it before dark, with help from a rural crossroads mechanic between Trieste and our destination. He raised the hood, listened raptly to the awful sounds, made fifteen minutes' worth of adjustments, smilingly refused any payment, and sent us on our way to what was then the one enormous parking lot on the outskirts of Venice (you left your car there, locked it hopefully, and walked across a bridge into town—*streets flooded* indeed). We splurged a little on a good dinner, had coffee on the piazza again, took as long a walk as our tired legs allowed, then headed to our separate lodgings for an early bedtime.

Being men of our time and place, Michael and I rose early next morning and dressed in jackets and ties for the occasion. Though neither of us was then a churchgoer, we reached the Piazza San Marco before our agreed-on meeting with Jane and Liz. So we waited for them near the main door of the cathedral, surrounded by the zillion pigeons who were plainly unwilling to believe our hands were empty on such a holy day. Then, as surprising as an unexpected gong-crash, a silent ecclesiastical procession rounded the corner to our right; and in its midst was the then-patriarch of Venice, Cardinal Roncalli.

In two more years he'd become the benign and astonishingly reform-minded Pope John XXIII, the convener of the Second Vatican Council which would change the church so irrevocably. Old, short, and agreeably stout, Angelo Roncalli—the son of tenant farmers—was physically a twin to my never-married cousin whose gift of money had bought the Volkswagen; and he passed within a few feet of Michael and me. Though neither of us had Catholic roots (not for the past four centuries at least), we were the only humans near at hand; and the cardinal gave us an especially generous blessing, smiling broadly.

He didn't say to us what an Orthodox Greek or Russian priest might have said—*Christ is risen!*—but his cheer was evidence enough. All my life, from the age of seven at least, I've bowed to the significant historical evidence that Jesus actually rose from the dead in bodily form, not as a mere actor in the dreams of a few disciples. In chapter 15 of Paul's First Letter to the Corinthians, he sets down what he's learned (presumably from Jesus' brother James and the prime disciples, Peter and John bar Zebedee, he records resurrection appearances to more than five hundred people). Of that small group, only another small handful can have moved onward—against enormous opposition from their own people and from Rome—to make, of their Lord's teaching and personal transcendence, a religion that in under three centuries had conquered the empire itself. I gave Roncalli a grateful wave back then; and on he moved to say a high mass for Easter Day and to become, so soon, one of the world's most powerful men—perhaps the most significant pope since the Renaissance.

Later in the day we saw Jane and Liz off back to Munich in their ruinous car—it actually made it—and next afternoon Michael and I took a train for Rome. The meeting of all four of us had been a big success. Michael and Liz clearly took to one another at once; Jane and I fit back together like the friends we'd been since the age of sixteen. There'd been no physical intimacy still; just the luxury of laugh-

Ruins adjacent to the castle at Duino. The castle complex is built upon the ruins of a Roman fortress. After our picnic nearby we didn't walk the few hundred yards from our lunch by the Adriatic toward the castle itself; but again I was especially struck by being so near the place where Rilke had begun work on his *Duino Elegies*, and I took this picture. My recent Christmas weeks in Rome had introduced me to actual antiquity—true ruins left over from the hands of human beings (back home, I'd been impressed by eighteenth-century buildings; and I did after all live in an Oxford quad begun in the fourteenth century)—but I can recall a certain thrill at spreading a picnic out on a rock in sight of something as old as this north-Italian ruin. The entirety is still in the hands of the Thurn und Taxis family, and the newer castle is open to the public.

ter and great ease in one another's company. So I don't think I'm entirely hallucinating when I mention here that I more than half remember writing to Jane later in the spring and, a little skittishly, suggesting that she and I might want to discuss the notion of marriage—how good an idea was it for her and me? I have no present memory of the thinking that lay behind my letter. But all these years later, I wonder if I'd gone weak-kneed about some aspect of my sexuality or the prospect of as solitary a life as I'd long foreseen myself leading? In fact, though, I think that my father's death in '54 had freed my mind to pursue its engrained course—a course that I still believe would not ultimately have disturbed that good man whose own life had no doubt reached into corners that he never had time to discuss with me before he was gone.

Shortly after the next millennium, Jane died of multiple sclerosis in pain so enduring and intense that it drove her to near distraction (she spent all her nights paralyzed and in an otherwise empty house). A few years before her death, Jane told me that she still had all my letters. Whether they survive, I don't know and haven't tried to discover. I can't then confirm the tone I took when writing to her more than fifty years ago. I'm certain, though, that she responded with the kind of good sense that characterized helpful stretches of our youth—no, marriage for us would surely not work. Her own eventual marriage—to a lawyer who moved her to a small conservative Carolina town—proved a failure, and she died in heartbroken loneliness.

Michael and I reached Rome to find that, incredibly, I'd made my second error in reservations there. Arriving just after dark, we went straight from the station to the student pensione whose address I'd somehow found. An enormous female proprietor met us at the door of the Pensione Università. Hearing our names, she told us at once that we were not expected till exactly a month from today. When I attempted to correct her, she produced my letter and showed me—inarguably—that I'd a made a simple but awful typing error and had reserved a room for thirty days hence. On Easter weekend—could Rome ever be more crowded?—I'd made that big a mistake.

Her face looked ferocious—what brand of fool was I? (when she wondered aloud if I was truly American, Michael broke down laughing). Still, given the hour, I tried at least to appeal to her Italian mercy. And when I confirmed my stunned disappointment and asked for her help with some solution, she melted a little. She'd have a room available in three more days; meanwhile we could sleep on cots in one of her hallways. But a large party of German tourists would rise before dawn for a trip to Pompeii (she whispered a reminder of the noisiness of Germans), and we'd be trying to sleep in their midst—a sufficiently awful prospect.

Earlier as we'd walked through the handsome postwar station, we'd been solicited by numerous men, loudly proclaiming the availability of inexpensive lodging. Now I suggested to Michael that we take a trolley back to the station and find a temporary room (the Milton was beyond Michael's present means). He agreed, I begged the proprietress to save space for us three days hence, she offered an enveloping handshake and off we went. It was well past ten o'clock. The Pensione Nazionale, with its ribald Christmas memories, was only a few blocks away; but I didn't suggest it. Still we quickly found a room in the Pensione Esedra, even nearer the station; and the flack carried our bags to the spot. The cost was daunting to us both, but I vowed to join Michael tomorrow in search of something cheaper till we could return to the Università.

Next morning we returned to the station. That early, there were no flacks in sight; but I happened to look down one aisle that ran off the enormous lobby and there—as I vaguely remembered from last night—was a sign that said, in Italian, "Society for the Protection of Catholic Youth." I turned to Michael—"We're Catholics, right?"— and led the way to a door beneath the sign. It was a small, severely unadorned room. To the right there was a long bench with two obviously pregnant girls, silent in their head scarves. They'd clearly come first, so we advanced to take a seat behind them. Suddenly, though, a woman's voice called us; a young nun beckoned us toward her desk. I told her the true story of our debacle, she listened (smiling) and never asked if we were Catholic. Before I could say that we'd have a room in another few nights, she was writing an address on a card. She handed it to us and, when I asked what the room would cost, she waved a pleasantly dismissing hand (ah, Italy!). There'd be no charge.

Another trolley took us to the address—a boys' boarding school, run by monks. The boys were away for Easter; and our room was what we might have expected—a bone-clean space, with two narrow beds (freshly made) and a crucifix centered on the wall. There was a running-water basin and a toilet with showers down the hall. A coffee-and-rolls breakfast was served, and for two days I don't recall seeing another guest. Even the monks were mostly invisible—though if encountered, they'd bow and scuttle. And as we'd been told, when the time came to claim our space at the Pensione Università, we took up our bags and left. There wasn't even a poor box by the door for a small contribution—something we just might have managed, given that our room at the Università cost $1.50 per night (including morning coffee, rolls, and jam but no more washing facilities than a basin in our room). We showered in a lower level of the grand train station, in the remarkably clean cubicles which proved to be rentable for showers—and whatever else was your choice.

The remainder of our time in Rome—was it ten days?—was much like my winter days with Jim, though the rain had mostly stopped. Among new sights I recall only seeing the older American film *All Quiet on the Western Front*—horrifically convincing (as it still is) in the portrayal of First War trench combat. At the prospect of our visit to the Vatican Museum, Michael quickly devised a new skill, one typical of his analytic mind. In those days the museum was arranged so that the Sistine was the final stop on your visit. Michael deduced that we should speed past the miles of ancient sculpture and paintings to the uncrowded Sistine, stay there as long as we liked, then amble back through the lesser collections. It was such a welcome discovery that we employed it on several other visits.

Again, the ceiling had not undergone the drastic cleaning which has left a spectacle whose colors look—in photographs—a good deal like early-twentieth-century French Fauve painting; so I've never felt deprived by my earlier experience of a reality filtered through the smoke of centuries. Any present visitor who regrets the experience of his elders should be assured that we saw a ceiling which amply attested to the genius of its creator and—for all its accretions—presented an entirely visible set of color compositions. In fact, *The Last Judgment* was far more beautiful before its cleaning.

And while the room's crowded content has never comprised one of my favorite works of art, I've taken every chance to see it again—most recently in 1980 when a family friend, a *monsignore* in the Vatican, allowed me and another friend to enter through the main door of the Sistine and study the ceiling and the often-ignored side walls at unsurrounded leisure (he also led us into the generally closed small Pauline Chapel which contains Michelangelo's final two frescoes—the conversion of Paul and the crucifixion of Peter; there we were literally face-to-face with the paintings, in easy touching distance, and the nearness was even more startling than I'd have guessed).

I'd alerted the Traxlers—Vieri and Nicoletta—to my planned return with Michael, and we spent a complicated Sunday with them. I don't recall where we met, though I know I was embarrassed—aside their usual restrained sartorial splendor—by the fact that I'd had to discard my Venice-ruined loafers and buy the only shoes I could afford—white canvas sneakers bought in a shop in the station. My Christmas friends were tolerantly amused by my explanation; and as ready as before with a thoughtful venture for their visitors, they revealed a plan. They'd always wanted to explore a deserted village an hour from Rome.

We piled into two small Fiats, then made our way out through the rolling campagna to the few brick, tile, and stone remains of a village called Santa Maria in Galera (or Galeria). It stood on a bluff above the small river; and from what Vieri had heard, the inhabitants departed more than a century ago, scared off by a plague. Since the site has shown evidence of occupation from Etruscan times till the eighteenth century, the discouragement must have been severe. Very little had survived from the abandonment till the day of our visit, except for what seemed to be the church tower (and in 1980 when I hired a driver and found my way back, only by proceeding to the tiny piazza and questioning the most ancient of the nearby villagers for proper guidance, I discovered that even the tower had collapsed).

As we loaded up to return to the city, one of our two cars got stuck in a gulley; and the four men of the party piled out to the rescue—and the virtual end of my new sneakers. Soon we were under way but as we approached the outskirts of Rome at dusk, a child (who'd been hesitating on the left edge of the road) all but flung herself into our car. I was sitting by Vieri on the front seat, and I can clearly recall the sensation of feeling a body crushed beneath our wheels. Thank God, I was wrong. We piled out to find a scratched and howling girl, maybe five or six years old.

A small crowd of men and women from the neighborhood materialized, and I dreaded an ugly confrontation. They all looked remarkably poor; my friends clearly weren't. But at once Vieri told the child's father that he'd drive them to the nearest hospital to have the daughter checked carefully. The rest of us waited in our party's second car; and in less than an hour, they'd returned—no broken bones, nothing worse than light scratches. Our eventual dinner was a little hungover from the strange afternoon—an hour's eerie ramble through a cursed deserted village, then a frightening collision with a live human child (the affluent adults and the wretched child). We finished early and bade a farewell that I've never since repaired, though my Italian publisher did get Olga Millo to photograph me a decade later when I was in Rome again.

Otherwise this second Roman visit deepened my involvement with the deep-stacked city and its characteristically dignified and mostly helpful modern men and women. Surely there's no other city in history, with the exception of Jerusalem, which has been ravaged by so many vicious invaders yet functioned so generously for so long. And it's been among my privileges—not to speak of pleasures—to visit Rome some five more times in subsequent years, always uncovering more and more and always welcomed with their peculiar hospitable yet self-possessed gravity by whatever Romans I met, from a bruised street-child to the treasurer of the Vatican.

When we'd spent all the money we'd earmarked for Rome, Michael and I took the train north to Florence for two nights at a pensione Michael knew of there. We invested more hours in the Uffizi, the Baptistery, the Duomo, the Accademia, the Medici Chapel and palace, and the Piazza della Signoria; and I was further reminded of my satisfaction in accompanying Michael to galleries and other sites—he enjoyed beauty in the way I most admire and find it easiest to travel with, which is to say he loved it rather silently; it affected his actions, not his chatter. When we departed Florence, I left it for good—and all its treasures. I've noted earlier that my southern heart had never quite warmed to the city and its citizens; and whenever I've had the chance to revisit Italy, I've headed south (I should add that I regret my inability to join in the later American access to the pleasures of rural Tuscany).

One more jam-packed express train—we dossed down to sleep on the corridor floor—sped us back to Geneva for our flight to London, then on to Oxford again. For my academic health it had been far too rich a time away (no fiction writing either). But a shared pleasure in unexpected wonders—and my own growing readiness to invest in a friendship that was skewed on its bases and Michael's own patience with the same reality—gave us each a lifelong relation with an unfailing friend: laughing, confiding, mutually supportive in all narrow straits, long decades without a single false move between us.

8

My third term began with an episode that might have proved grave. Just before I left for the Easter vac, I'd been using one of the Bodleian's many thousand treasures—John Milton's own copy of the plays of Euripides with marginal comments and emendations in his own youthful script (before his blindness obviously). Furthermore the volume, which was in excellent condition, had later belonged to Samuel Johnson; and it bore both Milton's and Johnson's signatures on the flyleaf (Dr. Johnson was born exactly a century after Milton's birth; and though the immensity of Milton's gifts was always a demon for Johnson, he nonetheless revered him, however querulously). Such a book would, even then, have brought a considerable price at auction—or by secret sale to an unscrupulous collector. I'd been surprised to discover then that, when I decided to study the volume, I had only to submit one of the Bodleian's routine call slips; and it was brought to my desk a few minutes later—no special security arrangements of any sort.

In those days volumes which a scholar planned to use frequently could be left overnight in a sort of cage from which they could be fetched the next day without the wait of a call slip. I'd left Milton's Euripides in the cage at the end of each day for several weeks before the vac, but when I knew I'd be gone for at least a month, I informed the relevant librarian that the volume could be sent back to the stacks in the event of some other scholar's need.

Shortly after my return, I submitted another call slip (I was especially interested in Milton's proposed emendations to Euripides's text, the only surviving record of his eagle-eyed study of the actual Greek; but since I knew almost no Greek, I'd seek the help of knowing friends like Tony Nuttall). In twenty minutes one of the usual book-fetchers—older men who'd clearly been instructed not to engage us in conversation—came to my desk and told me simply that the volume was presently in use by someone else. When I asked who, in hopes of sharing the volume, the fetcher said that it was in use by a Mr. Reynolds-Price (the class-conscious British of that era often tried to award me a posh-sounding hyphenated name—I was still then signing all three of my names, Edward Reynolds Price). The fetcher failed to smile—"Perhaps then, sir, you'd like to speak with Miss So-and-So at the desk there."

I spoke with her at once—a youngish woman but as little amused by our problem as the fetcher. She confirmed, in a minimum of words, that the volume was indeed recorded as being in my hands. My old winter call slip was still inserted in the empty slot on the shelf in the stacks. Given the solemnity of her look, I began to realize that I might have a difficult situation on my hands. Faced with the lax security of those days, it would have been entirely possible for me to have inserted the extremely valuable Milton/Johnson volume into my satchel and smuggled it out of the building (there were no briefcase checks, merely the assumption that all the library's users were ladies and gentlemen). I explained what I'd done—freed the book from the cage to return to the stacks some six weeks earlier—and the woman said "Then we have no choice but to wait and see what develops, do we?" The characteristic British "do we?" (or other similar question at the end of a sentence) can be alarmingly ominous.

For another month whenever I entered the upper reading room, I'd see a set of librarians lean to one another and whisper as I passed, no doubt some version of "That's the chap who's nicked our Milton's Euripides." Nothing overt was ever said to me, no imposing official called me in for a discussion of the matter, other kinds of service were never refused me, and I didn't feel spied upon, but my own unease deepened as time passed, and once or twice I asked at the desk for any developments in the mystery of Milton's Euripides. They'd generally shake their heads in the then-common English gesture of befuddled suspicion—"No, nothing whatever. Peculiar, isn't it?" and when I'd agree, the librarian would almost invariably say "Ra-*ther*" (I record all this truthfully and with an odd affection for the even odder behavior).

At last one early summer morning, a fetcher brought the volume to my seat—no comment. When I rose to inquire at the desk, the reply was as laconic as ever—"Turned up somehow, back in its place on the shelf." Since only employees of the Bodleian then had access to the miles of book stacks, I was left in wonderment. The book itself showed no signs of harm nor of what adventures it might have undergone in its months of silent abscondment. Well, it had survived Milton's long life, his blindness, London's dreadful plague epidemics, his danger of execution at the time of Charles II's restoration to the throne in 1660, and the Great Fire of London in 1666 (not to mention the later vicissitudes of Dr. Samuel Johnson's life and the recently avoided chance of firebombs from the Nazi Luftwaffe in the 1940s). So for as long as I used it thereafter, in the chill peace of the Duke Humfrey wing, the handy leather-bound volume—preserving, as it did, one of the three supreme epic poets' textual comments on one of the three supreme Greek dramatists—always gave me a welcome sense of elation to be the momentary proprietor of a thing as complex yet simple as itself, as nearly eternal, though so easy to lose, as both the Bodleian and I had recently learned.

More pleasantly, summer term also began with two surprises. In April, Soviet Premier Khrushchev and his colleague Nikolay Bulganin paid a state visit to Britain, with a side trip to Oxford for a little heavily guarded sightseeing. For the day, the city was in peculiar hands. In a morning walk up the High, I could plainly see armed secret-service guards on college rooftops, surveying the streets (there'd been rumors of men from Central Europe who'd just entered Britain with the avowed hope of assassinating their prime oppressors). Late in the afternoon, when I assumed that the Russians had left town, I set out in sunlight for Rhodes House on a minor errand. I walked up Longwall Street, which runs alongside Magdalen College's deer park; and just as I neared a small door in the high wall, a long black limousine pulled swiftly up beside me, the small door opened, and out stepped Khrushchev and Bulganin with a small covey of diplomats.

Astonished of course I froze in my tracks—careful to make no false move (but what would a false move be?)—and short plump Khrushchev looked my way with a broad grin on widely spaced teeth. I couldn't have been more than ten feet from him; and had I been armed (and so inclined) I could easily have shot him—and no doubt been promptly gunned down in return. Instead I matched his grin and—whoosh!—he was gone, as I likewise went on my newly cheered way, being surely a man of almost infinitely less importance to world history, not to speak of any control whatever over the fate of many thousand humans still in state prisons, than the ill-dressed fat man I'd just now greeted and who'd nonetheless only just acknowledged the monstrous reign of Stalin.

The second surprise was a small flurry of interest in my longish story "A Chain of Love." Diarmuid Russell wrote from New York to say that *The Virginia Quarterly Review* was interested in the story. At that point the manuscript was some twelve thousand words long; and the *Quarterly* wanted to give a prize in a contest it was running, but the rules had specified a maximum length of seven thousand words. Could I possibly cut it down to that length? I'd finished the first draft a year ago. Since then I'd continued with minor revisions—nit-picking—and though Diarmuid had been circulating it for less than a year, I'd experienced long stretches of beginner's nerves—wondering why no one had yet bought it.

And I've noted more than one night's dreams of going to the lodge and finding a letter from Diarmuid with a large check—my hopes and needs justified. But no, for all my impatience, the prospect of merely eliminating almost half the story couldn't thread its way through my brain. The disappointment at the impossibility was sizable, but at least I'd been given the first whiff of professional interest in my work. And Professor Blackburn at Duke had urged me to send the story to another old student of his, William Styron. I'd not yet met Styron, but Blackburn wrote me to say that Styron had promised to read the story and recommend it to *The Paris Review* if possible.

That long-since famous *Review* had started life just three years earlier, and Styron was one of its original advisory editors. So when I wrote Diarmuid to say that *The Virginia Quarterly* was not a possibility, I mentioned showing it to Styron who was still a young man himself—eight years older than I but already the author of a novel that had been a critical success in 1951, *Lie Down in Darkness*. I didn't know (and it was typical of Diarmuid not to tell me) that George Plimpton, the founder of *The Paris Review* and its chief editor for more than fifty years to come, was a client of Diarmuid's.

As spring moved ahead with occasional dry days, I began to meet with Miss Gardner again and attempted to get myself to work on the thesis. With the initial exam behind me, I was now very much on my own. I'd need to master my time, read the necessary background texts, and begin to write the thesis. If I was planning to win the B.Litt. and return home at the end of my second year, I had a great deal of work to do. Still there were sidelines, or lanes, that pulled me elsewhere.

The fiction was clearly one. The theatre, films, and music continued to be energy-hungry for time and attention in my life. Early in the term, for instance, Tyrone Power came to Oxford in a crackling revival of Shaw's American Revolution comedy, *The Devil's Disciple*; and in early May, Michael and I went down to London to hear Louis Armstrong and his band—an exciting introduction for Michael to America's greatest, though aging, jazzman (I'd heard him a time or two at Duke). But the sideline that became a virtual superhighway was the arrival, in late May, of my Volkswagen. With the slow increase of daylight, and a modest increase of mercy in the weather (the BBC was beginning to speak of possible "bright intervals" in our days), my car became—*alas* and *thank God*—an ever more tempting distraction from my academic work.

And two of my teachers began to become real friends. I've mentioned David Cecil as a teacher. Despite the fact that his wife and three children occupied his evenings at a pleasant home in north Oxford, he often invited me to meet him—for unplanned conversation—in his rooms in New College. It was there, late one afternoon that, without his knowledge, I crossed yet another of my old boundaries. He'd offered me sherry on all my prior visits, and I'd accept a small glass. But now from the drinks tray in a corner of his sitting room, he said "Whisky?" I doubt that my hesitation was noticeable; but to that point in my life—again—my family's history had braked me. Well, surely I was in safe quarters here, with a world-famed writer who was hardly likely to lure me toward a drunkard's doom. I quietly said "Thank you" and put out a hand to take the heavy weight of a large glass half full of Scotch whisky with no ice or water. Hard-core then, from the start. But no family gene lured me on into trouble, then or since.

It was in that third term that I showed Lord David my two completed short stories, "Michael Egerton" and "A Chain of Love." He responded with the kind of detailed attentiveness that I'd not yet had from any other reader—none of my good teachers at Duke nor even Eudora Welty. They'd all responded with welcome enthusiasm, but it immediately became clear that David had read my stories with a fellow writer's questioning eye. *Why did such-and-such happen at this point and not another? Was the young sister too young to justify her presence in a story as necessarily brief as mine? Did North Carolinians from a rural world speak with such calm eloquence?* His questions by no means always implied a desire for change; but even when they didn't, he elicited from me a new intensity of self-examination that was thoroughly healthy for the work itself and my own involvement in it (from his generous approval, I remember a particular phrase—he said that "Michael Egerton" "went like an arrow to the target").

Beyond that, he spoke of his own writer friends and acquaintances with a casual familiarity that made them seem real presences in the room and, further, made me feel that I might conceivably someday move in such circles with at least a sense of poise if not eminence— W. B. Yeats, Thomas Mann, Virginia Woolf, Lytton Strachey, E. M. Forster, Aldous Huxley, Elizabeth Bowen, L. P. Hartley, and more. And with his own always unmentioned aplomb, David discussed those eminences with no trace of braggadocio.

When we spoke (as we mostly did) of the classic works of fiction which I was then consuming wholesale—Emily Brontë, Tolstoy, Flaubert, Chekhov, Hardy, Woolf, Lawrence, and Forster—David reverted more than once to a major concern of his own: his concern for morality in art, for *moral* fiction. By *moral* he meant nothing so simpleminded as fiction which suppresses all concern with human sexuality or deals with sex in a pruned and scrubbed rhetoric. He wished only that a work of the imagination should be steadily conscious of its ultimate designs upon a reader and that its author should work to avoid secret or unconscious aims—ethical, moral, or erotic aims which advance on the reader in secret.

I'm afraid I no longer recall his examples of immoral fiction, though I do remember that he mentioned—with a smile—how Tolstoy had recorded his own condemnation of a passage in a story by Maupassant, a moment in which the author mentions soap bubbles on a woman's skin (and thereby aroused the ever-arousable Tolstoy to immoral thoughts). When I asked him to do so, he likewise expanded upon a recent essay of his own in which—without quite saying so, at a time when homosexuality in living authors was scarcely mentioned—he implied that E. M. Forster's novels suffered finally from an inability to portray, with ultimate degrees of success, romantic love between a man and a woman (a conclusion of David's with which I, and many thousand others, have never agreed).

With me from the start, David Cecil discussed homosexuality and gave no suggestion whatever of disapproval or condemnation (born in 1902, and a deeply devout Christian, he lived then and for many years longer in the midst of as happy a marriage as I've ever witnessed). So far as I could see, homosexual love appeared normal to him, though it seemed never to have been a need of his own. He'd noticed with considerable sympathy the serious problems it presented to homosexual writers of either gender (though in our talks, I don't recall our discussing my own particular sex life).

His oldest close friend, L. P. Hartley—the author of a brilliant then-recent novel, *The Go-Between*—was a repressed homosexual, and more than one of David's woman friends was drawn in the direction of same-sex love (Virginia Woolf and, at least once, Elizabeth Bowen among them). Adrian Wright's biography of Hartley makes it clear that, after David and Hartley met in Oxford, they developed an intense friendship; and for years after graduation (and before David's marriage), David often stayed with Hartley in Venice. But whether the relation was ever expressly sexual, Wright has insufficient evidence to say—my own guess would be no. In any case, David never discussed with me that aspect of any living author's life or work. We did, though, eventually begin to discuss my own growing love more candidly than I ventured with anyone else in my whole time at Oxford.

The other don who showed me special kindness in my first year was one whom I'd met when he joined Lord David in chairing my earlier class in criticism. He was Nevill Coghill who was then a fellow of Exeter College. His personal devotion was to the theatre (he directed frequent plays in Oxford); yet he most frequently lectured on Chaucer, Langland, Shakespeare, and Milton. And Chaucer was the poet whose *Canterbury Tales* he'd translated from the now-difficult Middle English for Penguin—a hugely successful book. I'd soon learn that Nevill had grown up in a family with various commitments to the arts.

His father was Sir Patrick Coghill, a member of the Anglo-Irish aristocracy who'd studied art in Paris in the late nineteenth century, lived on a sizable estate in Ireland, and painted a large number of high-skilled and often beautiful landscapes (several dozens of which hung in Nevill's Oxford rooms; I was always hoping to be offered one but alas no). One of his maternal aunts was Edith Somerville who joined with their younger cousin Violet Martin, whose pseudonym was Martin Ross, to form the lifelong writing partnership that produced, among numerous memorable works of fiction, *The Real Charlotte*. Nevill himself was born in 1899, served in the First War, married, fathered a daughter, then separated from his wife and lived a quietly homosexual life thereafter. He later spoke to me of several romances with men, but he apparently never established a residence with any of them; and until his retirement from Oxford, he always lived in his college rooms.

Our own friendship began when, after the late-afternoon class in criticism, Nevill asked me if I'd come to his rooms in Exeter for sherry. I went and we talked easily and pleasantly, though I recall only one moment of the hour—Nevill mentioned to me the name Antinous, the first time I'd heard of that fascinating figure from ancient history: the emperor Hadrian's young favorite who drowned mysteriously (suicide, murder, accident?) in the Nile in A.D. 130. Nevill was a fine laughter-loving tale-teller; and he'd been the teacher of W. H. Auden and Richard Burton, the actor, among numerous others. He'd even directed John Gielgud in a London production of *A Midsummer Night's Dream* ten years earlier. On this first meeting, by the way, I mentioned seeing Olivier at Stratford and praised his Macbeth very highly. To my surprise Nevill said "Olivier is a thoroughly clever physical performer; but Gielgud is a very great actor, right down to the *sockets!*" I'm quoting from old memory, but I think the memory is true to what Nevill said, certainly to his fervor. In any case, though I then profoundly disagreed, I didn't argue. And years more would pass before I began to understand Nevill's meaning and how much justice was on his side, though I've never relented in my sense of Olivier's very different kind of dramatic genius.

As I left that first meeting in time to race back to Merton for dinner, Nevill asked if I'd accompany him to a forthcoming evening in which the French composer Francis Poulenc would accompany the baritone Pierre Bernac in a recital of Poulenc's songs. I joined him for that good evening (good despite the appearance of the two performers—together they looked like nothing so much as a pair of senior waiters at a one-star restaurant in the provinces). Nevill and I went back to his rooms for a drink afterward; and a friendship slowly grew, one which lasted till his death in 1980. It was never an intimate relation, but the years were increasingly full of excellent fun and mutual consideration; and I learned a great deal from him about poetry, teaching, and especially about human life.

Though Helen Gardner had rescued me from the company of Mr. Leishman, and though she treated me warmly, I was never to have her friendship. I've noted that we met several times each term in her rooms in St. Hilda's (her sitting room was unusually bright, as dons' rooms went); and she always led me in challenging discussions of Milton and his contemporaries—our talks were punctuated by laughter and distinguished by a peculiar trait of Miss Gardner's. It was one noted by several of my male friends who likewise went to her rooms for tutorials—she generally wore some sort of pendant on a long chain; and in the course of a discussion, she was given to manipulating the pendant fairly constantly in the vicinity of her sweater-covered and quite nice breasts.

I knew, and still know, nothing of her sexual predilections beyond Stephen Spender's unconfirmed story of her falling haplessly in love with Henry Reed. I only know that her charming face (when she wished to charm), her beautiful eyes, and the ceaselessly moving pendant could leave me at the end of an hour with the sense of having participated in a semi-flirtation. Why not? The gesture was touching and surely no harm was done to either side—a single woman, a single man, alone together. Again, other male friends have reported their own odd hours with Miss Gardner; and one has just now written me from New Zealand (our first communication in fifty years and entirely unsolicited). With no coaching whatever, he mentions that Miss Gardner "sat opposite me, her skirt on her knees, her knees apart."

What was involved in these fairly unique gestures—a half-realized hope maybe that one of us would respond with some form of physical completion? When I took her out to dinner, toward the end of my Merton years, and brought her back to my rooms for after-dinner drinks, there was no sign of the pendant or any other form of seduction. I never heard a word of scandal about her from either her several ill-wishing colleagues or her students; and most of the male students known to me report Helen Gardner's carefully parceled-out portions of kindness and well-deserved criticism.

Late in my third term, I learned rather dramatically that she'd grown dissatisfied with my work. The word came in a small envelope addressed in her unmistakable clear script and sent through the university mail system (a Dickensian, bicycle-powered, and usefully prompt means of intercollege communication). She said, more or less literally—and very peremptorily—

> *Dear Mr. Price,*
> *When do you propose to get to work?*
> *Yours sincerely,*
> *Helen Gardner*

I knew I'd earned her rebuke. So I busied myself preparing several brief papers arising from my Miltonic readings; and soon enough I was back in her graces with a reading list for the Long Vac soon to come. And I took her out for thoroughly pleasant dinners more than once, but she never responded with a social invitation, even to so much as a cup of tea; and when I ultimately completed my thesis, our relation ended as though at the turn of a key—an instructive student-teacher interdependency but nothing more. Admittedly I can't recall ever telling her of my writing fiction; and when I began to publish stories, I never sent her a copy or wrote to her otherwise (I must have felt some guilt at owning up to rival pursuits).

My friendship with David and Nevill continued richly, largely by mail once I'd returned home to the States. I obviously never felt impelled to contact Miss Gardner, ever again. Perhaps she felt no particular desire to know me further. And my one receipt of a rocket from her pen, my awareness of the cool savagery of her professional pride when aroused (I recall a *Times Literary Supplement* public correspondence with a younger scholar about the textual editing of Donne's poems), and her own perhaps wary pull-back from a male student's life would eventually leave me discharged into cool outer space.

I acquired other friends among the university's various faculties. Merton's chief English tutor, Hugo Dyson, was a textbook specimen of his generation. Like Nevill he'd served in the Great War; and he moved slowly through the quads with a badly damaged leg, a severe limp, and a sturdy cane. I never actually studied with him; but as Merton's senior tutor in English lit., he took a persistent interest in my well-being. He'd kindly included me, early in my first term, in a dinner-jacketed meal for all the new Merton Eng. lit. students in a private room in college; and thereafter he'd stop me in Front Quad every few weeks and grill me cheerfully in his booming baritone—*Was I happy enough? Was so-and-so being generous to me? Too generous perhaps? How many times had I yet had pneumonia?* Our outdoor sessions would terminate in torrents of Hugo's laughter and a waving-off with his walking stick—he thought nothing of hailing me loudly with a personal question across the long quad. His own pupils were fond of him, and he even wound up with a small but imposing role in a popular English film of the 1960s—John Schlesinger's *Darling*.

A quieter man was the college's senior history tutor, Roger Highfield. For all his restraint he possessed distinct charm, a shy but smiling magnetism. His own specialty was medieval Spanish history, but he also knew a huge amount about the earliest life of Merton, and he'd ultimately co-write a history of the college. Roger was Michael's main tutor, the one who assigned his weekly papers and then sat and heard them read aloud. How I came to know him and, every few weeks, go to his rooms for sherry and good talk, I don't recall; but his friendship is among my warmest college memories.

An especially winning quality of Roger's was his ability to be right up to speed on whatever novel I'd just finished reading. With no boast or brag, he could hear you out on your own opinion of the work—Tolstoy, Wilkie Collins, whoever—then he'd nod slightly and say something that would prove memorable for decades. One evening I'd just completed a second reading of Prévost's *Manon Lescaut,* a novel that lies behind more than one opera; and I noted to Roger that I'd recently concluded a fascination with a beauty just as dangerous as Manon. Roger searched my eyes for the briefest moment; then said "Ah Manon, yes. The sort of person who absolutely always *lets you down.*" I suspected then, and still do, that something deeply personal must have powered that perfect observation; but I'd never have asked.

His younger history colleague John Roberts would eventually become Warden of Merton (the college president) and the author of, among other books, an immensely popular *History of the World.* John was only five years older than I and was the Principal of the Post- masters in my time, the equivalent of a minor dean in an American college. You went to him for permission to spend a night out of col- lege during term or to come in late (the gate closed at eleven), though you learned soon enough that climbing in was a simpler solution. You could either scale a nine-foot-high wall at the elbow bend in Merton Street and drop down into the dark interior of the college garden, or you could merely walk in illegally. That required a lengthy detour down St. Aldate's and then—just past the police station—you grabbed hold with both hands and swung round a rickety post that supported barbed wire and overhung a deep drainage ditch. From there you were free to walk through a spooky pitch-dark Christ Church Meadow for the equivalent of two blocks, then step over a low wall into the backside of Merton (that route, I'm told, has now been balked).

Somehow John Roberts and I soon knew that we shared common

interests; and I frequently had sherry with him, often turning an amused blind eye to the numerous attractive women who visited him at odd hours. As a member of the college, I never had the slightest behavioral difficulty with him. In fact my only problem with John lay in his possession of a pronounced facial tic. In any conversation he was likely at startling intervals to give a sudden, and surely unconscious, twist to one side of his face. Given my helpless lifelong tendency to mimic the accents of whomever I'm speaking with, I'd have to struggle when I was with John not to return his tic with a consoling wince of my own. I think I never did, but I can't guarantee it. He and his first wife eventually stayed with me in my first home back in the States; and he wrote me, most thoughtfully, years later when he learned of my cancer surgery (so did a mighty host of other Oxonians).

All these older friends—with the exception of Nevill and David, who were supremely important—are recalled here not so much because they proved helpful in my graduate studies (they did) but because they illustrate so likably one of my major early discoveries in the dim Thames Valley. For all the postwar bleakness of Britain then, and for all the British reputation for stiff-upper-lipped solemnity, my experience of Oxford—from the scouts at Merton on through my teachers and other academic friends—was an experience of high wit, often mischievous or otherwise boisterous laughter, and of infallible generosity if ever I asked for help.

As for my other experiences on that remarkably small island, my visits in recent years have been rare, mainly owing to the complexities of wheelchair travel; and I can't vouch for the atmosphere of the contemporary country, one that's altered in some ways unrecognizably since my time. But the whole nation in the mid-Fifties—close as it was to the horrors of the Second World War—is marked in my memory, like Oxford, by a warm and constant level of intelligence, and a widespread appetite for fun, a delight in the folly of the human race (as well as the silliness of one's friends and enemies), and above all one's own unquenchable absurdity. Even the joking American South of my boyhood didn't surpass that only-just-torpedoed and slowly sinking imperial center for discernment and laughter, though the players and the games were worlds apart. And no other region on the face of the planet—none known to me, including all other regions of the States—has evoked more enduring love in me than the literal ground and the class-sorted people of postwar Great Britain.

In the remainder of summer term (it ran from mid-April to mid-June), life went on much as I've described it, with only a few other standouts and with the added diversion of the new car. Once it arrived Michael availed himself of it for drives in the Oxfordshire countryside to ready himself for the driving-license test he'd never yet taken (those were still days when very few Britons owned their own cars). His learner status required the presence of a licensed companion in the car, and that was always me—three or four afternoons a week. In the process, rain or shine, I learned my way round a world of villages whose names I'd encountered in reading Matthew Arnold's Oxford poems, the only great poems which are specifically Oxonian—"The Scholar Gypsy" and "Thyrsis," the elegy on the death of Arnold's undergraduate companion, the poet Arthur Hugh Clough.

In their biscuit-colored stone, many of the villages looked virtually identical to what Arnold and Clough might have seen in their student wanderings through the county. My own favorites were Forest Hill, in whose church Milton almost surely married his first wife (Mary Powell, who was half his age and who left him a few weeks after the wedding to return to her family and then failed to rejoin him for nearly three years), and Godstow (where, on the opposite bank from the eventually famous Trout Inn, Mr. Charles Dodgson—a don at Christ Church—told two young girls the story which he'd later publish as *Alice's Adventures in Wonderland* under his pen name, Lewis Carroll). An even greater favorite was the small town of Woodstock which sported the vast Churchill family estate (presented by a grateful nation to the first Duke of Marlborough in thanks for his victory over the French and Bavarians in 1704 at Blenheim in Bavaria, hence the name of the house itself—Blenheim Palace, pronounced *Blen*-im in England). In those pre-tourist-flood days, the grounds were entirely open to random visitors—no tickets required. Michael could park us at one of the gates, and we'd wander the calmly natural park, designed by the apparently infallible landscape architect Capability Brown. Then we could lie by the lake with our books (weather permitting) and never be bothered by a single other human, reading till hunger or thirst compelled us into the nearby Bear Inn.

The addition of the Volkswagen encouraged thoughts of a summer trip to the Continent. Late in the term Michael got his driving license with no hitch; and given our good time in Italy, the two of us began to plan a long drive. We'd load the car on a ship to Norway, drive through Scandinavia, then down through Germany for a week with Jane and Liz in Munich, then up the Rhine to Holland and thence back to England. It was no doubt a half-insane project for a man who hoped to complete a substantial scholarly thesis by early in the autumn, then be successfully examined by a hard-nosed faculty board before I could win my degree and return home in the early summer of 1957. Well, at that point in my life, I still knew very little about my realistic rate of production in scholarship or fiction (though I'd already demonstrated my slowness during my final term at Duke when I completed my honors thesis—Milton's entry into politics—on the morning it was due). I guessed I could accomplish all the jobs before me in the time available; and without consulting Miss Gardner or the Warden of Rhodes House who after all signed my checks, I joined Michael in planning more than a month's wide loop round the Continent.

Meanwhile each of us also had the considerable problem of finding digs—lodgings—for the following year. In an increasingly crowded situation, Merton could only offer most undergraduates two years of in-college lodging; each grad student got a single year. We were soon to be thrown on the mercy of the city's digs market. There were numerous widows and assorted others who advertised rooms with a central university bureau; and lists of such providers were available, as was a lively oral tradition of affable landladies who'd previously accommodated Mertonians. But each man was very much on his own in the run for space.

How we discovered her I no longer recall; but Michael and I

Although I don't know the date of this photograph of W. H. Auden, it was taken by Erich Auerbach at what appears to be the time when I saw so much of Auden at Oxford—his Professor of Poetry years. He was in his early fifties by then; and while his face has begun its downward collapse into creasing, it's still a face that could—until almost the end of his life—be repaired by a smile (as it so often was in the middle years before a monumental sadness—impelled by drink, daily barbiturates, and a fading of the only love he'd wanted—overcame him). Only one thing is lacking here; there's no cigarette in his stained right hand. But isn't the open document in his lap a musical score, and isn't that a small piano in the left corner behind him? He and his partner Chester Kallman had written the libretto for Stravinsky's opera *The Rake's Progress* which had its premiere in Venice in 1951; and while it's one of the very few post-Puccini/Strauss operas to have a vigorous ongoing life, none of his and Kallman's several other libretti have met with such luck. Perhaps Auden holds another score here then, something for which he plans to write words (a complicated challenge) or a finished achievement. Above all, this is the heart and head that conceived and accomplished a quantity of poems surpassing all but a very few of the lines written by others in his lifetime—or since.

quickly found an extraordinary woman at 2 Sandfield Road in Headington, an eastside—and very stellar—Oxford neighborhood (it housed C. S. Lewis who'd never moved to Cambridge, J. R. R. Tolkien, and Isaiah Berlin). Our landlady-to-be, Win Kirkby, was the wife of a New College scout named Jack Kirkby; and she had two sets of digs to offer. They consisted of two ground-floor private sitting rooms with separate bedrooms upstairs, a shared upstairs bath (shared also with the two Kirkbys, no children). All that, with full English breakfast provided, would cost us each two pounds, ten shillings per week (the equivalent of $56 today or $224 per month, a substantial sum for men on scholarships). But the rooms were likable, the street itself was remarkably quiet; and Win would be our bedmaker and breakfast cook, as well as a huge source of educational entertainment—our first meeting with her suggested that strongly. No deposit was required, only our gentleman's word that we wanted the four rooms and would appear a few days before fall term.

Toward the end of spring term, one of the best surprises of the year saw the arrival in my pigeonhole of a small envelope—hand-addressed and bearing in the upper left corner a nearly illegible name. I thought it said W. H. Auden. I'd known that—the previous year, in a much-contested university election—Auden had been elected Professor of Poetry, a five-year appointment which required no residence in Oxford and only three lectures per year. I'd read a good deal about the controversy surrounding his election; and I knew that the fact he'd departed his native country for the United States essentially for good in 1939, as war with Hitler looked inevitable, hardly sat well with many of his former countrymen. In the interim, however, he'd become the most admired of still-working English-speaking poets—T. S. Eliot was no longer writing anything but occasional verse plays and critical essays. And despite a fierce campaign for votes, Auden's reputation overwhelmed all opposition to his apparent disloyalty and his not especially concealed homosexuality. I'd heard him called "a traitorous bugger" more than once before I received his letter, and I'd heard of his imminent arrival.

My envelope proved to contain a brief note, saying that our mutual friend Frank Lyell had suggested he should look me up upon his arrival in Oxford. Would I join him then, for a drink in his rooms, a few days from now? I accepted at once, acquired a volume of his poems, and consumed many with great admiration (I'd known some of them for years). I also read his latest volume, published only a few months earlier. It contained the poem that gave its name to the collection, a poem that would come to be seen by many as the lyric height of his enormous output—"The Shield of Achilles." In admiration but serious uncertainty then—I'd heard of his rudeness and, of all things, his silliness—I found my way up his tall staircase in the southeast corner of Tom Quad in Christ Church to meet a man who, whatever world-class strengths he'd attained in poetry, promised to be a strange bird.

Promptness has always been my sole major virtue, and I knocked on his door at five. Through the ensuing hour—Auden was downing a tumbler of gin; I chose sherry—it was clear that my host was as nervous as I. Was my presence the cause, or was it some disturbance in Auden's recent life? (He'd chosen not to bring his notoriously queer partner, Chester Kallman, even though Kallman had been Auden's serious collaborator on the libretto for Stravinsky's *Rake's Progress,* one of only two or three operas since Puccini's *Turandot* that has entered the ongoing repertoire of world-class opera houses). Auden had said in a recent interview that he felt, on arrival, like a new boy at a public school—a *public* school in Britain was an American *private* school. Or was he simply a poor companion for conversation? My own later experience suggests that, in attempted dialogue, Auden was hardly a companion. At Oxford he was a performer, awaiting his next moment to perform.

Whatever, I can remember only that he asked if I knew the work of M. F. K. Fisher. I confessed that I hadn't heard of Fisher. He said that she wrote entirely about food and was the finest living writer of prose (I'd soon learn that Auden was given to eccentric claims). When I mentioned my work on Milton, he had almost nothing to say. I mentioned my love of Emily Dickinson; he nodded with no enthusiasm— "Very little-bitty at times, don't you feel?" When he asked if I liked opera, I could honestly say I did—a lot. That seemed to get me to first base at least.

He asked for my favorite opera composer. I said Wagner; he grinned, shut his eyes in bliss, tilted his head back, and said "I'm having 'Siegfried's Funeral March' played at my funeral, and I long to direct a production of *Tristan und Isolde* with two large lesbians—no man and woman could ever carry on so fervently about one another" (a recording of the clangorous "Funeral March" would in fact be played just before Auden's funeral, years later in a gathering of his friends in the Austrian home he'd shared with Chester Kallman; but he never directed his ideal *Tristan*, though I later learned he'd told the story to hundreds of friends).

As I stood to leave at the end of an hour, Auden said he meant to have his coffee each day at eleven in the Cadena Café on the Cornmarket. I'd be welcome to drop by with any other students who might be interested. He also hoped we could dine together soon. Only a moment later as I was descending the stairs, it occurred to me—from earlier reading—that the nineteenth-century room and the famous rooftop photographic studio of Lewis Carroll must have been nearby. Well, Auden was at least as peculiar a fellow and at least as true a genius (in retrospect he seems to me, for all his flaws and late absurdities, to have been the greatest English-language poet since Eliot).

Unfortunately I waited too late to go to the Sheldonian Theatre on the afternoon of his superb inaugural lecture and was unable to gain entry—he'd packed the place. I did, however, take up his morning-coffee invitation more than once—well before other students were prepared to face such a formidable creature. And speaking of face, it's realistic, if inevitably unkind, to broach the problem of Auden's face; but since he allowed himself to be photographed often, right to the end of his life, he didn't conceal the fact. Pictures from his youth suggest that he was a near-albino in some respects—abnormally pale and thin-skinned. Perhaps that genetic endowment, plus the fact of long decades of chain-smoking—not to mention heavy drinking and pill-taking—had left the skin of his face phenomenally creased and gullied, though when he returned to Oxford, he was only in his late forties.

More than one joke on the subject made the local rounds. Even the kindly David Cecil said "If a fly were to walk across Wystan's face, it would break its legs." (I can vouch for David's invention of that one.) And Stravinsky was reported to have said "We're going to have to *iron* Wystan soon." I don't know that Auden ever heard the jokes; but for anyone with as keen a sense of physical beauty as he possessed, even the daily shave at the mirror may have been difficult. I can report, for what it's worth, that in numerous jokey remarks about himself, I never heard him allude to his wrinkles—maybe an indication of their painfulness.

The Cadena hours, with or without other students, were more relaxed. He'd have generally brought along a book in case no one turned up (incredibly it was often the case that Auden sat there alone amid the shopping housewives who'd paused for their own elevenses), and that lack of company gave him at least one thing he could volubly deplore, if a student appeared and nothing else surfaced as a subject for conversation. As a man who produced so much, and worked on a mercilessly regular schedule, he was addicted to midmorning and evening company.

Of all the books he brought, I remember only a volume of Rosemond Tuve's on English metaphysical poetry (I think she was visiting in Oxford that year). He admired it and, knowing of my interest in the same subject, he expatiated on it—especially the Christian poems of George Herbert. Since I made no notes, I remember nothing more of his lecture, for it did seem a lecture. One maybe relevant memory is that, while he knew I had serious hopes of a writing career, I never asked him if he'd read any one of my manuscript stories; and he never asked to see anything (a fact I can easily comprehend, after five decades of my own teaching; but then verse was his trade, not fiction, though he endlessly consumed mystery novels—as did Eudora Welty and Diarmuid Russell).

Term soon wound down without a dinner invitation; but by then I took that as no deprivation. Dinner on the Christ Church high table, and with a social reality as daunting as Wystan Auden, would not have been an occasion I sought fearlessly. I do recall that, after the official end of term, I was sitting in my car at the Carfax stoplight when I saw Auden walking up the High with a man whom—from some book-jacket photo maybe—I recognized as Chester Kallman. Kallman was fourteen years younger than his distinguished partner, blondish and fleshy, hardly a man I'd have called handsome, much less beautiful (as Auden implied, in a number of poems). So Auden had kept his self-administered vow; but today as he was no doubt packing to depart, Chester had arrived; and they both were laughing their way down the crowded sidewalk—Auden beaming at his friend.

Were they the first admittedly queer couple I witnessed in public life? Almost surely. If so, they were for me—devoted disciple of physical beauty that I then was—a sad introduction. Yet in their own complicated way, a way that included sexual infidelity on a steady scale for both men, a loyal partnership existed and endured till Auden's death some seventeen years later. Since the relation seemed—to many of Wystan's old friends—a source of prolonged unhappiness for him, its continuation was hard for those friends to comprehend. But aren't a great many enduring marriages, of whatever variety, incomprehensible to close observers? Thus *Love me, love my dog* is far too much for most married men or women to ask of their friends.

In any case, in my two remaining years at Oxford—and through the rest of Auden's life—I never met Chester Kallman; so I have no informed observations of a partnership that, after all, endured for nearly forty years. I did learn, though—as the interested world did—that Auden had left the whole of his hard-won considerable estate to Kallman with the instruction that, should Chester die before Auden, the estate would go to Auden's two nieces. If Chester should survive Auden, then the estate would be willed by Chester to the nieces. But the feckless Chester died intestate only two years later; and by default the Auden estate went to Chester's next-of-kin—his own father, Dr. Kallman, who was a dentist in New York, a man in his mid-eighties who soon remarried a younger woman. Not a penny went to Auden's two nieces. The absurd folly of such a conclusion might have amused the satiric Auden in his last years, prematurely exhausted with life as he was and deep in a miserable nightly drunkenness.

And to complete my own experience in the matter—the last time I saw Wystan Auden was in February 1969 when Nevill Coghill came to New York for the premiere of a musical based on his translation of *The Canterbury Tales*. He'd co-written the book with Martin Starkie and had himself written the lyrics. Nevill had recently retired from his long career at Oxford; and this was the first public display of a newly ongoing creative life from a man who'd done a great deal for scholarship and theatrical art and had been, above all, an endlessly encouraging teacher. For the opening night on Broadway, he invited three of his old students. The oldest was Cleanth Brooks, the critic who'd virtually invented the hugely influential, and now much lamented, New Criticism (lamented for its departure in the frequently incomprehensible wake of Critical Theory, a widespread disaster that presently blights most fields). The next was Wystan Auden, then me—I'd turned thirty-six only two days before and had flown up from North Carolina for the evening.

I arrived first at the Eugene O'Neill Theatre. Wystan, whom I hadn't seen since Stephen Spender invited us and Robert Lowell to lunch at the Algonquin a few years earlier—an extremely good-natured occasion with a keenly alert Auden still capable of leading the jokes and laughter—arrived next, huffing loudly in a thick black overcoat. He shook my hand, said a perfunctory word or two; then sat beside me, never removing the coat (he'd just turned sixty-two and would live only four more years). As ever, he proceeded next to replace his outdoor shoes with the carpet slippers he'd brought in a brown paper bag. I was shocked by his physical and apparent psychic decline in the short gap of time since our last meeting (later I'd learn that Kallman was now spending a great part of the year away from their traditional lodgings in New York and Austria and that Wystan was suffering from the separation).

Then Cleanth Brooks arrived with his usual Southern-gent courtesy, and the curtain rose on a performance that was not quite brilliant but was at least diverting—the young cast were attractive and scantily dressed when at all possible, generally a big help. Throughout the nimble stage action, Auden continued breathing stertorously. Sad to say, he also gave off the distinct odor of an old Oxonian who seldom used the facilities. We were invited to join Nevill later at a party—he'd only recently turned seventy—but midway through the first act, Wystan whispered to me a gruff "It's my bedtime" and was off in the darkness. Whether he ever saw Nevill again, I can't say—his departure from the theatre was inexcusably rude—but in the remaining years of Auden's life, I never saw the grand poet again, the man who'd written poems as indelible in the history of verse as his "Elegy for William Butler Yeats," "In Praise of Limestone," "Lay Your Sleeping Head, My Love," "The Shield of Achilles," and dozens of shorter lyrics and a handful of brilliant long poems like "The Sea and the Mirror" and "For the Time Being."

I've tried to make clear that I was never one of his friends. The innate shyness which his oldest friends frequently mention in their recollections may have been at work—a shyness often concealed by overbearing loquacity. Or maybe he just didn't like me, yet we often talked interestingly and laughed together a good deal in Oxford. Otherwise I saw him only four times, I think, thereafter—twice in New York and twice in Washington, occasions arranged by others (he recommended me for a Guggenheim Fellowship in the late Sixties, and my application was successful). I shared in whatever sense of a barrier he may have felt with me; in my case, he was too enormous for real friendship (that seemed a general response from other of my Oxford contemporaries). Still, I never doubted for a day that he was the only steadily productive genius with whom I've spent real time.

Even in the most relaxed moments in his Christ Church rooms, coming to the end of our first half-quart of martinis, he'd fall silent for two long draws on his endless cigarette; and in the brief silence that fell around us, I could hear his great mind turning like the wheels of a vast locomotive. Surely the barrels of alcohol and the kegs of amphetamines were, in part, mere means of damping that motion, the heat and light it steadily induced as it did its work—not to speak of its almost constant pain in the hope of loving someone as steadily difficult as Chester Kallman (that's of course to ignore the impossible challenge that faced Kallman daily—his attempt as a would-be younger poet to live with, and love, one of the great poets of the English language). And it should never be forgot that even the face Auden laid before us in the late photographs—that dreadful ruin— still concealed a brain that could issue, almost till the actual month of his death, the odd gorgeous poem.

In those days the British took a person's twenty-first birthday as a celebratory occasion far more regularly than most Americans. I'd observed my own twenty-first two years before, just as Dad discovered his cancer; but Michael's fell late in that spring term of '56. He'd met Pamela Redmayne on several rides with me to Burford. When she learned of his oncoming auspiciousness (and she said it coincided with an unspecified birthday of her own), she sprang into her finest military-planning mode. On the day in question, she said, we'd gather a few decorative girls and a number of Rhodesters from my class, several of whom had likewise bought cars. Then we'd proceed toward Longleat House, the home of the Marquess of Bath and the ancestral seat of the Bath family since 1580. Weather permitting, we'd search out a particularly beautiful hillside near Longleat. The place, it seemed, was known chiefly to Redmayne; and there we'd eat the enormous picnic she'd provide. As ever, all participants had preliminary duties assigned to them; and Michael and I spent the previous night at Pamela's house, performing various chores.

The great day dawned at last—gloriously sunlit, only the occasional cottony cloud lined with gray (imitating its predecessors in landscapes by Constable). As Michael and I ate Pamela's immense English breakfast, the tableside BBC weather report could—as ever in those pre-global-warming days—only muster its weakest threat: *Bright intervals interspersed with showers.* So in midmorning, off we set—John Sears from Massachusetts and Balliol, Rex Jamison, Jim Griffin, and Howard Reilly from Pennsylvania and Magdalen among others—in several midget autos, each car filled with smiling youngsters roughly our age, all almost infinitely grateful for such spring weather and the bursting hampers of guaranteed fine food.

Any trip with Pamela would include some modest detour to pay a brief call on a significant historic site. She never went in for lengthy tours, knowing (as she usually did) far more about the place than any official guide who was likely to appear. That morning she led us to the circle at Avebury, a prehistoric stone ring—only eighteen miles from Stonehenge—of incomprehensible complexity, the result of a gigantic effort from perhaps 3000 B.C. It's estimated that it took the equivalent of seven hundred men ten years to complete the task.

I regret to say that I was so involved in the beauty of the day itself—unmitigated sunlight after so much outer and inner darkness—and in Michael's delight in our birthday plans that I registered the marvels of Avebury less indelibly than I should have (I flagged it for a later return but never made it). From Avebury, Pamela guided us farther on to our destination—a spot on the Longleat estate called Heaven's Gate (or so she claimed; it certainly felt like a celestial entrance, and it looks that grand still in the color home movies I made at the time). The dozen or so of us sat down on a steep hillside—not in the usual picnic circle but facing Longleat House below us—and were told, briskly by Pamela, that we were in yet another nobleman's park designed by Capability Brown. Then hungry as dogs—the males at least—we seized upon Redmayne's first-rate chicken and salad, her English cheeses (which I still prefer to French) and homemade brown bread, all washed down with potent cider (wine and beer were mostly omitted from her battery of offerings but were seldom missed).

As we neared the point of abdominal ballistics, Pamela produced—incredibly—thirteen cakes, each made by her own hands. Then amid our oversated groans, we toasted our benefactress on her own birthday (I estimate she might have been sixty) and Michael on his newly confirmed manhood. Deeply reserved Englishman that he was, Michael laughed, then stood and bowed his formal thanks to Redmayne. I'd very likely not been happier in my life, not till then. And even now, turning back, I can think of very few days as full of harmless pleasure in the midst of an aristocrat's expensively tended grounds, entirely free to us, surrounded by friends of proven merit and with Michael, whom I more than half suspected was now an incomparable friend.

In short I'd come to trust the fact that I was fully committed. I'd told no one and wouldn't, for years—not even the object of my feeling. But *commitment* meant to me then that, so far as I could begin to foresee—since marriage and children were out of the question—I'd step forward without hesitation, if called, to lay down my life for the person in question. I don't recall having formed such an outlandish feeling, much less so dedicated a feeling, at Heaven's Gate; but I think it's true to my conviction that day, that point in the year. Fifty years later I may smile at my intensity; but I know I was not deluded. I would make that offer still, if called upon. The person had already proved his own loyalty and was giving as much as his very different nature could find a way to give.

To my further delight, when Pamela and several more of us stalked down the hill and approached the main door of Longleat, there stood the present holder of the title—a pleasantly ordinary-looking man of early middle age, greeting tourists (the house supported itself now on tickets). Redmayne moved forward and presented herself, by her own name and her father's, as a friend of the Bath family; and he greeted her with obvious recognition and welcome, waving us inward without bought tickets. After that, the interior of the house lay on the downward side of the day. Nonetheless we took the tour, with Redmayne correcting the hapless guide sotto voce but no doubt correctly. By the time we'd delivered Pamela back to Burford a few hours later and were safely back to Merton in early dark, I was more than ready for a long night's sleep. And the blessed Bill Jackson let me have it (no open curtains and "Good morning, sir" at half-past seven—how did he know?).

Also that spring William Styron responded to the manuscript I'd sent him at Professor Blackburn's insistence. He said at once that he was only an adviser to *The Paris Review* but that he'd already sent the story on to Peter Matthiessen, the fiction editor, with a high recommendation. He then went on to say the kinds of things any apprentice longs to hear from a respected professional—

I think it is a most beautiful and touching tale. The mood is set from the beginning, the tone is maintained throughout, and it all builds up, I think, to a wonderfully telling and poignant picture of life-in-death, with the background of the Piedmont South done with great accuracy, and humor, and versimilitude. (sic)

The only problem which Styron's praise presented, of course, was the fact that it gave me a powerful impetus to get on with new fiction when a thesis was still the abyss that yawned before me.

With a few other diversions then, the term—and my first academic year at Oxford—wound to its close. Michael and I and a couple of girls from St. Hilda's took a few Sunday afternoon drives down to Windsor Great Park to watch Philip, the Duke of Edinburgh, play polo in the presence of the royal women and infants—the younger Elizabeth II and her sister Margaret, as dowdy as ever then in tweeds and head scarves, and only the Queen Mother flying her usual banner of eccentric high fashion with ostrich-plumed hats and satin handbags in the midst of high-spirited polo (the Queen's children, Charles and Anne at eight and four, were the normal dressers of the family).

Then I went for an affable end-of-term meeting with Miss Gardner to confirm her recommendations for summer reading and writing. There was one more packing of all I'd brought to Oxford and all I'd acquired in the past eight months (Jackson had volunteered to store my trunk in his spacious pantry till I was ready to move to my digs). There were a series of coffees and sherries with my college friends— temporary farewells to tide us through the Long Vac. Then a visit to Brighton to spend a few days with Michael and his mother in her council flat—a pleasant six rooms with views of the sea and the town that had bloomed as a pleasure dome for the profligate Prince Regent (later King George IV) in the early nineteenth century.

RP with Wendy Stringer and Stella Kirk, photographed by Michael Jordan on the polo pitch at Windsor on a Sunday afternoon in June '56. Prince Philip (the Queen's husband) is a member of the horse melee before us; and the royal family are seated directly opposite us, some fifty yards away. Behind us is the black Volkswagen which I'd only acquired a month ago, and atop my head is the brown Borsalino porkpie hat I'd acquired in Italy sometime during the prior Easter vac. The two girls were cheerful friends from St. Hilda's College; and Wendy—in the middle here—would eventually marry an Italian and spend her life in his country. Note the degree of dress-up clearly involved in a visit to Windsor (the nearby Queen, in tweed skirt and head kerchief, is dressed less formally than we, though the Queen Mother is reliably dressed in pale-blue silk and a hat with modified ostrich feathers). In addition to the porkpie, I'm wearing a tie, the camel's hair jacket I bought in Venice, and—above all—the white socks that American college men of my era religiously wore. As grave as the three of us look—and Mike as well, behind the camera—we're actually thoroughly enjoying ourselves: in another two seconds, I'm sure, we'd have faced Mike and laughed.

9

Michael and I drove slightly east to Glyndebourne and heard Mozart's *Idomeneo*, my only visit to the famed musical shrine. The opera was seldom produced in those days; and the reliable resources of Glyndebourne—luxuriously cast and conducted operas in the grounds of a handsome country estate which the audience was free to roam during the long picnicking intermissions—went some way toward full pleasure (it was likewise a beautiful evening). The opera house of the time was small—the size Mozart had likely composed for—and decidedly plain in its décor, though the acoustics were superb and the music exalted.

Next I dashed some two hundred miles west to Plymouth to meet the ship of my Duke friend Deede Dort (I'd not yet reached the age when I could suggest that an able-bodied adult friend seek public transport). She and I sped back to Brighton, found her a hotel room on the seafront, and joined up with Michael for a jocular Sunday's drive to Canterbury where we roamed the cathedral which preserves the site of the murder of Thomas Beckett, the later goal of centuries of pilgrimage. Then we pushed on to Hastings and the nearby Battle Abbey where William the Conqueror had landed in 1066, killing the Saxon King Harold on the spot and proceeding to alter the fate of England and all its eventual descending cultures—their law and social structures and above all, the nature of the English language (an Anglo-Saxon tongue which gradually became at least thirty percent French).

After two or three days of good undergraduate memories and half-sad laughter as we walked on the front, Deede flew on to Paris where she'd study painting for several years; and I could finally bring myself toward something that represented, at least, the quiet solitude I'd treasured since childhood and needed now more than I'd realized in the midst of the past year's pleasures and struggles. That state of calm didn't, however, bring me back to a working scholar's desk. Instead I began a one-man drive westward to see a few things that had snagged in my mind during years of earnest reading and—earlier still—in my boyhood obsession with good King Arthur, his questing knights, and the Grail itself: their own mysterious gleaming aim.

In that first postwar devastated decade, with petrol prices phenomenally high by American standards, the roads were hardly crowded with privately owned cars. And few British roads were more than well-maintained but narrow two-lane concrete strips, going their remorselessly curving ways till—suddenly—there might be a mile or so of blessedly dead-straight progress. Such stretches sometimes proved to be laid on the tracks of ancient Roman roads (I recall hearing an old schoolmaster say that he'd once asked his boys why the Romans tended to build straight roads—for shorter distance obviously—but one boy eagerly raised his hand to say "So we Britons couldn't ambush them round the bends").

On most of my extended road trips, I couldn't plan to average more than thirty miles an hour. As an unadjusted American on my first long drive then, I had a good deal to learn. First, there were the old roads themselves. An impatient driver like me met with numerous scary moments when a two-lane road, in a curvy stretch, would unexpectedly narrow to little more than one lane; and I'd round the next curve to find myself in near-collision with an unhurried farmer driving some piece of antique farm machinery on to his next field. And in rural areas, which included most of southern England then, the high banks were often topped with dense hedgerows that loomed immediately at the edge of the concrete with no forgiving shoulders and made passing another car impossible. So anyone hoping to survive a day's travel, in body and mind, was soon compelled to learn a steady patience.

But soon the new tolerance became one more pleasure of the trip. Apart from guidebook-recommended sites, there were few of the obvious roadside stops to which an American and his bladder were accustomed—few petrol stations and absolutely no snack shops (even most Stateside highways were then devoid of franchise fast-food stops). The only chance of a small meal would be in a village tearoom, a good country pub (sandwiches and meat pies), or occasional uninspiring restaurants in towns. A man's needs to pee were easily met with the kind of unembarrassed roadside pause that was demonstrated to us on our first night in England; a modest woman faced more serious problems.

A generally reliable pleasure of the road—ultimately one of the memorable joys of my British years—was the average Briton's ready willingness to talk and chuckle with a traveling stranger. Within days of my arrival in the country, I was asking myself how the British Isles could have acquired their worldwide repute for frosty self-possession. If anything, I was having to employ courteous ways of disentangling myself from a talkative and hugely helpful man or woman whom I'd asked a simple question (and a Southerner was a trained employer of polite escapes).

In my first term David Cecil had asked me, during our first conversation after his seminar dispersed, how I was being treated—"Are the English being beastly to you?" When I assured him of the contrary, he said "Don't let them mislead you now. When the English seem cold, it's worth remembering that—frequently—they just *don't know you're there.* Call yourself to their notice, and I suspect you'll prosper." And so I had. In fact by the end of that first academic year, I was on the verge of a finding that would prove accurate for all my later experience of Britons, with normal exceptions, right into the mid-1990s—*The British are slower to declare a friendship than Americans; but once declared, they're nearly unshakable in their loyalty, far more so than the glad-handing but often fickle Yank.* And not at all incidentally, I think David's suggestion of blind self-absorption—as an analysis of British *beastliness*—is also an explanation for a large part of the human animal's rudeness and chill in whatever nation.

I drove west through the Thomas Hardy country of Dorset—especially the county town of Dorchester, with its city museum that then contained Thomas Hardy's reconstructed study. His novels had begun to interest me when I discovered *Tess of the D'Urbervilles* in high school. I'm sure that I didn't realize then how deeply I'd been marked by the fact that so much of my childhood and early teens was spent in a distinctly flavored region—the endlessly complex biracial society that had grown up in the cotton-and-tobacco countryside of northeast North Carolina, with its unadorned rolling hills, thick pine woods, and broomstraw fields, its sunbaked villages, and small towns with handsome white timber and redbrick homes from the eighteenth and early nineteenth centuries and the incredibly enduring hovels of black men and women who were, at most, only one or two generations out of actual slavery. Some seven decades might have passed since abolition; yet most of those men and women were still implicated in a dense involvement with their white overlords—an involvement that was, more often than we now acknowledge, as emotionally interdependent as the ruthless system allowed and had produced one of the twentieth century's great Anglo-African languages and the verbal and musical art that was still arising from it.

Though Hardy's world looked—to me, at first—far bleaker than my own, it had reflected in his novels an emotional complexity so much like the country of my early youth that it drew me powerfully in. And the fact that David Cecil was one of Hardy's distinguished interpreters and an enthusiastic guide to my reading and English travels was a help (David's father—and eventually his elder brother—were, in succession, the Marquess of Salisbury and were thus centered on an important Hardy town; and David himself kept a village home in the region almost all his life and died there).

I pushed on to Exeter with its fine small cathedral, much damaged by a German bomb; then on across the wide gloom of Dartmoor with—in the visible distance—its looming prison (you were warned then, as you still are in parts of the American southwest, not to run out of fuel in the area); and thence to Cornwall. My target was Tintagel and the ruins of its storied castle, and I reached the nearby village at dusk. There were virtually no tourists—to be sure, I dignified myself as a *traveler*—but there was a sad rash of Guinevere Tea Rooms and Lancelot Tobacconists. No motels of course and, according to the AA motoring guide, no hotel I could afford; so I entered a shop and asked if there was a local woman who could offer me an inexpensive room for a few nights. The female person at the counter took a long look at my face, then laughed, and addressed me in a thick Cornish accent—"You said a *woman*, didn't you now? Well, if it's a *lady* you're looking for, I could send you on to Mrs. Mason. She and her daughter Jill are just up the road. They can likely take you in."

A stubby woman almost swallowed up in her apron, Mrs. Mason and her antique suspicious spaniel welcomed me to the back bedroom—for a shockingly small sum—and in no time she and Jill, a pretty girl a year or so older than I, cooked me what they called "a meat tea"—four elegantly fried eggs, big rashers of Cornish bacon, bread and dripping (bread fried deliciously in bacon fat) followed by an eventual assortment of scones, cakes, and biscuits, accompanied throughout by cups of black tea strong enough to ream a radiator—and I was expected to eat their hearty dinner a little while later. In my three good days with the Masons, I spent so much interesting time talking with the two ladies in their kitchen that I finally had to force myself out into the gray drizzle to explore the ruins of my original magnet, the twelfth-century castle on Tintagel Head.

By what may be a complicated set of misunderstandings, the haunting landscape of the area, the masses of mossy stonework high above the crashing sea, an occasional now-empty grave chiseled into the live rock, and the one old church on the misty cliffs have conspired to win for themselves credit as the birthplace of King Arthur and, in some accounts, the site of Camelot itself. I'd read that much, often enough, in my childhood. And though I came here as a man disillusioned by his readings in the recent cold realism of Arthurian history, I nonetheless spent rapt hours roaming the otherwise empty array of this old place in simple awareness of visiting the same kinds of layer-on-layer of human habitation that had won me in Rome (there were fewer layers in Tintagel of course, but they were sonorous all the same).

Back at the Masons' alone in my small room, I turned for the first

time in months to serious thought about my fiction. I'd brought with
me copies of the three finished short stories which I'd sent off to
Diarmuid Russell. I'd also brought what I'd so far written on the story
I'd begun in Florence but had got nowhere near completing in the six
months since—"The Anniversary." And more in hope than certainty,
I'd brought my Florentine Olivetti. I can even remember some typing
in Mrs. Mason's kitchen, though I no longer know whether it was new
work or the endless recopying to which all writing veterans of the pre-
Xerox/pre-computer era were sentenced by the turtle-slow technology
of the time—the laborious retyping of all new drafts and a constant
reliance on the dreaded carbon paper if copies were needed. A further
writer's demon of the time was the never-quite-allayed terror of a lost
manuscript. No writer I knew, once he revised a draft, ever corrected
his carbons; so all our work was subject to fire, robbery, or the brand
of agony that Hemingway endured when his first wife lost forever the
only manuscript of his first book of stories (Lawrence of Arabia also
lost his original version of *The Seven Pillars of Wisdom* while changing trains in Reading, England—very near Oxford).

I'd meant, intently, to concentrate on my two kinds of writing that
summer—"The Anniversary" and then a very substantial amount of
work on my thesis, on which (despite the promise to Miss Gardner)
I'd managed very little, if any, work. The familiar yet incurable guilt
of the seasoned procrastinator seldom ceased assailing the lone hours
of my wanderings; but I consoled myself with the would-be writer's
assurance—relax, this is all invaluable *experience*. So after a glimpse
at a few more Cornish sites with Arthurian overtones (above all, the
ruins of King Mark's castle, as in *Tristan und Isolde*), I made a slow
way back from Cornwall for a few more days with Michael and his
mother. Michael had a brief summer job, to help with the expenses of
our forthcoming jaunt; but somehow it didn't prevent our driving the
hour north to Wimbledon where, according to a letter to Mother that
week, we stood "for some eight hours to see Ham play."
    Hamilton Richardson, as I've noted earlier, was my Rhodester
friend and was then a serious hope of American tennis. He was the

top-ranked American player that year and might well eventually have won the singles at Wimbledon had his diabetes not stood in the way. Still, Michael and I were at Wimbledon for at least two days in June, unreserved but patiently waiting in line for access to the free seats. Though the sunlight was the most relentless I recall from that era, and with all our standing up, Wimbledon was a decided pleasure, however eccentric—the tents serving strawberries and cream, the members of the royal family in attendance in Centre Court to see the startlingly handsome Lew Hoad win the men's singles (the finest eyes I recall on a man); and finally, the grotesque hats on would-be-fashionable Englishwomen.

I've mentioned that foreign students at British universities then had a real problem during the lengthy college vacs—where to stay. I'd moved out of Merton in June; and while I'd booked my Headington digs, the Kirkbys hadn't agreed to take me in during any portion of the Long Vac. But I didn't feel I should crowd Michael and his mother in their two-bedroom apartment for more than a weekend at a time. I could likely have offered Pamela significant help with the groceries, the grass, and the rain barrel for significant stretches in Burford; that prospect didn't attract me, though. Yet whenever I contemplated renting a temporary room in Oxford, I'd look at my budget for the pending continental trip and realize how close to the financial line I was steering. For the first time in my life, I was all but adrift.

So I took the chance to spend a free week, in a Hampstead hotel, with my last Duke mentor William Blackburn, who was at work in the British Museum's library on an edition of a particularly rich correspondence between Joseph Conrad and the editor of *Blackwood's Magazine*. Blackburn had taught me Elizabethan and Jacobean poetry and drama in my sophomore year; and when I'd survived a stunningly low grade on the first paper I wrote for him, he invited me to lunch and, over a plate of barbecue, asked whether I'd yet considered applying for a Rhodes scholarship in my senior year (he'd been a Rhodester from South Carolina in the 1920s). To that point, I had no such plans; but Blackburn set the thought at work in me.

William Blackburn in 1961, in his longtime office on the second story of the East Duke Building of Duke's East Campus. For some twenty years this enduringly successful but endlessly difficult teacher met his seventeenth-century literature class as well as his narrative-writing class in this small room. The few members of these deeply affecting classes sat in desk chairs along three sides of the office; Blackburn sat at his desk against the back window, with a view of the seated statue of Washington Duke just behind him. (The myth, in my student years, was that if a virgin walked in front of the bronze Mr. Duke, he'd be compelled to stand; very few girls took the risk. Nowadays no one even seems to recall the myth, much less fears risking a revelation of her sexual adventures.) Taken by John Menapace, who was then the art designer at Duke University Press and a photographer of real power, the picture is a forceful memory of Blackburn's large head, nose, and hands. Even now, more than fifty years since my last class with him, I note with some degree of jitters that he's reading one of the booklets in which we then submitted our final exams. If he looks up now, he'll either grind his teeth in the deep despair of a lifelong teacher or break into his rolling bass laugh—a sign of rare pleasure from a troubled man.

Furthermore his classroom demonstrations of the degree to which a thoroughly robust man could respond to the power of lyric verse at its pinnacles—Thomas Wyatt, Walter Raleigh, Spenser, Marlowe, Shakespeare—were crucial to my own already strong hope to write and teach. It may sound Mr. Chips–like; but many more of his students than I (Styron among them) attest to the fact that William Blackburn was the kind of magus who could give his class an oral performance of, say, Spenser's "Epithalamium" in his richly modulated baritone—sometimes accompanied by his own silent tears—and teach us more about Spenser, and poetry as a benign life force, than any number of lectures.

In my last year at Duke, his pioneering two-semester course in the writing of prose narrative—which he refused, admirably, to call creative writing ("All good writing is creative," he'd say)—became the forum of my first two successful short stories. Blackburn himself could scarcely write a postcard. His own prose was stamped by the hulking awkwardness of his tall stout body. But he had the born teacher's gift for identifying ability and authentic passion in a student and for zeroing in on those incipient qualities to produce ultimate results.

That very rare strength helped propel more than one man to the eventual publication of good fiction—William Styron and Fred Chappell were two of his other successful writers. He seldom encouraged female students, on the grounds that they were so seldom able—in their careers as 1950s wives and mothers—to find the time to write. In retrospect, while his explanation had a certain validity, my guess is that he more likely feared some romantic involvement (on his part) with a gifted young woman.

The fervor he was capable of pouring into his support of a particular male student—and his ability to reject fervently the same student if some never-declared, and apparently paranoid, limit were passed—eventually suggested to me, through a sometimes mysteriously interrupted friendship of more than twenty years, that there might be a deeply buried but troublesome erotic component in a few of his teacher-student relations. I recall for instance that he once spent almost an entire class hour demonstrating to us—very dubiously, to

say the least—that Shakespeare's most indubitably homoerotic sonnets could not in fact be homoerotic.

But none of the three other male recipients of his backing has ever
mentioned to me any moment of overt word or gesture. On the contrary, so controlled was his support of me that after my father's death
in the winter of 1954, Blackburn became for me not only a respected
teacher but—for almost a decade thereafter—a surrogate father (so
much so that I ultimately regretted, in silence, giving him a handsome
sport jacket that my father had bought a few months before his death;
it fit Blackburn perfectly and gave him, at times, an unnerving resemblance to Dad).

I was glad then to spend those inexpensive summer days with him
in London. By that point he was an enormously lonely man in his late
fifties. He'd ended his own first marriage in the late 1940s; and despite
often comically desperate efforts, he failed to find a second wife for
another twenty years. In that time he was isolated from his teaching
colleagues by what they perceived as a degree of paranoia that only
grew more disabling as he aged. Even with his few adult friends and
favored students then, he could often be grim company. He once told
me that his father "died in a madhouse"—an assertion I've been
unable to confirm. So perhaps he was burdened by a genetic tendency to severe melancholia. Yet despite his depressions, and his
suspicions of the loyalty of even the most devoted friends, he worked
with gargantuan energy at his teaching. And his often sardonic but
irresistible wit could make him a frequently rewarding companion
(weeks after our time in London, he spoke in a letter of "our week of
laughter at the Sandringham [Hotel]" as the high spot of his English
summer).

Of our time together, I recall mainly a continuation of the sunlit
weather I'd had at Wimbledon and the chance to make some return
on Blackburn's many prior generosities to me—it would be years
before he accepted my addressing him as "Bill." On the night of July 1,
1956, for instance, I treated him to a genuinely first-rate musical occasion. At the almost-new Festival Hall, we heard the Verdi *Requiem* conducted by Guido Cantelli, a superb young Italian conductor.

Toscanini's much-loved protégé, Cantelli would be killed in a plane crash a few months later. On this warm and tranquil night on the south bank of the calm Thames, though, he led the Philharmonia Orchestra with Elisabeth Schwarzkopf, Ebe Stignani, Ferruccio Tagliavini, and Giuseppe Modesti in a performance of blazing splendor.

Blackburn's love of music was one of the chief consolations of his solitude, but his taste ran—as it did in his choice of poetry—toward the leaner textures of sixteenth- and seventeenth-century Italian and English composers (secular ones above all). Yet for all his love of early music, and his general avoidance of opera, even Blackburn was demonstrably moved by Verdi's mammoth eloquence in a *Requiem* which unflinchingly confronts the worst possibilities of death and remains bowed but upright and still rapt in the face of life's final mystery, imploring God's mercy on those who've preceded us beyond the veil of eternity. Only some eighteen months after my father's death, the performance worked as a sovereign final distancing of that powerful man from my own grieving mind.

10

SOON THEREAFTER Michael and I—with the fledging beards we'd just begun growing—loaded my car's tiny front-end trunk with our travel provisions (engines in VWs then were located in the rear): a minimum of clothes, and a case of canned corned beef that Michael's mother had bought us, wholesale, for roadside lunches. Then we aimed ourselves due north. We spent a night above a quiet pub in the town of York (where Constantine was proclaimed Roman emperor in A.D. 306 and Auden was born in 1907); then a morning in the nearby York Minster. It remains to this day the grandest ecclesiastical building I've seen, the one that stands for me as a thoroughly convincing demonstration of the overwhelming reality, somewhere beyond us, of a watchful creative existence—something called *God* in the absence of some deeper comprehension.

Later that day we spent an hour in another grand building, tall above a river—Durham Cathedral, even older than York in its present form, with piers down both sides of the dim nave, massive in girth as the magnified legs of the Norman builders who set them up (I was mainly drawn to the bizarre face on the main door's knocker, a place of safe harbor for runaway convicts). Then we pushed on for a night and a day with our beautiful Oxford friend, Stella Kirk from St. Hilda's. She led us on a visit almost to the Scottish border to see Alnwick Castle, the home of the Percys and their rowdy son Hotspur (clearly one of Shakespeare's favorite characters); then a roam through the ruins of Dunstanburgh Castle, the seat of John of Gaunt (gifted also with Shakespearean eloquence).

Then on to Stella's welcoming family in the village of Felton, a few miles from our port, and a happy evening which included my introduction to cold poached salmon with fresh mayonnaise as a dinner dish, all at a big table with family and friends in the clear late light of a far-northern country—a further blessing poured round us. Next morning—July 12—Michael and I stood in Newcastle in further unblemished sunlight and watched my Volkswagen hoisted off the pier, straight upward through what seemed an infinity of dangerous air, then safely down aboard our ship for the calm all-day and overnight voyage across the North Sea to Norway: five hundred miles north, beyond the undersea Viking Bank.

Then the long-planned journey and our first week in Scandinavia. We claimed the unscratched car in sunbathed Bergen—which seemed a glistening toy town, the birthplace of the composer Edvard Grieg, though we hardly paused—and began our drive toward Oslo. Again it was little more than a decade since Western Europe had been freed from a state almost unimaginable to an American—the long grip of the Nazis and the worst of all wars that destroyed them. Norway reflected that recent history in many ways. Most striking at once was

the fact that the roads, except in a few towns, were still dirt roads—
well maintained but unpaved.

And there were few towns along the way—and over the mountains—
from Bergen to Oslo, only the occasional village with, often, small
squads of boys who seemed to be collecting license-plate numbers
from the scarce traffic (as British boys then often collected locomotive
numbers). My plate was QG-2166, as I well recall—largely because I
can still hear the raucous young voices shout it out in Norwegian as
we passed, waving their wild enthusiasm while we vanished eastward in a light cloud of dust. And almost anywhere we stopped—for
gas or water—there'd be a single striking framed photo on the wall: a
young man accepting the surrender of an imposingly uniformed
Nazi officer.

The young man in the picture appeared to be in his early adolescence, and he seemed to be dressed in something like a Boy Scout
uniform. I can't recall that we ever got an authoritative explanation of
the widespread scene, but a friendly drunk outside the Oslo city hall
one later evening told us that the Norwegian government-in-exile had
decided upon this moment as a final humiliation for its defeated
enemy—the forced surrender of a proud Prussian officer to a mere
Nordic boy. God knows, valiant Norway had earned the moment; and
I hope that's more or less the true story.

Whatever, on that first long day on the road, we bought fresh
bread and small ripe tomatoes in a village shop; then stopped by a lake
farther on in the countryside and opened our first can of corned
beef. Even now, framed in my room among my fiercely selective
gallery of Heroes and Worthies, I have the picture I took of Michael
that day, handing me a plate composed of those elements. If I'd felt
rewarded more richly by life than on that bright evening, more so
even than at Heaven's Gate six weeks before, I don't recall it—the
beautiful place unoccupied by others (so far as we could see) and the
simple offer from a tested friend, as good to see as the far-northern lake
and the trees beyond it, of all I needed to nourish me through the
remainder of daylight.

I'd completed no fiction since leaving the States, though "The

Michael Jordan by a lake in rural Norway, July 1956. We're consuming, at lunch each day, a can of corned beef from the case Mike's mother bought us in England, plus the fresh bread and ripe tomatoes we buy on the road in some village by the smooth dirt roads which cross that admirable country, only just then repairing its Viking heart from the long night of Nazi oppression. Of the many dozen photos of Mike I've taken in a friendship that's lasted more than fifty years, none speaks more eloquently of my friend's undemonstrative generosity and the silent help he's rendered many times when I've encountered problems ranging in seriousness from wretched food poisoning in the Merton dining hall to the paraplegia that felled me irreparably thirty years later. No other man I know of has had so loyal a friend through so many years.

Anniversary" was well advanced; and I'd laid my thesis aside to be where I was. Yet I was sure I wasn't deceiving myself when I felt I was doing the right thing for me—and doing it on Cecil Rhodes's money, that steely empire builder who was almost surely queer (I regret that these occasional revelations may strike a reader like rabbits from hats, but I offer none that don't seem relevant in their present context). What I was doing was laying down, by the hour, ardent life beneath me, achieved experience that would serve my future life and my work so long as I had a mind to use and time to use it in. And it was all happening with one even-tempered laconic, and loyal man. All these years later, however long I delayed the completion of my B.Litt. thesis, I can confirm the rightness of the choices a young fool made in the midst of his early twenties (the fool was me of course).

By dusk that day—past nine o'clock, far north as we were—we'd reached a small ski resort called Geilo. Half-dark was enfolding us on all sides; we were tired and it seemed unwise to push deeper into evergreen woods as dense as any forest in a Brothers Grimm tale. A small hotel loomed beside the road. Its surprised manager—surprised to have guests in early summer—took us in for a reasonable fee and, next morning, served us our first near-endless Scandinavian breakfast: mountains of impeccable open-faced sandwiches grandly displayed on a rising series of pewter racks, and for no guests but us apparently (no one else was in sight but a single waitress with a rosy complexion as flawless as any porcelain doll's). Then off to Oslo on further dirt roads through denser forests past more boys shouting my license number at us.

On the outskirts of Oslo, Michael proved the existence of an innate skill I'd not known in anyone before—he possessed, as perhaps a genetic endowment, an apparently infallible internal compass (my mother had a good "sense of direction," but Michael's was amazing). In most cases that summer, our hoped-for first stop in a new city would be the railway station; and Michael could guide us straight there with no hesitation at any crossroads. We'd read somewhere that continental stations all had information windows which could give us the names of individuals, mostly widows or spinsters, with inexpensive rooms to rent in their homes. And lo! we found our Norwegian widow in no time, right at the city center: a clean room in an almost uncannily quiet apartment for the equivalent of eighty-four cents per night (I still have the receipt).

After a quick wash-up we walked out in search of dinner. Strange as it feels after five decades—and with no help from diaries—I can see the cafeteria we found and the entrée I bought—a hearty beef stew with potatoes and beans. *Carbonade*, it was called. The other eaters around us were likewise male—generally middle-aged and not quite destitute maybe but solitary and still wearing their overcoats, though the evening was warm. Maybe we'd stumbled on food largely patronized by the homeless; I've somehow always thought our fellow diners were veterans of the recent war, likely the underground (especially active in Norway).

In the next few days we ticked off the obvious local sights. First, the unique Gustav Vigeland park with the native-son sculptor's swarm of figures—men, women, and children in every decent posture. Then the National Gallery with its numerous paintings by Edvard Munch—Norway's great painter had died only twelve years before, and the dedicated Munch Museum had not yet opened. What was most imposing to one who knew his work only superficially—I'd studied it at Harvard two summers before—was the revelation of what a wide and deep range of response he'd displayed to so much human life, far beyond the riveting *Scream*. From the array of pictures in the National Gallery, it seemed he responded chiefly to female life, from his famous near-vampiric nude women to sick and even threatened girls.

The National Gallery also included a host of considerably less striking landscapes by other Norwegians, mostly in the shrill pastels that led Michael to take all he could before saying—some thirty seconds before I'd have said the same thing—"Enough, I think." What was perhaps most striking about the best work in the city—Vigeland's sculptures and Munch's pictures—was the degree to which they had an immediately obvious personal flavor, a thoroughgoing originality that had somehow fought off the influence of other European art yet was nonetheless not provincial in the usually denigrating sense.

To clear our heads we found the local beach at Huk, near the center of town; and shoulder to shoulder with crowds of the locals, we surrendered our pale hides to a warm sun. And while I'd suffered the dark Oxford autumn days, now I could note in a letter home that "It's still vaguely light at midnight and dawn begins at about 1:30." I never stopped wondering how the birds stood it; when could they sleep? From three or four more days in Oslo, I've retained a memory of welcome warmth from the townsfolk we encountered, mainly in the outdoor café in the central square; yet just under the warmth was a rough-textured nature that seemed ready to fight for whatever it needed to remain itself.

It was surely no accident that all these people had once been the Vikings; and when we'd noticed the young Italian and Spanish men who'd already been drawn, in a lemming rush northward, to seek their polar opposites—the tall blond girls with fetching smiles who awaited them like vaguely superior doe-deer at the edge of a clearing, threatening to speak before they bolted—I trusted in their survival, though I've never had a chance to return and see.

In 1956, though, I could chuckle at the all-but-panting dark-haired boys who always seemed to arrive in packs, descending in their droves from tiny Fiats like circus clowns (thirty clowns from a minuscule car).

I'd begun to notice how both Michael and I were refusing to see ourselves as any brand of tourist. With tilted noses we claimed superiority to that. But how, in my own estimation? Well, I saw myself as a silent benign witness, hoping eventually to convey in useful words what I'd seen. I hope I had the honesty also to grant that a man who managed his combined hope to write and teach as badly as I was so far doing was a creature as open to loud derision as any priapic visitor from the south, but it's taken me more than five decades to do so. Nonetheless, fifty years later I'm recording some memories of those days; and I'm nurturing the ongoing hope that—like the Italians who've survived so many millennia of invasions with ample grace—the Norwegians haven't lost the trait I treasure most from my visit:

their gradual readiness to smile with a slowness that made a grin, once it dawned on their strong-boned faces, seem a genuine victory you could add to your file of on-the-road achievements.

A few miles after we crossed the border into Sweden, we paused to spend a night near Säffle (near the great Lake Vänern) in the home of an elderly woman to whom we'd been recommended by a Brighton friend. The lady was plainly wealthy and gave us a guest room in her handsome country house. Our room alone seemed nearly the size and height of a high-school gym, and our kind hostess fed us well. Most memorably, she sat with us on her front porch in the after-dinner dusk and described—in carefully formed English sentences—her enduring shame, as a Swede, to have sat in that same spot at the start of the Second War and watched German tanks, trucks, and thousands of soldiers pour past her into hapless Norway (it was apparently a condition of Swedish neutrality in the war that Sweden would accept this hateful passage into an even smaller country, its eternal neighbor). Over breakfast next morning before we departed, she asked us please to remember what she'd told us last night. She didn't say why and I didn't ask; but her ramrod spinal dignity is clear in my memory, along with her story of what she well knew was an appalling human betrayal.

Through the station window in Stockholm, we found a private room in a fairly high-class youth hostel on the outskirts of town (the clerk pointed down the street toward the birthplace of Greta Garbo). On our first whole day in the city, we entered a downtown department store. Walking past its windows the night before, Michael had seen a necktie he liked; and we went in while he inquired about it. Since we spoke no Swedish, someone immediately fetched the store's translator.

She was a woman a little younger than we—Birgitta Leander—and as the tie was wrapped, she talked excitedly of her plans to visit England and the States. Then by coincidence, as we explored the artist Carl Milles's sculpture garden later in the day, we encountered Birgitta and her parents. They promptly invited us to dine at their home that night and soon dispelled any rumors we'd heard of Swedish coolness.

Next day we continued to learn our way through the handsome

city—its old quarter and the noble spaces of the city center with the royal palace, the opera, and the broad canals. No other modern Western European capital has seemed so grand to me—grand without ostentation (I've never seen Paris, odd as that may be). We must have stayed there nearly a week; and apart from a museum or two and a Birgitta-led Sunday in the nearby university town of Uppsala where we drank mead in a tavern near some tall Viking mounds, my best memory of the time is an evening when we arranged to meet Birgitta at Berns's nightclub. She'd be coming with her pretty friend Eva, whom we'd met at her parents' dinner party. At the club, Eartha Kitt—then at the height of her fame—was to be the performer. And the plan was that Michael and I should go early to insure a ringside table, and the girls would join us at the end of the workday. As promised, they arrived well before the floor show and found Michael and me at an ideal table.

The girls were laughing as they spread a newspaper before us and said "Who is *this*?" I've neglected here to chart the growth of our beards; but there undeniably we were—our heads, large, on a page of that day's *Aftonbladet*, the afternoon paper, under a Swedish caption that said something like "Summer beards are blooming again." Our beards had indeed progressed remarkably since leaving England (had the near-constant northern light been fertilizing?). Mine was near-black and Karl Marxist in its profusion. Michael's was a tawny blond and more spiffily shaped. How the picture was taken we never learned; but for us four—pleased with ourselves to be in a nightclub, sipping wine in the midst of worldly adults—it proved a cheerful curtain opener for Eartha Kitt, a sassy South Carolina native who gave us way more than our money's worth in the course of a long evening of stage hijinks and song (the waiter let us sit through two shows).

When we left Stockholm soon afterward, Birgitta rode with us as far south as Copenhagen to visit friends (I never saw Birgitta again, but I know that she later came to New York and held an important position in the United Nations translation department). My memories of the then-smallish and quiet Danish capital include driving out to visit

Hamlet's handsome castle Elsinore (Helsingör), then the celebrated flea circus in the teeming midtown amusement park called Tivoli. Who but the Danes could keep an amusement park tasteful, and am I hallucinating when I recall that the flea circus featured a jumping-insect version of the chariot race from *Ben Hur*? Mainly, though, I recall long walks through an old city without the grandeur achieved by Stockholm but also, surely, with no such grand ambitions.

Mainly I recall our sitting in an outdoor café one late bright evening, surrounded by well-dressed Danish ladies who were smoking cigars as the news-in-lights crawled round a nearby building to inform us that Premier Nasser of Egypt had just seized the Suez Canal from its international keepers, the French and the British. Ah, there was a real world after all. Would it lean on us now (surely the West could hardly allow the canal to be closed)?

My car lacked a radio, our ignorance of Scandinavian languages had shut us off from printed news in recent weeks, and Michael and I shared the general oblivion of the young to news that didn't directly affect our bodies. So the bad news came as a mild surprise, but neither of us was alarmed. Michael was the only child of a British war widow and may thus have been exempt from any draft (the same was true, in those days, of the only sons of American war widows). And again, I was in Britain on an annually renewable permit from the U.S. Selective Service authorities. In those years the American draft system had been sympathetic to serious students—my grades at Duke had saved me from the Korean War. While I could theoretically be summoned home for military testing and induction, any implications of this latest news—even in the tinderbox of Middle Eastern politics—hardly seemed likely to require my presence in the American armed forces. So our trip continued on its untroubled way with a few more days in Denmark; but why did I say, in a letter home, "The Danes are friendly to a fault"?

And before I depart Scandinavia entirely, I should record that another soused but amused Norwegian told Michael and me this not entirely unfair joke one evening as we strolled past the Royal Palace in Oslo—he conveyed it as urgent news we'd need for the trip. Two Norwegians, two Danes, and two Swedes are shipwrecked on a desert island. A whole year passes before they're rescued. In the twelve long months, the two Norwegians have had a fight; and one has killed the other. The two Danes have formed a cooperative and are doing very nicely, thank you. But the two Swedes have not been introduced yet. Well, apart from our better experience with a few of the Swedes, the joke held water.

From Copenhagen we crossed by late-night ferry into northern West Germany and plunged straight down toward Jane and Liz in Munich. I have dim memories of bypassing Hamburg and Nuremberg in the dark — on the remains of Hitler's pioneering autobahns (Michael was a faster driver than I) — and reaching Munich in early daylight. Having no notion of the girls' location (Michael's internal compass was on hold), I told him to pull over at the curb where two policemen were standing. Their uniforms were almost alarmingly like German uniforms of the recent war; I assumed they'd be helpful, though. But when I rolled down my window and — in English — asked for directions from the more lupine of the two men, he turned away from me to his colleague. They shared a dry laugh. Then, together, they said a few N words — words that I, with no German, heard as entirely negative (like *nein* and *nix*); and they waved us onward, out of their sight, with no trace of help.

As we stumbled toward our friends, I continued to see the word *Dönitz* on numerous walls and hoardings. I was old enough to recall that Admiral Karl Dönitz was designated by Hitler, in the last days of the war, as his successor. What I didn't know was that Dönitz had, ever since, been in the Allied prison at Spandau and would be released in two months. It seemed at least possible that the men who'd scrawled his name on walls were awaiting his freedom with vague hopes of a Nazi return to power, if they were not in the grip of some grimmer dream. I began to wonder just where we'd come to.

The week in Jane and Liz's bright American-style apartment was a welcome change from our stays with the impeccable and inexpensive but mostly silent landladies of Scandinavia. Liz was preparing to return to the States to complete her college years in America, and she'd already finished her work with Radio Free Europe and was ready to join Michael and me in some local prowling. There was an indelibly memorable venture to Dachau, the site of Hitler's first concentration camp, built in the year of my birth, 1933.

The town of Dachau was a virtual suburb of Munich, some twelve miles away, giving the lie at once to those citizens of the larger town who claimed they'd known nothing of the camp's eventual murders. Dachau was not primarily a death camp but a holding-site for political prisoners and, not at all incidentally, the 110 homosexuals who were counted on the day of the last roll call in April '45. Nonetheless some 32,000 prisoners died there, some of them as the result of the typhus epidemics which swept through many of the Nazi camps. Since the liberation of Dachau had occurred only some eleven years before our visit, there had been very little decorating of the premises. The present national-park atmosphere most definitely did not prevail; and I still have the photos I took, showing the raw realities of the site on the day of my visit with Liz.

My and Liz's visit? Unexpectedly, on our arrival at the gate, Michael declined to enter with us. I tried, in one sentence, to persuade him; he shook his head in a silent No. And I knew to go no further, but that was all I knew. I left it at that, and in all the succeeding years have never asked why he refused. He waited outside in the unblocked sun as Liz and I wandered for a slow hour through the near-deserted spaces. What we saw were wide and unadorned barbed-wire enclosures, long frame barracks, and long low redbrick buildings that had housed the incinerator ovens that consumed many corpses—outside, by the covered trenches that housed many more, the plaques said with stunning economy (in German)—*The Grave of Nameless Thousands.*

A few old women lingered, apparently even more baffled than we, near the crematory. A few old men wore their Jewish prayer shawls and murmured prayers; a very few guards watched us but no one else. Years later I wrote a long story called "Waiting at Dachau" that arose from the experience. More immediately, in a letter home soon after the visit, I described Dachau as "one of the two most impressive things I've seen"—the other was the Sistine Chapel, and the claim still holds.

A night or two later, the four of us drove a swift eighty miles east to Salzburg for as near an antidote as one could imagine to so much horror—a festival performance of Mozart's *Le Nozze de Figaro*. Conducted by Karl Böhm and sung by (among others) Elisabeth Schwarzkopf, Irmgard Seefried, Christa Ludwig, and Dietrich Fischer-Dieskau, it was a long but sublime evening. The fact that both Mozart and Hitler were Austrian, and that the conductor and more than one of the brilliant cast of singers had likely been members of the Nazi party, only complicated the richness of the evening.

Given my youth, I'd heard a rewarding number of great performances at the Met and on the surprisingly distinguished concert stage in Raleigh—where I heard Flagstad twice, Melchior twice, Marian Anderson twice, Pinza and Steber once—but as we drove back on another splendid highway, I silently reckoned I'd never hear a more nearly perfect ensemble effort in the service of a greater stretch of music. On that return to Munich, we spent most of our remaining energy laughing at something we'd heard at a polite Salzburg bar to which we'd retired after the music. Two older classic-American female tourists, straight out of a *New Yorker* cartoon, were discussing what we'd just heard. The larger of the two said to her friend, "I'm not really sure we got our money's worth." When her friend looked quizzical, the unsure lady continued, "Listen, when I hear *great* music, something in me just *swells up*; and tonight it didn't swell."

Three other events linger on from the week in Munich. Liz took Michael and me, for a drink, to the large beer hall—the Bürgerbräukeller—which was locally famed as an early meeting place for Hitler and his cronies and the scene of their failed putsch of 1924. It was clean-scrubbed and as charmless as a vast tile toilet, but did I expect charm from a Fascist cradle? Another day, Liz, Michael, and I returned to Salzburg for a morning's walk through the old town, cli-

Jane Savage, dancing the Charleston in a dress of her mother's from the 1920s. Jane sent me the picture in the 1950s, and almost ever since it's been framed at my bedside. It was taken by a friend of hers at Radio Free Europe in Munich where she was working when Mike and I visited her and Liz McNelly in the summer of '56. Jane had meant a good deal to me since we met in high school in the late '40s, and there were times when I thought marriage might be a possibility (she may never have shared my thought). In any case, we brought each other a lot of pleasure and laughter till she married, moved out of easy reach, then succumbed to the slow ravages of multiple sclerosis, and died in her midsixties. In this costumed picture, she suggests—without obvious effort—both her gift for self-parody and her genuine grace.

maxing in a visit to Mozart's birthplace—another hard-scrubbed site but one whose walls at least surrounded the authentic space in which one of humanity's supreme benefactors began his life. Then we downed a big lunch, ending in my second chance at Salzburger nockerl, one of my lifetime-favorite desserts.

Finally, the night before Michael and I were to leave Munich, the third memorable event came down. We went with Jane and Liz to a loud and eventually drunken party given by their colleagues at Radio Free Europe. By midnight, my childhood fear of drunks—their noise and the unpredictability of their hate—had sent me onto the porch to wait out the remainder of the evening. A patient soul always, Jane came out and joined me in an effort to turn my dislike of her friends. What always seemed my prudery at such occasions embarrassed me, and I surely had no problem with the fact that these oddly homeless Americans and exiled Easterners were sub rosa employees of the CIA—I've always thought that Radio Free Europe was one of the agency's better ideas—so I unburdened myself of a good deal of the emotional history of my Oxford months.

I'd suspected all week that Jane had realized how much Michael's friendship meant to me, and she'd shown no sense whatever of rivalry. I know I came near to broaching the matter, but ultimately my sobriety curbed me. So with her usual will to be defenseless, Jane moved into one of our first silences to tell me of the recently ended affair she'd had with an Eastern European at RFE—a man I'd liked in recent days. I was partly glad to hear of it—she and I, like most of our friends, had been so absurdly celibate all our lives—but I also felt a sudden steep wave of recalling how much she'd meant to me in the past ten years since I'd met her in our Raleigh neighborhood. I came very near a second proposal of some sort—marriage, whatever, I didn't quite know. She was seated on the redbrick step just below me. I leaned way down, set my chin on the crown of her head—her blond hair—and dug right in. My hands didn't reach out to turn her toward me; she didn't turn but her head did press back hard into my sharp chin. I'm sure I thanked her—the few plain words.

*   *   *

Michael and I proceeded along the sunny Rhine for a good part of our way northwest. I recall bypassing Stuttgart, Frankfurt, and Bonn; then stopping for a night in Cologne. After the lack of obvious war scars in Munich and Salzburg (the Marshall Plan had done brilliant work in the hands of the notoriously able-handed and ambitious West Germans), it came as a surprise to see the condition of Cologne. More than ninety percent of the city's buildings had been destroyed by Allied bombs in a total of 262 air raids; and at the end of the war, when West Germany was divided into zones of jurisdiction, Cologne lay in the British zone.

The British had, understandably, slim enthusiasm for encouraging the rebuilding of a country that had plunged them into war twice in twenty-five years. So the city we reached in late afternoon—the central city in any case—was a warren of only partly reconstructed single- or double-storied buildings, towered over by the giant cathedral that had also been damaged and was black with smoke but still strode triumphant above a huddled skyline. We stayed in a cigar-box-size room with a bombed-out widow for only one night, took a walk round central Cologne in the morning; walked slowly through the cathedral whose survival may well have been miraculous, and then were off.

Late the next afternoon—of a gray day—we crossed into Holland; and once we'd braved a literally incredible swarm of end-of-work bicycle traffic (hardly a car in sight but thousands of bikes), we found another widow's room—a hilarious old woman—in downtown Amsterdam and ate a fine supper in an Indonesian restaurant (the Dutch equivalent of British Indian restaurants—colonial survival). Then we strolled through narrow streets in the dedicated red-light district. Informed though we'd been—like so many million tourists—we were quickly shown the reality of numerous attractive young women seated in windows a few yards from the sidewalk, polishing their nails, straightening seams in their fishnet stockings, meeting our eyes with the blank penetration of alluring cats but never once smiling (was a smile illegal?). One especially young girl did turn politely aside from my smile and dissolve in laughter; I stopped in my tracks, but she never looked back—not at me. I was tempted more than once to enter the open doors by the windows, if only to prove that the women were live and could actually talk. But neither Michael nor I took the bait, maybe because by then we were very near broke.

Like several other small but site-rich countries (Israel for instance), one of the numerous likable realities of a visit to Holland is that you really need to rent only one room. Then on public transportation you can easily venture all round the country—in Holland, nothing is much more than an hour from Amsterdam. So we stayed on in Amsterdam for several nights and submerged in a piece of amazing luck. The summer of 1956 was the 350th anniversary of Rembrandt's birth. I take it as beyond debate that Rembrandt is as great a painter and draftsman as ever lived and that, further, he was at least as specifically Dutch in his vision as Praxiteles was Greek.

And Michael and I were now in precisely the right place on the planet to absorb two enormous celebratory exhibitions of Rembrandt's work. In Amsterdam we saw as many of his drawings and etchings as could be gathered back to Holland for display at the Rijksmuseum. And in Rotterdam a comparably exhilarating wilderness of paintings was gathered. A two-day gallery visit was called for in either city; and we gave them that (only the gathering of Michelangelo's work in Rome had provided a similar chance to see so much genius in so little space—and all of it near the scene of its creation).

What was almost equally astonishing was the fact that the Van Gogh family's enormous collection of Van Gogh paintings and drawings was on display in Amsterdam's Stedelijk Museum (there was not yet a dedicated Van Gogh museum). And almost as an afterthought, in another wing of the Stedelijk stood (temporarily) the original of Picasso's huge *Guernica* in the midst of a lavish display of related sketches and plans. As one who'd already begun to immerse himself in the depths of seventeenth-century Europe, I'll confess that Rembrandt and Vermeer reached me in ways that Van Gogh and Picasso didn't, not in my early twenties. Of course I admired the more recent painters; but I wasn't yet deeply moved by them. Still I bought a full-size reproduction of Van Gogh's very late *Crows in a Cornfield* and would soon hang it in my room in Headington.

The pleasure that spread in rings round the silent landing in my mind of a genius as comprehensive as that of Rembrandt or Vermeer has never ceased nor diminished within me. But time would ripen me for a greater vulnerability to the often hectic, sometimes serene, art of the more nearly contemporary men. Even now, the older painters still move me most—largely through their power to console. I take it that any sane human life, as it moves on past—say—the age of fifty is grateful for literal help in learning that its pains, griefs, delights, and hopes are shared; and the older painters offer such experience, steady and clear.

There were further Dutch sidelights of the Rembrandt summer. Despite our happiness with the jokey widow in Amsterdam, we soon discovered a reason to move to the Hague. Because of the crowded gallery conditions in the two large cities, all the Vermeer paintings that still belonged to Holland had been gathered in the Hague in—can my memory be right?—a single middle-size room of the Mauritshuis: among them, the *Girl with a Pearl Earring*, the *View of Delft*, *The Little Street*, *The Milkmaid*, and the *Woman in Blue Reading a Letter*.

For three nights then we found a room in the home of a large and thoroughly warmhearted family—the Sanderses. In our evenings we dined with them and then played quietly ferocious games of Monopoly with the parents and children. Otherwise we walked through the small leafy city and spent as much time as possible with the Vermeers. Among those immaculate and immensely complex pictures— each of them apparently breathed effortlessly onto their canvas or panels—the *Woman in Blue Reading a Letter* would work steadily in my mind after the visit and play a crucial role in suggesting to me the subject of my first novel. The picture shows what appears to be a pregnant young woman dressed in blue, standing before a large map (of what distant place?) and facing a well-lit window as she reads a letter (from whom?). In the Mauritshuis I'd stand and study the picture as I've never, before or since, felt compelled to study any image—setting my eyes to prowl the relatively small surface with the relentless thoroughness of a spy-in-the-sky satellite.

In our final days in Holland, we visited Delft for the small-town sense of Vermeer's life (he was born and lived there always). His father's narrow house still stands on the spacious central square, crowded though it is with Delft-blue porcelain shops which may nonetheless provide a clatter similar to the one through which Vermeer persisted, daily, in his creation of the phenomenal silence of his pictures. And as a fitting end to the trip, we took a long walk on the vacant and windy beach at Scheveningen where Van Gogh had often worked. Then five weeks after our departure from Newcastle, we returned on choppy water from the Hook of Holland to Harwich on the southeast coast of England.

Fine as the days and the long miles had been, I was ready for a stretch of solitude; no doubt Michael was also. We each had almost two months of the Long Vac left. I'd be faced again with the question of where to stay; we'd both need to get down to concentrated study. Meanwhile it's worth noting that we'd completed that rarest of travel ventures—a long car trip, with all the enforced closeness such a trip entails, yet one without a single falling-out. If either Michael or I felt the need of a free breath, we wandered off for an hour of reading beneath a tree; or we sped up, two rooms ahead in a museum and indulged in private viewing.

One of the travel skills I learned from Michael was the wisdom of declining to discuss paintings, cathedrals, or even mountainscapes while we were in the act of viewing them. Discussion, if called for, could occur over our next meal; any disagreements would have cooled by then. Michael's natural quietude had no doubt engendered the skill in him years earlier—later I'd learn that he likely acquired the trait from his mother, a woman who'd spent much time alone since her husband's death, if not before—but through a trip as long as ours, his taciturnity damped down my Southern tendency toward instantaneous babble and thus any number of on-the-road wrangles.

11

IN ATTEMPTING to reintroduce my car to England, late on an August Sunday afternoon, I experienced a first brassy taste of British bureaucratic superiority. I'd bought the car, under the strict tax regulations then prevailing, without paying the large amount of purchase tax that a Briton would have paid. I was spared the tax on the understanding that I'd export the car forever within a year. Now the customs men at Harwich attempted to assert that I'd exported the car forever when I took it to Norway and that I could only import it now if I paid several hundred pounds of tax on the spot. As I attempted to explain myself to the increasingly livid agents in a shed in Harwich, I realized that I'd exported the car for a summer journey without sufficient inquiries, on my part, as to my freedom to bring it back. I assumed my year of grace-from-tax still had more than half a year to run.

Maybe the agents were annoyed at having to work on a Sunday—and work with a university student, at that (I was getting my first whiff of British class antagonism). But faced with their demand either for hundreds of pounds I didn't possess or else the temporary surrender of my car, I finally asked to speak with the supervisor on duty. The request further infuriated the men who were dealing with my return; but a supervisor did indeed materialize, one with even more braid on his cap. I tried a last impassioned plea for an understanding pardon, and the man relented—not of course before he read me a lengthy and increasingly chauvinistic lecture to the approximate effect that "You Americans"—shades of Mr. Leishman!—"think you can rewrite our laws for your own benefit anytime you wish. This country suffered a world war for you, we're suffering still; and here you're swanking around with your dollars, flouting our troubles."

I heard some degree of justice in his lecture; but I kept silent, then apologized for my oversight in not seeking the correct prior permissions. I made no attempt to defend my military compatriots who, even as I spoke, might well be climbing aboard willing girls in Gropecunt Lane—or an alley adjacent to the very pub nearest this customs station. No doubt, by their own lights, the customs men were correct; but since my prior experiences of the English had convinced me of an extraordinary lack of the prim self-importance and the moral superiority I'd faced for the past hour, I was briefly stunned. But the instant the supervisor waved us onward, I floored the pedal and was out of his shed before he could dream of changing his mind. I should add that the car had given us perfect service on the continental roads— needing only gas, oil, and an occasional windshield wash. In fact it would give me cheerfully reliable service for the seven years I owned it—by far the most reliable car I've owned, in fifty-one years of cars.

A supper of the famed, and first-rate, oysters from the nearby beds at Colchester set me back up; and before midnight I'd returned Michael to his mother's flat. I stayed there with them another day or two. Michael was facing his third, and final, year at college; so once back home he betook himself to the books he might have been reading all summer. And I, who also might well have spent the past five weeks in the Bodleian, merely drove myself to Oxford and surprised the landlady who'd expected me no sooner than October 1. I asked to occupy my rooms for at least the time I'd need to shave off my beard, get my clothes truly clean again, select a few books of my own to read (mainly a few unread novels by Hardy and Forster and my increasingly annotated text of *Samson*), and change the oil in my car.

While I'd been on the Continent, Mother had finally undergone a surgery she'd long needed—a hysterectomy and the necessary work to repair the damage done by the delivery of two very large baby boys and a near-fatal stillbirth some twenty years earlier. My letters from the time reflect a good deal of worry for her health and the guilt I experienced for having been on a European lark while she suffered. They also show that I was beginning to think of the doctoral degree I thought I'd need after my B.Litt. In the summer before my senior year at Duke I'd spent a rewarding ten weeks at Harvard, studying with the

My mother Elizabeth and brother Will in 1956 on the porch of the Rodwell house in Macon where Mother and I were born. Between them is my cousin Marcia Drake Bennett, and another family member sits in the swing which had been such a welcoming feature of my long boyhood visits. I've mentioned the degree to which I missed Will and Mother during my three English years (we called him Bill then, and note his white socks). The many similar photographs which they sent me in their letters did little to assuage my longing for home, nor did my frequent spells of homesickness greatly dilute my pleasure in the British and continental years. Knowing that I'd be home, essentially for good, in the summer of 1958 kept me mostly even-keeled.

first-rate, amusing, and friendly Howard Mumford Jones—among several others. And now I wrote home to say that "I'm pretty determined to try to get into Harvard next fall" (the fall of '57)—yet I was still working much harder on my own fiction than on Milton's poetry.

Having dispatched those concerns to North Carolina, I stashed my belongings at the Kirkbys' and headed to Burford, after all, for my longest stay yet with Redmayne. A briefly resident friend did a good life-size drawing of me and the beard. Pamela fed me well and recounted her sometimes amusing, often plainly apocryphal, recollections. In return I mowed her lawn, trimmed the shrubs, attended Sunday church at the small but beautifully detailed Burford parish church, and rode with her to Tewkesbury to see its magnificent and cavernous Norman abbey church and the nearby field where in 1471 a crucial battle in the Wars of the Roses was fought, one in which the eventual Richard III led the Yorkist forces which killed the young Lancastrian Prince of Wales.

Then encumbered by grateful affection for Redmayne's kindness and by semi-homicidal tendencies in the face of her increasingly elaborate confabulations, I struck out alone for the Gower Peninsula in the south of Wales near Swansea. In another of her bountiful good deeds, Pamela had put me onto a couple—a working stonemason named Harry Bevan and his wife—whose small ad she'd discovered in a magazine. They offered the large upper room in their rural cottage for a strikingly low weekly rent, all meals included. My family name Price (from *ap Rhys*, "son of Rhys") is among the most frequently encountered Welsh names; and while my father's family had kept no strong Welsh tradition, I'd learned—in some genealogical prowling of my own—of our Celtic roots. I was at least double Celtic; one side of Dad's family was Welsh, another Scottish/French Huguenot. His mother was a Scot by name, a McCraw, thereby doubling my connection to that strangely imaginative and often violent brood. As I drove southwest then in early September (with $15.42 in my checking account) and slowly approached my hosts near the village of Oxwich Green, in sight of the sea, I felt slowly absorbed back into a world my genes had departed centuries ago but recognized now, in every rock and tree.

And the Bevans' isolated cottage—no others in sight—seemed the first real home I'd inhabited in the eleven months since I left my mother's (Michael's mother worked outside their apartment all day, and their flat had an oddly unlived-in air). The Bevans had no children; but Mrs. Bevan was in the cottage all day, involved in the usual work of a homemaker. When I worked or read upstairs, the quiet sounds of her kitchen jobs—cleaning, polishing, and asides to the dog—were welcome accompaniments.

So in memory I seem to have stayed a long time—sleeping late, then eating Mrs. Bevan's rich breakfast, going for long walks down to the beautiful deserted beach or the ruined castle or rides into nearby Swansea with its lively outdoor market. There I talked a good deal with the merchants at their stalls—the musical accent of that part of Wales was very near to song or chant—and I bought yards of the stout light-blue wool from which local miners' shirts were made (I still have the fabric, folded in a closet; no shirts were ever made for me). Most redeemingly, I worked on my stories. I'd still begun nothing new but was content to teach myself how to write as I worked at my endless revisions of the four stories I considered worth owning—"Michael Egerton," "A Chain of Love," "The Warrior Princess Ozimba," and "The Anniversary."

Most vividly I recall a particular quiet tap at my door—I was napping in early afternoon. It was Mrs. Bevan and she spent a long minute begging my pardon; then said that their dog, an ancient terrier, was ill. Could she pay me please to drive her and the dog to Swansea to see the vet? She was not an old woman, maybe in her early forties, with a distinct but gentle dark beauty—chestnut hair, eyes so brown they were nearly black, perfect skin with no wrinkles yet.

I was lonely that afternoon and glad to accept her request, assuring her that no money could be involved. On our way into town, she stroked the sick dog asleep in her lap; and she talked of how she and Harry had tried and tried for a child and how "old Barrett" had taken the place of a younger human creature to love. No tears, no tug at my arm for brotherhood; yet almost no memory from that first year abroad is stronger for me now than the drive into Swansea with Mrs. Bevan and Barrett.

Yet strangely I barely recall the sequel. We brought Barrett home, alive though not healed. Oddly a very similar situation arose a year later when the Kirkbys, my also childless Oxford landlords, would ask me to be with their only dog Peter while a vet "put him down." Old Peter, who looked like a bag of dirty feathers, had lunged for my ankles, fangs bared, a hundred times but was too blind to catch me. Now he was riddled with cancer, in moaning pain; so I went to the back room where he was all but immobile on his pillow. The vet was preparing her lethal hypodermic. Till Peter died quietly, I warily rubbed his neck (if he'd rallied he might have torn off a finger). From the two occasions, with Barrett and Peter, some dozen years later I wrote a story called "A Dog's Death."

And in retrospect now I more than half think that the incident in Oxwich Green—intense as it was—kept me from returning to the Bevans' perfect quarters during later vacs, despite Mrs. Bevan's kind letters of invitation. Maybe though more than two years had passed, I felt too near the vigil I'd kept on Dad's awful death, and the cancer dread I'd encouraged a few months ago, to return to even a sick dog's home. It would be almost another decade—Mother's inescapable decline—before I felt adequate to face such trials (the completion of three related short stories was a crucial help).

So I wrote to my forthcoming landlady and begged the right to return. Then after ten days in Wales—and giving her no chance to say No—I turned back up on her doorstep. Despite griping steadily for the first two days, she folded me in. Her name, again, was Win Kirkby. In many ways she and her husband Jack were classic instances of the upper-working-class Briton of their time and place (I continue to specify matters of class because they were so vitally important at the time). Win and Jack owned their home in Headington—a clean and orderly Oxford middle-class neighborhood of two-story brick and occasional stucco houses. Their next-door neighbor to the right was a physician;

farther down the road at number 76 lived Professor J. R. R. Tolkien and his wife (as yet his trilogy was by no means famous, in Britain or elsewhere). Win added a one-car garage while I lived there; and once I returned to the States, she paid for driving lessons, purchased her own Morris Mini; and of all things—considering her sizable tendency to battiness—she took to the roads with considerable aplomb.

The Kirkbys were dedicated members of the Labour Party and worked for the party in various minor connections—organizing and serving at spring and summer fetes, for instance. Win was also a full-time housewife (her aged mother lived alone elsewhere in Headington, and Win took loyal care of her in several daily visits on her bike). In his longtime job as a scout at New College, Jack was a man of considerable dignity—maybe also in his mid-fifties, handsome in a retired-RAF-pilot way—though he'd never been a pilot. He sported a luxuriant grizzled black mustache, a blazer with the New College emblem, and the patience of Job—which he needed.

Win was in her late forties, with an often laughing demeanor but a settled ruthlessness when crossed (I never crossed her, though I witnessed occasions when others did).

Her hair had been red, likely helped along now by a little dye; and both she and Jack spoke one of the few authentic noncollegiate Oxfordshire accents I heard in my time—an accent with none of the harshness of Cockney and none of the facial contortions required by certain other English dialects.

I mentioned Jack's patience, and sometimes I found his tolerance in the face of Win's headstrong impulses all but incredible. As an instance, in Oxford there was a public dance-hall near the downtown crossroads at Carfax—the Carfax Assembly Rooms. From her girlhood days, Win would often recall, she'd "evermore loved to dance." And even in my time, maybe one or two nights a week, she'd go down on the bus and dance till midnight. If my downstairs study light was still burning, she might tap on my door and ask if I'd like a cup of cocoa. I'd always say Yes and, delivering it a few minutes later, she'd have a chance to tell me—in a stage whisper—about her evening (Jack would be twenty-five feet away, down the hall in their own sitting room).

She might regale me with a story of the "lovely young chap"—a student, a townsman, a soldier—whom she'd danced with for hours and how he might have got "all het up" when he pressed her close on the dance floor. I never saw Win in any state approaching inebriation, but some nights she'd grow so amused by her memory of the evening that she'd seem a little tipsy, laughing deeply and going on further—"He was so het up, it was rising and rising till I thought it was coming out of his blooming collar next: blimey O'Riley!"

And she did once tell me that, a few years earlier during the war, she'd come home unusually late one night to find Jack waiting for her in the pouring rain at the corner bus stop. She stepped off the bus to see him standing there, soaking wet. He'd brought her rain boots along to protect her through the final block-long walk to their home. Win said "He looked so silly standing there in the bus light that, like a dirty dog, I burst out laughing right in his face. He took a step back, looked me right up and down, then flung the bloody boots straight at me—cut me lip and all too. I bled for hours and was ever so angry for days, but of course I knew he was right to do what he did. Old Jack, he's a good un, he is" (whatever their privacies from one another and the ensuing peeves, their mutual devotion was clear as clean water).

She also had endless stories about prior students who'd lived at the house. She had especially fond memories of someone she always called "The Honorable Thomas Pakenham" (likely the son of Lord and Lady Longford, and the brother of Antonia Fraser—a 1955 graduate of Magdalen who eventually succeeded his father to the title, as eighth Earl of Longford). She might laugh about somebody's laundry habits or a girl someone had smuggled in through the window one night; but she never deplored her old gents, not once in my hearing. If they'd completed a year or more at Win's, they were safe in her head forever after. And her head was subject to confusion—rackety schedules, odd requests, but—again—never a real lean on us. Despite her lack of a car, for instance, she never once asked me to drive her here or there, though I'd sometimes offer.

So far as we roomers were concerned, her day was generally regu-

Win Kirkby, my landlady in the Headington suburb of Oxford—2 Sandfield Road. It was a neighborhood not far from the home of C. S. Lewis, and J. R. R. Tolkien lived just down the road from Win and Jack Kirkby's house. Mike Jordan and I—and once Mike left for Princeton, Tony Nuttall and I—had two sets of rooms (a bedroom and sitting room for each) in the boisterously warm surroundings generated by Win and Jack with their ancient and would-be-vicious dog Peter. Here, Win sits in her own back garden in unusual sunlight, more formally dressed than was usual for her—no doubt because I'd hauled out my camera and asked her to pose. Her red hair escapes note in the picture, but her grinning eyes go a long way toward recording her undaunted taste for the Wife-of-Bath world she'd inhabit almost any Saturday night in the dance-hall palace at the center of town—the Carfax Assembly Room, a gently rowdy city dancing place (where the Beatles later made their only Oxford appearance, in 1963).

lar. She expected us downstairs in our sitting rooms for breakfast no later than eight—Michael and I always met in my front room, though Michael had his own. Invariably Win provided the customary huge English breakfast with fried eggs, fried tomatoes, fried bread, sometimes fried mushrooms, toast and marmalade, and coffee or tea as we wished. While we were eating and getting down to the morning's reading or writing, she'd go upstairs, lightly dust the various surfaces, and make our beds—clean sheets once a week. Also once a week she'd vacuum the carpets ("Hoovering the rug," it was called, after the Hoover vacuum cleaner). There was never a complaint about our own housekeeping—though I'll have to say that Michael and I—and once Michael was gone, Tony Nuttall and I—were neat, as young men go.

And all that, again, for two pounds, ten shillings per week—an extra shilling for hot water if we had a bath, though she'd frequently donate the baths or forget to charge for them. By nine she'd be done with us for the day ("I don't do teas—you can make your own damned tea"). Then she'd head out on her bike for the morning chores in the village of Headington, ten minutes uphill on her bike; or occasionally she'd take the bus downhill to Oxford itself, a quarter-hour ride. Later in the day, or in the evening if she stayed in, she might stop for a moment's laughter; but between Jack, her old mother, her own household chores, her Labour Party duties, and her dancing, she was too busy to donate further time to the lodgers.

When I did see her, however, she poured out such a wealth of expressions I'd never heard that I kept a list of the most striking, many of which I eventually used in short stories that transformed her into a centrally important character ("Scars" and "A Dog's Death" chiefly). If I was looking gloomy, she might say "What's wrong, Mr. Price? Your face is as long as a wet week." If I mentioned that a friend's fiancée was especially homely, Win would say "Well, you don't look at the mantel while you're poking the fire, now do you?" A married friend of hers named Mary was involved in a cheating love affair with a young man, and I said "She'd better be careful or her husband will know." Win said "I told her that meself; and Mary said 'Well, a slice off a cut loaf is never missed, is it?'" I've assumed that few of the sayings were original to Win (some may well have been; she had a verbal flair), but her immediate zest when she produced them in conversation was worthy of a comic actress with brilliant timing. Having few places to go during my remaining long vacations, I spent more time with the Kirkbys than most of their gents had done; and they became important parts of my English years. In retrospect, I've been especially grateful for the chance they gave me to participate in, at length and in depth, a genuine piece of an old working-class England that few Americans of my era ever encountered.

For the remainder of that first summer, I stayed on at the Kirkbys' and finally got down to serious daily work in the Bodleian. In addition to my immersion in Milton scholarship, I was also reading widely in Italian Renaissance criticism, especially in the matter of what those early critics took to be Greek drama (there were strong indications that they thought Greek tragedy was much like early Italian opera or vice versa—and in many ways it probably was).

In the process my own knowledge of Italian grew rapidly, and I was even challenged to expand my two years of high-school Latin. I likewise read a good many of the Italian plays which Milton might have incorporated into the dense web of knowledge out of which he'd eventually weave his own Greek tragedy in English. Despite my conviction that my future work would consist—way more than half—of writing fiction and poetry, I'd begun to discover, with a certain amount of silent surprise, that such esoteric studies gave me considerable pleasure. More than once I told myself that if my fiction failed, I'd have a worthy second profession waiting; but once I got my first novel well under way, I could look back and see that those moments of contentment in the Bodleian were more nearly a form of impersonation than genuine identity. I doubt I could ever have succeeded as a full-time scholar, though I've admired many scholarly colleagues in later years.

Unable, as ever, to take books home from the Bodleian, I recovered some of my old self-protections as a solitary. When the building closed at sundown, I'd generally drive past the extensive Clarendon

Press on Walton Street and eat a curry dinner at the Bombay Restaurant. I was already a friend of the waiters there—boys younger than I, hardly off the plane from southern India—and I almost always ate alone during the vac. Before long I began to realize that they were often silently halving my bill or simply whispering "There is no charge tonight, sir." I'd bow gratefully and then conclude the evening with a film at the nearby Scala Cinema.

There I saw a wealth of pictures I'd never known of—*Les Enfants du Paradis, La Ronde, Quai des Brumes, Salaire de la Peur* among many others—German, Italian, and American included. Their complexities of form, human behavior, and exotic emotion would often occur to me years later—in images, even in flashes of dialogue—as I worked at my own plots and the relations of fictional characters. Incidentally when literary critics discuss the influences upon a given writer, they're inclined to limit themselves to books they assume the writer has read. In the past century however more and more of us have been as profoundly influenced by the films we saw, especially in our youth, as by any particular book (childhood reading is another much-overlooked influence).

Some of those evenings I'd share with a friend who'd, like me, come back to town early—Jim Griffin remained my chief friend among the Americans; and two of my Merton friends from New Zealand, Kees Westrate and Jeremy Commons, were often in town to join me for a still-bright short drive out across Port Meadow to the Trout Inn. It was nowhere near so famous then as now, with its present busloads of harried tourists; and it was easy enough to arrive there before dusk when the place was empty and sit on the pub's river-edge and gaze across the narrow stream to the opposite grassy bank where Alice had in fact begun to enter Wonderland.

Though I'd loved the book since my eighth-grade teacher had read it to us, I'd only recently learned of Mr. Dodgson's powerful love for Alice Liddell, the child for whom he'd told the tale, and the poignancy of his offering this ingenious work to her as a token of his deep devotion (she was only ten when he told the story). The chance to be so near the site of this enduring invention on a series of beautiful summer evenings, and with likable friends, was yet another privilege of the past full year.

A number of evenings, though, were spent in contented reading of the fiction I felt so bent on acquiring to feed my own hopes as a writer. I'd read voraciously as a child and a young man; but fired by David Cecil's enthusiasm, I read all the Tolstoy I'd not previously known and, again, almost all of Hardy. Among David's other prime loves were Jane Austen, Emily Brontë, Joseph Conrad, and Henry James (David had after all been sixteen when James died; and his father-in-law had known the man, two fairly incredible discoveries for a student like me to whom James seemed as old as Fielding and a good deal harder to read). So I proceeded through *Emma* with pleasure and admiration; but as I tried to push on, the next two or three Austen novels failed to lure me in. More accurately, I failed to be lured by their obvious skill and their persistent concern with the early plights of young women. It was both a matter of limited taste on my part and a maybe understandable lack of interest in her subjects; in any case I managed to conceal my failure from David. And while there were acres of Henry James which mostly failed to move me (though oddly the difficult late novels did, most powerfully), Conrad has remained a lifelong favorite as well as Defoe whom David had rightly made so irresistible in his lectures.

There were one or two more visits to Redmayne in Burford. By then I'd begun to wonder about Pamela's own personal life—her sexuality (if she had an ongoing sex life) and the apparent isolation which she worked hard to combat with the sporadic company of each year's new crop of Rhodesters. She had a particular friend named Katherine Watson who seemed to be in her early forties. Katherine was sometimes mutely present in the house and at the table when I'd stay. A woman with prematurely white hair and obvious intelligence, when she could be lured into conversation, the nature of Katherine's own life never clarified; and I came to wonder if she was a romantic partner of Pamela's. I hope they had delights, that I never witnessed, in one another; but they're both gone now and

I'll never know. It's certain that I never felt the slightest sexual interest on Pamela's part in any of us young men, but I'm compelled by a recent discovery to admit that I could have been wrong. I was astonished to learn from one of my Oxford friend John Bayley's memoirs that he was at one time engaged to Katherine, not long after she'd left the convent in which she'd been living.

On otherwise unplanned evenings—weather permitting—I'd drive up to Woodstock and, as I've noted, lie out by the gorgeous lake, with the Churchills' great palace looming to my left, and read till the late dark of summer forced me back to Headington. By early October, though, my cravings for solitude had waned into outright loneliness— almost a sense of abandonment, so far from home (my letters to Mother and Bill, reread now, have caught me unawares with the intensity of my longing for home). Without quite knowing it, I was slowly being inducted into the writer's life with its unavoidable isolation and its demand for internal resources that can so easily be replaced by drink, other drugs, and the supreme narcotic of other human bodies.

12

THEN MY SECOND YEAR commenced with Michael's arrival in his own two-room set at the Kirkbys'. I've dealt with the first year in such full detail because it was, till then, the most important year of my life—emotional, intellectual, and (surprisingly, given the slim amount of fiction I completed) likewise so far as my writing was concerned. When I recovered—in the previous autumn—from my imaginary cancer, I'd managed to get as close as I'd ever come to a final peace with Dad's death. The terrible memories of his last two weeks, when I was with him in the hospital most of the days and all

Mike Jordan and I, at the gate to our Headington digs on Sandfield Road. I was always mildly baffled to note the British insistence on surrounding one's living quarters with walls, fences, and gates. However small your plot of ground, you enclosed it with an unmistakable indication of your right to privacy within your walls—and that in a country which seemed, to me in the 1950s, the epitome of safety compared with the States. The picture was taken by our landlady at my request. Mike's papers and necktie indicate that he's off for town to study; my open-necked shirt suggests that I'll be reading and/or writing in our digs. My display of an incipient but unmistakable belly marks my growing addiction to the tasty Indian food (with a great deal of fried rice) which we've discovered. It also marks me as my mother's son—the men in her family, the Rodwells of Warren County, were known for "the Rodwell paunch"; and I'm clearly bound in that direction, even at age twenty-three.

the nights, are still capable—five decades later—of replaying themselves in my mind; but they no longer bring on my old desperation at
being so helpless to ease him or my still baffled guilt that, there at the
end of his life, he seemed to want only me—not Mother—with him
(my brother was then considered too young, by the family elders, for
hospital visits in such a dire situation). And by the fall of 1956, that particular shackle had mostly dissolved from my ankle.

Meanwhile my friendship with Michael had gradually become—
for me—an old-fashioned romantic friendship of the sort I'd read
about in the school and college lives of Milton, Tennyson, or
Matthew Arnold (with the addition of a cooling reality which those
earlier men may or may not have experienced in their connections—
and I'm referring to Milton's intense friendship with Charles Diodati,
Tennyson's with Arthur Hallam, or Arnold's with Arthur Clough).
Michael's sense of our bond was always distinctly different from mine.
What we had was not a sexual relation; and all these years later,
despite the fact that we live on opposite sides of an ocean—and that
he's content in a second marriage with three grown children—we
meet at least annually and have still never got down to a thorough discussion of what we've meant to one another.

But that's a situation with which I've long since been at ease. From
the start I was the professional communicator; Michael was the agreeably taciturn, though frequently laughing and always strong-minded,
Briton. I think there must have been times when my attachment to
him was briefly onerous. But his unquestioned loyalty, over so long a
stretch, and his obvious enjoyment of our times together have spoken
more resonantly than any more analytic words he might have offered
about the value of our friendship.

By the end of our first year together, it was clear that, outside my
family, no other relation in my life had been more rewarding in so
many ways; and despite occasional mild disappointments, that's still
the case, I'm glad to say. The friendship had already taught me an
enormous amount about affection, love, steadfastness, wit, and
patience—not at once but slowly and largely in reflection. I'd never
been an especially patient person, and the necessity to learn the art of

self-restraint in a close relation—and to learn it from someone who taught me equanimity by quietly stepping back from any disagreement or unreasonable expectation—proved both difficult and invaluable (and I was never expected to provide a female emotional response, whatever that might be, in our relation; I was always another man, contentious when need be but peaceful by the end of a day).

The day Michael Jordan looked into Mob Quad 2:1 and said he didn't suppose I was interested in soccer was the most educational day, then, of my Oxford years. So far as my having, then or later, an active interest in the much-alleged homosexual crowd of Oxford under-graduates, I literally knew no other student who claimed to be queer (or appeared to be—it was some time before queer confessions became as common as weak jokes); and I couldn't have told you, till late in my third year, whether or not there was a queer pub or other gathering place in the city. The life I lived was my own rich satisfaction. (Despite the general heterosexual drift of the university, by the way, there was very little in the way of romantic connection between male and female students—partly because all colleges were then single-gender but also because it seemed to be a long-standing Oxford custom.)

I was further supported by the seriousness with which elders like David Cecil, Nevill Coghill, and Helen Gardner received me. The very structure of Oxford education in those years—with its imposed distance between teacher and pupil—meant that I could trust the friendship those teachers offered me and, yes, the liking which the two men expressed for my fiction. But the interest of David and Nevill came from men who were themselves widely respected writers; so I felt I could trust them in ways that had made it difficult to trust the aesthetic commendations of my American teachers of literature, none of whom was such a writer. That's not to demean the sincerity or the intelligence of my generous countrymen; it does say, however, that I'd always felt a sense that they were pushing my writing onward in at least a partial necessity to do so. I sat just under their eyes in class somewhere between three and five times per week. I was maybe the most serious student they had in a particular year, and I was so obviously hungry for affection and praise that they could hardly have refused me without overt cruelty.

Again, in Oxford I was a plainly grown man who was running his own life, though my teachers knew little about my incompetence to do so. I'd see those dons maybe six or eight times in a two-month term; and they each possessed a natural English reserve that had not come naturally to my sometimes fervent teachers at home. I knew what a small amount of good writing I'd accomplished by the age of twenty-three, I knew it was not all first-rate work, but I felt I could trust what lay just behind me and push on for much more. Now in case I seem to claim that I'd grown miraculously better in the course of a year, I'll add that some of my American friends found it a little amusing that I'd grown hyper-British in a very short time (not so British, though, as one of my American colleagues at Merton; he'd become a virtual rolled umbrella). I can say again, in defense, that through my whole life a certain family gene for sympathetic mimicry—my father was a master mimic—had led me, unconsciously at first, to assume the voice and sometimes the physical mannerisms of anyone whom I especially liked and spent much time with.

Partly I wanted my interlocutors to understand my words, so I'd use no outlandish Americanese in those days before American accents were common on British television, but mainly—I think—I almost wanted to *become* them. Was it a characteristic of, say, someone bound to be a writer—or at least some brand of constant observer? In childhood, for instance, I'd assume the dialect and tones of black people who worked in our family homes. If any one of them minded, they never told me, and those men and women freely told children to correct any out-of-line behavior. At Duke I'd do it with friends from the northeast, people whom we Southerners still thought of as Yankees (the Civil War, after all, had ended only sixty-eight years before my birth).

Now I was doing it with the British—and in a variety of British accents, from various regions and social classes of the whole United Kingdom. Never mind; I've had far worse temptations and have yielded to many. The moment an American friend stepped into the room, I was once more from North Carolina or New Jersey or Iowa, depending on their origins. Nonetheless in two further years of Oxford life, I'd worn out or outgrown my American clothes and acquired British trousers and sweaters from Marks and Spencer—or Marks and Sparks, as people called what was then Britain's most widespread cut-rate clothing chain.

I too owned a bamboo-handled umbrella (bought in New York two years earlier), I'd largely settled on an upper-middle-class accent, and sometimes I could feel my actual movements becoming British. I was growing less rangy and loping, more self-contained in my walk and gestures—the actions of a man on a small crowded island, not claiming excess space for himself. Never once, though, did I think of becoming a British subject. I could eventually see that my friend Jim Griffin was tilting in that direction. I loved where I was, at Merton and on Sandfield Road; but even in term time, surrounded by friends, I've noted how that pleasure nonetheless went through spells of missing home badly.

In my first year I'd splurged on the two long trips to Italy and the continental summer. The second year was spent almost entirely in town and at the university. Early in the first term of my second year, then, it became clear that—to do an adequate job on my thesis (and the B.Litt. was considered a two-year degree)—I'd need an unusual third year in residence. Apart from the academic reality—and why hadn't I seen its inevitability sooner?—I'm sure that my interest in Britain (the country and the people) had grown so genuine that I wished to extend my stay so long as the Rhodes Foundation would support me. A possible third year was the previously announced extent of their largess. Michael was due to leave Oxford in the coming spring; but other friends would remain—David and Nevill lived there, plus a clutch of the undergraduates I've mentioned—and by now the Kirkbys were becoming both fascinating to observe and warmhearted in their friendship. I felt more and more like a foster son of theirs, which was something I still needed to feel.

But I knew that my mother would be painfully disappointed by news of my intention to stay, and I waited till I'd settled various questions before telling her—would my application for third-year funding be successful, would Win Kirkby agree to my staying on with very little time away from Sandfield Road, was my academic work likely to prosper (I'd begun to think of turning toward work on a D.Phil. degree once I'd completed the B.Litt.); and could I find promising subjects to complete a volume with the seventy-odd pages of more or less finished stories I had in my drawer?

First, though, I plunged into the thesis. Miss Gardner met with me early in the fall term and discussed the shape of my work to date. I'm not sure whether it was her personal practice with graduate students or an overall practice of the English faculty; in any case she let me know that she'd eventually read perhaps the first third of my thesis but no more. By way of explanation, she noted that there was the real chance she might be appointed as one of my final examiners; and she didn't want to examine a thesis which she'd thoroughly influenced throughout its length. That struck me as a healthy procedure. We sketched out a possible plan for the chapters I was likely to need in an adequate study of a poem as complex as *Samson.* Then we agreed to meet once a month, for sherry if nothing more; and I was on my way.

Given that the play is composed on the models of Greek tragedy as written by Aeschylus, Sophocles, and Euripides, I knew that I'd now have to read all their surviving plays—some for the first time. Though the surviving Greek texts are only a small proportion of what we know to have been a far larger treasury of plays by the three men, it was clear that Milton had read all the Greek tragedies we presently possess and was continuously guided by them, especially in matters of form. As far as my reading was concerned, there was one large hitch—I didn't know classical Greek and would not have time to learn it. Nor did Miss Gardner expect me to do so (I doubt that she herself knew Greek well). As an English major at Duke, to be sure, I'd read four or five of the most famous plays in translation. Now I entered the long tunnel of consuming a variety of translations of all the surviving others.

Various prior essays on *Samson* had suggested that Milton was more influenced by Sophocles than either of the others. In my own reading, however, I began to see that, not only was Milton hardly subservient to any one ancient master, he had in fact invented a quite original role for his Chorus, one that lent a new emotional depth to his tragedy and made it not merely a modern imitation of an older model but a devastatingly fresh study of human failure and gradual redemption (salvation in the act of suicide).

Soon Miss Gardner declared that my findings were of considerable interest. She likewise endorsed my readiness to commence writing the thesis. So I began—and at once encountered a roadblock, one that many scholars encounter at a similar point in their work. Because I'd set out to answer a question—what's the role of the Chorus in *Samson Agonistes?*—I soon discovered that, in my extensive prior reading, I'd answered the question. The fact that I now had to write a thesis of nearly two hundred pages—a watertight argument that laid out the means by which I'd come to my solution—soon balked me. The writing became harder and harder because it became more and more boring by the day. Near the end of the first term, I had few finished pages behind me; and with much relief I drove to Brighton to spend Christmas week with Michael and his mother.

The fall term had not been devoid of worldly concerns, though they seem to have had little effect on me or my friends. In late October '56, Hungary launched a popular rising against Soviet occupation. The rising was brutally repressed by Khrushchev's tanks but not before many young Hungarians fled the country. Numbers of their best students arrived in Oxford and promptly began to study in various colleges. One of them was named George Radda, a quiet but winning man. He was quickly absorbed by one of the groups whom I often joined for coffee after lunch. And by the kind of eventual action of a fate to which many of us are subject (often without knowing it), George would become one of the Oxford scientists crucially involved in the development of magnetic radiation imagery—the now omnipresent MRI—a revolutionary mode of soft-tissue imaging which would be used importantly by my neurosurgeon in the removal of a large malignant tumor from within my spinal cord some thirty years after George's flight from Hungary.

Also in late October '56, Britain joined with France and Israel to retake Suez from the Egyptian control which had ensued upon Nasser's seizure of the canal in July. Those allies were quickly forced, however—largely by pressure from the United States—to withdraw from the canal in humiliation. Meanwhile Egypt sank numerous ships in the canal, leaving it impassable—with oppressive results on the transport of vital fuel oil to Europe. The Cold War had seldom felt colder; yet I don't recall that I was especially depressed (why, I can't recall, considering my tenuous relations with the American draft). The chief difference felt by any resident of Britain who owned a car was the start, soon after the Suez debacle, of petrol rationing. It didn't affect me drastically, though I did have to apply to my local rationing board for an extra coupon to permit me to drive down to visit my Merton friend Ron Tamplin in the TB sanatorium near Windsor Great Park where he was spending a few months, dealing with a recurrence of boyhood tuberculosis.

The third important world event for Oxford Americans during that same fall was the presidential election. Adlai Stevenson was running, for the second time, against Eisenhower; and I sat up through the night with many other Rhodesters at Rhodes House and watched the slow returns on TV. With his elegant command of the spoken language and his sane liberal proposals (in the face of an Eisenhower White House that had often seemed listless, if not gravely somnolent), Stevenson had been the favorite candidate of almost all my friends in the university; but however late we sat up near radios and televisions in Rhodes House, we couldn't hand him victory. He lost, with the same valorous grace he'd shown at the time of his loss in 1952; and only when he came to Oxford for an honorary degree the following spring and was entertained at a Rhodes House reception did I get a mild shock to my sense of his famed degree of civilized discourse (I took Auden to the party and introduced him to Stevenson; the smiling man shook Auden's hand but gave no other sign of knowing who W. H. Auden was).

*   *   *

More helpfully in those externally unnerving months, Lord David invited me for the first of my high-table dinners with him in New College. Such dinners then were truly high occasions—the best kind of English cooking, followed by an actual dessert in the Senior Common Room, complete with not only dessert but numerous fine cheeses, much old brandy, and—of all things—an offering of snuff. You sprinkled it along the side of your thumb and snorted, hard. With my long history of uncontrollable sneezing, I declined (I doubt that a dinner for eighteenth-century gentlemen would have differed significantly, though the empire then would have been growing, not shrinking as now).

Till then, I'd not heard the full force of David's conversation with his contemporary colleagues, men such as John Bayley, who'd soon marry the novelist and philosopher Iris Murdoch (and eventually publish eloquent memoirs of his care for her through years of premature Alzheimer's), and most strikingly, the philosopher Stuart Hampshire who could engage David at his own level of intelligence, wisdom, and wit—many sharp edges on all sides and a great deal of laughter. I noted that, in response to some colleague's objection to a dubious claim of David's, his lordship's thumbs fidgeted at hummingbird speed, his narrowed eyes blinked as fast; and he said—in a reply worthy of Groucho Marx—"Ah, but I stop at nothing!"

Earlier in the fall in New York, Diarmuid Russell had experienced a heart attack but was still able to inform me, in the midst of international bad news (and his own), that *The Paris Review* was accepting "A Chain of Love." I was greatly cheered by what felt like a certified stamp on my forehead. There was no certainty when a fledgling quarterly might use such a long story, and it would hardly pay much; but maybe now I could cease the frequent dreams of acceptance letters in my Merton pigeonhole, and I could tell anyone with doubt on his face that, yes, I was now an official young writer. The other stories in Diarmuid's hands, however, were not yet finding homes (and those were the glory days of American magazines; far more of them than now published serious fiction).

13

IN THE FACE OF those realities, I'd recalled my and
Michael's sightings of Stephen Spender the previous Easter in Venice.
In addition to the writing of his poetry and a large body of essays and
reviews, Spender also co-edited the magazine *Encounter* which had
rapidly become one of the liveliest literary and political monthlies of
the time. In the fall then I sent him three of my short stories and
brashly suggested my willingness to come to London and discuss
them with him. He replied to say that he'd be out of town for a good
while but would contact me on his return. And he did. So in mid-
December, just before the three-hour drive to Brighton, I went to
London and met with Spender. Till then I'd read a number of his
early poems and, above all, his autobiography *World Within World*, as
much admired today as it was fifty years ago.

I was clearly contacting him in the hopes of placing a story in his
magazine. Almost as much I was hoping for more professional comment on the work, which is why I included a copy of "A Chain of
Love." Though I'd learned in his memoir of an early history of intense
male relations, I'd also read that he was married for a second time and
had two young children. He'd implied in *World Within World* that
marriage had shut down his intimate male relations; and I was naïve
enough in the understanding of erotic realities to believe the implication (most of the world, then, was as uninformed as I). I certainly
had no intention of reigniting banked coals; my own emotions were
firmly committed.

I called on Spender in his office then, in Panton Street just off the
Haymarket, two blocks from Piccadilly; and we went out at once for a
good lunch at an amusing all-vegetarian restaurant nearby—he was
not a vegetarian. We laughed a good deal when he ordered (and
commended to me) an item called nut cutlets which proved to be

delicious. I can't recall the name of the restaurant, only that the conductor Antal Dorati was seated nearby (as though nut cutlets exerted widespread magnetism on distinguished artists) and that Spender's response to my stories was encouraging. Like David Cecil, he'd turned a working writer's eye on my pages; and he asked if "A Chain of Love" was available for publication. I told him of the interest of *The Paris Review*; but faced with an apparent interest on his part—and given the distinction of *Encounter* (and the chance of its paying a good deal more), I may have said that its fate was not sure. I'm fairly convinced that I didn't reveal the fact that Diarmuid had said the story was accepted at *The Paris Review*.

At this point, so many years later—and in the absence of a diary or other records—I'm entering here on an honest uncertainty. I've mentioned *The Paris Review*'s youth (it was three years old) and my awareness, at least, that little magazines died with the speed of fruit flies. *Encounter* was virtually the same age; but it had already won international notice for its superb offerings in poetry, fiction, and political commentary; and it seemed to be firmly financed (it would be years before I knew that it, like Radio Free Europe, was largely funded by the CIA). Furthermore it was an English magazine; and I was living in England, surrounded by English friends. Its famous co-editor was my host at lunch, I'd sent him my manuscripts months earlier, and he seemed to be showing genuine interest in publishing my till-then best work.

So I think, again, that I told Spender "A Chain of Love" might be available—I'd need to check with my agent. I was vaguely aware of differences between U.S. and English rights in some literary publications. Mainly though I was flying blind, and I made a bad mistake in waffling on the matter of the story's freedom. Whatever, Spender did say that it would be difficult to sell such a long story to his colleagues on the magazine (his co-editor was Irving Kristol, and Dwight Macdonald was spending a year in London as a visiting editor). He'd have to let me know as soon as he could present the story to his colleagues. A little sheepishly, I nodded my powerfully conflicted hopes for his success. In the face of the very real poverty visited on me by a previous year of expensive gallivanting, a good deal of my silent conflict centered round the fact that Spender had mentioned what *Encounter* might pay for such a long story—the present equivalent of $865, an almost literal stack of gold to a man in my situation.

By then we were at the end of a winey lunch; and Spender suggested that—since I had my car, and his day at *Encounter* was done—I could drive him to his house, meet his children, and see his pictures (we'd talked a good deal of our interest in collecting art, an interest I'd lacked the funds to realize, except for a fragment of a marble Roman Venus which I'd bought for fifty dollars in Cambridge, Massachusetts some three years ago). We drove north then into the respectable, but hardly glamorous, district called St. John's Wood and on to his pleasant nineteenth-century house on Loudoun Road. The children were still at school, as I recall; but Francesca, the live-in Italian maid, served us coffee in the comfortably furnished sitting room. Its chief feature was a concert grand piano, the prime possession of his wife Natasha Litvin who was still performing publicly and who'd be in America doing just that for several more weeks.

When the children soon arrived, we struck it off at once. A married friend of mine—the father of three—always says "Only bachelors have ever known how to rear children, and they forget as soon as they marry." I've mostly had good luck with children—mainly because I've tended to treat them, benignly, as if they're adults. Since their parents almost never think of them as grown-up, the youngsters can hardly avoid liking me. The Spenders' son was Matthew; the daughter was Lizzie. In fact it became uncannily clear, in the course of the afternoon, that we were arranged in a remarkable set of chronological stairs—Stephen was forty-eight, I was twenty-four, Matthew was twelve, Lizzie was six, and Francesca's son Dimitri (who was playing among us) was three. The numerological reality seemed a Jungian blessing on our day, and Matthew was especially impressed.

Matt—then also known as Matteo—had the grave seriousness of a lanky boy just on the edge of puberty, but he welcomed chances to laugh; and when he accompanied me on a tour of the numerous paintings, drawings, and etchings in the house, his comments were often keen (of a Henry Moore drawing of his father as a lean, almost hypnotically focused young man, Matt said "It makes me see how much I wish I'd known Dad then"). Lizzie was a lively charmer, much given to laughter and a normal young girl's fantasy-love of horses (she didn't yet have a horse). Like most children, what they eventually seemed to enjoy in my company was my tendency to tell them stories from my own childhood in quite a different world. I'd noticed, long before, that children find it impossible to imagine that their elders were ever really young. Any narrative proof of the fact is generally welcome to them and can prove magnetic, if the narrating adult is even mildly amusing.

When at last I said I must head back to Oxford, Stephen and the children asked me to stay for dinner and I did. The four of us lingered in the downstairs dining room; and Francesca served us a grand meal—roasted lamb chops, risotto, salad, and a silken crème caramel. The chance for Italian home-cooking was again irresistible (though after college food, dog chow might have proved welcome); and the air round the table was relaxed and frequently hilarious. When the time came for the children to retire, they seconded Stephen's invitation for me to stay the night—the drive back to Oxford would take an hour and a half. I'd brought nothing by way of sleeping equipment, so I promised them—Francesca included—that I'd come back soon for a night. Their enthusiasm for a weekend's visit seemed, and ultimately proved, to be genuine; and my exile's yearning for family was again aroused.

Back in Oxford in mid-January, I was in my sitting room on Sandfield Road, reading a month-old copy of *The Warren Record*, the county weekly from my most-native-of-all-heaths (my aunt Martha Reynolds Price had sent me a subscription). As many small newspapers then did in December, the paper published a column of children's letters to Santa Claus with the usual requests for Christmas presents—toy guns, baseball mitts, dolls, tea sets. As I proceeded through the familiar details, I suddenly saw how to end a story I'd been thinking of for more than a week. It would be a story about an illegitimately pregnant girl; and my sudden apprehension was that the story would be about a young woman whom I'd portrayed, in her adolescence, in "A Chain of Love."

Her name, again, was Rosacoke Mustian; and she, like me and my parents, was from Warren County. Her reluctant boyfriend was named Wesley Beavers; and somehow I'd narrate the details that brought Rosa to her realization of the unwanted pregnancy and her eventual decision, I knew at once, would resolve itself in Rosacoke's mind as she played the familiar role of the Virgin Mary in the kind of small-church pageant in which I'd participated more than once in my childhood. When I recorded my finding in the notes I kept for possible fiction, I added this—

If I finish the story and it's fine, then when I have a whole book, I can put "A Chain of Love" as the first story and this one as the last.

Quickly the entries in my notebook began to multiply, all concerned with the new story. And a week later the entries are dated from London. As promised I'd returned to the Spenders' house to spend a few days with the family. Stephen, his children, Dimitri, and I spent a Sunday with a good long walk on the rolling terrain of Hampstead Heath (with another glimpse of the Vermeer at Kenmore), and a drive past the house where Stephen had spent his boyhood. Then he and I passed a bibulous and cheerful long evening with his friend the distinguished essayist Cyril Connolly. I would see Cyril a number of times in the next few years, but that first meeting is especially vivid for me still.

He and Stephen had worked together in the early days of their celebrated and historically important magazine *Horizon*; and their work now was separate—Stephen at *Encounter* and Cyril as a regular book columnist for *The Sunday Times*—but their mutual affection was apparent, despite the fact that Cyril's slight seniority (and his murderous wit) still laced his remarks with ironies and insults which Stephen appeared to enjoy without reservation—at least he laughed heartily and never riposted in kind. Cyril took the classic British

Stephen Spender and RP on Hampstead Heath, January 1957. Matthew Spender, who was then twelve, took the picture in the midst of a long walk on the Heath one bright Sunday morning (Lizzie Spender, age six, was also with us, as was Dimitri, age three, the fine Italian cook's son). It was my first visit to the Spender household and a happy one—as they'd all prove to be. Here Stephen looks half a head taller than I but he wasn't. Maybe he was standing on a small hillock or a root of the tree behind us—he was six foot, two; I was five, ten and a half. Some of the excitement I read on my face in the picture results from the goodness of the visit; the remainder comes from the fact that I'd only just conceived the story that would—some five years later—become my first novel, A Long and Happy Life.

Older School Boy role in their friendship, Stephen played the Hapless New Boy; and they each clearly relished a conscious assumption of their roles, especially in the presence of a new consumer like me who'd never heard their best tales.

At our first lunch together, Stephen told the story Leonard Woolf had told him about his first outing with young Virginia Stephen, the daughter of Sir Leslie Stephen. They took a train trip to somewhere in the country, the day went well; but on the way home, in their private compartment aboard the train, Virginia was struck by a dreadful need to pee. It was one of the old carriages with no corridor, thus no hope of a loo. Of course Virginia didn't speak of her pain till she reached the point of cutting loose in her floor-length skirts. Only then could she burst out—"I'm dying, Leonard." When he understood the cause, he took his copy of that day's *Times* and made a huge circular funnel with no open end. Appalled but overwhelmed, Virginia turned her face to the landscape, squatted above Leonard's improvised loo, lifted her skirts, drained her bladder, and threw the loaded funnel out the window. "There was no way not to get married after that," Leonard had said.

In fact even in private I never heard Stephen say worse about Cyril than the incontestable fact that you had to be careful with your prize books when Cyril came to dinner or one of the most valuable might be inclined to follow him home.

In all our meetings I was lucky never to come in for one of the Connolly barbs, though when I told David Cecil of my first meeting with Cyril, David paused at length, put his long tongue firmly in one cheek, blinked rapidly as he did before launching a sudden discovery, and then said "Cyril is not as nice as he looks"—a thoroughly complicated Cecilian warning: Cyril was notoriously ugly, with a short plump body topped by a head that looked almost comically more like a Greek satyr (or the satyr-like Socrates, amazingly so) than anything remotely British.

And speaking of prized books, eventually Stephen would give me a first edition of the intensely personal and self-demeaning but wise document *The Unquiet Grave*. It was initially published in 1944 by

Horizon under the name Palinurus, a pseudonym soon penetrated by all its literate readers. And many years later, I note that the inscription in the copy which Stephen gave me says, in Cyril's large clear script—

> *For Reynolds Price*
> *with affection*
> *admiration*
>   *And in the*
> *expectation of*
>   *benefits to come*
> *from his friend*
>   *Palinurus*
> *'he is not dead, but sleepeth'*
> *London 1961*

An even more substantial work had long been awaited from, and by, Cyril (who semi-promised it for years); but it was never written. And long before he could have known of my interest in the Gospel of Mark, his "he is not dead but sleepeth" is a paraphrase of Jesus' remark near the apparently dead body of Jairus' daughter in Mark 5:39 (the King James version), "The damsel is not dead but sleepeth." I'm glad to note that Cyril remains—with David Cecil and my father—one of the three most continuously intelligent, originally witty, and verbally elegant talkers I've known.

On that first weekend visit, I met another of Stephen's friends, considerably younger than he but also funny and famously gifted—the painter John Craxton. John had come to public notice in his early twenties, along with his then friend Lucian Freud, through his haunting quasi-surreal drawings and paintings of British landscape. As soon as the Second War ended, and continental travel was possible, John made his first trip to Greece and seldom looked back. By the time Stephen took me to meet John, he was living on the top floor of his parents' house in Hampstead, sporadically at work on several large oils of Greek shepherds and fishermen.

On that first visit, John also showed me dozens of small and inexplicably economical portrait sketches of Greeks whom he met briefly in cafés and wherever else, young men who (not yet entirely Westernized) could easily have stepped from Homer's battle scenes, the somber tragedies of Aeschylus, or even the raucous ithyphallic comedies of Aristophanes—their adamant dignity and craving for life was still that firmly intact and vividly conveyed in a few pencil lines. My first turn through John's sketchbooks was among my earliest experiences of the true collector's longing—at once, I wanted almost all these drawings.

Meanwhile, since I'd ultimately spend a good deal of time there, I'll note a few characteristics of the extraordinary Craxton household. John's father was Harold Craxton, one of the most respected piano teachers of his time at the Royal Academy of Music. Between pupils, he wandered round the large three-story house with the distinctly vague air of a cartoon character—say, Mr. Magoo. Likewise in residence were John's sister Janet, principal oboist in the BBC Symphony, and—somewhat later—their brother Anthony, a senior producer for BBC Television, frequently in charge of programs involving the royal family. John's mother Essie—who often seemed harassed but was never less than quietly masterful—somehow managed to hold this unparalleled artistic menagerie together. Among them, almost from our first meeting, John became a valued friend.

Stephen himself became, in the few days of that first visit to his home, a friend who'd remain impeccably loyal for the rest of his life (and he died peacefully a year after I last saw him, when he was eighty-six). I've noted that I learned, from his autobiography when I was hardly out of my teens, how his past had been marked by a complex sexuality. Without burdening the reader unduly, I can honestly condense the nature of our early relation by recording that, from the day we met, I was aware that Stephen was signaling the possibility of a sexual intimacy.

The signals, though, came from the other side of the room (literally) in nervously laughing and thoroughly shy remarks. As hints, the signals were never pressing—they seemed offered almost idly as tests of a particular situation—and when I, first, ignored them and then made it politely clear that my feelings were otherwise involved, the cloud quickly dispersed with no ill will on either side. Despite the fact that Stephen was then twice my age—and knew so many men and women who were far more accomplished than the young man I was (Auden and Isaiah Berlin had been his closest contemporary friends since their undergraduate days)—we nonetheless had so much in common, in our lives and work, that an enduring friendship grew when one of its possible directions was shut off at the start.

By far the chief subjects of our earliest conversations were our reading, our love of music, of the great masters of twentieth-century painting, and our friends, eager to laugh at almost any moment—sympathetically, ironically, or mercilessly. In retrospect I'd note that my first responses to Stephen were virtually identical with my last. In 1994 I made my first return trip to England in many years—ten years after I'd taken to a wheelchair with the remains of spinal cancer—and saw Stephen back in the Loudoun Road dining room with Natasha (he was eighty-five; they'd been married for fifty-three years, and whatever waves had troubled the marriage seemed mainly calmed in mutual old age).

Stephen had a passion for the workings of the independent liberal mind, with all its most harmless foods and pleasures, like that of no one else I've known (the Spenders were an old liberal family). A department of that passion was his constant search for something that's grown increasingly impossible to find—the kind of romantic friendship with which I'd also been increasingly involved since my own early days at Oxford—the physically imposing friend who'd share one's deepest enthusiasms and engage with one in adventures that might range from physical love to dangerous gestures in the effort to aid another friend or even helpless strangers.

In *World Within World*, Stephen describes just such a gesture. When his former partner, whom he calls Jimmy Younger (the real name was Tony Hyndman), feels abandoned by Stephen's impulsive first marriage, Jimmy flees to Spain to fight with the International Brigades in the Civil War and is promptly caught and threatened with execution. Stephen quickly follows him to Spain, and considerably endangers himself, in the attempt to rescue Jimmy (the rescue succeeded, Stephen's marriage promptly failed, and the remainder of Jimmy's life was a sad downslide).

The fact that Stephen's poetry was always subject to almost violently opposing views from his readers—a paradox that virtually silenced his publication of poems in the 1950s and '60s—was a humiliating sadness for him; and I can only be glad he wasn't alive to read the recent British reviews of his posthumous *Collected Poems*. For an American who's loved, studied, and written poetry with attentive passion for more than six decades, it was astonishing to see how almost completely those reviewers failed to recognize the kind of poem Stephen Spender was always trying to write and often did—a neo-Romantic lyric, all but anti-Modernist in its tones, rhythms, and actual vocabulary and profound in its feeling. It's my conviction that, in time—when the enemies he accumulated so readily in the course of a long and politically stormy public life in Britain and America have likewise died (he published a number of intemperate and often hilariously sardonic reviews in both countries and thereby earned a portion of his treatment)—several dozen of his poems will be seen as strikingly original and piercingly true to a particular time, place, and extraordinary mind. Of how many continuously anthologized poets can we say more?

During the remainder of my first stay on Loudoun Road, there was a dinner with Malcolm Muggeridge, who was then editor of *Punch* and by no means the doctrinaire Christian he later became. Toward the end of a good deal of wine, I recall his saying to Stephen words to this effect—"Don't you know how fond you can become of a man whose wife you're fucking?" Stephen laughed nervously and nodded. There was a dinner with Cyril Connolly and Lionel Trilling, who was in England without his widely dreaded wife Diana (Stephen and his friends had heard with relief that she hated flying). Trilling himself was quietly polite, though he gave off a soberly academic whiff of disapproval of these laughing English writers; and they of course could never forget that he'd written an entire humorless book about E. M. Forster without perceiving that Forster was queer.

Still, I enjoyed a Sunday afternoon's visit to the Royal Academy show with Trilling and Stephen and a Sunday-afternoon lunch at Loudoun Road with Trilling, Cyril, and Rose Macaulay, who was by then an ancient-seeming woman (only five years older than I am now but as shrunken as the Cumean sibyl); her recent masterpiece, *The Towers of Trebizond*, was a novel I'd much admired and have continued to read. Also at the table for Francesca's ample spread was Sonia Orwell, the widow of George Orwell. I'd see Sonia many more times in my last eighteen months in England and always found her good-looking, warm, and funny—never the difficult and inscrutable person she apparently became in her last years. Toward the end of my visit, I began to wonder at the furious pace of Stephen's social life and slowly came to realize—over many years—that he literally craved the mental stimulus of very bright friends: fine conversation, in a single word. I also learned that—infallibly—at the end of the busiest day, he'd go down to the cleared dining table and work till the early hours—on poems, his journal, or a short novel he'd just begun. It was ultimately published as *Engaged in Writing* and concerned itself with the grave, and comical, Cold War–cultural problems that arose in the Venice conference which he was attending when I first saw him.

So my first stay at the Spender household—some ten days—ended with our attendance at a performance of Beethoven's *Fidelio* by the Sadler's Wells Opera. *Fidelio* had been among Stephen's highest pleasures since his early visits to Germany and Austria. This performance in January '57 was sung in English by competent British performers. And while it had—almost unavoidably—stretches of musical and dramatic excitement, it was no match for my own prior *Fidelio*, a thrilling performance with Kirsten Flagstad which I saw and heard Bruno Walter conduct at the Met in March '51. Nonetheless the evening provided a useful marker for the start of a friendship that would help us both powerfully through four more decades of life and work.

A final marker of that long week was the fact that, on my last morning in London, I went with Stephen to the Zwemmer Gallery to see a small show of the etchings Picasso had made, years earlier, as illustrations for an edition of the *Metamorphoses* of Ovid. Those uncomplicated line drawings of superb elegance were so cheap that Stephen bought several; and even I, broke as I was, bought one: the fall of Phaeton in the chariot of the sun for only twenty guineas (a guinea in the currency of the '50s was a pound and a shilling, hence twenty-one shillings). I also got to meet Mr. Zwemmer himself, a white-haired and distinguished feature of the London gallery world whom I'd eventually see more than once again.

14

B ACK IN OXFORD by mid-January '57, Michael and I were hard at work on our separate chores—his final exams and my thesis—but we often met for lunch in the Open Market off the High near Carfax. There was an upstairs diner called George's Café (pronounced "cafe" to rhyme with *strafe*) run by a burdened, though cheerful, family with a lovely tall daughter. Their clientele, in a space no larger than the average American living room, consisted of workingmen—masons, lorry drivers, and dustmen among them—and students. Each day there was a single menu with no more than two choices for your meal, inscribed on a blackboard by the door. You paid your small sum of money in advance, sat at one of the few long green-painted tables with whomever might have got there before you, and waited till the lovely daughter brought your plate. Whatever the blackboard had said, what you got was mainly potatoes, the odd slice of carrot, a few bits of pastry, and maybe a lump or two of boiled mutton.

Fairly wretched food if truth be told; but the attraction for most of the student patrons was twofold—a belly-filling plug of hot edibles for very little money and a certain sense of matey mingling with the working class. A bulky man in his workman's cap might jostle your elbow, grin, and ask for the mustard in his country-Oxford accent (there were virtually no immigrants working in Oxford then). Ah, you were living!—and on a plain that stretched far below the base of your Tower which, however you denied it, was indeed carved most meticulously and magnificently from the finest ivory available in the Western World at least.

Yet with all that suspect sense of camaraderie, my most indelible memory of George's is that a red-haired American from another college entered the café in late January and told me that he'd heard on the BBC just now that Arturo Toscanini had died in suburban New York only two months short of his ninetieth birthday. For educated Americans of our generation that was genuine news, and for me it has its own special pitch and pathos. Younger readers may not know that Toscanini was among the two or three supreme orchestral conductors of the twentieth century. After a long maturation in Italy, primarily as a conductor of opera, he'd come to America and conducted a brilliant seven years at the Met; then departing from the Met—primarily it seems because of a love affair gone bad with the queen of the house, the American diva Geraldine Farrar—he spent an equally superb nine years with the New York Philharmonic. He returned in the early 1930s to Europe for extraordinary productions of Wagner, Mozart, and Verdi at Bayreuth and Salzburg (a number of those performances can still be heard on surprisingly listenable recordings).

And when fascism triumphed in Europe, he was lured back to America where the National Broadcasting Company created a first-rate orchestra for him. In weekly Sunday-afternoon broadcasts (which I began to hear, without fail, in my early teens), he proceeded to bring to an enormous radio audience often astonishing performances of the standard repertoire of what we now called classical European music. I recall the first afternoon when I sat on our living-room floor alone and heard him conduct Brahms's First Symphony; that great opening sweep was likely my initial revelation of what such music held in wait for the remainder of my life. And Toscanini continued to retain that eminence—in my life and the nation's—on into his eighties, and in 1950 he took the NBC Symphony on an unprecedented tour of the States.

As a high-school senior I seized the opportunity; drove to Richmond, Virginia and stayed in the ornate Jefferson Hotel (which still had live alligators in the lobby), and heard the maestro lead his ninety-odd men in the Mosque auditorium. Though he was then eighty-three, he conducted a demanding program that included memorable performances of Beethoven's *Eroica* and Tchaikovsky's *Pathétique*, followed eventually by a single encore—an unannounced but instantly audience-rousing performance of "Dixie." The song had not then acquired quite the political significance it now exerts (the Civil War, which destroyed much of Richmond, was not a century behind us). Nonetheless it was a performance that—despite Toscanini's international standing as a public enemy of Hitler and Mussolini—would now be impossible to play, both for the conductor and much of his audience.

I joined in the clamorous ovation, featuring Rebel yells, throughout the old Confederate anthem and for long after the beautiful old man tottered into the wings—no conductor has ever rivaled his physical beauty or perhaps his often gratified hunger for beautiful young women. Among my strongest memories, now in my own old age, is that he left the stage finally with a ramrod-straight back after so much exertion in the cause of beauty, passionately pursued (through the long evening he had never once touched the supportive railing round his podium).

The news of his death, then, was the first time I'd experienced a shocking tear in the fabric of my love of the arts. Here early in the twenty-first century there are persistent detractors who've attacked Toscanini's old unchallenged eminence. And of course he had his faults—an occasional hyperfeverish propulsion—but an immense archive of his performances survives; and while I sometimes hear the faults, I also hear an unrivaled clarity of texture, a gorgeous awareness of the powers of varied rhythm (when appropriate); but above all his burning conviction that the finest music—orchestral, operatic, or choral—is the highest form of human expression.

How lucky I was then, like millions of other Americans, to learn in youth so many of the supreme cornerstones of Western music at the hands of a purveyor of such genius. And how I wish he were still available on weekend afternoons—or whenever—to reach new generations of young listeners, the vast majority of whom are enslaved to kinds of music which (however good some of it may be) have left them ignorant of the culture's greatest treasures. In George's Café, when I was two weeks short of my twenty-fourth birthday, I could hardly see this far; but I had a strong sense of what I'd lost.

In the remainder of that winter and spring, I went on dealing with two personally urgent matters—the thesis and any future I might have as a writer. In mid-January Stephen told me that he'd established, with his co-editors, that *Encounter* now definitely wanted to publish "A Chain of Love." And only a few days later, Diarmuid informed me that *The Paris Review* would publish the story in the next issue—or the next issue thereafter (not a heartwarming commitment, it seemed to me). At that point I made up my own wobbly mind and let Stephen know that, given my American agent's involvement in the sale of the story to *The Paris Review*, I felt committed to allowing the story to go forward there. Should *Encounter* like any of my other stories, it would be most welcome to them. Stephen didn't seem to feel cheated in the matter and said he'd let me know about the other stories.

Meanwhile, with the selflessness that would mark all his dealings with me for nearly four decades to come, he endorsed my work so generously to British and American publishers that they began to contact me directly. In the course of that winter term, then, I had a visit in Oxford from Cass Canfield, a famous senior editor at Harper's in New York (who happened also to own the company). He took me out for a sedate but enormous lunch at the Mitre Hotel on the High, treated me and my work with apparent seriousness (though I couldn't tell how much he'd read), and contacted Diarmuid as soon as he was back in the States, offering what Diarmuid called a *lien*—presumably an option—on my work-to-date. Diarmuid thanked him but didn't like liens and said that, for now, we'd wait.

Then Hamish Hamilton, the eponymous proprietor of a British house of considerable eminence, asked if he could come to Oxford and see me. Six years earlier he'd published Stephen's autobiography to considerable success (and was, as I'd later learn, one of Vivien Leigh's oldest friends). I took him for a long walk round and round the Merton gardens. He seemed to me mildly chilly; still I could tell that he'd read the few existing stories and said he liked them greatly. As I recall, though, he made no prompt offer. But his visit was followed quickly by one from Peter Calvocoressi, an editor at Chatto and Windus in London. In a letter home I noted that he was "the nicest of the three publishers I've met."

After another garden walk at Merton and a long conversation on the bench at the height of the wall above Dead Man's Walk, Calvo-coressi returned to London and informed Diarmuid that Chatto would offer an immediate contract for a book of short stories—no lien or option but a real contract with a cash advance, the present equiv-alent of $700. After a longish pause to consider the offer, Diarmuid rec-ommended that we take it—for a British edition—and by midsummer we signed the contract. Clearly at age twenty-four, I was more than pleased by the commitment. I'll note, as well, that the publishing world which I encountered first—Canfield as a representative of an old American house, Hamilton and Calvocoressi as younger Britons—was much more like the world known to, say, Henry James and Edith Wharton than anything that's available today when a young writer begins to hunt for attention. It was a staunchly all-male world of panel-walled men's clubs and restaurants, excellent wines, fine tailored suits, and dignified but—if they'd gone so far as to ask you to lunch—dead serious interest in your work. This was, after all, a time when what we now call "serious fiction" was treated a great deal more seriously by publishers and reviewers than it is now (my first novel, when it was ulti-mately published in 1962, would receive almost *ninety* individual newspaper reviews in the States and Britain; today even the most admired first novel would be lucky to rack up twenty separate reviews). With a fully executed contract in my drawer, I could settle back in, a little more confidently, to write my thesis before returning to my fiction for the final pages of a book-length manuscript.

As ever, all the same, I varied my academic labors with further reading in the classic prose fiction I'd come to need, like some vital mineral, for my own eventual writing. And my surviving notes also demonstrate how steadily I continued thinking of the story that would narrate Rosacoke and Wesley's difficult courtship and final commitment. But by then my thesis work had become an established daily routine. By way of a regimen, Michael and I would generally head downtown soon after our giant's breakfast. I'd park on Merton Street, we'd check for mail in the college lodge, then Michael would head for either the college's own library or the Radcliffe Camera (the handsome eighteenth-century reading room set beside the Bodleian like nothing so much as the full-scale dome of a Roman baroque church neatly lifted off its home and set on a small green space in the midst of Oxford). He'd spend the day there, reviewing the required history texts for his coming exams.

And I'd head into the upper reading room of the neighboring Bodleian for my own final investigations of the history and theory of Greek tragedy and the beginnings of English tragedy in medieval and early-modern Britain. Even in my scholar days, a fair amount of batty anthropological speculation on the nature and origins of tragedy was available; so my reading was often less dull than it might have been (for instance, the word *tragedy* apparently derives from the Greek words for "goat" and "song," and acres of trees have fallen to provide paper for the mad speculations those two roots have spurred).

During the spring of '57, when Auden had returned for his annual three lectures—all of them superb and with their own sometimes batty moments—I might pause to have elevenses with him in his usual stand at the Cadena. Then I might lunch with Michael and other friends at George's; and he and I would generally meet for dinner in college, at the Bombay, or at our hands-down favorite—the minuscule Tudor Cottage with its maybe six tables, a few miles outside town in the village of Iffley with its rock-ribbed and remarkably well-preserved Norman church. There we could eat the best kind of English cooking, prepared with great care for the nature of the ingredients and served in the preternaturally quiet rooms of a thatched-roof cottage (no Ye Olde Englande tarted-up stage set but an actual home with a low fire burning, when needed, in the rough-hewn chimney by its deep inglenook).

In the spring of my second year, Michael learned that he'd won a fellowship for graduate study at the Woodrow Wilson School at Princeton; and I learned from Rhodes House that my request for a third year of funding had been approved. I'd stressed that the completion of my ambitious thesis was a major goal; and more important, I said that I'd then begin serious work on a D.Phil. —work that would lead to a dissertation on the history of the short story in English. And since in those years, as now, it was virtually impossible to land and keep a teaching job at a respectable American university without a Doctorate of Philosophy, my proposal to Rhodes House had been honest enough (I'd even won David's agreement to guide my work). The two developments meant that Michael would leave for the States in August, and I'd stay on at the Kirkbys' for most of another year.

Very strangely, I don't recall when I got a job; but at some point late in my second year (or early in my third), I received a letter from the chairman of the English department at Duke. He was contemplating a new program in freshman English and was in the process of hiring eight or nine young instructors who'd staff the course. We'd teach on three-year contracts with no hope of renewal thereafter, but the job *was* a start. A smallish salary was mentioned and normal academic working hours. But at least I could relax on that one pressing matter and not have to begin the enormous task of sending out dozens of applications to American colleges and prep schools (in the absence of affordable phone calls and e-mail, nothing would work but hardcopy letters). Obviously, I accepted at once and assured the chairman that I'd be available by September 1958, as he'd specified.

Meanwhile I accumulated still more notes for my long story. It was becoming obvious, finally, that the remaining reading for my thesis would prevent serious work on any new fiction in the immediate future. So I reckoned on returning to stories as soon as possible after I returned to America, which now promised to be the summer of '58. Travel and the kinds of entertainment that had consumed so much time the previous year were more than a little curtailed, both by my academic duties and the fact that, with Michael's upcoming finals, he was less available for assorted hijinks. But he continued his involvement with the Merton soccer club and our occasional evenings at the film society. He'd meanwhile begun to see a lovely raven-haired woman at St. Hilda's College; and in the same spring season, he entertained in town an attractive young Vietnamese woman he'd met in Brighton (all his life, like me—though in an opposite direction— Michael's been an unrelenting acolyte of physical beauty, though age has greatly slowed us both). These relations, as I recall, caused me no enduring pain—my relation with Michael had always assumed such developments.

My friendship with Stephen Spender grew further, chiefly by frequent letters between Oxford and London. When I felt I could take a little time from my work, I'd drive down to London for lunch or dinner with him—a concert or an opera with him and Natasha, an evening in the theatre, or a party involving his literary friends (we heard two memorable performances at Covent Garden—*Meistersinger* with, of all people, Joan Sutherland as a towering and lantern-jawed but powerfully sweet-voiced Eva and then a full-length revival of Berlioz's gorgeous *Les Troyens* with Jon Vickers and Blanche Thebom).

And when the Spender family got access to the writer Rex Warner's country house near Burford, I'd sometimes drive out to visit them there. One hot Sunday Michael rode with me, and I noticed how Natasha welcomed a chance to see that I had friends other than her husband—that I was a young man half Stephen's age, very much embroiled in a life of my own and no threat whatever to her standing. Any domestic uncertainties seemed further eased by the fact that all our meetings were strung with the normal amounts of laughter. By then, incidentally, Stephen had acquired a secondhand tan Jaguar which Lizzie named *Teddy*; and while we commented gratefully on Stephen's recent mastery of driving skills as opposed to Wystan Auden's hair-raisingly awful performances at the wheel, the skills were strictly relative—there'd be more than one bad accident on Stephen's record, though nothing that resulted in significant harm to anything, or anyone but *Teddy*. The main problem was a tendency to engage so deeply in front-seat conversation that Stephen forgot the existence of a road beneath him and other cars speeding toward him; David Cecil was even more alarming at the wheel.

If Natasha had needless concerns about my and Stephen's friendship, I also learned of worries from my mother. Her friend Carolyn had lent her a copy of *World Within World*, and Mother promptly relayed her candid concerns to me as soon as she'd read Stephen's account of his early relations with Tony Hyndman. I replied at once with honest reassurance; and in time—on several of Stephen's many visits to North Carolina—she came to be especially fond of him. Her worried letter in the winter of '57, by the way, was the only time in the remaining eight years of her life when she expressed the slightest concern to me about my friendships with other men.

In fact she mentioned marriage to me only once, when I was well on in my thirties. She said "Son, if you're ever planning marriage, don't wait till you're as old as Boots." Boots, whose name was Wilton Egerton Rodwell, was her own favorite brother, born in 1890 and thus fifteen years older than she; and from various bits of family narrative, I've assumed that he was born queer. Then when he was in his late forties, and a significant executive of the Seaboard Railroad, he married for the first time; the bride was his longtime secretary. To my great surprise, Mother proceeded to tell me that she knew Boots had waited too late in his marriage because—when he died of a ruptured appendix, not long after his wedding—his wife Lida told her that Boots was initially unable to consummate the marriage (after the honeymoon she'd undergone a surgical removal of her hymen).

My own guess has always been that he married late when he realized that his ongoing career, in that era, required a respectable wife.

Matthew and Lizzie Spender and Dimitri, taken by me in January '57 on Hampstead Heath—Stephen and Natasha Spender's son and daughter and the even younger boy, Dimitri, who was the son of Francesca, the family cook. The occasion was the same as the one recorded previously—Stephen and RP. Lizzie in the fork of the tree between the two boys has always looked to me, here, much like one of the enchanting but mysterious girls in the pictures taken so lovingly by Lewis Carroll (Charles Lutwidge Dodgson), the author of *Alice's Adventures in Wonderland*, in his Oxford studio some hundred years before this day in London. I've seen Matthew happily in recent years and admired his paintings and sculptures (he lives in Italy). I haven't seen Lizzie since she was maybe ten, though we've spoken on the phone lately. I've missed seeing Dimitri on my later trips to England.

He may also have felt increasingly lonely; and Lida—a beautiful woman, by the way—seemed the ideal candidate for partnership. Whether there was any psychic component in his death not long after the marriage, even I won't speculate. In any case, the peritonitis which followed the rupture of his appendix killed him rapidly in those last years before the availability of penicillin in the States (my mother had survived the same infectious assault in her late teens—the early 1920s—but she had the vigor of youth on her side).

My own early childhood memories of Boots are of a large, too-loud, always laughing giant; but my mother adored him, as did her three sisters, the eldest of whom once said to me—in innocent delight—"Lord, Bootie would rather wear Mama's clothes, especially her hats, than eat when he was hungry!" For what it's worth then, I can see that—in Boots—I almost surely had a queer maternal uncle. On my father's side, there was a wealthy lifelong bachelor cousin in Chicago whom I met only once in my early adolescence but have always assumed was queer. At present I know of one other queer male cousin besides myself, one apparent lesbian, and a now dead cousin from Chicago. That makes five of us in two generations—four on Mother's side, one on Dad's. Potent genes may well have been at work.

I spent a second Christmas with Michael and his mother in Brighton—Anne Jordan and I grew closer as I missed my own mother more—but the quick trips to London and an occasional Sunday lunch with Redmayne constituted my travels. Otherwise during the vacs, I stayed on in my digs and was mostly working there now that my library research was largely complete. When I'd moved back to Sandfield Road in the fall, it seemed to me that Win's décor in my sitting room was depressingly representative of the time, place, and social station—dun-colored embossed wallpaper, a dull tan carpet, comfortable overstuffed brown chairs, and tan tiles around the fireplace. But she offered no objection when I asked to replace her garishly colored landscapes with pictures of my own. So the space gradually felt hospitable; and I could write there in uninterrupted quiet (the house had no telephone), or I could ask friends in for the occasional tea or sherry.

I underwent no severe yearning for further trips to Italy or elsewhere on the continent. The first year's journeys—and the purchase
of a car—had made a cavernous dent in my small personal savings,
and only a recent reading of my weekly letters home has reminded me
how nearly broke I was a good part of the time. That condition, hard
as it often seemed, was an academic blessing in my second year
since, again, I urgently needed to sit very still and complete the
degree for which my scholarship was so uncomplainingly paying.

Through all my early problems with Mr. Leishman and my laggard
progress with the thesis, I'd heard no grousing whatever from Warden
Williams in the requisite once-a-term meeting with him in his large
and calmly deluxe office in Rhodes House. Through clouds of aro-
matic pipe smoke, he'd turn his bemused gaze upon me and kindly
inquire about my life, my work, and (very occasionally) my diversions.
Given that he presided over the funding of more than half my Oxford
career, it was no doubt intensely English of him to award me my
social privacy. It would be demeaning to a good man to call it a
purely dutiful relationship—he taught me nothing—but I knew that
Bill Williams had no real continuing interest in me beyond that
imposed by his job. He and his even more severely English wife Jill
had their favorite Americans, and they made no effort to conceal the
fact. That I was not among them caused me no single minute of
regret. Dutiful child of the Fifties that I still was, though, I could
always grin through the haze and assure him of progress, however
glacial, in my work.

And speaking of *glacial*, I've hardly expanded for some time here on
the two perennial problems I faced as an American from the warm-to-
blistering and generally sunlit upper South. I've noted my tendency to
melancholy through at least five or six months of the dark English year.
And I've spoken of my hilariously inadequate electric space heater in
the medieval fastness of Mob Quad. At the Kirkbys' I at least had an
Aladdin stove—a circular heater some thirty inches tall which burned
kerosene (called "paraffin" in Britain). It would build up a likable,
though oily-smelling, fug in whichever of my two rooms I set it in.

Mostly I kept it in my downstairs sitting room, and it burned up its two-gallon tank every few winter days. The range of outdoor fall and winter temperatures in Oxford then was similar to the climate in my part of North Carolina; the difference of course was that the indoor temperature in Oxford was alarmingly similar to the outdoor.

Only in the most frigid onslaughts then would I haul the heater to my upstairs bedroom and burn it all night—with the single window tightly shut. Why I didn't die of carbon monoxide poisoning—I was unaware of the threat and no one warned me—I still don't know; but I did sleep warmly, especially given Win's tendency to give my door a single peremptory knock around midnight and rush in silently to thrust a hot-water bottle under the covers beside my feet. That was a service I hadn't requested and for which she made no extra charge, only another instance of her native kindness. However spoiled I sound, none of that diminishes the severe effects of the cold and the dark. I've noted my college contemporaries' indifference to the problems; but the older Britons—recall David Cecil's long underwear—seemed to share my discomfort, if not my melancholia (for which they'd had long centuries in which to prepare genetic defenses). The standard greeting from virtually any of my older friends would be "Wretched weather we're having, isn't it?"

When at last I came to pack my great quantity of belongings to head back to America, I noticed—a little to my surprise—that I'd bought a number of sweaters in England; and as I wondered why, I concluded that there could hardly have been a day in the previous three years when I hadn't needed a sweater for a least part of the day. As I listen nowadays to the BBC weather reports on the radio, I'm keenly aware of what temporary blessings Britain has won from global warming in the past fifty years. Even so, when student friends of mine from Duke go to study in England now, they invariably report on problems like mine with the outer and inner climate; and when very recently I phoned an English department colleague who was back in southeast England for the summer and eventually asked what he was doing at the moment, he said (and he's British born) "I'm typing in my mittens."

＊   ＊   ＊

Nonetheless my second year was not devoid of occasional elations. Easter came in April that year; and Jim Griffin, Howard Reilly, and I spent the holiday very pleasantly at Redmayne's cottage. For some reason she was away the entire time, so we did our own cooking and driving around in the Cotswold neighborhood—and a good deal of the late sleep with which young men of our time were afflicted (as young men still are, whenever possible). I've mentioned that Jim was the single member of our Rhodes class to spend the remainder of his professional life at Oxford. Howard invited me to his rooms at Magdalen once for a drink and took some delight in telling me that they'd been Oscar Wilde's undergraduate rooms. He made no reference to any awareness of his own homosexuality; but once he'd returned to the States and won a law degree, he quit the law and spent some years in minor acting jobs on stage and in television commercials (he was strikingly handsome). We had almost no contacts in those later years, but I took him to see the splendid Chagall production of *The Magic Flute* at the Met in the late 1960s. Then there was little else—and no discussion, ever, of our private lives. Sadly, he proved the only one of us to die of AIDS, at the height of that disaster, when he was well into his fifties.

I've mentioned Auden's return for the spring term and my inevitable midmorning coffees with him. This time he had a set of rooms in a Christ Church annex across from Tom Quad on Brewer Street, and shortly after arriving he sent another intercollege message to invite me for a drink. This was the time when he left me my favorite of his nearly illegible scrawled messages. I'd been asked to have drinks at his inflexible time, 5:00 p.m.; and of course I was poised on the pavement to be sure of my punctuality. As the great bell in Tom Tower began to strike five, I was advancing down the hallway toward Wystan's door when I saw a piece of typing paper with a hole torn in it, jammed over the doorknob. When I reached the paper, I could see my name; and unwrinkling the message I could just read the following (in effect)—

Reynolds, Have gone to an unveiling of the Dean's bust, back shortly.
Come in and pour yourself a drink.

Wystan

I obeyed and in fact he appeared shortly and apologetically, huffing and puffing as ever. Old Dean Jenkins was being honored in Christ Church with a commemorative bust, and it would have been insulting had Wystan not appeared. I recall almost nothing else from that meeting or most of our other numerous later meetings (strange that the most gifted person I met in Britain left so few traces in my memory beyond the startling sight of his face and a few donnish jokes from his formal lectures).

I think this first of our meetings in '57 may have been the occasion for the only reference I ever heard Wystan make to his own sexual life (he never once alluded to mine; so far as he seemed concerned, I might have been finished off smooth below the navel). As he poured our second drinks, he launched into a grinning narrative of having brought an American airman home from White's Bar on the High. White's was a louche weekend hangout of airmen from nearby bases and their whores—girls who came down by train from London every Friday for lucrative weekends. The more affluent girls kept flats in Beaumont Street, one of the city's tonier addresses—home of that jewel among small museums, the Ashmolean, and birthplace of Richard the Lionheart in 1157 and his wretched brother (later King John) when a royal palace was located on the site. Both Wystan and the airman were surprised in bed by Auden's scout next morning when he entered to start the day. Wystan was a little concerned at the discovery and thought he must offer a word of apology and a handsome tip. But before he could mention the incident, the scout himself brought the matter up very succinctly, smiled broadly, and said that Mr. Auden was not to give a thought to the matter, not a thought.

In the remainder of the spring, apart from attending Auden's three public lectures and joining him for an occasional morning coffee or afternoon drink, I recall mainly only a few events from a distinctly pruned-down array of music, theatre, and—what?—the literary arts. The first was a solitary drive to London in May to see Laurence Olivier in yet another phenomenal performance, this time in a contemporary play. As the third-rate vaudeville comedian in John Osborne's new play *The Entertainer*—a play which Olivier had requested from Osborne—he astonished even a seasoned admirer like me, and virtually all reviewers, with the imaginative originality and virtuosity of his acting. I'd see him in the same play twice more that spring and eventually in the disappointing film. But it would be years before the public knew that, at that very time, his long marriage to Vivien Leigh was coming to final shipwreck on the combined rocks of her intermittent bipolar psychosis and his cold self-absorption—a private agony which he fed so brilliantly through the needle's eye of Osborne's portrait of a worse than mediocre performer, a character with the emotional stunting which Olivier may by then have perceived in his own offstage life.

The second especially memorable event occurred when I invited Auden to dinner at the Bear Inn in Woodstock. I drove the two of us up, and of course the tiny interior of my Beetle was dense with his cigarette smoke in only those seven miles, but I'd grown up in a home with chain-smoking parents and was hardly bothered. As we were seated in the helpfully bright dining room, Wystan said—in his most likable schoolmaster's-lecturing way—that he was delighted to be my guest but that I must let him at least buy the wine. Knowing the sophistication of his taste, I promptly agreed; and he proceeded to order a bottle of Château Lafite Rothschild. At the time I was way too inexperienced to realize what an investment he'd just made and what a tribute to our times together—one of the best and costliest of wines—but at my first taste, I realized that a sizable moment had arrived in my life: now I knew how good a first-rate wine could be.

Again our conversation is lost to me. I can assert a strange reality, however. In all our times together, Auden never spoke with me about Stephen (and almost never about Nevill; and he never said a word of even the mildest criticism of any friend we shared). His undergraduate friendship with Stephen had only strengthened through the years, unmarred by Auden's baffling departure as the Second War loomed; and in the postwar years, Loudoun Road was always Auden's resting place on trips to London. But though he knew of my quick friendship with Stephen, he never mentioned it and never remarked on any aspect of his old friend's life or work. And it occurs to me at this moment that our conversations may have proved so unmemorable because, in fact, they never concerned any single human being known to me nor his own work.

It also interests me that, on our trip to Woodstock, I didn't suggest to Auden that we walk the few yards over to one of the entrances to Blenheim Palace and at least look down at the grounds and the pond. I'd silently gathered that landscape was of no serious interest to so indoors a man (I did have the pleasure, months later, to walk there with a younger student at another college—David Korda, the son of Zoltan Korda, one of the famous Korda brothers of film-making fame. We never came to know each other well, though I'll have to say that—early in his college years at least—David, with his Hungarian-Jewish genes, was as princely in his person as any man I've known).

After we left Woodstock that evening, I drove Wystan to my digs. We went to my sitting room and, again, talked unmemorably. To repeat, this was a time in Auden's life when he'd only just published *The Shield of Achilles* with the eponymous poem still widely agreed to be among his finest. In this especially long evening, can I have had no questions or comments which elicited remarkable replies from him? Did he ask me nothing about my Milton thesis or my fiction? Apparently not—and partly maybe owing to the evening's quantity of drink. In that department, I recall that—back on Sandfield Road—I produced a bottle which a friend had brought me from a recent recuperation on the island of Madeira. The old woman who'd sold it to my friend had told him that it was one of her own family's finest vintages of the island's famous wine, and indeed the heavy brown bottle had no label but was hand-lettered in spidery white paint.

Wine-innocent as I was, I showed it to Wystan and asked if we should try it. He readily said Yes, uncorked it himself, and poured us big glasses. At his first taste, he said "It's turned to gin." I didn't understand what he meant and still don't. I took my own first sip and agreed, though, that it tasted a little exotic — it was dark red but characterless. Still we'd finish the bottle soon enough — our second of the evening, in addition to our predinner gins in Woodstock (a lot of drink for me, even now). By then it was past eleven; and shortly we heard the sound of Michael returning, by bus, from his studies. I stepped to the hall and asked him to meet Auden. He joined us, Wystan poured him a glass of the remaining "gin" from Madeira, whatever it was; and when Michael mentioned to Wystan that he'd be attending Princeton next fall, Auden said very simply that Dag Hammarskjöld — then secretary-general of the United Nations — was a friend of his and maybe Michael would like to meet him (he never mentioned Hammarskjöld's very discreet homosexuality, of which Michael and I then knew nothing).

Awhile later there was a tap at my door — Win Kirkby was checking to see if all was well. She'd known I was bringing the world-famed, as she'd have said, Professor of Poetry in after dinner; and she was ever a great respecter of titles, despite her Labourite convictions. So she too came in to meet the thoroughly boozed poet who of course rose to meet her. Then she politely declined a glass of our "gin" and went on cheerfully to bed. The seven- or eight-hour evening ended on those pleasant notes; and in the early hours of the morning, I drove Wystan back downtown to his digs. I almost knew at the time that — in a later life of excellent meetings with distinguished artists, some of them great — I'd have no other such privileged hours with a human being who was that supremely gifted, however withholding in our private conversations.

In the spring I noted, to Mother and Bill, a memorable evening when Stephen came to Oxford for a dinner at the Tudor Cottage with Michael, Tony Nuttall, and me — followed by a visit to the Oxford Playhouse with Stephen and Tony for a not very distinguished undergraduate production of Marlowe's *Dr. Faustus*, directed by Nevill and starred in by Vernon Dobtcheff who'd eventually have a long career of film roles as sinister males. Later in the spring, Stephen brought Rosamond Lehmann—a good novelist and a once-famed beauty and lover of Cecil Day-Lewis—to Merton to see a college production of *Two Noble Kinsmen*, a likable Jacobean drama co-written by Shakespeare and John Fletcher. The longish comedy was produced by students in the Merton gardens, at their most calmly luxuriant in early June; and Tony Nuttall (likewise at his most imposing) assumed the important role of Theseus. With his fine dark looks, his reliably deep voice, and his already masterful delivery of dramatic verse, Tony might well have had a classical stage career if he'd chosen to pursue one. In any case, the rough-and-ready college production was ultimately more enjoyable than Nevill's indoor production of *Faustus* (as flawless a friend as Nevill always was, I'm compelled to say that his theatrical productions—including his hoped-for pinnacle, a 1967 film of *Faustus* with Burton and Elizabeth Taylor, as the silent Helen of Troy—were often torpedoed by a garish excess).

Also in early June, the university was excited by the arrival of Robert Frost for an honorary degree. The great poet was then eighty-three years old; and because I was an agreeable student who possessed a working car, I was marginally involved in two aspects of the visit. On one of his three days in Oxford, Willie Morris and I were scheduled to collect Frost from the Warden's quarters in Wadham College and drive him some four blocks down the street to Rhodes House where Frost was to be feted by the Rhodesters and assorted other Americans in Oxford. Our knock on the proper door was answered by the Warden himself, Sir Maurice Bowra—the "Warden of Sodom" as he was often called, a man who was simultaneously a widely known, if superficial, critic of ancient Greek and Roman literature and the author of remarkably skillful and amazingly scurrilous poems about his academic colleagues and public figures (poems that have only recently been published). He was expecting me and Willie, invited us into his foyer, and at once whispered to this effect—"The old gentleman went upstairs after luncheon here to have a brief rest in his room but has not reappeared; and when I just tapped on his door and listened, I heard no response nor any sounds of movement."

To my and Willie's chagrin, Sir Maurice pointed us upstairs ahead of himself—"Perhaps you should knock and call out to him in your own accent." I looked to Willie in mute amusement—he was from Mississippi, I from Carolina, and Mr. Frost was from New Hampshire (though named after Robert E. Lee by his Confederate-sympathizing father). What chance did he have of hearing our *accents*? Nonetheless we preceded Sir Maurice up the stairs and listened at the firmly shut door for a moment. Then I (as Willie's slight elder) summoned my courage—Frost was known for his testy humor—and called out "Mr. Frost, we've come to take you to the reception at Rhodes House."

An all-round agonized minute of silence passed; and Sir Maurice, who was there behind us on the landing, whispered again "Oh God, has the old man died in my house?"

Then the door opened slowly and there stood the grandest head of straight white hair in the hemisphere—and the toughest face. His famous old-bear growl emitted a word or two, inaudibly. Well, at least he was alive. His hand came out to shake mine and Willie's; and we got him safely down the Warden's stairs and into the Beetle, on the front seat beside me. At the crowded reception he was, of course, a huge Yankee success.

Next afternoon my poet friend Ron Tamplin and I collected Auden and drove him to Beaumont Street where he was to introduce Frost's only local reading at a packed lecture hall in the Ashmolean. It was the only occasion on which I saw Wystan markedly nervous before an appearance, but he introduced Frost most handsomely. In fact, he praised him in an unexpected way, saying that Frost was the living poet whom he most *enjoyed* reading. That didn't entirely please the old man, and he let Wystan—and the entire audience—know as much in his opening words. I won't attempt to recall them closely here (a recording may survive), but he let us all understand that he'd noted how Auden hadn't called him the most *admirable* living poet. Then he proceeded to give a first-class reading.

I'd heard him read in Chapel Hill three or four prior times; before an American college audience he'd indulge in the sort of cracker-barrel New England country-philosopher imitation which was much enjoyed in the States—never reading his darkest lyrics, for instance. But at the Ashmolean he spoke of his own early days in England, with Pound and Edward Thomas; and he read a few of his jet-dark poems, especially my own two favorites, a longish poem called "Directive" which ends "Drink and be whole again beyond confusion" and then "The Most of It" which, almost literally, might have been written by Sophocles—it ambushes you that severely yet leaves you gap-mouthed with admiration. So despite the old man's peevish remark about Auden, I left the big room happy, knowing that there could seldom have been a time—since, say, fifth-century Athens—when two poets of such extraordinary distinction had performed in the same room in immediate succession (one in introductory prose, the other in verse); and I was glad for the modest success of my chauffeuring duties in recent days.

The climax of the academic year, for 2 Sandfield Road at least, came in June with Michael's final examinations. In those days a young Briton's entire life—if he chose to live in the United Kingdom and work for a British employer—could be forever affected by the outcome of a week of exam papers, written in vast rooms filled with other candidates and with proctors roaming the aisles. A First would come as close to insuring early career success as anything could, a Second would prove a useful door-opener, a Third was essentially a disaster (Auden had got a Third, and Stephen had left without taking the exams; attendance at lectures and seminars counted for nothing). Calm as Michael mostly was, his anticipation of Schools had begun to build fairly visibly as the spring months advanced.

The first days in the gloomy Exam Schools, on the corner of Merton Street and the High, seemed to go well for him. On the night before he was to rise early to head down Headington Hill for his final day of papers, we'd dined at the Tudor Cottage; and Michael turned in early. Then I was awakened just after daylight by a light knock at my bedroom door. I opened on Michael in his pajamas, looking uncharacteristically daunted. I attempted an agreeable "Good morning," but he only said "How do I look?" At first I laughed at the oddness of his question. Then I realized he did in fact look under the weather, and he went on to say "I've been awake most of the night; I think I have a fever."

Win's thermometer confirmed a high fever. From that point on, what felt like real drama ensued—the stakes were that high; we had to move quickly. By then it was nearly seven. I sped Michael down to the college doctor who discovered a long scratch on his leg. Michael and I quickly recalled an entanglement in riverbank thorns a week ago when we'd gone punting. Ah-ha—at once the doctor diagnosed the problem as erysipelas, an acute bacterial infection. From the doctor's office Michael phoned his presiding tutor, Roger Highfield. When he learned that Michael was upright and conscious, Roger urged him to turn up for the day's papers and do the best he possibly could. Allowances would ultimately be made; if Michael were to quit now, however, he'd almost surely get an *aegrotat* degree, one awarded without class ranking but in acknowledgment that the exams could not be completed because of illness.

We raced back to Sandfield Road, Michael got himself into the requisite Schools attire (dark suit, white bow tie, commoner's gown, a mortarboard); and I delivered him to the Schools building by nine. Then I took myself to the chemist's for the prescribed antibiotic (the doctor had given him an initial injection). In brief Michael made it valiantly through the last of his five days of papers; and when he returned to Oxford in midsummer for his viva voce exam (the oral), the committee of examiners "vivaed" him through to an honorable high Second.

15

I SPENT THE LONG VAC almost steadily at work, initially in Oxford. Stephen had asked me to write an omnibus review of several novels for *Encounter*; and I readily undertook the task—reading Camus's last novel *The Fall* and Iris Murdoch's second and writing about them with the deplorable condescension so endemic to the reviewer's trade. The fact that Camus might have read my review before his early death only some three years later has always troubled me—*Encounter* was widely discussed in intellectual France; and while no one there would have heard of me, any bad review is a bad review. And at Redmayne's in Burford, I'd soon meet Iris Murdoch with her recent husband, my friend John Bayley from New College. If Murdoch had read my notice, she cheerfully forgave me as the twerp-in-training I'd soon decline to be again.

I knew that Stephen would leave in late August for a long lecture trip to Japan, and I made a few evening efforts to see him in London before his departure. Much the most impressive was a chance to see Peter Brook's production of *Titus Andronicus* yet again when it was revived at the huge Stoll Theatre in London for a few weeks in July '57. It was my third chance at this revelatory production of a play that had for so long been considered unproducible tripe. Before the performance Stephen sent a note backstage to Vivien Leigh, saying we'd like to come round at the final curtain and see her. Not ten minutes later a young man came to Stephen's aisle seat and said that Lady Olivier would welcome us with pleasure.

Her performance as Titus's daughter Lavinia, earlier at Stratford, had been derided by Kenneth Tynan—Leigh's pursuing critical nightmare—as a travesty of the role's demands for horror. In contrast to her husband's sulphurously powerful Titus, with its great speech "I am the sea" and his quite credible amputation of a hand, Leigh's portrayal of Titus's daughter—raped, with her tongue and hands shorn away—was far more unreal. Her Lavinia was balletic in its stylized beauty and enforced silence in the face of Olivier's bellowing realism. As Leigh saw it, Lavinia had more than half preceded her father already into some imposing but fearful afterlife; and from here, my memories of her appalling grace are stronger than my surviving pictures of him.

Backstage she greeted us in her dressing room with a Scarlett O'Hara brand of hospitality, telling Stephen that she'd merely told her assistant to go into the stalls, find the best-looking man, and it would be Stephen. We talked on with her awhile longer, and I found it hard to do more than focus on her face—to this day, the most beautiful woman in my well-populated experience. When I heard someone behind me, I looked round to see Alec Guinness and his wife. Guinness had been Olivier's Fool in an earlier performance of *Lear*; but tonight he seemed present as a fellow actor's duty and was otherwise polite but cool, almost cold-fish cool.

When it was time to leave, Stephen and I both kissed Leigh's cheek; and Stephen asked her to give his compliments to Larry. She pointed to a nearby shut door and said "He's just there. Do speak to him." Stephen tapped on the door, one of the world's famous baritone voices said "Come in," the door opened; and there stood Laurence Olivier naked as a jay. He was obviously changing into street clothes and was talking with his old friend John Mills, one of my favorite film actors ever since his performance as the adult Pip in David Lean's *Great Expectations*. As Olivier stepped into his underpants, we stood beside him, exchanging a few pleasantries about a play that hardly bore pleasantries. I'd never met him before, and he seemed exhausted and distracted in a way that his wife hadn't. But then, I thought, he'd had the larger role; and we'd caught him in his unattractive starkers (as my Oxford friends might have said).

What I learned only years later, when various biographies appeared, was that the Oliviers had just returned from a tour of the Continent which had carried them as far east as Yugoslavia. Along the way Leigh had undergone one of her most intense and prolonged manic seizures. Manic depression had begun to trouble her at the time of her triumph in *Gone With the Wind*, and its ravages from the mid-1950s onward (though amazingly well concealed from the public and even her closest friends) had grown more disturbing as the years passed; and these were years before the development of effective treatments. Only a day or so before we spent our calm time with her, she'd very improperly risen in the gallery of the House of Commons and loudly protested plans to demolish St. James's Theatre, a building that had been important in her and her husband's careers. She'd been ushered politely from Parliament and told us candidly about a very kind message of chastisement she'd just received from Winston Churchill, an old friend.

Following our pleasant meeting with them—they were, after all, great *actors*, superb concealers—the Olivier-Leigh marriage had a few tormented years left; and her troubles slowly ebbed once he'd left her. In any case, she worked on to the end—especially in memorable productions of Jean Giraudoux's *Duel of Angels* with Claire Bloom and with Gielgud in Chekhov's *Ivanov*—and she died of recurrent tuberculosis while preparing to rehearse the female lead in Edward Albee's *A Delicate Balance*. As great a force as Laurence Oliver exerted on the British and American stage, and in more than one influential film, I'm convinced—after many watchings through the decades—that Vivien Leigh's Scarlett in *Gone With the Wind* and her Blanche in *A Streetcar Named Desire* are comparable to one another in their dark power and the generous heart they display. And in her Anna Karenina she managed effortlessly to surpass Garbo's famous performance; in fact Leigh's Anna may be her greatest work, though in too short a film.

What's clear above all is her utter willingness to burn herself as a kind of sacrificial fuel for her ambitious art right before the eyes of an audience, crowds of strangers down into the future wherever films are shown. But the husband who left her, superb as he was, also left a resonating narcissistic chill on much of what he touched (in fact, of all the stage and screen roles I saw him in, only his Titus, his Macbeth, and his Archie Rice approached Leigh's greatest work).

In the spring months, I'd had a few more chances to see, and like, John Craxton and his teeming family household; so when *The Paris Review* contacted me urgently in late July—they sent a telegram—and asked if I could get an illustration for the story immediately and rush it to the printer in Nijmegen, Holland, I thought of John. The obvious implication was that the issue was on-press and a drawing was needed at once. Innocent of the strapped and understaffed ways of a youthful literary quarterly—run with some apparent confusion from both Paris and New York—I hurried to London and asked John if he could

quickly provide a drawing. He agreed, read the story, and promptly produced a striking pen-and-ink drawing—Rosacoke in the final scene,
delivering her flowers to the hospital room of an unknown family
across the hall from her own sick grandfather. As instructed, I sent the
drawing off, in considerable enthusiasm directly to Holland—and
eagerly awaited my first professional publication: these young editors
really meant business.

Wrong. In early August they sent me proofs of the story but added
that publication had been delayed—no indication of when I should
expect it. More than ever, I felt that Diarmuid and I had made the
wrong choice (even if George Plimpton was also Diarmuid's client).
But when Stephen left for Japan some two weeks later, I don't think I
mentioned the delay in Paris. Only a few days later, though, I heard
from the Paris office again.

They wrote to say that the Craxton drawing was inappropriate and
could not be used. They enclosed it in the same envelope—no protective cardboard, the drawing folded, no apparent awareness of Craxton's eminence in Britain, and no offer to pay him for his prompt work.
I was foaming at the mouth in no time; but I kept my own counsel—
no immediate contact with Diarmuid or John Craxton. Then in early
September I wrote to Paris and, in the face of their astonishingly cav-
alier response to the fine Craxton drawing, I withdrew my story.
Whether or not *Encounter*'s interest would survive, I couldn't know,
especially now that Stephen was in Japan—which in those days was
virtually the moon—but I felt that, given the treatment my work and
my efforts had received, I had no other choice. A wiser young writer
might have discussed the matter with his agent or his original contact
at the *Review*, William Styron; but what I saw as justified wrath drove
me ahead. Plimpton and I corresponded later, and peacefully, about
the dustup, and (in the patience of time) he arranged in 1991 for me
to be interviewed for the *Review* in its famous Art of Fiction series.

Toward the end of August, I drove to Brighton and shared a farewell
dinner with the Jordans and a few of their friends whom I'd grown to
like. Then I drove Michael and his mother to Southampton for his

departure to the States on one of the smaller Cunard liners. To be sure, I was sad to see him go. The first two years of our friendship had been as nearly flawless as friendships manage to be. And by the end of that second year, I'd visited in Anne Jordan's flat so often that she told me—as we drove back from Southampton—to feel free to stay on with her as long as I liked now that Michael's room was empty.

I've noted that the flat, with its airy balcony, was mostly vacant all day; and it became my working place for the remainder of the vac—on to early October. Through September I'd write away at the thesis from the time Anne left for work till midafternoon. By then I'd be near blind with discussing Milton and Greek tragedy; so I'd take a break in downtown Brighton, then return to Anne's for a quiet supper and a couple of hours of television with her. On weekends we'd take short jaunts in the Beetle through green rural Sussex; and I'd enjoy visits from her friends and (especially for me) from her aged mother, Mrs. Almond.

Mrs. Almond was then in her late eighties; and though she was friendly with me in her native gentleness, her memory had failed badly. Anne would leave her office at midday and race, by bus, to her mother's house to feed her; and getting her to eat was becoming a problem. She was seeing herself in a large mirror, thinking another woman was with her there in the room, and saving most of her own food for the woman in the mirror—demented no doubt yet employing the same kindness she'd imbued in her daughter. On her visits to Anne and me on weekends, whenever tea or supper was served, Mrs. Almond would always open her purse and try to pay as if we were out at a restaurant or tearoom.

The sweetness with which she seemed to recognize me at every meeting contrasted as boldly as possible with the equally old woman who lived directly across the street from Anne. That woman likewise lived alone with no apparent care and no visitors; and she'd frequently rush out into the street and shout her lurid fantasies—mostly sexual—to surrounding houses, shaking her fist in impotent fury at the windows behind which her watchers (me included) lurked. None of us ever went to help her.

What would help have been, barring a phone call to "the authorities"—who were they; and what could they do but haul her off from
the place she knew and lock her away? The sight was my introduction
to hopeless senile dementia, which I'd never before witnessed, as the
sight of Mrs. Almond's calmer confusion was likewise new to me
and pathetic though closely cared for. But the writer in me watched
both women closely. I even recorded, in my notes, a few of the wild
woman's shouted words out on Prince's Crescent.

I've mentioned late-day pauses. Almost every afternoon I'd drive
downhill, park on the seafront, and take long walks. In those days the
town of Brighton, and its adjacent neighbor, Hove, came in several
varieties. There was the seafront with its elaborate piers and their
sideshows. There was a long spread of hotels, ranging from the thoroughly upper-class to the lower-middle or the decidedly sleazy. There
were the handsome nineteenth-century residential crescents, the
bolt-holes of well-off London businessmen and theatre folk. And of
course there was the sea itself, though the English Channel at that
point was more nearly a large gray lake lapping the shore like an
elderly and halfhearted spaniel. The shore itself consisted of shingle—
large rounded stones, no sand whatever—and seemed to me so
uninviting that I never once sampled its offering.

Immediately inland there were the Lanes—virtual paths past
dozens of shops that, again, ranged from excellent antiques purveyors
to tourist junk shops peddling the usual seaside rubbish. But I loved
their array of postcards and collected those with drawings of hugely
busted women and spindly puzzled men engaged in comic action
with ribald implications—ribald but not quite pornographic: *We are
British after all!* In those days opportunities for food ranged from seaside stands with winkles, through good pub food at any number of
saloons, to expensive restaurants for those with the money and the
inclination. I roamed through many of them but seldom paused—
again my cash was all but gone.

Apart from Michael's mother and a few of her middle-aged female
friends, I had not a single local acquaintance, despite the obvious
availability of sexual merger with any number of female prostitutes—

some of them beautiful, some classically whorish—and men of all ages, most of whom appeared to be offering their sometimes attractive services free. I can honestly report that I touched no one; and in retrospect I'm mildly sorry (I've never paid for sex in my life; what might I have learned if I had?). So my afternoon roaming through a quiet but crowded city served to deepen my solitude.

At first I missed Michael badly; and staying in his room—his actual bed, with his books and some of his clothes at hand—deepened my sense of the absence of someone who'd mattered more to me than anyone but the closest of my kin. Yet again I'd never been led, by him or myself, to expect another outcome of our two years together. I trusted that those years were bound to come to something else for us, wherever we lived thereafter: enviable tokens of loyalty that they were, of reliability in whatever straits, promises of occasional reunions with lashings of nostalgic laughter. Yet I worried about Michael's welfare when there was no word in nearly a month. At last a letter, addressed to his mother, arrived while she was at work; and for the only time in my life, I steamed the air letter open, read his uneventful but safe news, and resealed it in a manner that might have won me a job in the better divisions of the CIA.

Solitary though I was then, I don't recall that solitude as loneliness— even as, with shut eyes, I'd roam a strange and always abandoned- seeming spot called the Scented Garden for the Blind in a park near Anne's flat. After my midafternoon walk I'd return to the flat to write another page of my thesis before I'd welcome her back and begin to help her with dinner. Not only had my hundreds of hours of child- hood solitude prepared me for such life, I was also bolstered by my confidence that I now had at least one friend I could love as calmly as I then needed to love. The fact that the friend had been plainly, from the start, set for women was somehow a part of my attraction. And when I say *somehow*, I'm not withholding any degree of my own understanding. The fact that a few straight men have been, for a while, the responsive loves of my life is a large mystery for me, one that has sometimes produced real sadness but ultimately great

reward—a reward that proceeds from a kind of love that I go on failing to understand.

In his remarkable preface to Shakespeare's sonnets, Auden dis-
cusses what he calls the Vision of Eros. Auden asserts that in the real
world there exists a rare and divinely inspired vision which can suddenly endow one person in the eyes of another with extraordinary radi-
ance and thus produce a mysterious union that is otherwise unheard
of, and he sees such an endowed vision in Shakespeare's otherwise
inexplicable love of the young man who's addressed in at least 126 of
the sonnets (though Auden later regretted his parallel assertion that
Shakespeare's love never found physical consummation). Such a
claim of supernal magnetism is clearly not incredible; there's a great
deal of evidence for its validity in thousands of lives—if we think that
Auden's enduring love of Kallman proceeded from something other
than foolishness, then it would seem quite possibly to proceed from
some such vision.

I also feel that I underwent such a relation in those first two years in
England. But why should anyone be inspired—by God or whatever
power—to love someone who cannot spend his life with you? Shakespeare's answer might well have been "The answer is here in these
beautiful sonnets; these poems are the lasting product of that vision,
surely an adequate reward for both partners." My own answer—one
that's always satisfied me—is simply "Why not? Is any ultimately
harmless love not better than no love?" And finally it's been the for-
tunate truth to say that anyone I've ever really loved is still of profound
value to me.

Toward the end of that second year in Britain, I couldn't have claimed
to foresee that reality; but I know I felt no desperation, no sense of
abandonment by God or man and, again, no guilt in being launched
on a love life which so many believe to be anything from absurdly
wrongheaded to abominable. I partly regretted the silence enforced by
society; but since my solitary childhood, I'd always been a thoroughly
private person. What I didn't relate, even to my kind parents, was the
majority of what I thought and felt. My life felt like such an endless

process of *becoming* that I could seldom pause and say *This is where and who I am at the present moment*. I was also a collector-in-training. I was saving the best of my inner life for some future offloading, some useful revelation that might detain and amuse my tale-telling kin as I'd seen them detain one another and thereby earn what seemed to be their faithful love. When I was a child, could I have explained to you any of that long-term hope for my life? No, but I honestly think I felt something very like all of it. And isn't at least that much the burden of all my work—some thirty-seven full-length volumes to date?

In my sophomore year at Duke, I read Joyce's *Portrait of the Artist as a Young Man* and came across a phrase which perfectly defined the way in which I might manage my own vocation, the life of a writer— an instructive and broadly useful writer. It comes near the end of something Joyce's alter ego, Stephen Daedalus, says to his friend Cranly.

> You have asked me what I would do and what I would not do. I will tell you what I will do and what I will not do. I will not serve that in which I no longer believe whether it call itself my home, my father-land or my church: and I will try to express myself in some mode of life or art as freely as I can, and as wholly as I can, using for my defence the only arms I allow myself to use . . . silence, exile, and cunning.

As I aged and learned how Joyce's ultimately cold heart had deadened so much of his work after the *Portrait* and the short stories in *Dubliners* (his concluding story there—"The Dead"—is still the finest I know in this language), I nonetheless kept to his motto for the inner life: *silence, exile, and cunning*. I exiled myself for three years—and eventually a fourth—to a country that was then very different from my own, I kept my silence about the most intimate concerns of my own heart (including my homeland's increasingly appalling reactions to the inevitable progress of the civil-rights movement—in September '57 President Eisenhower had sent in federal troops to insure the

Anthony Nuttall, punting me on the river Isis (the Thames, as it passes through Oxford, is called the Isis). Propelling a punt is a thoroughly tricky bit of survival-on-the-water. What's required is first-rate personal balance in an upright position and the strength to use a long pole to send the flat-bottomed boat onward—and all without propelling one's self into the water or the punt in an undesired direction. Provided the punter can deploy the necessary skills; and given a beautiful day (as Tony and I clearly are), few river trips can be more enjoyable. Tony Nuttall was as fine a master of punting as he was of Greek, Latin, Anglo-Saxon, ancient Greek and Roman philosophy, ethics, and poetry and—in time—the details of English literature. After he and I had shared a year's digs at 2 Sandfield Road in Headington—and seen each other often in my fourth year back in Oxford—we parted company amicably and eventually lost touch, though we sent occasional copies of our books to one another (we were the book-machines of our Merton generation). Then in the '90s, the realities of e-mail brought us back together most pleasantly—long messages recalling shared memories, almost all of them hilarious. Though this picture is hardly well-focused, it preserves two of Tony's memorable gifts—the strength of a fine torso and his ready joy in a rare splendid day as he punts the two of us beyond the last of the grand old college boathouses (themselves rotting barges, soon to be replaced by dismal substitutes). That he was buried on my seventy-fourth birthday was a shocking sadness.

integration of public schools in Little Rock, Arkansas; and white townsfolk turned out to malign the young black students). As for cunning—I did what it took, short of physical harm to another, to foresee and then finish my work.

16

WHEN I RETURNED to Oxford for the fall term of my third year, I'd completed well over half my thesis; and when I met with Miss Gardner, she was pleased with the chapters which she felt free to read. The next two months were as devoted to work as the end of the summer had been. I'd occasionally go for coffee or a curry with one of my younger college friends. I've mentioned Peter Heap and John Speaight, who were especially enjoyable for their quite different qualities. (Peter had done his two years of national service before coming up to Merton and had good stories of Her Majesty's army in stations as far-flung as the old Gold Coast just before it was Ghana. John's father was British ambassador in Bulgaria; and the droll John would return from endless train-trip vac visits to Sofia with astonishing stories of life behind the Iron Curtain and of what a tin of Nescafé could be exchanged for in Sofia.)

Another always welcome companion was Tony Nuttall. Tony had moved into Michael's rooms at the Kirkbys' and was proceeding toward the completion of the unusually demanding course of classical education called Literae Humaniores or Greats, a course which consisted of a four-year immersion in the Greek and Latin languages, plus their surrounding history, philosophy, etc. and which remained— even in our time—Oxford's greatest offering to undergraduates. Greats would be only the start of a training that led Tony onward into graduate degrees in English literature and then toward a career as one of the very few first-rate scholar-critics of his generation in Britain and America. Over many years as a devoted teacher at the University of Sussex and back at Oxford, he wrote voluminously on a wide array of subjects in the literatures of the English language and concluded his career with *Shakespeare the Thinker,* one of the rare books entirely worthy of its incomparable subject.

In our year together on Sandfield Road, Tony's chief alternate commitment was to acting with the Merton theatrical group called Floats and to entertaining friends at various women's colleges—he was always fine to look at, with a deep-voiced wit ever ready to chuckle—but the two of us had Win's breakfasts together daily, plus occasional films, plays, and dinners. And that was the extent of our friendship in my first Oxford stint. I never wanted an atom more from him, and it's only been with the ease of e-mail that we returned lately to occasional nostalgic communication.

You can perhaps then measure the extent of my shock and grief when I note that—not receiving Tony's usual immediate reply to an e-mail question as I prepared the long paragraph above—I checked the Internet to see if he might be away on a tour with his new Shakespeare book and discovered that he had died very recently—quickly, alone in his room in New College, of a ruptured aorta—and been buried, literally, on my seventy-fourth birthday (only three months from his own seventieth). The numerous obituaries in the English press are the warmest I can recall for anyone.

Aside from those therapeutic meetings with friends, I was otherwise buried in work. Throughout high school, Duke, and the summer at Harvard, I'd finish an assigned piece ten seconds before it was due, then race to my teacher's home with a steaming hot paper and abject apologies. With my B.Litt. thesis, by now I'd prepared a detailed schedule that would have me delivering the requisite three copies to a bindery up the Cowley Road early on the morning of the day it was due at the university registry—I had a promise from the binder. In my heedless youth I was pleasantly confident, but of course I'd neglected to allow for trouble. And trouble struck fiercely in early October.

I'd driven out to Burford on Sunday for lunch with Redmayne. No one accompanied me and as I was returning to Oxford in late afternoon, I entered the roundabout at the top of Banbury Road when — like a sizable house collapsing on me without ten seconds' warning — I was struck by the Asian flu. I'd heard that by now, even in Britain, the viral infection was approaching pandemic stage yet I felt invincible (like much of the public then, I was suspicious of the flu shot and had avoided it). It's now thought by many epidemiologists that this strain of influenza infected more people than the Spanish flu of 1918, but the availability in 1957 of antibiotics to treat the secondary infections that killed so many in the earlier pandemic suppressed the death rate (even so it killed some seventy thousand in the United States alone). In 1957 the infection was known to strike suddenly, without warning — as it did me. I hadn't noticed so much as a sneeze nor any coughing, not till the crucial moment.

As I drove on down Banbury Road, I quickly guessed what was wrong and realized that I had to focus very intently if I hoped to get back to the Kirkbys'. With another two or three miles to go, I bore down hard. My vision was affected and as I passed through the main business district — nearly deserted on Sunday afternoon — I felt as though I might go unconscious at any moment. A sane man would have pulled to the curb and somehow called for help; but with my fever I was hardly sane.

Still I made it through town and into my narrow bed on Sandfield Road. Tony must have been away from the house; but thanks to her fearless soul, Win Kirkby promptly took over and nursed me through an eventual whole bedridden week. My fever stayed too high to think of getting up for any long stretches of work — nothing essential remained but checking a few footnotes and the typing. With her brusque but generous heart, Win fed me and brought me those English-homemaker panaceas — hot-water bottles and hot drinks. Whenever I was clearheaded enough to mention the disaster that had struck my thesis schedule, Win would cluck and say "Listen, His Lordship will somehow save your blooming neck." Far-left Labourite though she was, she still trusted in an actual lord — David Cecil — to save me. He'd come to my digs once for tea; and she'd managed—again—to knock on my door while he was there and to meet him, most respectfully (she all but curtsied).

He might well have moved ahead with the saving; so might Miss Gardner for that matter, though she wasn't yet a dame; but I hoped not to lean on either don. So I got up as soon as I could stumble downstairs to the task that lay strewn about my study. I'd finished the actual writing of the thesis—some 175 mostly handwritten pages lay on my desk, waiting only to be typed out in fair copy with three carbons. My strapped budget was requiring that I myself man the typewriter—the nifty but featherlight small-gauged Florentine Olivetti.

That first day back downstairs, with hot-drink help from Win and Tony, I managed maybe ten pages. My keyboard skills had been learned in a high-school typing class (I've often said that the two most valuable courses of my lifetime were Latin and typing); but my lingering fever was causing more mis-strikes than usual. I doubt that anyone younger than forty even knows what carbon paper is—or was. In the century before Xerox however, it was the only practical way to make multiple copies of a typescript; and a huge mess it was for anyone but the most deft professional stenographer. Even at my best I was surely not that; so with the necessity of carbon paper, any mis-strike would cause a significant wait while I carefully erased my original, then each of my carbon copies (taking care not to rub carbon onto my corrected pages) before I typed the corrected word on my original. In the course of the next two or three days—I still hadn't risked driving into town—I typed another twenty or thirty pages. Then I felt the necessity of dressing and driving into college for a breath of air, the mail, and tea with my friends. That small excursion went so well that I decided I could accept Stephen's invitation—he was recently back from Japan—to join him and the children at Bruern, near Burford, where they were staying in an immensely likable loaner house, lent them by Michael Astor.

Mainly I recall sleeping a lot, then going with Stephen next door to dine in the Astors' enormous house with them and a dozen of their friends. It would be my only evening, ever, with that many English aristocrats and plutocrats at a single table, though I remember only two things—first, I learned from an overnight guest as new as I to such rarefied surroundings that the morning papers were delivered literally warm to each overnight guest's room (some soul on the large staff literally *ironed* your *Times* before it was delivered); and second, at the dinner table I encountered lemon wedges individually wrapped in lemon-colored netting to avoid an accidental dousing of one's self or one's neighbor while spraying an early course of shrimp (or *shrimps*, in the plural, which was then the British form unless they called them *prawns*).

I returned to Oxford feeling a little restored and ready to return to the final assault on typing the thesis. Alas, I'd collided with another lurking microbe; and my departing flu made room for a full-scale new infection. I tried to ignore it and cough my way onward through the typing; but after a poor day's work, Win's thermometer confirmed a return of my fever. Tough as she was, Win said I truly must now see the college doctor. She guessed it right—"Here you gone and brought us all a case of pneumonia, you pitiful dog." I obeyed, the doctor listened to my chest, confirmed Win's guess and sent me out with a bizarre prescription: a transparent yellow liquid which I was supposed to gargle for one whole minute, then swallow the entire mouthful. I've never since found an American doctor who recognized any such therapy.

If it worked, it worked slowly. Thoroughly weak again—and feeling like Milton's version of Hell in *Paradise Lost* (alternate spells of fire and ice)—I returned to the Olivetti and way more than half of my waiting pages. With frequent pauses to nap on the couch, I moved ahead. But my absolute deadline was striding down on me. I got to three a.m. of the final day—no real sleep for three straight days—with some ten pages still to go, plus a detailed bibliography; and my limited supply of endurance quit. My exhausted mind and body simply told itself *Forget it. So what if you don't get the damned degree, this year or ever? To hell with the nightmare.* I lay down on the sofa again; the thought of climbing upstairs to my actual bed was too chilly a proposition at this point. The Aladdin stove had at least warmed my sitting room to, say, fifty-five degrees. I pulled Win's crocheted afghan up over me and fell deep asleep.

Not so deeply however as to bury my apparently ineradicable Protestant conscience. My mother and brother, our extended family, the Warden of Rhodes House, Helen Gardner, David Cecil, Nevill Coghill, Michael and his mother, Win and Jack, Tony and a few other Merton friends would learn of my defection and shake their heads in degrees of emotion from bafflement to disappointment to "I told you so" conviction—*This sorry lad, amusing though he might have been, lacked the shoulders to bear a scholar's burden. He passed through here like a restless moth. Pray he manages to be a writer at least.*

So after a twenty-minute nap, I rose, completed the job, and drove up Cowley Road to find my binder waiting—a stubby square-jawed yeoman Briton of the sort who fired the first volley at Agincourt, then awaited further orders (if I'd failed him, he'd have been there all the same, having made a promise to some bloody young Yank and turned up an hour early to keep it). I returned to my digs for a shave and a whore's bath, collected my regulation bound copies, parked illegally outside the elegant Clarendon Building on Broad Street, raced dizzily in, and laid them in the hands of the University Registrar five whole minutes before the town clock at Carfax struck an unmistakable noon (the final twelve hours of the crisis had been my own version of a Buster Keaton film). I slept through what was left of the day and the whole next night.

A week later Jane Savage came from Spain to stay in Oxford a few days (after leaving Munich a year ago, she'd worked in Spain meanwhile and now felt ready to return home). During her visit, I drove us once to London where we saw Olivier in *The Entertainer,* my third time with the play and his unfaltering sensational performance. Then bent on keeping my promise to Mother—that if I stayed for a third year, I'd come home for Christmas '57—we took the train to Southampton. On November 29 then we boarded the old French liner, the *Liberté.* The ship had started life as a German liner—the *Europa*—in the early '30s; the Americans had used her briefly as a captured troop ship in the

'40s, then handed her over to the French as part of the massive World War II reparations. The French line changed her name appropriately and refitted her for transatlantic service (and since a more modern reader may wonder why we didn't fly, I noted in a letter home that a round-trip airfare would then have cost $550 ($3,850 now), a shared cabin on a good ship would cost $350 (or $2,450).

The *Liberté* was hardly as glamorous as other French liners of the time—the *Ile de France* and the forthcoming splendid but short-lived *France*—but she was thoroughly adequate for our young purposes; and since she gave me only my second trip on the North Atlantic passenger run, I'll expand a little on the nature of the old liner crossings. First, the experience was radically different from what's offered by present-day cruise ships. Since the majority of passengers were hardly prosperous and were headed purposefully from Europe to America (or vice versa), there was none of the cruise-ship air of endless food and drink, on-deck swimming pools, and frequent ports-of-call for exotic shopping. In short the ships were not entertainment devices.

On all the six liners I ultimately experienced, if you were traveling third class, you had your bunk in anything ranging from a small four-passenger cabin to a private cubicle. You had the use of all third-class accommodations, barred as you physically were from access to the other classes aboard. The third-class provisions included pleasant lounges with adjacent bars, reclining chairs on deck for earnest reading or conversation (with occasional visits from attractive young members of the crew bearing trays of hot bouillon), on-deck shuffleboard or badminton, a free nonstop movie theatre with brand-new films, and above all the dining room. Even on the British Cunard line, third-class food was good—far better than Oxford food to be sure. On the French ships, of course, the food—even in third class—was first-rate; and as with all the lines, you could eat as much as you liked and drink as much of the proffered wine. Then if you sat up talking with some likable stranger, sipping your drink slowly, you'd be able to wobble to your cabin after midnight and sleep through the appalling snore of your venerable cabin-mate—from Cornwall, Provence, or Poland (Jane and I didn't share a cabin).

Also since most ships took about five days to cross in either direction, you set your watch back or forward one single hour each midnight. Then when you reached New York, Southampton, or Cherbourg, your body was on local time—no jet lag. To my surprise in the late fall on the *Liberté*, I confirmed that I was a good sailor. By the mid-1950s most of the large liners were fitted with anti-rocking mechanisms that made stormy waters less a passenger threat than they'd previously been; and only once did I feel a mild case of queasiness.

The turbulence lasted one afternoon and evening, so I missed a single meal. In fact my anticipation of the excellent cuisine was a potent cure and preventive, as was the fact that—owing to their thoughtful design—none of the ships ever seemed crowded, at whatever season. If you wanted to be alone at any point, you had no problem finding a secluded spot. I even resorted now and then to childhood play. If approached repeatedly by someone I dreaded, I'd eventually reply in a fluent but entirely made-up foreign language, thereby preventing further discourse. I thought I sounded vaguely Balkan. In any case it always worked.

December at home was nearly its familiar self, despite my father's absence. Shortly after settling in at Mother's, I drove to Durham for a meeting with my future department chairman at Duke. With marked enthusiasm, this small man with the nicotine-stained toothbrush mustache—Charles Ward, a biographer of Dryden—explained the details of the program he'd personally devised for the perennially impossible task of teaching the composition of clear and cogent English prose to mobs of eighteen-year-olds, many of whom were very much at sea in the skill. How do you teach their native language to virtually grown men and women who still can't employ it in writing (in those days English was indeed the native language of virtually all our students)?

While back on campus I called on two of my old faculty mentors—Harold Parker in history, a monkish bachelor than whom I never had a better teacher (and who married happily in his old age), and of course William Blackburn with whom I'd stayed in Hampstead. It was especially odd, greeting them now in a new hat, only three years after I'd been their respectful student. They appeared to welcome me, though Blackburn—in his innate old-Southern formality and wariness—made me feel more like the boy I still was than I enjoyed. I'd be moving back to Durham in another few months, and I'd also need to find living space. With my small salary ($4,800 annually—$33,600 now), I wondered if I could find so much as a dry shoebox; but it was way too early to search.

From the month at home, a few more details linger. The worst came with a knock on our front door at three a.m. on the morning of December 26. I was sleeping in the front room upstairs and went to the window to see who was there at this unlikely hour. No one but me had heard the knock, and soon I saw by the streetlight that one of Mother's nephews—the family's favorite drunk—had stepped back and was looking toward the front of the house, imploringly. Then he tried a second round of knocking. Still no one but me heard him. We all knew that he'd disappeared from his wife and daughter a few days earlier on one of his endlessly recurrent jags, and Mother had often rescued him in the past.

In the early morning dark, I made a silent decision against rescue. It was the first consciously heartless adult decision I'd made. But apart from sheer blood mercy, why should I offer this man—who'd refused every effort our family had made to help him—the chance to ruin our Christmas? Finally I saw him drive slowly away. In another ten minutes our telephone rang. I knew it was he at the nearest pay phone; and I raced to lift the receiver and set it off the hook unanswered. A day or two later, we heard that he'd gone back to his wife and child, and I realized that I'd made the first thoroughly adult decision—however unlikable—in the matter of my troublesome relatives.

The second memory is better. Michael came down by train from Princeton for Christmas week. We all drove up to Warren County to dine with the remains of our kin. Their inexhaustible and unsurpassed skills at recounting family history amused Michael with the evident novelty of the memories—his own family kept few such narrative traditions—and the opportunity to see my older kin at their best convinced me once more of the rightness of my decision to wait till I'd come home to stay before commencing my own long story—I needed the voices of these subtly precise verbal masters in my ears (and even that late in '57, the bitter feelings in the face of an ongoing thrust for civil rights that would rile half a dozen of my older male kin had not bit deep).

Michael and I also drove a few hours north to Williamsburg, Virginia to see the hard-to-believe reconstruction there of the royal capital of Virginia as imagined by millions of Rockefeller dollars. In our superior youth we regaled ourselves with condescending shots at the easy targets of thoroughly modern American faces (complete with bifocal glasses) poised atop eighteenth-century dresses or knee trousers ending in calf-clinging hose. We were more impressed at nearby Jamestown, site of the first permanent English colony in North America and the home of Pocahontas, Powhatan, John Smith, and John Rolfe (Pocahontas's eventual husband and, alas, the founder of the American tobacco industry and a billion lung cancers).

In Virginia we found one of our 1956-style local households offering an inexpensive guest room for rent; as Michael and I had parted only four months earlier, it felt entirely natural to resume our Oxford conversation right where we'd left off. Above all I was interested in Michael's immediate reactions to life in the States. So far he seemed to have enjoyed himself thoroughly—one of the grounds of our friendship, from the start, had been an appetite for pleasure of all harmless sorts—and he was already hinting at the possibility of searching for at least a temporary job on this side of the Atlantic. His intellectual tilt was aiming him now in the direction of international economic affairs; and in those still green days of numerous good jobs across a wide board, his chances seemed better than promising that he could go more or less anywhere he'd like to be.

Apart from the foiled late-night visit from my drunk cousin— which neither I nor the cousin ever mentioned to one another or to Mother—it had been a good visit. Home still seemed home, a relief for us all (Dad had been dead for three years now); and the thought of having Michael only a few hours up the eastern seaboard was welcome. If only I could find an affordable country house, then I'd hope for a quick introduction to the arts of teaching (since Oxford had nothing resembling the American system whereby graduate students teach lower classmen, I'd never taught a class). Three years of life in the traffic and endless dialogue of Oxford had left me ready for a stretch of country quiet. Surely the thousands of acres of evergreen forest that surrounded Duke could fold me in—me and my hope to begin the story I thought would complete a volume.

In early January '58 I returned to New York and boarded the original Cunard *Queen Mary* for the return to England. She was a huge vessel but—in the dead of winter—she was nine-tenths deserted; and we intrepid few were a whole day at sea before encountering rough weather. It was only then that I learned that the fine old vessel—she'd entered transatlantic service in 1936—was not fitted with the stabilizers which might have counteracted the pitch and roll of a winter sea. So by the second morning most of the other passengers in third class (surely no more than a hundred souls) had absented themselves from breakfast—and from almost all subsequent meals, bar visits, and strolls on the rainy decks. But the ship went on, undaunted, in her pendulum rock as the cheerful staff strung ropes along the corridors for us to grab when necessary, and waiters dampened our tablecloths in the hope of preventing slippages of our plates and cutlery.

Even now I have an indelible memory of a kitchen door swinging open on a young waiter, with a full tray of loaded plates, just as our tilt went deeper than usual. His face registered a kind of amused horror as he realized he was helplessly falling. It was too late for him to do more than offer a Chaplinesque grin as he—and all his plates of English breakfast—pitched loudly to the floor. Somehow I managed to eat on (might I, at this point in an earlier century, have signed aboard a whaler or even a corsair for a few years of seasoning?).

One passenger who shared a resistance to seasickness proved to be a thoroughly enjoyable man in his mid-fifties, named Alan Campbell. I met him on our first evening at sea, and we took to one another at once—partly because he was a Virginian. Even after a long night in the bar, it was clear that he was no braggart; but eventually he said he was bound for England to accompany the English playwright and actor Emlyn Williams on some sort of theatrical tour (likely Williams's astonishingly convincing impersonation of Charles Dickens reading from his own fiction—I'd already seen it twice, at Duke and then Stratford). It was at least another day before it became clear that this Alan Campbell was himself a successful screenwriter, one who'd worked largely in collaboration with Dorothy Parker, the famous— even notorious—poet and wit. Their most famous film was the first version, in 1937, of *A Star Is Born* with Janet Gaynor and Frederic March. Further, as I'd discover when I reached Oxford and looked him up in *Who's Who*, Campbell had twice been married to Miss Parker—married, divorced, remarried.

The two of us spent a good part of the remaining week's journey in the otherwise abandoned third-class saloon and did our best to amuse one another—I with stories of peculiar Oxford types like Mr. Leishman, Alan with memories of Dottie's finest moments (she was still very much alive, they appeared to be still married, and he always called her Dottie; but later biographies of Parker indicate that their relations were always complicated by mutual alcoholism, an aspect of Alan that I never witnessed). An occasional memory of some other friend might flicker through his conversation—Hemingway, Somerset Maugham, Dashiell Hammett, Scott Fitzgerald. But he proved that very rare American—one who'd known well a number of deservedly famous men and women and could mention them rarely and casually but never in the wearisome tone of a mere name-dropper. David Cecil, Spender, Auden, and Connolly shared the trait; but they were from a far older culture and could speak quickly of, say, Virginia Woolf, Eliot, or the Queen Mother Elizabeth as naturally as you might mention your favorite rural aunt and her delicious gooseberry jam.

Alan was likewise interested in my accounts of scholarly research at Oxford and my pressing hopes to write good fiction, and he asked to be alerted when I began to publish. On the fifth afternoon we docked in France—Le Havre (or was it Cherbourg?)—for just long enough to unload a few passengers and for Alan and me to take a brisk walk round the port, one of the only two visits I ever paid to France. Then we headed back for Southampton but were delayed for almost a whole day, by adverse winter winds, in proceeding up the river past the Isle of Wight to dock again.

When we landed at last, Alan and I said goodbye with the genuine hope—on my part at least—to meet again. We never did, though we corresponded pleasantly, at widely spaced intervals, after he'd returned to Los Angeles and life with Dottie. Then in June 1963 I learned of his death in a newspaper obituary, a suicide at the age of fifty-nine. I never learned why (if anyone knew) and all I've learned since is something I read in a magazine years later. A neighbor of Dorothy Parker happened to be in Los Angeles when Alan died. She went straight to Dottie and said at once "Is there anything on earth I can do for you?" Dottie said "Yeah, get me a hot pastrami on rye; hold the mayo." Alan would have relished telling me that in the third-class saloon if he could have looked some five years forward.

What I have left of him now are these vivid shipboard memories, then a startlingly tacky card he bought on a day trip to Tijuana and mailed to me (a huge bouquet of unimaginable, stinkingly perfumed flowers), a few brief notes, and a memorable letter containing a fresh anecdote from an evening with his wife—an account that offered me a first-class Parker remark that, to the best of my knowledge, never saw the light till I published it in my novel *The Good Priest's Son* in 2005. It bears repeating here—for the billions who've yet to read my novel— in the hope that I can lodge it in the treasury of classic Dorothy Parker remarks.

Sometime in 1962 she and Alan had been invited to a preview screening of *The Chapman Report*, a film based on Irving Wallace's novel about a door-to-door survey of the sexual behavior of American women. It had, apparently, the sole distinction of being directed by George Cukor. In any case Alan and Dottie managed to sit through the entire two hours; and as they were glumly departing, a flak from the studio approached Dottie with a tape recorder—"Oh Miss Parker, the studio would be so honored if you'd give us a few words about the film." Alan said that, without breaking stride, Dottie said "In my opinion, *The Chapman Report* will set fucking back fifty years."

17

RETURNING TO A COLD wet gray Oxford, it felt entirely natural to reconnect the battery on my Volkswagen and rejoin Win and Jack Kirkby, Tony Nuttall, a few other student friends, and of course my faculty friends—David, Nevill, and (to the cool extent she permitted) Helen Gardner. I even recall my usual failure to connect with Professor Tolkien. At least once a month, I'd be climbing into the Beetle just as I saw Tolkien heading toward me from his home at number 76. I'd always ask if I could give him a lift down to Merton, and he'd always give me nothing more than a broad grin—"Thank you kindly, Mr. Price; but I think the walk will do me good" (by *the walk*, he meant another fifty yards to the bus stop on the brow of Headington Hill; now that I'm older than him at the time, I understand—he didn't want to have to make small talk with a student; and by the way, he pronounced his name *Toll-KEAN*, not *TOLL-kin* as most Americans miscall him).

While I waited for my oral exam, I dutifully began to think of what lay before me if I undertook serious work on the D.Phil.—a history of the short story in English. From midway through high school onward, I'd consumed hundreds of such stories and, in recent years, an almost equal number of the Russian, French, and German stories which had deeply influenced the best writers in English. Guided now by David Cecil—who almost literally seemed to remember every word he'd ever read, certainly every plot and character—I began more reading and rereading: the often ramshackle but generally powerful stories of D. H. Lawrence, the perfections of James Joyce, stories by Hardy, Forster, Woolf; even a few living writers like V. S. Pritchett and of course Hemingway, Fitzgerald, Faulkner, Porter, and Welty (I'd hardly thought yet of immersing in the brief English prose fictions that came before the nineteenth century).

Truth is, though, that while the reading was often pleasing—and occasionally exciting and instructive—by then I was far more interested in the possibilities of my own work, especially now that I was freed of the weight I'd worn for two years—poor blind shackled Samson. The surviving notes for my long story show how much time I spent that winter and spring in contemplating the technical problems of what would be my first venture into long narrative. Reading those notes so many years later, I can see how clearly I was coming to realize the degree to which the story of Rosacoke and Wesley's relationship was beginning to absorb the core of many emotions of my own and the questions my feelings raised in my own life and in the world around me. The history of fiction famously contains many instances in which male writers have successfully invented central female characters who go on to express intense thoughts and feelings in which the author himself is profoundly invested.

Flaubert's Emma Bovary, Tolstoy's Anna Karenina, and Hardy's Tess are the most enduring such characters; and while a few feminist critics have attempted to demonstrate that these characters are unconvincing portrayals of "real" women, they've hardly stemmed the flood of conviction by generations of readers, female and male, that these novels—and a good many more—produce a rich sense of complex female life. Wouldn't almost any well-equipped novelist of either gender be to a large extent psychically bisexual—as were Mozart, Verdi, and Wagner in the narrative intensities of opera?

Why that's so is hard to define; but when I asked the question of David Cecil, he said virtually the following, "Men are reared by women; so are women. Each of us has a mother; and in almost all societies, children are raised in the essentially exclusive company of women till they're at least adolescent. Therefore observant men learn a great deal about women before they begin to desire women sexually; female writers are put at a disadvantage perhaps because, while they're reared by women, they happen to be women themselves and thus spend little time in the close company of men till they're courting or married." I can understand why some women find such an observation difficult to accept; but if they reject it, then it would be interesting to

Peter Heap, early 1958, at Inkpen Beacon, the highest point at the northern edge of England's chalk downs. The gallows that stand only a few yards from Peter in this picture were first built in 1676 to execute a man and his mistress who had, nearby, clubbed the man's wife and son to death. When the brutal couple were hanged, it was claimed that their chained remains could be seen from surrounding counties, suspended from the gibbet. Peter had arrived at Merton a year after me; and though I was a graduate student, Peter's two years of prior service in the British army left him only two years younger than I in his freshman year. We'd set out idly from college after lunch for a brief country ride to help us dispel winter grimness, but good talk took us farther and father onward till we wound up in Berkshire at this spot, grimmer than the weather in which I took this picture. In the years after his degree in politics, philosophy, and economics, Peter's work in the Foreign Office would prosper; and by the time of his retirement, he was British Ambassador to Brazil. Shortly thereafter, he was knighted—Sir Peter Heap, a grateful but unexpected thing to call this cheerful old friend.

hear why they think there are so few distinguished novels written by women with central male characters. David had earlier noted in an essay on Jane Austen that, in all her novels, she has no scene in which a man is portrayed alone and in thought; and he added that she apparently doubted her ability to achieve such a moment convincingly.

The numerous lingering events of that final term included a drive with John Speaight and Peter Heap to Peter's family home in Bristol. I've mentioned Peter's army experience, which left him with a fund of amusing memories but also the familiar English hunger for amusement from others, a hunger which renders them among the planet's great listeners. I've also recalled John's wry wit. With that gift (plus the fact that he was a perfect stereotype of the learned young man who has agreed to look funny: large ears, huge glasses, an irreparable cowlick, and a slow but winning grin), he was always a welcome companion. A few days then with two such friends, quite different from any Americans I knew—and quite different from Michael—added a helpful late set of touches to my sense of the early-postwar Englishman.

Those days in Cary Grant's hometown (his real name was Archibald Leach, and he was born there in 1904) included visits to Bath and the nearby small city of Wells. I've noted my visit to York Minster and its lasting impression on me as the grandest of ecclesiastical buildings. Wells Cathedral remains for me a structure with similar irresistible power. A considerably smaller medieval space is rendered haunting by its solution, found some two centuries after the building's completion, to the problem of supporting the weight of the tower when signs of strain began to develop. Three inverted gothic arches were introduced at the crossing which bisects the altar; and the resulting solution to a potentially disastrous problem is not only ingenious but entirely original and ultimately a witness to an initial human failing that was met with a practical imagination that ended in startling beauty.

The remaining crucial event of those last months in England was the eruption of a first quite fervent erotic relation, this one with a man eight years my senior. He taught elsewhere in the university, and I'd met him on several relaxed social occasions early in my third year. For honorable reasons that I won't spell out, he'd been separated from his family in Eastern Europe, had spent hard months in a prisoner-of-war camp, and had reached Britain soon after his liberation (by then his home was in Soviet hands). The experience had not only all but starved him, it was my eventual sense that it left him with intense emotional hungers and a baffling fear of feeding them.

For whatever reasons, he seemed to fend off his obvious needs. Nonetheless in some thirteen prior years, he'd worked his way up the formidable British academic ladder to a safe position. Yet I was far more drawn by a physical appearance that distinguished him, in any room, from even the most striking nearby Briton. In his strong head and face, I aroused my attraction by assuming—maybe rightly—that there was a whiff of genetic memory of the passage of Attila and his Huns through medieval Europe. In any case his appetite for long sessions of philosophical conversation could grow complicated by his insistence on dominating a round of exchanges—there was a genuine air of the warrior about him—yet he laughed often, if a little reluctantly, when sufficiently entertained; and his spoken English was perfect, though firmly accented.

After we'd talked at a couple of student parties, we began to meet for dinners, movies, and country drives—trips on which I was soon giving my second round of Oxford driving lessons. Soon I could hear the familiar sounds of a strong magnetism clamping down on my mind. His name was Matyas and in late February he invited me to join him on a trip to London for a luncheon with Sir John Gielgud—he'd met the great actor a year or so earlier. It was a small party in Gielgud's narrow house on Cowley Street just behind Westminster Abbey—four guests in all, I think, including the young actor Brian Bedford who'd been Ariel to Gielgud's recent Prospero in a London production of *The Tempest* (which I'd seen with another Oxford friend).

There was excellent food served by an all-purpose butler; and of course there was much laughing theatrical talk and banter followed by coffee upstairs in the sitting room where a beautiful, perhaps Pre-

Raphaelite portrait of Gielgud's great-aunt the actress Ellen Terry in her exquisite youth, hung over the fireplace (I'm unsure whether it was by Millais or by her first husband G. F. Watts). I was agreeably surprised by the fact that, as we all sat—eased by modest amounts of midday wine—Gielgud began calmly to tell us about his notorious public shame only four years earlier.

There'd been no comparable scandal in the upper reaches of the British theatre since the trials and imprisonment of Oscar Wilde half a century ago (and Gielgud had been the peerless actor in postwar revivals of Wilde's comedies). Sitting in the warm safety of his home, hearing an eminent artist describe a personal disaster—and no later account that I've encountered contradicts it—we learned first that Gielgud's knighthood had apparently been delayed by the government's fear of his discreet but well-known homosexuality. Olivier, who was three years his junior, had been knighted years earlier, as had Ralph Richardson; and Gielgud was arguably their superior, certainly their equal. But in the swirl of artistic events and honors that attended the coronation of Elizabeth II in the summer of 1953, Gielgud at last became Sir John.

Then early in the fall, he was arrested for importuning a plainclothes policeman late at night in a men's room in Chelsea. I recall only one thing he said about that moment of entrapment. He smiled slightly and said "I looked at the gentleman standing there and said to myself 'Not my type.' Then I told myself 'Who am I to say "Not my type"?' " Since no physical contact occurred, the punishment was merely a small fine rendered in a magistrate's court a few hours later. The significant punishment descended in a flood however, as news reached the papers.

In recounting the story to us—four younger men, only one of whom I knew—our host focused on the immediate aftermath of the revelation, as he returned to his Cowley Street house alone. In Sheridan Morley's authorized biography of him, Gielgud says that his first thought was suicide. I doubt he told us that. What he did say, without an audible trace of self-pity, was that—when the early edition of the *Evening Standard* hit the streets—he waited and waited for the phone to ring. Where were all his friends from the highest echelons of the-atrical life? None of them phoned, though he did allow that "Many of them, to be sure, were likely still asleep."

At last Dame Sybil Thorndike—the elderly doyenne of the British stage and Gielgud's colleague in an immediately forthcoming play—phoned sympathetically and refused to hear of his not attending that evening's rehearsal. He went, the scandal mounted to hysteria in some quarters; but he somehow survived and continued, not merely in A *Day by the Sea* but in the succeeding months. In Gielgud's after-lunch account, there was a coda that tasted a little bitter after his report of Sybil Thorndike's kindness.

Shortly after the play opened, the Queen Mother Elizabeth was scheduled to attend a performance. Just before the play began, the stage manager entered Sir John's dressing room and asked if he'd please send the Queen Mother his regrets and not appear with the remainder of the cast when her Royal Highness came back to greet the actors (she was, by the way, known for liking queer men). Having no wish to embarrass a royal, Sir John of course sent a polite message—he was physically indisposed. When the great lady had said all her greetings, however, she turned to the bumbling stage manager, handed him her armload of flowers, and asked that they be taken as soon as possible to Sir John. And they were (the word *bumbling* is my own; Gielgud did not characterize the little man's timorousness).

The entire account of his humiliation can have taken no more than twenty minutes before he smiled again and stood to offer brandy. If I ever knew, I no longer recall why Sir John chose to tell us—surely none of us asked him. Reading Sheridan Morley's careful chapter on the episode and its lifelong effects on a man of such distinction, I can imagine at least that Gielgud was unburdening himself of a heavy weight (he hadn't mentioned that his mother was alive at the time of his shame). With how many others in the London of 1958 could he speak of the episode? Perhaps even more important, he was offering us, his young guests, a serious warning—a by no means uncalled-for warning.

Morley gives considerable evidence for thinking that the British

London 1961

Jeremy Grayson

John Gielgud, who shared eminence with Laurence Olivier as a classical actor on the British stage of the late twentieth century. I saw him in *King Lear*, *The Tempest*, and in Graham Greene's *The Potting Shed*; and among several meetings, I spent an extraordinary afternoon with him (and a few others) in his London home near Westminster Abbey in the winter of '58. This studio photograph, from 1961 by Jeremy Grayson, captures his famous profile with the imposing nose which he always called "the Terry nose," a gift to caricaturists. Through his mother, Gielgud had inherited the genes of the Terrys—an enduring English family of distinguished actors, including Ellen Terry, Sir Henry Irving's partner through decades of distinguished Shakespearean performances (Gielgud was her great-nephew).

police of the early to mid-1950s were engaged in an all-out assault on homosexual behavior, perhaps exacerbated by the arrest and conviction in 1953 of Lord Montague and three of his friends for alleged relations with two airmen. I can't speak to the possibility that Gielgud was implicitly warning us; I don't recall hearing any warning from him (nor from any other queer friend at the time). Morley spells out in painful detail the degree to which Gielgud—despite the enormous successes, especially in films, of his later years—was forever blighted by his arrest and left unwilling to discuss it, or his own sexuality, publicly however widespread the awareness of homosexuality became in the decades before his death.

What I do know is that, after all these years, those quiet minutes—in a thoroughly private space—are the only time I'd yet heard an unquestionably great artist (and a great man) uncover the core of a personal tragedy. My gratitude is still considerable, for the trust involved, reckless as it might have been. I was after all a stranger, brought to his home by a man whom he hardly knew. We might have abused his confidence and caused him further embarrassment. What I've brought forward here, seven years after his death, is plainly meant by way of praise (and while my relation of Gielgud's private account differs in a few minor details from Morley's, I confirm my own memory).

For some time John Craxton and I had harbored vague plans to drive to Cornwall and take a boat out to the Scilly Isles. After another trip to London during which I introduced Matyas to John, back in Oxford I urged Matyas to make a party of three with me and John in the islands during the Easter vac. The Scillies were scantily inhabited then, not the tourist resorts they've since become; and John had stayed before on the island of Tresco with a warmhearted fisherman's family—the Bill Gibbonses—in their small cottage. Matyas pled hopeless busyness but at last agreed, so John made the arrangement with Cathy Gibbons; and though Matyas tried to cancel at the last minute, I laid siege for his company and prevailed.

John joined us in Oxford, and early one morning we set out for Cornwall—Penzance and Land's End—in gloomy damp weather. At the time I was the only one with a driver's license, so I manned the wheel one whole long day and night on a good many two-lane roads that were even more excruciatingly slow than usual. Still we made only occasional stops for pub food, toilet calls, and stretches. We were aimed for an early-morning mail-and-supply boat that ran every few days from Penzance to the islands, and we just made it—parking my car in a waterside lot and boarding the boat almost as it pulled away from the dock (how could I trust that my much-loved Beetle would still be there when we returned?).

The crossing lasted for a turbulent three hours as we entered the Gulf Stream that flowed north past Land's End and rendered the Scillies not merely the westernmost outpost of Britain but quasi-tropical in their climate, by comparison with southern England at least. Matyas managed to sleep on one of the small boat's inside cushioned benches. John and I spent most of the time on deck, absorbing the chill spray and waiting impatiently for the first glimpse of the islands. At last the boat beached us and our slim luggage unceremoniously on Tresco, and John led us toward our lodgings. The walk took us past the island's lush garden adjacent to the local manor house and chocked with almost alarmingly healthy palm trees, large cacti, and various other entirely unlikely seeming plants for such a latitude.

Our hosts and their children met us with an equivalent warmth. And a fine ten days commenced—lots of reading, naps, walks round the mainly empty island: a few more cottages, a tiny village center with a post office, and one or two miniature shops, a small church, and numerous areas of shoreline that would have been ideal for swimming had the early spring water not been dauntingly cold (Gulf Stream or not). Otherwise we had one another's affable company and Cathy's good plain food—huge breakfasts, elevenses, lunch, high tea, and a big supper which was always centered on whatever fish Bill brought in from the sea that afternoon. I recall that he returned once with a fresh-caught bucket of anchovies—small long silver fingerlings. Kathy boiled them up quickly, mashed them into a kind of butter, and served them with our tea on her homemade bread. I think I heard, years later, that Bill had drowned at sea.

In the attic room of the cottage, I had also the fulfillment of my main hope in the trip. Matyas and I turned our prior uncertainty into an actual intimacy. Despite the fact that I'd turned twenty-five in February, it was my first experience of employing my body in one of its grandest jobs. There was, in a single important sense, no future for the acts in any true marital way (we could obviously propagate no children); and since I'd be departing for the States in June, our acts—however expressive of desire and affection—were hardly likely to be one of the main fuels of an enduring love. But as I already knew, any form of physically harmless sexual union between willing adults may well breed—literally—a number of good things. My writing had already greatly benefited by a few such affections; and the heated relation which Matyas and I chose to begin on Tresco would likewise prove fecund in very different ways (sex between two men is, in one pure sense, the ideal male sex act, productive of possible affection and a quick intense pleasure—an act that's therefore profoundly different from female sex, likely as that often is to result in the commencement of a child's life).

And when I speak of fecundity, I'm not at all suggesting some vaporous metaphysical ecstasy—some seventeenth-century fantasy of souls uniting in midair above the bed, the grass, the sandy verge of an ocean beneath the little flesh with which I'd so far joined. What I knew by the spring of my third year in England was the vital relevance for me of intimate union, not only for its powers of simple invigoration through the heights of physical pleasure (with accompanying talk and laughter) but also for my own adult self-respect and the ongoing growth of my work. That pleasure affected deeply the rhythmic vigor of sentences on a page as they attended closely to the precise moral implications of my subject at any given moment in my story. The fact that the unions I longed for were then gravely illegal—in Britain, through much of continental Europe, in the States, and most of Asia—was a fact that hovered at the edge of my awareness of a powerful need; but I was hardly deterred.

Even when love was out of the question—love in the sense of a relation that's likely to endure, ripen, and alter with the decades—my realization that a sane and mainly admirable creature was desiring my body (and outright using it for his own purposes) helped me award myself at least a minimum of self-esteem. And that's a quality which I, like most everyone I know, am generally a quart low on. I don't think I've been much of a self-hater, though my adolescence had the usual stretches of in-turned self-consumption. Neither have I often stood before any of the available mirrors and preened in the glow of my imagined perfections. But my reflection, through the years, in the eyes of a sane lover—sane and not self-loathing—has taught me considerable amounts about my deplorable qualities and failings and has likewise encouraged me to shore up whatever genuine benevolence is left in my soul.

Through my remaining weeks in Britain, I packed in all I could while still pursuing the excitement of knowing Matyas (he no longer gave serious signs of resisting my aim). I also kept a steady amount of reading under way. I saw as much of David Cecil as he and I could manage. I worked on my notes for the pregnant-girl story, and I learned a great deal from a small passage with Nevill Coghill. In the post-Christmas weeks, thinking that Nevill might well be one of the three oral examiners of my thesis, I avoided the friendly evenings we'd become accustomed to having—in Oxford, Stratford, wherever. Eventually he sent a note and asked if he'd somehow offended me. He likewise invited me to tea. When I went, he asked again about any offense he might have caused; and I explained my recent disappearance—I didn't want to press my friendship to the fore in any decision he might have to make on my thesis. He heard me out, frowning; then smiled his tooth-filled grin and said "But Reynolds, you've been my honored friend for nearly three years. You don't think that if your thesis were poor, I'd fail it, do you?"

If anyone had asked, I'd have denied possessing any shred of whatever Protestant Puritanism might lie among my origins; but no, here and now I was momentarily shocked by Nevill's question. Smiling though he was, I could hear that he was dead earnest; and suddenly I realized that what he said had been clarified in a sentence I'd encountered in an E. M. Forster essay—"If I had to choose between betraying my country and betraying my friend, I hope I should have the guts to betray my country."

My own later years of teaching, and life, have sometimes left me unsure of my total agreement with either Nevill or Forster (though when I insert the word *mother, father, son,* or *daughter,* then disagreement would prove impossible); but sitting on the other side of a Coghill family teacup, I'd glad I thanked my friend for his brave and instructive wisdom. (Years later I read about the 1980s revelations of treason among a group of Cambridge faculty and students—spy activities involving the betrayal of British and American military secrets to the Soviet government—and then I've had even more complicated situations in which to test Forster's maxim: one of the notorious Cambridge spies, for instance, was later a firm friend of mine, though I scarcely knew of it till after his death.)

In mid-February 1958, Nevill indeed proved to be one of my examiners—the other two were strangers—and at the end of a lively hour-long viva in the lobby of the Examination Schools, all three of them approved my thesis with no apparent pressure from my loyal friend. I was an unofficial Bachelor of Letters; the official award would occur in a begowned ceremony in Christopher Wren's Sheldonian Theatre later in early May. I'd made my return, however belated, on the generous trust of the Rhodes Foundation, my teachers thereabouts, and my kin and friends at home. Further I'd proved to myself that I could stand in countervailing winds, most of them self-generated, and complete a job that had grown increasingly baffling for me—baffling in the sense of *Why should I be doing this?* But now—whether or not my high-school decision to pursue a lifetime of writing and teaching would prove feasible—much remained to be seen.

18

IN ANY CASE I'd celebrated my first professional publication in March of '58 when *Encounter* published "A Chain of Love." It was a long story for any magazine, and it won a good deal of attention to itself. My Oxford friends and teachers were especially responsive, the BBC's weekly magazine *The Listener* (whose literary editor was the distinguished writer J. R. Ackerley) took brief note of the story, a rare form of praise; and responses from the States included an offer of a contract for a book of short stories from Hiram Haydn, the famous editor in chief at Random House. Diarmuid recommended immediate acceptance, though he'd declined Cass Canfield's from Harper's. Hiram's offer came with a five-hundred-dollar advance—serious riches in comparison to my recent bare fortunes. After the slow progress of my academic life, my literary life felt suddenly transfused with high-class hope.

It's clear, I trust, that what remained of my three-year residence in one of the Western world's most distinguished and venerable universities would hardly be spent in academically intense pursuits. A considerable amount of time was spent with Stephen—and in a hard period of his life. Through a good deal of '57–58, he'd been attending various maddeningly pointless cultural conferences, especially in Japan. It had been his first visit to that opulent and almost incomprehensibly contradictory culture; and while there, he'd met a young man in whom he'd rapidly invested a great deal of emotional energy.

The man, Osamu Tokunaga, had likewise quickly attached himself to Stephen; and in Stephen's letters to me and in our later conversations, Stephen made it clear that he himself was in a personal dilemma. There were two problems—he felt an intense attraction to Osamu; he also felt that his home life was becalmed. From what he told me—and from the fact that he made a second trip to Japan on the heels of the first—I began to feel that only the youth of the Spender children, and the necessity of making the money to support an estranged family, was restraining Stephen from a drastic new arrangement.

Given the fact that we'd met little more than a year earlier, I was complimented by the trust Stephen seemed to place in my advice (I see now that he had few older confidants for such a crisis, perhaps only Isaiah Berlin who stood high among respected British intellectuals of the time). I was still twenty-five; Stephen would soon turn fifty. I hadn't then grown as familiar as I've since become with a Western middle-class male tendency to midlife crisis—what I've since had reason to believe is a true male menopause (probably a psychic rather than a physical change; I know—I eventually had one). In any case I'd never met Osamu; but I was compelled to tell Stephen that, quite apart from the inescapable nature of his family commitments in England, his persistent thoughts of a future with a young Japanese man—perhaps even life with Osamu in another country—seemed to me hopeless.

I doubt I added the other relevant words, *reckless* and *cruel* to everyone involved, himself included. I could see he knew them better than I and recited them many times an hour. Still, he agonized for months; and as the next ten years would play out in Stephen's life and work, the brief confusion surrounding Osamu seemed a major forecast of the humiliation attendant upon Stephen's confirmation of rumors whose roots he'd pursued for years—the possibility that the CIA was in fact the principal founder and continuing support of *Encounter,* a support whose admission many of his far-left friends and enemies had urged upon him well before he at last believed it.

Whenever Stephen was in England, I'd drive to London for more lunches or dinners and evenings at the theatre. We saw, for instance, Graham Greene's *The Potting Shed* with John Gielgud and Irene Worth, a mediocre play and a good performance marred by a smattering of audience laughter when Gielgud's character began asking questions on the order of "What can be wrong with me?" At that time, for professional reasons, Stephen was seeing a good deal of Irene Worth, a native of Nebraska who'd succeeded in the British theatre (he was then translating Schiller's *Mary Stuart* for Worth); and I joined the two of them in several talkative dinners, at one of which I confronted my first boiled artichoke—the culinary equivalent of encountering your first fried Gila monster: how do you approach it? Worth's friendliness was always, and often tiresomely, laced with the standard actor's fury—in her case, at such-and-such an acting colleague or director. She could well have used an awareness of Helen Mirren's later remark about herself—"I'm famous for being cool about not being gorgeous."

I've noted that Stephen and I heard Joan Sutherland in *Meistersinger*. Before the spring was over, my Merton friend Jeremy Commons took Stephen and me to hear Sutherland again, this time in Handel's *Alcina* in St. Pancras Town Hall (as I remember). Handel had long been among my prime composers; and Sutherland herself sang memorably, without the mannered drooping diction that would spoil so much of her later work. But several of the surrounding cast were amateurish, and the sets were minimal (Jeremy would later become friends of Sutherland and her husband Richard Bonynge; and though he returned to his native New Zealand to teach, he's managed to work frequently with Bonynge on textual and historical questions relating to eighteenth- and nineteenth-century opera).

In those last months I relished Wystan Auden's annual visit—his usual superb lectures and a hilarious evening when I hosted a four-man dinner at the quiet Tudor Cottage in Iffley. Apart from Auden, the guests were John Craxton and a friend of his called Brin who'd come from London for the occasion. Brin was an Irish country boy and a member of the Queen's Irish Guards, quartered in London. Possessed of a recognizably Celtic gift for tale-telling, Brin regaled us with stories of the means whereby many of the Guardsmen—miserably paid as they were—scrounged a fair amount of spending money by making themselves available for sexually active evenings with well-to-do male civilians whom they met mostly in pubs around Piccadilly Circus. His best story—and I can tell it here because Brin died many years ago—involved his beginning an affair with a well-known American film director whom he met in Hyde Park (decently, he declined to give us his name).

The director was then making a film in London; he and Brin began at once to meet for sex. Soon the director introduced Brin to his wife; and in short order Brin and the wife were meeting for their own intimacies. Brin assumed that these encounters were secret from the husband; but when the director completed his film, he invited Brin to a dinner in the couple's hotel suite; and as the climax of the evening, the director and his wife jointly presented Brin with an engraved gold watch which made it quite clear that both husband and wife had, at some prior point, learned of one another's meetings with Brin.

For me, it was a fascinating glimpse of a wholly new world when I realized that this Irish country boy, born into grim poverty, saw all such meetings—the one-on-one Piccadilly dates and the involvement with an American couple—as exhibits in a personal and highly comic Vanity Fair. Yet for all the comedy, and its pictures of human beings at their most helplessly abandoned to desire (a state about which I'd lately learned a fair amount), Brin anointed his accounts with a patently genuine degree of affection. He had clearly felt some degree of understanding of his clients' needs and had been glad to be of service. Even his account of evenings with "the Mad Major," whose exotic requirements I'll spare the reader all knowledge of, was astounding but accompanied by Brin's quiet chuckle. His short strong body and cheerful face were among the few possessions he could offer an interested world (he had a steady girlfriend, all the while—a Cypriot, I believe).

Late in the spring term, David Cecil gave a small dinner in his rooms in New College—six guests. Auden was guest of honor, and the others were undergraduate writers and perhaps John Bayley. This may have been the occasion on which I met Julian Mitchell who'd later become a successful writer of plays, films, and novels. Years later he'd visit me several times in the States and become a close friend. John Fuller, the poet, was likewise present; and the evening went ahead pleasantly—late sunlight poured through the windows—with a good deal of good-natured jokery.

As we neared the end of the wine and poetry, Auden lifted his head a little backwards—a sure sign, I knew by then, that he was about to deliver either a serious Auden dogma or a witticism. He then proceeded to tell us that he was proposing an emendation in Milton's supreme pastoral elegy "Lycidas." In the penultimate line, the traditional text of the poem has always said (and I give it in its seventeenth-century spelling; the word spelled *blew* is our word *blue*)—

> *At last he rose, and twitch'd his Mantle blew;*
> *To morrow to fresh Woods and Pastures new.*

"I've always suspected," Auden said, "an error in the line; and I propose the insertion of a semicolon after the word *twitch'd*." He then stood in place, gave an exaggerated twitch of his head, swept an imaginary mantle behind him with a broad wave of the hand, and began to say his goodbyes. I took the joke as a reference to my Miltonic interests. It was also clearly an adolescent textbook-Auden parody of the donnish absurdity he'd been teasing (however quietly) since his return to Oxford. We all stood, laughing, to see him off—tottering a little dangerously as he descended David's stairs, entirely alone in the still-bright early summer evening.

A further deep look into Auden's nature came at the end of term when he asked if I'd drive him and his sparse luggage to the station for his train to London and thence to New York. When I went to collect him from his rooms in Brewer Street, I asked him to sign a copy of his collected shorter poems. He signed himself "*With love, Wystan Auden*" which touched me—I hadn't expected so much. But as I stood waiting, I looked round at two rooms in a state of disarray that I'd never before seen generated by any human being. And Wystan had only been in residence for two months. The desk, the floors, the tables, and every other surface were inches—if not feet—deep in abandoned books, magazines, clothing, galley proofs, dirty dishes, whatever. My face may have betrayed my literal shock; but Auden only gave a brisk wave above the chaos and said "If you'd like to come back later and see if there's anything you want, by all means do" (in those days Oxford rooms were almost never locked).

I drove him to the station, sat with him there in the gloomy café for a heavy mug of tea and twenty minutes of the very one-sided talk I'd always had with him—friendly on his part but entirely self-centered. Toward time for the train, I asked if he had any advice for the start of my teaching career; and rather surprisingly he said that if I felt attracted to any of my American students I must be especially careful in arranging private meetings. He expanded by saying, as I recall, "An English or European boy will politely decline an invitation if he suspects that a pass is likely to be made and is sure that he'll wish to decline. A young American may knowingly accept the invitation, then appear surprised and even shocked at a pass."

I nodded my bemused thanks for the information, then helped him and his tattered bags aboard the train. Straight afterward I returned to his rooms as he said I might. In the end I couldn't bring myself to look for long through the indescribable and, in places, filthy mess. I collected two or three paperback books with penciled notations in his near-illegible hand, then abandoned the job. If I'd had more patience, I could likely have gathered a hundred pounds of lucrative items for future years but, foolishly, no.

As I left I wished only that I'd brought my camera, if only to have future proof of this great poet and critic's potential for private disorder (later I read of Beethoven's own notorious shambles in his frequently changed Vienna lodgings, the only parallel I've since heard of to Auden's chaos). How does the mind of a genius—and Auden was the single unquestionable genius I've known—function in the midst of such external confusion? He's known to have said he hated the self-generated havoc but found it inevitable; and it seems to have accompanied him throughout his life, wherever he paused for more than a day. Stephen was bad enough—when he left at the end of any stay at my home, I'd spend half a morning collecting his left-behind clutter; but compared with Wystan, Stephen was obsessively neat.

In the bright warm weather of May and June, Matyas and I continued our relation with trips to London to see the Moscow Arts Theatre in Russian-language productions of Chekhov's *Uncle Vanya* and *The*

Cherry Orchard. I read the plays carefully again before seeing them; and the performances were so splendid that I had the illusion, through-out, of understanding every sentence—if not every word. Back in Oxford we took long country rides (Matyas would soon be ready for his driving test); and we sometimes shared our delight in each other with the clouds and weeds. Such sharing was hardly wise, considering that male-male contact was still punishable in Britain by substantial prison time. And though the famous Wolfenden Report had appeared the previous year, recommending that sexual contact—in private between consenting males over the age of twenty-one—should be decriminalized, it would be another ten years before those recom-mendations became law and another forty-three years (in Britain) before the legal age was reduced to sixteen, the same as for hetero-sexual acts.

Before those weeks I'd been a thoroughly private man. Now, though, I carefully filed away mental images of places where physical delight reached memorable heights for Matyas and me. There was one particular Sunday afternoon on a flank of Boars Hill. The hill was a sedate but still-posh Oxford suburb, the sometime residence of dis-tinguished turn-of-the-century poets and scholars. Robert Bridges, the poet laureate who's now remembered mostly for having edited and published the great poems of his college friend Gerard Manley Hop-kins, had lived on the hill for many years and died there in 1930. Arthur Evans, the archaeologist who either discovered or invented (as some scholars believe) Minoan culture in ancient Crete and pub-lished an exhaustive four-volume account of his findings, had survived till 1941. And Gilbert Murray, who'd long been the presiding scholar of Greek literature, had survived till almost exactly a year before the day I'm describing.

Bridges died at eighty-five, Evans at ninety, and Murray at ninety-one. In my own time there, yet another poet still lived nearby—John Masefield—and Nevill had recently told me of a visit to the old man. As tea ended and Nevill rose to leave, Masefield handed him a small new volume of poems. Nevill had not heard of their publication, and he expressed surprised pleasure. Masefield said "Ah yes, you see I'm like an old clock. My hands have fallen off, and no one tells time by me anymore, but I go on ticking." So he did—to almost eighty-nine.

Yet for all the hill's placid suburban air, even in the Fifties it harbored wild fields covered with new summer weeds and their various flowers. Matyas and I laid ourselves down there on a particular warm Sunday and took the nearest we could come to full pleasure in sight of the sky and anyone who might have happened to pass. In those high-class purlieus, no one seems to have done so, though I've wondered more than once if there could be a snapshot lurking in an aging box of someone's scraps, recording the moment of two young men far gone in gravely illegal affection. In any case, there's a vivid picture in my own skull still, safe behind my good eyes.

Not long after, I drove Matyas north to St. Andrew's, the Scottish university where he'd agreed to serve as an examiner. We proceeded as speedily as we could manage on the highways of the time till we landed in a handsome seaside town. While Matyas examined students nearby for several days, I roamed the town's lanes and numerous bookshops in surprisingly balmy weather and ate my take-out pub-sandwich lunches among the ruins of a medieval cathedral. Then when it was clear that Matyas would need more time for his local job, I turned back toward Oxford.

On the return I felt so sad to be alone that I paused on the long slow trip only for gas. I even sped past the tourist-hallowed sites of Wordsworth and the other Lake poets, and I was a man—still am—who revered Wordsworth second only to Shakespeare and Milton. The eventual dizziness of hunger did stop me once somewhere in the grimly industrial Midlands for a truly ghastly meal in a laborers' café. When I entered and sat, the locals and the waitress were loudly enjoying themselves; and I seemed to be invisible to them. Only when I indulged in a loud stage cough did the waitress step over, tell me that there was still toad-in-the-'ole; but "All vegges are off." I usually enjoyed such surroundings; but now I could only bolt down the barely warm meat pie and return to the road, aiming to reach my own narrow bed before another dawn. I was not only dead-tired but like-wise on the outskirts of falling in love.

Compelled as I was, by the time I'd threaded my way through Coventry I knew I was dangerously exhausted. I'd already fallen briefly asleep at the wheel more than once. When I was back in the countryside then, I pulled into an apparently unoccupied clearing sur-rounded by dark trees. It was nearly one a.m. I locked myself in the car and slept for maybe three hours—dream-harried sleep—till an unnerving nearby sound woke me—gentle England had never seemed so threatening, and I drove back onto the highway.

A little later still, once Matyas returned to Oxford, and learned that I'd never seen Cambridge (Oxford and Cambridge seemed then as psy-chically far apart as Moscow and Cleveland), he insisted that we go there for a weekend. We drove over then, in more fine weather, to see welcome sights in a small but majestic university town that's famously more distinguished for its writing alumni than Oxford (Cambridge taught a quartet of the supremes—Spenser, Milton, Wordsworth, and Tennyson). Oxford had harbored more than one great writer—Walter Raleigh, Philip Sidney, John Donne, Samuel Johnson, Matthew Arnold, Lewis Carroll, Gerard Manley Hopkins, Oscar Wilde, Auden, and Philip Larkin among them—but it's specialized in philosophers and statesmen (the joke has long held that Oxford excels in prime min-isters because the schedule of trains from Oxford to London is far bet-ter than that from Cambridge).

I was glad to take us through Milton's small college—Christ's (which I'd never visited)—and from photographs I'd seen, I was able to point out the traditional site of Milton's room. We had the compulsory outdoor tea in the Orchard in the nearby village of Grantchester; then back to Cambridge in late afternoon where, on the sidewalk, we ran into—of all people—John Gielgud who was also in town for a quiet moment. The meeting was so unlikely that I wondered briefly if Matyas had somehow arranged it; but that was past belief. And surely Gielgud hadn't followed us there. Britain was, after all, a country smaller than many American states; such coincidences were inescapable.

We had a drink with Sir John in a nearby hotel bar (by then I was calling him John at his insistence); and despite his lordly countenance—suspended round an enormous but imposing aquiline nose and the world-famed cello of a voice—his gossip and theatrical anecdotes were as likable in Cambridge as in his own home. He said he'd be playing Cardinal Wolsey in a soon-opening Old Vic production of *Henry VIII*; we must be his guests. It was an invitation we hoped to accept (I've mentioned seeing both his Lear and Prospero earlier).

To have seen Gielgud in both those roles and Olivier in Macbeth, Titus (three times), and Malvolio in a span of three years was a theatrical and literary privilege of as high an order as I could imagine—a privilege impossible in subsequent decades. Their Shakespeare was twentieth-century university-trained in its accents and physical effects, though Olivier was more of a stage gymnast (to the point of flash exhibitionism) than Gielgud whom Kenneth Tynan once called "the world's greatest actor from the neck up." And of course no one really knows how Shakespeare's own actors pronounced his lines; but the large-minded grasp of the two men's imposing intelligences, the eloquence of their quite different voices, and the power of their gestures and general body-movement was incomparably memorable.

I've noted the genuinely unnerving power with which Olivier portrayed the slow crawl of pure evil across Macbeth's soul and, eventually, that soul's physical face till the actor's very eyes and hands seemed splotched with the same lethal, and contagious, fungus—even ten rows from the stage, I felt endangered. And the appalling strength of King Lear's too-late denunciation of his wicked daughters in Gielgud's portrayal, the near-comic tragedy of his night in the storm on the heath, and the pathos of his final recovery, his begging pardon from Cordelia, and his pitiful death were at least as potent as Olivier's other interpretations and far more so than the television film which Olivier made so late in his life that memory fails him in numerous spots, as does the power of his voice. Since Shakespeare's death in 1616, there can have been very few times—if any—when the English-speaking stage has offered two such actors, who were simultaneously at the top of their form, for the supreme tragedies of the language and were eager to portray them in theatres.

Soon after Cambridge, Matyas busied himself with plans to revisit his birthplace for the first time since his imprisonment fourteen years earlier. He'd be gone from Oxford all summer; and by the time he returned, I'd be back in the States, teaching my own first classes. As he launched those homeward preparations, I knew I was in love; and while Matyas didn't seem as emotionally involved as I, he'd nonetheless expended a great deal of affection—as well as physical intensity—in our times together.

I understood that his career was established in Britain and that his whole life was anchored there (he'd had occasional affairs with other men and women well before I appeared). But I had no intention of attempting a long-term Oxford career of my own. Still I was young enough to think that somehow our relation could go on growing as we parted, deepening to the point at which we might each become the other's chief emotional commitment. Academics, after all, get long vacations; and surely we'd be able to see one another.

Matyas's emotional life seemed to me, as I've said, cored out by his imprisonment in late adolescence and then—after his liberation—by an inability to return to a family trapped in the Soviet East. Now I'd come to believe, however unrealistically, that I might begin to offer something like a long repayment for his years of emotional deprivation in a frozen-up postwar Britain. Whatever my hopes, I was rational enough not to express them aloud to Matyas, even when I drove him to London where we spent another two days together before his flight east. We made an attempt to accept Gielgud's invitation to see him in *Henry VIII*. By phone he told us that the particular performance we'd hoped to attend was sold out and that his house seats were already committed. But he asked us to join him in his dressing room at the Vic before the play, by which time an opening might have developed in the theatre's very limited space.

We sat in his tiny dressing room then as he made himself up for the overweening Wolsey, then stripped to a jockstrap and donned the cardinal's voluminous (and very hot) scarlet robes. Watching a friend— even a new friend—slowly become someone else before my eyes was like nothing I'd experienced. At last a messenger tapped on John's door to say that even the theatre's standing room was now overcrowded. John said that he'd gladly speak with the stage manager and perhaps we could watch from the wings; but in fact he didn't recommend it, especially for such a long evening and with so many bulky costumes passing in and out beside us.

We bade the kind man goodbye. He left for the stage in full regalia, and Matyas and I went out for our last night together. I'd encounter the peripatetic Gielgud once more before I left England, in the Randolph Hotel in Oxford when John Craxton was in town. Again, over drinks, he was prepossessing and funny in his uniquely distant way— warm, but warm from behind a perfectly polished glass screen (by the way, I never saw him indulge, even for a moment, in camp tones or gestures; and I never heard him drop one of his notorious sarcastic bricks—perhaps they were reserved for other actors). After that, I never saw him again, not face to face—though his belated decision to have a film career gave me numerous chances to see him again and again on screen, never more brilliantly than as Charles Ryder's father in the TV production of *Brideshead Revisited*.

I no longer know all that Matyas and I did for the rest of the night. I do recall that his plane was due to depart early next morning, and each of us finally slept very deeply. My eyes opened though, just at dawn; and I lay in our narrow bed, preparing myself for another farewell. By then at twenty-five, I'd reached the age when (as I'd read) catabolism likely begins—the human body's slow decline. And I'd said more enduring goodbyes than I liked, so I knew no real preparation for the sadness of another such farewell was possible but I braced myself.

And what I recall considering then, and for some days to follow, was the unaccustomed word *rapture* and its role in my life for the past few months. The English word derives (as *rape* does also) from a late Latin word for "seizure" or "seizing." In the best of my unions with Matyas, I'd felt seized away—not by anything so simple as a form of physical gesture, certainly nothing with a hint of sadism. What I'd suddenly discovered was a synonym for *rapture*—with little doubt I'd tasted *ecstasy* (which derives from Latin and Greek roots meaning "standing outside").

In the initial delights of plain physical nearness and the ultimate release, I'd frequently begun to feel outside my body's and mind's concerns—and for more than a few postcoital minutes. It seemed, then and now, a blessed acquisition; and like most forms of intense pleasure, it would ultimately lead to spells of dependence—a gratification most fully described in "The Closing, the Ecstasy," the final poem in my *Collected Poems*, one written long after my first Oxford years and after actual paralysis had seized me.

Then a porter knocked to alert us. We shaved, dressed quickly with few words said, ate another inescapable breakfast; and I left Matyas at the in-town terminal for the bus to Heathrow. As he passed through the gate, I thought he seemed bereft of a great deal more than me (though in a few years he'd have a fine wife and likable children). By then my Beetle could virtually drive itself back to Oxford; so I set it on its invisible rails northwest and was on Sandfield Road again in hardly more than an hour.

The final days of those three years are a blur of packing and further goodbyes. I called on David Cecil in his home for a late-morning sherry. I'd been to his family home on Linton Road many times before, but I'd never quite noticed two revealing things. First, despite his family's wealth, the house in north Oxford was much like the homes of a number of my teacher friends in the States (good furniture, good pictures; nothing ostentatious, though Glyn Philpot's profile portrait of David as a young man was all but Edwardian in its muted *Yellow Book* flamboyance—I recalled that David had told me he'd been fascinated, during the sittings, by the fact that Philpot actually wore a gold earring). Second, David's study—where we usually

Nevill Coghill's imposing profile is on the left. He was one of two unfailing pillars-to-lean-on during my Oxford years. The man on the right is Richard Burton, the powerful and celebrated actor whom Nevill virtually discovered in 1944 when he was casting a student production of *Measure for Measure*; and Burton (then at Oxford for a few months on a military course) turned up to read for whatever role might be possible. Nevill told me, years later, that he'd very nearly cast the role of Angelo with another undergraduate before he heard the eighteen-year-old Burton read. That plangent Welsh voice proceeding from that impressive pockmarked face was at once irresistible, and Nevill changed his mind. Burton never forgot the chance he was given—the first of many of the great Shakespearean roles—and he honored Nevill, affectionately, on numerous occasions. In fact when I spent a day with Burton in Rome in 1962, he told me at length about the detailed advice he'd got from Nevill in advance of a Broadway production of *Hamlet,* under Gielgud's direction, two years later. I saw the performance and thought it unvaried in ferocity.

This picture was taken, by Terence Spencer, on the most notable occasion of Nevill's work with Burton—in 1966 when Burton returned to Oxford to join Nevill in a co-directed production of Marlowe's *Doctor Faustus* (with Elizabeth Taylor, Burton's second wife, in the silent role of Helen of Troy). Following a successful run of performances in Oxford, virtually the entire university cast decamped to Rome and filmed the production in 1967. At the time of the film, Nevill was sixty-nine. I hadn't then seen him for four years and never would again, though we corresponded faithfully till forgetfulness overtook my loyal friend.

met—was upstairs among the family bedrooms (I'd met young Jonathan, Hugh, and Laura); and I sometimes made my way through relaxed family business as I climbed toward David's study. Once I'd even met up with Rachel hoovering the carpet, hardly the household duty an American might have expected from the wife of an English lord.

The notion of an eventual D.Phil. under David's supervision was still alive in my head, and he and I discussed again the possibilities of my returning in the not too distant future to complete that task. Then he took a long pause and urged me "not to court extreme loneliness"—I think I remember his phrase exactly. I thanked him and said I'd do my very best. As I stood to leave, David also rose and seemed on the verge of a parting embrace; but a spell of nervous blinking overtook him. He reached to his table and handed me a signed copy of his book of essays on Victorian novelists, apologizing for "a slender old book" which is nonetheless perhaps the best of his critical volumes. His now seldom-mentioned essay on *Wuthering Heights*, a book that he thought far and away the greatest English novel, goes deeper than any other known to me. At the time his lordship was fifty-six; my father had lived two years less. Considering how generous-hearted David had been in all our dealings, and given his apparent frailty, I thought for a moment we were parting forever; and I almost offered the embrace he declined. But not in England, not in 1958.

That same afternoon my farewell meeting with Nevill was more relaxed. In the past year he'd been voted into the Merton chair in English literature, then one of the few professorial chairs in English studies at Oxford. F. P. Wilson, his predecessor in the chair, had won it over C. S. Lewis; and Lewis had decamped for Cambridge. Nevill had won it over Helen Gardner. To a few, Nevill's elevation seemed based on slender scholarly credentials. Miss Gardner was especially bitter at having been passed over, as she showed me in one of our last meetings. I was sitting beside her, in her study, as she read through one of my thesis chapters. In it, I referred to Nevill as Professor Coghill, though his inaugural lecture was a few weeks away. With her pencil she firmly struck through the word *Professor* and darkly muttered "Not *yet.*" Whatever her qualifications, she must have known that her great defect for the Merton chair was her gender.

The new post permitted Nevill to move, from his modest rooms in Exeter, several hundred yards across the High to Fellows Quad in Merton, the largest and most elegant of our quads. There he'd decorated his two-story suite of rooms in what one of his Merton faculty fellows described to me as "pansy modern." To be sure, the décor was a little elaborate in spots; but I never reported the pansy opinion to Nevill, and he and I laughed over more sherry at my account of the recent disastrous state of Wystan Auden's rooms. It was then that he told me a story from Auden's student days. When Nevill had taught him some thirty years ago, he once returned to his study at Exeter to find the prematurely arrived Wystan rummaging through the papers on Nevill's desk. The older man chided the younger on such behavior, but the adolescent Auden merely said "How do you suppose I'm to become a poet if I don't know how people conduct themselves on paper?"

In late afternoon when I felt the need to move on, I asked Nevill for some wisdom to take home with me. All the years later, it seems a quaint request; yet he took it seriously and paused for an appropriate answer (despite his heretical sexuality he'd been described accurately by C. S. Lewis in their student days as "a Christian and thoroughgoing supernaturalist"). His answer for me was a story. Years earlier he'd been summoned to his mother's deathbed. Lady Coghill had chosen an inconvenient time to die since Nevill was, I believe, serving as a Schools examiner—whatever, he had urgent duties in Oxford. He hired a small airplane to fly him from a tiny field in Oxfordshire to the family estate in rural Ireland; but when he arrived, his mother was in a final deep sleep or coma. He waited with his other muted kin as long as he possibly could before having to return to his professional duties; then he went in to kiss her sleeping head goodbye. She showed no response and he turned to leave quietly. As he touched the latch of her door, though, there came the sudden sound of her voice—"Nevill." He turned to see her behind him, half-risen in bed. She lifted a frail hand and pointed toward him strongly. "Nevill, remember—I only regret my *economies.*"

As he finished his story in the dimming room, I could see that his bright eyes had filled. I stood to leave, knowing that I'd heard a crucial sentence—wisdom indeed, from a dying woman, brought forward by her son who was way past old enough to be my father. Few things I've heard have ever been wiser or of greater use in my own long life; and I pass the story on, every chance I get, to my younger friends and students—the story and the words it embodies (with a pronoun change): *You'll only regret your economies.*

Nevill stood also, taller than I—not the first reminder I'd had of his time in the trenches of World War I where tallness was a danger—and folded me in. He was pushing sixty, he had a grown daughter somewhere far off, his marriage had ended decades ago, and I'd recently met what he called the great love of his life (a married man with children). Yet for all his cheer and competence and his legions of friends, Nevill had always seemed to me a lonely man. Still I knew he'd heeded his mother's last words. He'd lavishly poured out his own deep mental and spiritual gifts; and however depleted the well must have seemed at many times, it had always refilled—as it had in all his unfailingly generous dealings with me. Another piece of parting wisdom then, to set by Auden's characteristically peculiar observation, while I continued the complex labor of shutting the lid on three years of vital importance in my life.

In the few days left, I visited Stephen in London and spent two nights on Loudoun Road. One night we had dinner with his only surviving younger brother, Humphrey, who is only now being celebrated as the extraordinary photographer he'd been in his early years. I took to Humphrey right away, over dinner and through a long bibulous evening; but Stephen had never once mentioned his brother's photography to me, and we didn't discuss it that evening. Later I was often reminded how little Stephen's surviving siblings—Humphrey and their sister Caroline whom I never met—figured in his present life, though he'd written (in the Forties) some of his finest poems about the last illness and death of Humphrey's first wife Margaret. Enduring family devotion (apart from his immediate family) had got essentially omitted from his childhood skills, owing maybe to the early death of his mother and, thereafter, to his father's lack of involvement with the children—all of whom were reared by a pair of exemplary hired sisters. (Surprisingly, after our dinner, I was sitting on the floor near Humphrey's chair; and whenever Stephen left the room to pee—which was always often—Humphrey would lean forward and massage my neck or scratch my head. It was only in his obituary in the London *Independent* that I learned that he always told his three successive wives of his bisexuality).

From that visit to London I drove my Beetle on to Manchester for shipment to the States; and it seemed I'd make that long trip alone, despite the fact that the headwaiter at the Bombay Restaurant on Walton Street had asked to come along with me, just for the trip. He was a virtual twin to one of my childhood heroes, the film actor Sabu (the headwaiter's name was Shamsul, and he was about my age). I'd never seen him outside the Bombay, though he'd kindly given me more free dinners in my recent near-bankrupt weeks. Maybe I feared beginning another intensity too late in my English stay, despite this young man's small-bodied physical perfection. I also felt a certain familiar human need to deepen my own sadness at parting from the scene of so much learning, so much education in the most useful senses.

The nearest feasible port to my home in North Carolina was Charleston, South Carolina; and when I left the Beetle in the clamorous freight yard of a Manchester shipper recommended by my Oxford travel service, I more than half expected never to see it again. Nonetheless it had made my time in Britain—and through the continental summer with Michael—far richer than either might otherwise have been. I spent one solitary night in an enormous Manchester hotel, also commended by my ever-resourceful travel service. And by the time of my next-morning train back to Oxford, I'd indeed intensified my tangled compound of sadness and withdrawal. I'd also stirred into the mix a bracing awareness that, if I were ever going to become the professional fiction writer I'd told the world I was on the verge of becoming, then a return to home-ground central (northeast North Carolina) was my surest means of taking an even more serious step on into that venture. All I needed now—I told myself—was a safe voyage westward and the quick location of a quiet country house.

Back on Sandfield Road, I spent a last three days repacking my trunk with semi-lunatic care. When I'd wedged in (with elaborate jigsaw-puzzle assembly) every acquisition from a manically acquisitive three years—every new book, framed picture, sweater, all the other clothes, souvenir tickets, and theatre programs, all the saved letters from valuable friends, and on and on—then I called British Railways to come and collect it for shipment to dockside Southampton and the French line, bound for New York. (I'd sold dozens of books to Blackwell's, including my near-complete Columbia set of Milton, in order to purchase a few pictures that were still available at startlingly low prices. I'd seen Kenneth Clark, for instance, a few weeks earlier on TV; and he said that original Rembrandt etchings, printed during the artist's lifetime, could still be bought for "less than the television set on which you're watching this program"; so even with a beautiful Craxton portrait of a young Greek soldier, I thought I had a lighter load than I'd brought with me three years ago.)

In response to my call then, two strong-armed men came to my study, took one look at the trunk, gave a hasty pull at the leather handles, and said "No way, mate. If we can't lift it, we don't have to take it."

In considerable shock I said "What do you suggest then?" The larger of the men said "Saw the bloody thing in 'alf," and then they were gone. So much for the reliability of a nationalized railroad (it was the most substantial rudeness I'd yet experienced in Britain; the customs men in Harwich were after all responding to an error I'd made). A little desperate, I bussed myself into town and asked my travel agent for help. He at once suggested a local private trucking company whose polite but suspiciously undersized men came, took one slow look at my trunk, said nothing to one another nor to me but (without further ado) proceeded to heave the deadweight burden onto their lorry and bear it briskly away—nearly seven hundred pounds as I'd learn to my amazement when paying the freight bill later that afternoon.

*   *   *

Oddly I don't recall my last night in Oxford. Did I dine with a friend (almost all undergraduates had left for the Long Vac)? Did I eat a farewell complimentary curry with my Indian waiter friends at the Bombay (that would have required a bus transfer)? Did I drop in at St. Hilda's and see if Miss Gardner was available for something (about as likely as calling on old Queen Mary herself with a similar proposal, though a few weeks earlier I'd taken Miss Gardner out to dinner and brought her back to Sandfield Road for a convivial last glass of wine and a good deal of talk)? Or did I simply stay in Headington, eat bread and cheese, make the odd joke with Win as she looked in at intervals, apparently abashed to show any feeling invested in my departure, and make my final preparations for tomorrow's train to Southampton and the better part of a week at sea—if we made it safely? An Italian liner, the *Andrea Doria*, had after all sunk almost exactly two years ago with the loss of some fifty souls.

In the absence of any specific memory, it seems right to recall my final dinner with Stephen. He'd come to Oxford some two weeks earlier, and we'd met—for dinner maybe or at least a good talk. We realized clearly that a first round of our friendship was ending. Again we both knew—silently—that despite the difference in our ages, I'd been promoted to a new rank when Stephen consulted me about his domestic options in the crisis he precipitated during his concern for Osamu. The immediate change in our relation was that I'd no longer be within easy reach of London; but while it eliminated our chances of meeting often for theatre and music, that was surely no great problem. Given Stephen's restless circling of the globe, we were bound to meet again soon.

And there were always letters. In those last good days before the telephone largely consumed the art of letter writing, we'd go on with our regular correspondence. Stephen had told me more than once how he felt that the best of him was contained in his journals and his letters; and now—twelve years after his death—there must be thousands of his letters that survive and remain to be collected and published. His brilliant biographer John Sutherland has written that

"The largest private collection of Stephen Spender's correspondence and literary papers is held by his friend of many years, Reynolds Price. It is deposited (under restriction) at Duke University Library." They're letters which—for intelligence, wit, and emotional and narrative coherence—equal any I've read since Virginia Woolf's. He himself almost never kept copies, saying that he liked to cast his bread on the waters and leave it at that. There are more than three hundred in my files alone.

The deepest-cut memory from that late Oxford meeting was Stephen's saying how he worried about the very thing that gave me most hope—the fact that I was returning to my old home ground (at Duke I'd be little more than an hour from my birthplace). His own intensely cosmopolite view—plus his lack of any real knowledge of the realities of life in my old world and, even more crucially, his lack of any strong ties to a parental family of blood kin—was that I might now proceed to write only about a few past realities, abandoning the new lines I'd pursued as my angles of vision expanded in England.

Mightn't I eventually dry up (he feared a certain Medusa power at the heart of American culture)? Without ever having told his two oldest friends apparently, he felt that America had, to a large extent, sterilized the early gifts of both Auden and Isherwood. I didn't mention that they'd exiled themselves from fertile home ground, whereas I was returning from temporary absence; and of course I didn't point out—and never would—the clearly painful fact that his own poetry had virtually ceased.

What he was telling me was something he'd plainly thought a good deal about; and coming from such a canny and benevolent friend (one capable of an unpretentious wisdom that often ran in tandem with his personal confusions and defeats), his question lodged in my mind at once as a warning worth perpetual attention. Since I had no guarantee to offer him that I wouldn't likewise succumb to some nameless cauterizing American plague, I could only assure him of an ongoing awareness. Wouldn't a three-year immersion in a culture as profoundly different as the Britain of those years have insured me, for life, against the pointless provincialism that Stephen seemed to dread?

Young as I was, I felt he was wrong; and I was young enough to say so. It was one more of my brash replies which he absorbed into the wide and silent blue-eyed German-Jewish gaze with which he filed away refusals that he fully expected to meet again when the person whom he'd warned eventually realized his rightness.

Well, I came from sanguine stock. Both my parents had owned very little to bank on but persistent hope; and here now I sat, their healthy elder son, all but straining at the bit with the goodness of my already-annotated plans for a longish fiction. I'd even recently acquired a title. A few months ago I'd gone to an Oxford showing of *The Bridge on the River Kwai*. I'd seen the powerful film, brand new, on the rolling *Queen Mary* with Alan Campbell; but on a second viewing, I heard more clearly one brief—and near final—speech of William Holden's.

It comes near the film's catastrophic ending, when Holden and his young accomplice are deploying their explosives. As they're almost done, Holden turns to the young man; and here's the note I made that evening, back in my study—

> There is a line in *Bridge on the River Kwai* which might give a title for the Rosacoke story—"Let me wish you *a long and happy life*."

I was too early in my writing career to realize how crucial titles would become for me, how they'd crystallize my central meaning and lure me onward. But here, more than eighteen months before I began really writing my story, I'd found its heart. Though I couldn't yet know it, I was off and—was I running? I was moving onward in any case—and not only toward a story that would become a novel but toward a further life of my own, one as happy at least as what I'd yet lived through (despite the sadnesses to which I've alluded, I'd known a great deal of unmitigated joy).

With a sense of silent drama then, and the baggage of hope that was natural for me, this native son began his return to the bright orange clay and dense piney woods of his early life, the home of so much of his eventual work. On July 23, 1958 I faced back west and put to sea again in another old but agreeable French ship, the *Ile de France*—

launched as long ago as 1927—entrusting myself, mind and body, for five more days to the all but bottomless surging breast of the North Atlantic.

19

Near the start of these memories, I recounted a shipboard meditation on my life as I headed for England in the fall of 1955. And while I don't recall a similar spate of nocturnal reflection on the starlit decks of the *Ile de France*, it's hardly misleading to indulge here in a parallel account of the man I thought I was as I headed home with three years of Britain and Europe packed into my skull and heart. Among many uncertainties I can guarantee that I felt huge relief at the thought of assuming a teaching job in September—an interesting-sounding commitment and a regular paycheck. And while that small sum would be gutted by the usual tax deductions, it would at least be a sum I'd earned. I could set up my own establishment, however modest, under no one else's roof. And at least as important, I could contribute finally to my mother and brother's expenses and begin to become—in my own eyes at least—something besides a bright and aging schoolboy.

I must also have thought of my prospects for love and companionship. I hope I've made it clear above that my relation with Michael Jordan had firmly, and almost painlessly, settled into the groove of close friendship, a groove that might offer its own disappointments. But even in America—where friendship between grown men seems limited to hunting parties, bowling teams, wallowing golf carts, and smoky poker nights—we seemed to have a fair chance at remaining available to one another as reliable wells of laughter, good stories, and all-but-silent support in times of trouble.

And I've laid out earlier here my hope that the brushfire intensity of my three months with Matyas had, near its core, so many chances for further thoughtful dialogue and—again—our frequent resorts to riotous laughter that had fueled our second-strongest mutual attraction. Surely there was a chance of turning our present separation into an eventual permanent reunion. At sea I understood the near-impossibility of my hope, but when did near-impossibility balk such hope? Whatever, deep-dyed romantic that I was—and a sexual wolverine by now—an enduring partnership was not among my immediate projects. And again, odd as it seems, I (and virtually all my few queer friends, from wherever) had way too little awareness that an overwhelmingly vital need in our lives was criminal according to the law.

Given the stack of notes for a long story, one I trusted would complete the volume contracted now with Chatto and Windus and with Random House, my urgent enterprise was the commencement of work on *A Long and Happy Life*. After docking in New York, I'd spend a few days in her big apartment with Nancy Jo Fox, a stunning Duke friend as given to hopeless love as I. Michael would join us briefly from Princeton for an evening or two on the town; and I'd hope to meet with Diarmuid whom I hadn't seen for a full three years. Then I'd pass through the soon to be brutally destroyed Roman splendor of old Penn Station—grimier by now than Rome can ever have been—and board the Silver Meteor, the Seaboard's crack express train for Florida via Raleigh.

Once semi-unpacked and well-fed at Mother's, I'd begin my search for country quarters near Durham. I'd introduce myself to a few of my colleagues-to-be; and by the third week in September, I'd have begun to teach my first classes. I'd learned already in a letter from my chairman that my three courses were scheduled for Tuesdays, Thursdays, and Saturdays (Saturdays would be howlingly unheard of today)—two sections of freshman composition and a sophomore survey of English literature. If at last I could wrestle my perennially rambling attention into line, I'd have four whole days for writing (I hadn't yet learned to take Sundays off). With any luck couldn't I finish *A Long and Happy Life*, a story of—say—seventy-five or a hundred pages within six months? All provided, of course, that the draft—the government's draft—didn't want me.

But for all his recent denunciation of the Stalin years in Russia, Premier Khrushchev remained a formidable counter to the United States, its allies, and all its interests. The still-divided city of Berlin was a steady flash point. Our ground forces were kept at a high level of readiness for any threat that didn't involve intercontinental ballistic missile attacks on our mainland or on any of our numerous partners in the NATO pact. My return could conceivably be the moment for my homeland to require at least two years of my life in military service. My draft board in Raleigh had the date of my return on file; and at times I could feel that reality ticking ominously. I had my flat feet and my lifelong affliction with severe hay fever as possible disqualifications. So till further notice, the plans for beginning my adult work remained in force.

On board ship with no close friends to divert me, I also looked round at the recent past and wondered what my English years had meant. How much had that investment of a thick slice of my life amounted to? I'd left home in the hopes of enlarging my abilities to write and teach. So far as the writing of fiction went, I'd completed four short stories—"Michael Egerton," "The Anniversary," "The Warrior Princess Ozimba," and "A Chain of Love," which I'd seen published with considerable reward; and now I'd started work on a fifth story, "Troubled Sleep." More promisingly yet, I'd elaborately planned the rest of the book.

So far as the goal of teaching literature in a good university, I'd completed an intermediate graduate degree; and I'd made a reading-start on the work for a doctorate. But until I'd finished my Oxford degree and was homeward bound, I hadn't fully considered how that hardly brutal stint of work on *Samson* had often felt too much like hauling a deadweight across a wide river. Granted, I still loved the poetry of Milton. Granted, I'd watched enough good teachers in my nineteen years of formal education to know that I'd almost surely love teaching (and I hadn't yet foreseen the special rewards which annual roomfuls of students can bring to childless teachers).

Yet given the fact that what I wanted most to do—the writing—
might well be compromised by the teaching, as the scholarship had
compromised it at Oxford, could I bear to return home now and
divide my time between teaching and writing—and all with the
prospect, dead ahead, of another two or three years of doctoral work
just to earn myself the essential union card for college teaching?
What other choice was available, though? I had to make money, for
myself and others; and surely there was no more likely job than the one
that had landed unsought in my lap—three working days a week, nine
months a year, at a first-rate university (even if the salary was minuscule). Well, the army would pay me a great deal less for donkey work.

I've mentioned coming from sanguine stock—good-humored hard
workers. So for now I prowled the dark decks of the sleepless liner with
the same pleasure I'd felt heading east three years ago. I seemed as
sure as I'd been, in '55, that I was headed for an outcome as promising
as it was new (no doubt I'd even learn something in the army, if it
spared my life). In many directions I'd changed remarkably in ways
that even I could see. My hair was longer, my accent was Oxbridge
British in spots (I recall my mother's puzzled "The *what?*" as I
announced that I was headed for the *baaath*; life in Carolina would
soon erase that protective mimicry). My wardrobe—such as it was—
was all English now, though by no means Savile Row in quality. The
bamboo-handled, tightly rolled umbrella that I'd bought at the end of
my Harvard summer four years ago had survived a thousand chances
to be lost; for a while to come then I'd sport it as a cane (it bore no
banner saying *Ex–Rhodes Scholar*—De Voto's warning had stuck in
my craw).

Three years in Britain had been the best time of my life till then; I'd
experienced more pleasure (which can only come from acts, large or
small) than in all the prior years. Yet I wasn't Anglophile in any
unreasonably altered way. I'd bear those skin-deep signs of Englishness
for the months it took to settle back into a far older life—my first
twenty-two in the upper South of the United States, years that followed far nearer than I yet comprehended on General Lee's ride out

of Appomattox, the murder of Lincoln, and the actual freedom of four million slaves.

That stretch of the world, which I'd loved enough to choose as the source of my early work and the ongoing scene of my daily life, was poised on the rim of a revolution at least as crucial as the war that had freed us from Britain two centuries ago and the even more devastating War between the States. The people who'd tended so many days and nights of my childhood—descendants of the African slaves my forebears had imported and owned—were stirring to a new life. With all I'd read in British newspapers and occasional issues of *Time* magazine, I had no real understanding of the power in the storm that was breaking and that would only grow till it wiped away many traits and tones of a world I'd cherished and begun already to preserve in fiction. Gone with the wind indeed.

Much of what I'd known, and at least silently accepted, was evil at the core. Whatever I'd learned in the ancient university I was leaving behind—an institution that, among a thousand other things, had played an indispensable role in manning the largest empire ever assembled—still, I hadn't entirely identified the central errors in what I'd adhered to and honored in my prior life. Among the skills and understandings which lay ahead for me, that admission would be the largest and, in painful ways, the hardest since it would mean acknowledging that many of the people whom I loved most (my kin and oldest friends, not to mention myself) had been intricately incorporated into the tragic ongoing machinery of racial oppression—and worse.

T W O

THE UNITED STATES
1958–1961

1

We were all buck-naked, wearing only our watches, maybe our potato-sized high-school rings, and toting our wallets. We were almost surely hapless American citizens, summoned for pre-induction draft physicals in our time and place. We were upstairs in a dim building in downtown Raleigh. I'd got home a couple of weeks earlier to find, on the night of my arrival, the letter I'd dreaded. It was waiting on the desk in my boyhood bedroom among welcome letters from English friends (no one, in those days, corresponded with the ferocious loyalty and promptitude of the English). The return address said, in letters of flame, *Selective Service System*.

And here I was, obedient to the call. Some two hundred of us—black, white, and a very few others from one of the surviving eastern Tar Heel Indian tribes—had appeared with astonishing unanimity at seven in the morning. As I entered the dark room and looked round for any encouraging face, I glanced into the farthest corner and saw an old high-school classmate. He had a magnificent name—Brutus Bloxton—and looked exactly like such a man—tall, built like a three-story brick warehouse, and blessed with a likably handsome face. I went toward him, and Brutus and I soon caught ourselves up on our lives since high school—a long seven years.

I've forgot what Brutus had been doing meanwhile—and now he's long dead—but before we were summoned to the first event of an ominous morning, he reached into the watch pocket of his trousers and slowly drew out something apparently precious. He whispered "Look here." When I looked, he was half concealing a small pill, much smaller than an aspirin. I had to ask what it was; and Brutus whispered again—"See, I've got the high blood" (a regional term for hypertension). "This is just to make sure it *stays* high today." With that, he put the pill in his mouth and swallowed hard—just as a tiny corporal called out that we must now assort ourselves under unmistakable letters of the alphabet, hung from overhead wires. We obeyed in the usual semi-distracted Southern fashion (some of us slowed by an uncertain knowledge of the alphabet).

Then we were led upstairs and slotted into small rooms. There we spent a silent hour answering two kinds of printed questions. First there was a straightforward intelligence test of the sort many of us had taken from grade school onward. Next came a page headed *Do you now have or have you ever had?* That question was followed by several dozen Yes/No possibilities—*measles, epileptic seizures, syphilis,* and so on into a final sweep of more complicated choices like *nervous breakdown, prison sentence, homosexual relations.* I had no trouble answering all the questions honestly, though several of them had never confronted me before—not in writing at least.

Next we were herded into a wide room that seemed to run the length of the building, back toward the State Capitol (some two blocks away). Here we were told to remove all clothing—barring jewelry, watches, and wallets—and leave the clothes, with the shaving kits we'd been told to bring, in a row of unlockable lockers. Then we passed down, one by one, before a line of doctors and medics and were given further brief commands. First, we were weighed. A short black man, who'd cheerfully introduced himself to me as Bernice, stood immediately ahead. He climbed on the scales, and the arrow slammed past the maximum weight—300 pounds. The unamused medic looked at my new friend's paperwork and said "Bernice, estimate your weight." Bernice admitted he didn't know but allowed it was "Bound to be more than three hundred." He looked back at me and winked. The medic said "Nothing funny about this. Move ahead."

Already Bernice was disqualified for service; but his wink helped me onward in the grim process (we'd been commanded to bring a shaving kit since, if we were found fit, we'd be instantly inducted and shipped out). My robust friend and I were parted at that point, but several other laughs proved helpful. One doctor said to another man before me in line, "Bend over and spread your cheeks." The man bent way forward, inserted two fingers into his mouth, spread his facial cheeks, and looked back at the doctor before he could be told to spread his *buttocks* for a rectal exam.

I provided no amusement to anyone wearing a uniform but performed all commands abjectly—trapped already in the prevailing atmosphere of semi-civil, total control. When I turned to proceed through other physical tests, I nearly collided with a small cot. On it was lying Brutus Bloxton, likewise naked and surrounded by medics with blood-pressure sleeves. The pill seemed to be at work; and when Brutus saw me standing above him, he gave me my second wink of the morning. I silently mouthed "Good luck" and kept going, half expecting to hear Brutus explode behind me.

As little as I wished to serve in the army for several years—quitting my job at Duke and my hopes of writing—I was nonetheless moving forward here, in typical American-boy fashion, as passively as a castrated ram, a wether. Other than obedience I had only one choice—I could quietly dress and walk out. Likely no one would stop me. But sooner or later I'd receive another letter; and if I failed to obey at that point, I'd presumably be arrested and compelled either into service—if acceptable—or confinement in a federal prison. In any case, after twenty more minutes of simple challenges—a blood test and a chest X-ray—we were shepherded into short lines before three open doorways.

Three yards behind each door, a military physician was seated with a pencil. We waited three yards outside the door and were waved forward as the prior man concluded his interview. My particular doctor wore navy whites, a pleasant-looking man, not yet thirty. When I stepped to his desk, I remained upright—still naked—as he found my papers in a short stack before him. He spent a silent minute glancing at my intelligence-test score and my answers to the *Have you ever* questions. At closer range I could see he was young, hardly older than I and likewise black-haired; and he spoke very softly as though to prevent the next man from hearing us. Finally he beckoned me nearer still, and his pencil pointed to the question about homosexual relations. He said "Edward, do you know what this means?" (Edward is my first name).

I said "Yes sir."

It took him twenty seconds, looking down all the while, to frame his next question. "Have you consulted a psychiatrist about this problem?"

I said "Sir, I've never felt the need." I'd thought from the start, with Bernice at the scales, that it was odd to be addressed here by our first names; was it a studied attempt to calm us?

At last the doctor could look up and face me.

In my wallet I had a letter from my local physician attesting to the true fact that I had a lifetime history of serious respiratory allergies. I handed the letter over. The doctor read it slowly, then handed it back. He opened a small black book to his left, consulted several pages, and entered a long line of coded information at the bottom of one of my forms—a total of maybe ten letters and numbers. Then he faced me again—"You can dress and go to the next room." I assumed that my exam was finished; my fate was sealed and, for now, encoded in that penciled formula. Soon I'd know what it meant, so I dressed as told and went to the next room, a smaller space. Some dozen men, mostly younger than I, waited on a long bench against the wall. I joined the others.

A condensed, muscle-packed man sat opposite—five yards away. Soon he called my name, *Price Edward.* The reverse order seemed bad news, but I advanced to face him and surrendered my papers.

He wore army khaki and had every physical characteristic of the ultimate hard-assed drill sergeant. He confirmed that I was Price Edward, then looked down at the crucial line of code, opened his own black book, consulted a few pages slowly, entered another line of code beneath the first, then looked up with what I've always remembered—maybe unfairly—as a look of pure despisal (though maybe he faced his wife and child identically at each predawn breakfast; he was not a happy man). "Price, you've been found unfit for military service. Take your kit and leave." He didn't specify my failings, but I doubt I've ever heard two more welcome sentences in conjunction. Of course I concealed my elation.

But Brutus Bloxton—who'd filed in behind me, still undressed—called out "All *right.*" I'd seen no one all morning who couldn't have been curled into pretzel shape by Brutus, so I gave him a V sign in unalloyed thanks. Then I quietly drove to Mother's house and phoned her at the store with welcome news. Later in the week I tried to phone Brutus, reached his mother, and learned that the high blood pressure (native or not) had apparently saved him. In any case, the army had sent him down to Fort Bragg to rest overnight under observation before concluding he was too big a risk.

Classes had almost started and I still hadn't found the country dwelling I wanted. I was staying mostly with Mother and Bill in Raleigh; but I also spent as much time as possible in Warren County—our poor and underpopulated but beautiful home place an hour to the north on the Virginia state border. Lifelong affection for kinfolk on both sides of our family, and the hope of real news about our shared past, led me first to my aunt Ida Rodwell Drake. She'd reared Mother, when their parents died in Mother's childhood, and was living still in the village of Macon in the rambling white house built by my grandfather John Egerton Rodwell in about 1886.

I'd been born in the same house and had spent a good many of my happiest days there with Ida in the 1930s and '40s. She was eighteen years older than Mother; and in the absence of a maternal grandmother, Ida had always been—in effect—my grandmother. She'd borne and raised three sons of her own, each of whom had devastated her hopes again and again with their alcoholism. For a good part of my childhood then, without knowing why, I'd gladly received—and, I think, reciprocated—a quantity of love that had lain untapped within her. We'd written each other often in my years abroad; and her husband had died while I was in England, so she was now alone in the old house.

Freed at last of army dread, I felt more than ever poised to complete a volume of stories with the long account of Rosacoke and Wesley; and before my teaching duties began, I was hell-bent on moving Oxford and Britain far to one side of my mind and filling all available space with the materials of language and narrative I'd need—the languorous words and rhythms of eastern Carolina in those last days before the universal blighting eye of television had begun to substitute itself for the rich old speech that had built itself on seventeenth-century British English and a single other great contribution.

The site of the first permanent English colony in North America was only some ninety crow's-flight miles from Macon, and it was at Jamestown that African slaves were first bought in 1619 from Dutch traders. The brand of the English language that those inventive captives (and their two or three freed generations of descendants) had made for their own daily intermingling with owners and neighbors was another rich influence on my early speech and thought—an influence I was especially eager now to recover, both for my pleasure and for use in my story. Few places in the South preserved as rich a brand of black English as Warren County, North Carolina.

As late as my return home, many black people were living there in conditions that—so far as housing, food, and clothing were concerned—were often worse than those maintained by any slave owner concerned with protecting his largest investment. Still the vigor of black English thereabouts—the rising pitch and the endless wit of its sentences—was intact, thank God, wherever I turned: perhaps the most potent of several inventions that had kept these people alive and stable for so many years.

I'm well aware that such a description may read like a long-outdated defense of the slow years of oppressed segregation that followed abolition. It's not. It attempts to describe honestly the convincing welcome I always got from black men and women in Macon as long as I was known there (I mainly stopped going in the mid-1980s when paraplegia ended my driving). But did that apparent sincerity from those welcoming African-Americans conceal degrees of hatred or hostility? No doubt many of them had long practiced the deployment of intricate layers of concealment in their dealings with white folks, yet don't all human beings search out an inner core of kinsmen and friends to love or like (or tolerate with amusement)? Those older natives of Macon had surely found occasional whites whom they could like, however selectively. They'd also developed wary skills for selecting the few likable characteristics of highly prejudiced whites and acknowledging those traits in the language of daily discourse.

I could sit in Ida's kitchen, for instance, and talk with a black woman who'd blessed my childhood with ceaseless generosity. Her name was Mary Lee Parker, and she'd cooked there as long as I remembered. Her father was a prominent local white man; and Mary Lee knew it, though the paternity had never been publicly announced. I'd occasionally witnessed, in my summer visits, rare brief flare-ups of temper between Mary Lee and Ida. But I never came in for the least trace of whatever resentments this more than half-white woman had stored; and until her death some twenty years later, Mary Lee and I remained in good touch.

While I doubt she ever read more than a few pages of my subsequent fiction (pages that transformed the death of her daughter in childbirth), I know that she had some sense of participating in it through years of the free-flowing talk between us. Free-flowing as it was, however, it was only on my last visit to her—in her sweltering house with the Kennedy postcard propped on her mantel—that she asked me finally, as though I might know, "Reynolds, why do the white people hate the black people so much?" I could only tell her it was the deepest mystery we had, and she gave a one-note chuckle at my helplessness.

After a kitchen morning with Mary Lee or an afternoon on the porch with Ida—asking her to tell me, one more time, some story from the past she'd actually known (it extended to her birth in 1888 and far beyond in her memory of stories told by others)—I could ride out into the country in Mother's car (my own had yet to land) and find old black friends of my mother and father, most of whom met me pleasantly on my return from "over the pond." One still-active man who might have been born a slave—that was a question you didn't ask—wanted to know how I liked Mr. Churchill (pronounced as two distinct syllables, *Church-hill*). But not once did I encounter a whiff of rancor or indifference, only the same old readiness to surround me, submerge me, in magically looping tales of the past—their own, my mother's girlhood, my infancy hereabouts. My difficult birth and my dangerous escapade at the age of two in a runaway goat cart was still a memory of considerable vitality and laughter (and in numerous versions).

I could drive five miles to Warrenton, where my father's three sisters still lived. There I could stay with two of them in the old Price place where the two kept house for themselves and an aged and difficult maiden aunt who—whatever problems she presented—was never committed to a nursing home. In fairly typical American fashion, the mother repeatedly takes the children to visit her own family home, and the father passively agrees. Thus my brother and I had seen little of these women in our childhood. By the time Bill and I were on our own, though, we quickly learned that the Price women—famous for their sharp tongues (the two oldest had experienced monumentally sad marriages)—could give us fascinating company in a good many ways, at times even more so than the Rodwells. They shared the Rodwell willingness to speak quite freely of family calamities, including our scandals; but the Prices spiced their stories with even more wit and humor—tendencies that were perhaps endowments of their mixed Scottish, Welsh, and French Huguenot blood.

In short, with the personal tragedies receding into the past, they could recount the lives of others—all of them were our kin and nearby friends—with a detailed and not-quite-cruel delight in the spectacles of human folly (they loved nothing more than a joke on themselves). As a grown man I'd just begun to comprehend and join them in that delight, a skill that had been unavailable to me in childhood; and once I possessed their tales, I could pass them on with the only narrative skill my aunts lacked. That final skill was a gift of my father's to my brother and me (is it chiefly a male trait?)—we could mimic the voices and manners of our subjects to apparently startling, and laughable, degrees.

In addition to those human reconnections, I spent long hours simply driving through the county. In those days its fields were mainly devoted to raising tobacco (cotton had mostly moved farther south); and its apparently endless clusters of pines were providing pulp wood for the manufacture of paper just down the road in Halifax County, where one paper mill offended the air on any damp evening. Peanuts were grown also but it would be nearly two more decades before the diminished number of American smokers made peanuts and pulp-wood the county's substitute main crops.

What I was mostly seeking on my rides was the solitude that had been such a gift to my childhood—the dappled silent woods and streams through which I rambled, well before I could drive, and kept long company with nothing but my own mind, stocked as it then was with little more than the books I'd read, the movies I'd seen, and the dreams of becoming a grown man with power to make my particular art (not till I was sixteen or seventeen did I turn, as so many writers have, from being a painter to the writing of fiction and poetry). Apart from the care I'd received from my parents and other kin, that country silence—a substance as real as trees and sky—had brought me to where I was then and there. I was a hopeful man who'd nonetheless reached his mid-twenties with no large piece of public work, no partner I hoped to trust forever, no children, no money, and no job that promised regular pay for more than three years.

Yet a close confrontation with those realities left me oddly happier than maybe it should have. By then in the States, a middle-class man at twenty-five was still a young man (not the post-adolescent he often is today). But no one I knew had managed to say *Get your ass in gear and finish this book you've promised to any number of well-wishers.* When I headed back to Mother's to search the classifieds for a country dwelling in easy reach of Duke—a residence I could both afford and soon turn into my usual cocoon of books and pictures around a central desk—I did so with more than a few nightmares suggesting that my aim was misguided if not ludicrous. My father had been well on into his thirties before he managed to quit his drinking and hear his life click down on the track it could follow with any degree of rewarding response. How long would life take before I heard a similar click?

Again the hard thing was—and I didn't realize it was hard because I didn't know it existed as a problem—I didn't truly know *how* to proceed with my writing (and I've still never heard of anyone who was taught a useful means of managing the problem). If nothing else, the work on my *Samson* thesis should have shown me this. I hardly doubted that I had an endowment for words and rhythm, and I'd already looked down into a deep potential well of subjects. How, though, could I persuade my mind—my actual hands—to put the words and their story on paper, day after day? It was as real a problem as if you told an apprentice potter to persuade a lump of damp clay to rise on a wheel and form a sturdy but handsome bowl—not a question of technique but of sheer procedure: how to move from *one* to *two*, A to B, without losing force, and how to do it *daily*. The answer wouldn't come to the potter, or me, till we'd worked and failed a good many times.

Soon after my liberation from the draft—and numerous discouraging visits to country landladies with airless garage apartments to rent—Professor Blackburn phoned me one evening at Mother's and said that he'd seen a promising ad in that day's paper—a trailer/house combination on the edge of Duke Forest. There'd been no further details in the ad, though in his paternal way, Blackburn had already phoned the listed number and got directions for seeing the place if I was interested—he clearly thought I should be. His own hunch fired my hopes in the matter.

In an hour I'd got to Durham, collected Blackburn, pushed on west of town, and entered the dense dark that surrounds (and still encloses) the west side of the university—seven thousand acres of evergreens and hardwoods. With some initial difficulty we found the landlord's house at the junction of two dirt roads just on the edge of Orange County, four miles from campus—the southwest corner of Kerley Road and Cornwallis. Henry May proved to be a talkative middle-aged alumnus of Duke and a teacher in a local junior high (we didn't yet say "middle school"). From the moment we arrived, he assumed I'd already rented his property—he thought it was that irresistible. And in deep dark anyhow, it was. The dwelling itself was thirty yards from the house where he and his wife lived.

It consisted of a faded blue pre–World War II trailer (maybe ten yards long with a built-in bed and a convertible sofa); then a three-foot-long connecting passageway led into a brand-new pale-green cinder-block house that sat parallel to the trailer and contained a small living room with a salvaged car-seat sofa, built-in bookshelves; a kitchen with a sink, a stove, a shower stall, a toilet; and outside was a separate garage. There was no air-conditioning, and the only heat would come from a huge oil burner in the living room—two matters that seemed of little importance to a recent dweller on Sandfield Road. I couldn't yet see the alleged adjacent pond or the nearby woods, but the rent and Mr. May's confidence in me turned the deal. I'd pay the monthly sum of forty-five dollars, less than ten percent of my monthly check; and I could move in tomorrow. A few days earlier I'd gone down to Charleston by bus and rescued my car. Amazingly it had survived its own Atlantic crossing with literally no scratches, and the customs duty turned out to be small.

Next morning then I loaded a few things at Mother's and began to move myself into the first freestanding house of which I'd be the master, however bizarre its architectural components. I awarded myself a long walk in the ample, and amply promising, adjacent woods (Mr. May had purchased more than a hundred acres, on a schoolteacher's salary during the Depression); and that night Blackburn opened a bottle of Almaden Pinot Noir, baked two large potatoes, and broiled a thick sirloin in his bachelor apartment near campus. That was the launching of a friendship that built on our old teacher-student days, our 1956 week in London, and would become an enduringly supportive and unintentionally draining long-term experience.

In Raleigh I'd busied myself, harvesting from Mother's excess a sturdy worktable, a few dishes, minimal eating and cooking implements, plus sheets and towels. My cousin Mildred Drake cheerfully volunteered to make the plain curtains for my several windows; and a day or two before I'd teach my first classes, I hung my English-acquired drawings and etchings, and laid out my sizable table. Though I could only hope for it then, it would be the surface on which I'd write all my first book and a good part of the second and third. I especially liked the fact—and read it as a good omen—that the table had been a family dining table for numerous years.

Then I set down my short stack of completed fiction. It consisted of "Michael Egerton," "A Chain of Love," "The Anniversary," "The Warrior Princess Ozimba," and the last story begun in England—

The view from my trailer/house in Orange County, North Carolina in one of the oddly frequent snows of the late 1950s. I'm back from Oxford, living in the country four miles from Duke where I teach full-time. I'm also writing my novel *A Long and Happy Life*; and that job is greatly benefiting from the woods around me and the nearby pond. Small as it is, it nonetheless harbors a ferocious snapping turtle, a loyal great blue heron, foxes, raccoons, deer, and other wildlife. In the far distance of this picture, the hillside will eventually become the site of the house which I'll buy in 1965 and where I'll live and work ever since—much the most enduring residence in all my life.

"Troubled Sleep"—which lay uneasy, awaiting the last light touches for completion. Thin as the stack might be, I still believed in the goodness of what I'd achieved so far (and I still didn't know that it's, in many ways, more difficult to write a good short narrative than a long one—a novel). To the right of the stack, I aligned a few filled fountain pens. It had always been crucial for me to have an orderly desk—orderly to a fault, with the various items of my work laid out in parallel spaces to one another as if I might go blind in the night and be forced to fumble next morning for some way to write a few lines till I found someone who could take dictation.

2

FOR THE NEXT SEVERAL DAYS, I could do my last tinkering on "Troubled Sleep." Then once I got my teaching under way, I'd take up my favorite pen and, on unlined white paper in permanent black ink, I'd attempt to handwrite the opening sentence of *A Long and Happy Life*. First and last sentences have been absolutely crucial for me, then and now. And while I didn't know the right words yet, I knew what my characters were doing with their bodies—Rosacoke was on the back of her boyfriend Wesley's motorcycle. She was forcing Wesley to take her to the church where her black friend Mildred was being buried, dead in childbirth. A funeral is hardly Wesley's idea for a fine summer Sunday; so he's speeding up on the bumpy dirt road and loudly passing the numerous cars of the funeral procession, including a pickup truck with the coffin. The clear look of their bodies in my mind—the young white couple's—tells me who they are and how they each feel: Wesley exuberant yet silent, Rosa ashamed and cowed. Now I only had to carve out that one sentence, but first I had to learn how to teach my first class.

So in mid-September—still sweltering weather with no air-conditioning on Kerley Road—I resumed modified academic dress, the American version. With the first-day-of-school nerves I'd always experienced since entering first grade, I drove to campus for the formal beginning of my life as a teacher. In a new light-blue seersucker suit and my Merton College tie, I parked in a faculty-assigned spot on Duke's Georgian redbrick East Campus. In the West Duke Building I'd been assigned a kind of milk-carton office, very small but very tall. The building's local fame was that it continued to house not only a sizable portion of the English and philosophy departments but also the laboratory of the world-famed parapsychologist J. B. Rhine (when I first reached Oxford and said the word *Duke*, everyone would immediately say "Ah, Dr. Rhine!" and with serious interest).

Rhine was then by far the best-known member of the Duke community—many would have said the most notorious (he'd attracted visitors as distinguished as Aldous Huxley and Arthur Koestler). Having died in 1980, Rhine is now a far less noted man than he was in my early faculty days; and his field is subject to widespread rejection for what are now thought of as scientifically questionable methods. In fact even in my own student years, I seldom heard a good word spoken about Rhine's work by my teachers; and while I never met the man and am uninformed about his work, I directed many lost campus visitors to his office. More than a few of them told me of the urgency of their need to tell Dr. Rhine of a personal experience of ESP—extrasensory perception. And more than one described to me, before I could slip away, a ghostly manifestation of some kinsman long years after his or her death.

Waiting in my pigeonhole that starting day in '58 were the first of many years of even more nervous-making revelations—the names of my students for the coming semester. In that precomputer era, we learned the number and names of our students by way of packs of small registration cards. In the Duke of the late 1950s, almost all freshman classes were segregated by gender (that they'd also be all-white was a long-foregone conclusion); and since my office was on the

Woman's College campus, all the names for my two classes of fresh-man English were female—eighteen women in each of two sections.

A quick flip-through showed no names I recognized. I'd already got my free textbooks and had been glad to learn that, in the fall term, we'd be reading prose which might prove especially congenial to my own writing hopes. We'd start with an anthology of essays—such brief but worthy chestnuts as Virginia Woolf's "The Death of the Moth" and E. B. White's "Once More to the Lake." Then we'd lead our charges into three unquestioned cornerstones of modern fiction—Conrad's novella *Heart of Darkness*, Hemingway's *A Farewell to Arms*, and Fitzgerald's *The Great Gatsby*.

It was considerably too early in the development of the male American psyche for me to consider how unremittingly male those long fictions were—there'd be no Edith Wharton or Willa Cather, no further Woolf. But the structure of the freshman course was radically new for Duke. Once weekly a senior member of the department would lecture to all the freshmen, divided into large groups in various big lecture halls on the men's and women's campuses. The lecturer would give an overview of the book under consideration. The point of assigning the mass lectures to senior professors, we were told, was to give the freshmen a view of our stellar performers in full action, thereby tempting them into an eventual English major. Alas, the chairman's faith in the senior members' ability to lecture clearly and arrestingly was misplaced; and within a year more than a few lectures were assigned to promising younger members.

One such senior lecture, on *The Great Gatsby*, was so appallingly bad that I returned to the trailer foaming mad; and in my furious attempt to drive a picture-hanging nail into the concrete-block wall, I broke the nail. It flew into my left eye with the near force of a bullet. I fell to the floor, covered the eye with my fingers, and slowly drew back a handful of blood. It was late afternoon but I phoned a local eye hospital which urged me to come in before it closed at five. By four-thirty I'd managed to get the Beetle within three blocks of the hospital when a sudden great jet of what seemed black octopus-ink flooded the vision of the wounded eye. But I managed to see a doctor who told me to return home and lie flat on my back for a week. Otherwise the retina might detach and the eye be ruined. My brother came out and helped me with cooking and other chores, and at the end of a week the doctor took another look inside the eye and sent me home for a second week of lying down. After two weeks I was allowed to return to my teaching; and though I experienced unnerving flashes of light for years to come—and floating black blood cells—the eye slowly repaired itself. And I never allowed myself thereafter to react so realistically to a senior lecturer.

Once past the mass lecture, in any case, we junior instructors would meet with our two sections separately and lead a more detailed discussion of the book (or essays or stories). Then we'd assign a topic related to the book, and each student would write her best effort at a five-hundred-word theme. Then—and here was the truly demanding part for the instructor—we'd hold private twenty-minute conferences with each student. With the student at our elbow, we'd read, discuss, and grade each theme. There'd be ten themes per term—10 times 36 students, thus 360 themes per term x 20 minutes per theme = 120 hours of conferences per term. And those were hours that could well be fraught with student unhappiness, not to mention tears, if the instructor disliked a particular theme.

Even at best, a twenty-minute conference could feel infinite if the student wasn't already a semi-competent talker about books and the difficulties of prose composition in midcentury American English; and since I was determined (for the sake of my writing) to do all my teaching on a three-day weekly schedule, I could stagger home exhausted after that many hours of conferences. What was most demanding from me in those private meetings was not the total time spent but the new skills required by every such contact. The first required skill was mere attention. As a man with no children of my own, I had to learn quickly how to sit and listen sympathetically, but not without misgivings, to a young person's self-explanations. Then harder still I had to learn to explain my misgivings and, finally, the grade I gave a particular piece of work at the end of the conference.

And in those days of seriously uninflated grading—ah, the rigors of

outright *honesty* about the quality of student work!—my explana-
tions often had to justify a grade of D or F, even to the hypercourteous
students of those days. (In contrast, fifty years later such low grades are
all but unheard of in the humanities in most American universities;
and the present higher grades almost never reflect a significant
improvement in the quality of student intelligence. A teacher award-
ing such grades now, even when they're entirely justified by the quality of the student's work, is likely to find that his or her classes have
grown massively unpopular—classes that almost no one will take.)

My third class would generally prove my favorite—Representative
British Writers, a course required of all English majors. In those days
we thought we knew who the major British writers were (I still think
many thoughtful readers do, though I'm not sure *representative* is the
word for a series of writers, at least three out of four of whom were
geniuses). In my first year we divided the fall semester among Chaucer,
Shakespeare, Donne, and Milton. Since our students were mostly
sophomores and juniors, they were no longer separated by gender; and
the classes were often a good deal larger than the handily small freshman classes. From the start I'd concentrate on drawing my students
into group discussions of the poems and plays. And because of my
Oxford experience of such talk, I sometimes succeeded, though I'd find
almost invariably that a small clutch of the students would simply
refuse to commit themselves to speaking aloud, and in the presence of
their peers, to the slightest opinion or question. Even five decades later,
I usually find that ten percent of a class will simply refuse to engage in
class conversation, even when they've been told at the start of the term
that my evaluation of their part in class dialogue will constitute, say, a
third of their final grade (I always specify that any student who has difficulty with such contribution should discuss the problem privately
with me, and we'll make special efforts to ease the difficulty; very few
of the silent ten percent ever come to discuss the problem).

Those early freshmen, however, would absorb far the greater portion of my energy. My first class met in another tall, but enormous,
room in the same building with my office—a nineteenth-century

Anne Tyler when I first knew her, in the Duke Gardens in the fall of 1958. She's sixteen years old and already endowed with the gifts which made it such a pleasure to teach her—though *teaching* is hardly the word. In retrospect, I can see that—at age twenty-five—I was far more nearly a kind of household steward for the start of a career that was longing to start. In her Raleigh high school, which had been mine also (seven years earlier), she'd thought of painting as a likely life's work; but when she reached Duke and began to respond to a few vague suggestions offered by her freshman composition teacher, the powder trail of prodigious feeling which had waited silently within her ignited and burnt its way forward. When I recently asked her if the dress she's wearing in this picture might not have been a little conservative for the late 1950s, she told me "The dress I am wearing was made by my mother, who made every single one of my clothes until I went away to graduate school, at which point I found out that I was actually two sizes smaller than the dresses she had been sewing for me all those years." The spit curl, however, was entirely in fashion, as was—and is—the thoroughly winning smile.

limestone survivor of old Trinity College which had preceded James B. Duke's vast endowment and then named itself after his father, in understandable gratitude—and my first set of eighteen girls were banded in the midst of the space in the jittery uncertainty of novice college students (we called them *girls* or *boys* then with no sense of insult). My own nerves would have been even more high-strung if I'd thought the students knew it was my own first day of teaching.

From the moment I sat at the desk and looked up with my best imitation of the unsmiling authority that had always impressed me in a teacher, a particular young woman caught my attention. She sat at the head of the row on my right, and she faced me with the same grave self-possession I was struggling to show her—a beautiful clear face, long black hair, and dark eyes. I opened my stack of cards and began to call the roll, asking the girls to tell me which of their given names they preferred and where they'd grown up. In those days I almost never had to ask for help in pronouncing their names—then they were at least ninety-nine percent Anglo-Saxon—and unlike my present students, they'd almost all grown up in a single town (unless they were "army brats").

The imposing girl responded to the name Anne Tyler with a surprising blush—"Anne is pronounced *Anne*, and I've lived in Raleigh since I was a child." I nodded and decided to wait for our first conference before revealing my own Raleigh connections. As I moved on through the name cards, I couldn't have known what a vivid stroke of beginner's luck I'd just been dealt.

Our reading began with the previously required anthology of essays, and my first assignment to the students was a theme on the subject of their very earliest memories. I asked them to describe as honestly and pictorially as possible—in however many words proved necessary—the oldest moment they thought they'd preserved. I told them that my own first memory appeared to be very brief but clear—a sunbath in the yard of the house in which my parents were renting rooms; I was three or four months old and heard the approach of a grazing goat who'd soon begin to eat my diaper. The majority of my freshmen women brought me descriptions of moments from around age three—normal enough, as I learned from psychologist friends. But Anne Tyler gave me 150 words describing a shaft of light that fell on her crib when she was some six months old (I've convinced myself I can still see the half-page, though I didn't save it).

When she came to my office for her first conference, I learned several interesting things. First she'd spent a good part of her late childhood and adolescence in her parents' house, only two blocks from my own parents'. She was sixteen years old now, when most of her fellow freshmen were eighteen. And she was a graduate of my high school in Raleigh—Needham Broughton High, widely acknowledged as the best public high school in the state—and there she'd studied with my own remarkable English teacher Phyllis Peacock, a woman marked by an outlandish but ultimately irresistible intensity of love for her subject (I've noted that Mrs. Peacock had been crucial to my decision at age sixteen to pursue a life of writing rather than painting).

It turned out that Anne had been similarly tempted; and even here in her first days of college, she still possessed a strong urge to draw and paint. Her brief description of such an early memory struck me, not so much by its few clear words of evocative prose as by the remarkable earliness of her small scrap of memory. (It would be years before I learned, and oddly from Anne's eventual husband—Taghi Modarressi, a psychiatrist who was himself a distinguished Iranian novelist—that an unusually well-stocked early memory was characteristic of dedicated writers. He even suggested that the act of writing might be a form of relieving, and unburdening ourselves of, the pressure of such memory.) That early in our acquaintance then, Anne Tyler and I shared several important things in our past experience; and our meetings could proceed with an ease that was not always native to freshman conferences, despite the fact that I was then nearer to the age of my students than to most of my teaching colleagues.

As my two freshman classes continued to read from the volume of essays, my next assigned subject for the theme was the production of an actual essay. I mentioned some possible subjects, most of them no doubt characteristic of my own recent concerns and maybe a little morbid for young women of such apparent good health and spirits. I suggested for instance an essay about their first encounter with death, a grandparent's funeral maybe. And while I don't remember any other single piece from that week's crop of thirty-six essays, I do recall Anne Tyler's. In fact I still possess a copy.

She called it "The Galax," and it describes an event from Anne's childhood when she and her three brothers lived with their idealistic parents in a quasi-pacifist community called Celo deep in the North Carolina mountains. In the short piece Anne joins a group of mountain women for a foray through woods to gather wild galax, an evergreen vine which they'll sell for Christmas decoration. With remarkable subtlety, for such a young writer with so few words allowed, Anne clarifies the degree to which she differs so profoundly from these embedded mountaineers. When I'd read the theme several times, and gone over it with her in conference, I acted on impulse and told her that, thereafter, when I assigned theme subjects to the other class members, she was secretly to feel free to write whatever she wished. It was my first impulsive move as a teacher and one that, most obviously, I've never regretted.

If only I'd kept copies of her work in the course of that freshman experience, I'd have an instructive and compelling portrayal of a gifted apprentice writer's rapid self-discovery and growth. And if I'd done discreetly what one of my colleagues has done throughout his equally long career—that is, photographed each student for future reference— I'd have another picture of the engaging woman Anne Tyler was becoming. In the absence of an early photograph, however, I attempted to preserve that memory in a poem which I wrote shortly after a visit to Baltimore in 1995 (the last time I'd see Taghi alive—that good man was dying of lymphoma); and here are the opening lines of my memory—

> *Thirty-seven years ago this month,*
> *You entered the first class I ever taught—*
> *The gray-eyed Athena, straight as a poplar.*
> *Tall, dark-haired and far more gifted*
> *Than a tasteful billionaire's Christmas tree . . .*

To have had the pleasure of such a presence—with the mind that moved it—in the first class I taught seemed, in my tyro's innocence, almost normal. How was I to know that it wouldn't happen often? Time, though, would tell me what an initial godsend I'd had—a gift of sufficient richness to constitute one of the ultimate reasons for my spending, throughout my life, a part of each year at a teacher's desk. An unmitigated appetite for hope—not money, surely—is the fuel. Anne Tyler would graduate from Duke in only three years at age nineteen, but she'd be a member of one other class I'd teach.

In my second year back at Duke, I was asked by a stingy-hearted colleague (not Bill Blackburn) if I'd teach his writing course for a semester while he was on sabbatical. Maybe a better descriptive word is *parched*—once he returned, he failed to offer so much as a word of minimal thanks for my work, only the flat assertion that he'd never have his course taught again in his own absence. Well, I'd taught it with great pleasure; and (for what it was worth to them) two of the students went on to become world-respected novelists. My colleague had no such luck, ever.

In the expectation of an interesting semester, I silently divided those older writing students into two sections. Those with whom I hadn't previously worked were in one; in the other I assembled an especially promising group of students with whom I'd either worked previously or had known well. Anne Tyler was prime among the group I already knew—as were Fred Chappell and Wallace Kaufman, among three or four others. That second group would meet for one extended evening each week at Fred and Sue Chappell's apartment near the Woman's Campus. I'd met Fred in 1954 during my last undergraduate year and had published his first story and at least one of his early poems in the student magazine which I was editing then. When I was in England, Fred's drinking ran him afoul of the deans; and he retired to his home in the Carolina mountains. There he married his girlfriend Sue, who accompanied him on his successful return to Duke. They gave the class a warm welcome each week, and the group proved as remarkable as I'd hoped.

I'd often begin the evening by reading a few pages from whatever I'd written that week, and we'd discuss my problems before moving on to their work (given the closeness of our ages, I had no trouble in getting them to speak candidly about my faults). As we moved on to their work, we witnessed the start of Fred Chappell's always moving and frequently hilarious fiction that reinvented his own memories from a boyhood life in a large Appalachian family. Wally Kaufman had begun to deal, in stories, with his world of blue-collar north-shore Long Island. And in the course of the term, Anne completed a short story that still seems to me astonishing. It's called "The Saints in Caesar's Household"; and while it would appear in the student magazine, and years later in a creative-writing textbook, it's never appeared elsewhere (Anne has always resisted collecting her short fiction).

When she'd given me the manuscript at the end of a previous meeting, I'd gone straight home and read it in my trailer bed with climbing excitement. I'd known this girl was good, but now she'd taken a long stride onward. When she read it aloud at the next class meeting, the other members sagely granted the strength of the story; but no one was prepared to say—or perhaps to *see*—what a first-rate thing she'd made: first-rate, I knew, by any standards. It was the first adult writing class I'd managed, but raw instinct prevented my trying to tell the whole class how high the story stood.

I suspected it was my complex duty not to discourage any of the other gifted students by praising one of their number disproportionately. But later, privately, I told Anne what I thought and asked her if I might do what Eudora Welty had done for me some four years earlier—submit the story to Diarmuid Russell. With her sometimes unnerving self-possession—or was it genuine shyness?—she only said "Yes." So I sent the story off and Diarmuid responded Yes in his own laconic way. He never managed to sell that one story, but in only a few more years he'd sold Anne's first novel, and one of the most successful careers of the past five decades in American fiction had begun. With no false humility whatever, I can add that I make no claim to have taught Anne Tyler anything significant about narrative writing. The fact that, despite the eight-year difference in our ages, we met in parallel starting-gates may have produced a certain mutual excitement in those early years; but if so, that effect was benignly accidental, not managed by me. It might even have helped us both more.

I can recall, for instance, that in the summer after our first year's work together, Anne sent me a new short story. I can only guess that it had something to do with a young man and woman at a dance (maybe I'm wrong). I know that I wrote back in response, and I know that—once she'd left Duke and completed a year's work in Russian studies at Columbia—she returned to campus and worked for a year as a cataloguer of Russian books. I saw her a few times then at student parties, and I met the young Iranian resident in psychiatry at Duke Hospital whom she'd ultimately marry. But I don't recall seeing her privately. My apprentice teacher's sense—learned from Professor Blackburn—that a responsible male teacher must be very circumspect in his dealings with female students rather absurdly hindered my early relations with Anne, who spent all her college summers very near my mother's house where I could have seen her often (four years later, that same excessive circumspection affected my dealings with Josephine Humphries, the next greatly gifted student with whom I worked).

The friends who were roughly my age in those first years back in Durham consisted mainly of two couples—Dick and Charlotte Quaintance and Bill and Marie Combs. Dick and Bill were a few years older than I and had essentially completed work for their doctorates at, respectively, Yale and Harvard. Each of the couples had two children; and while it appeared—unostentatiously—that Dick might have a little money of his own, all of us seemed strapped each month to make it through till payday (we'd often borrow a dollar or two, from whichever one of us was still afloat, to feed ourselves till then).

The Quaintances and Combses provided almost all my social life—weekend dinners, with good food and drinkable cheap wine, that would last till two or three in the morning. Our gatherings were further fueled by intense but ultimately laughing discussions of the novels and poems we taught and the films we saw (the best of the Ingmar Bergman films, for instance, were opening then with powerful frequency); and all our meetings were seasoned with sometimes hilarious, occasionally heartbreaking accounts of the students we were learning to know in the exhausting yet somehow exhilarating hours of conferences.

It's more than interesting, in retrospect, to consider that most of those close friends were either from the northeast or the Midwest; yet the subject of civil rights—and specifically of Duke's all-white student body—seldom arose in our conversations. Was the explanation as simple as the fact that virtually all of us had simply settled, long since in most cases, into an acceptance (however sad) of the realities of segregation? Surely we were not that massively indifferent to so great an injustice. Still, the only one of us whom I can recall as participating in any of the peaceful marches and demonstrations that occurred regularly in Durham was Bill Combs, who'd been reared in Mississippi. And our undergraduate students showed less interest in the civil-rights movements than we, a great deal less—though there was none of the obviously vicious environment of governmental resistance to oncoming change that one heard of from the deep South. For that, we had the complex history of North Carolina to thank and the governorship of Terry Sanford (and ours was a state which had lost more men than any other Confederate state to the Civil War).

As for social companions, I don't recall a single "date" with any woman but Dorothy Roberts, the phenomenally capable secretary of the English department. She'd begun that job in the late 1940s and, with only a single assistant (an older woman who primarily typed and filed), Dot Roberts did, with impeccable professional pride, the job that's now done by some five or six employees. She was some fifteen years older than I; and she tended to contribute excessive talk to social situations, small or large; but she was good-looking and unquestionably loyal to any man or woman who earned her respect (her standards were old-fashioned Southern but high—she hailed from south central Virginia and had graduated from the University of Richmond). Starting shortly after my return to Duke and continuing till she retired from the department in the late 1980s, she was my frequent partner at lectures, dinners, whatever. To the best of my knowledge, no one thought we were lovers; and neither of us forged that appearance, not once in the thirty-odd years of our devoted and affectionate friendship.

This may be as good a time as any to recount a relevant fact—the fact that, in all my life, I've lied only once about my sexual proclivities. In fact it was to one of my old college friends that I told—I still believe—the only lie I ever told about my sexuality. I later declined to answer the question from a very few others whom I thought had no right to ask it, but I lied to no one else, and that was long ago.

Late in our senior year, one of my closest friends came to the office from which I was editing the student literary magazine and quietly said, in private, that he'd heard a disturbing rumor from an acquaintance of ours—the claim that I was queer. Since the acquaintance had no firsthand knowledge of me or any of my actions, I was puzzled as to the origins of the rumor (especially since, till then, my very low total of sexual acts would have shamed a robust Chaucerian friar). It was the first time I'd faced the rumor; and in response—and in the barest minimum of words—I lied. I said I was not; and I never corrected the claim, not to that friend. It would be another twenty years before any number of queer Americans felt safe in openly discussing their exotic sexuality. To have advertised it in the 1950s or early '60s would have endangered anyone's hope of a stable career, not to mention his standing with kinfolk and friends—or the police.

Otherwise I spent increasing amounts of evening time with Fred and Sue Chappell. Slowly I was learning that Fred was very close to being the best-read young American I knew (better than I); and finding an early and near-supreme literacy at the roots of his rural fiction and intensely intellectual poetry—all in a man who was ready to talk till dawn, as his long-suffering wife Sue poured us endless coffee—was a genuine help to my prevailing solitude. At least once a week also, I'd accept an invitation from Bill Blackburn and join him for a sirloin steak, a huge baked potato, and salad—served atop the desk in the living room of his four-room apartment.

By now Blackburn was in the vicinity of sixty, was entering his second decade of bachelor life, and the loneliness was plainly drilling in on him. The extremes of mood which I'd watched as his student were even more vivid at close range. Belly laughter at his own fine jokes could turn in a moment to indigo silence. After a long wait, he might rise and refill my wineglass, put a record on his turntable—a succession of Monteverdi madrigals, say—and we'd sit in a further bottomless quiet through a rapt half-hour of a kind that I'd never experienced with any other music-loving friend.

Even at a public concert, one friend might whisper a comment to the other but not with Bill. If anything had replaced the missionary-parent religion of his childhood, it was music. To him the notes and voices that poured from his state-of-the-art speakers mattered most desperately. Few of his friends can have more nearly shared his love of a certain kind of music than I (Fred Chappell would later be another), but the unbroken solemnity of the listening sessions eventually grew hard to endure. They were never as hard to attend to, though, as his steadily delivered opinions of our departmental colleagues.

Almost anyone who knew Bill Blackburn intimately in the final two decades of his life was aware that he descended slowly but with no turn-back into what can only be called grave clinical paranoia. Many of his colleagues—most of whom, I came to realize, thought of him with wary admiration and slightly bemused affection—were, he came to feel, his sworn enemies, dedicated to destroying his good name in our community and, somehow, to endangering his employment at the university (despite the fact that, tenured full professor as he was, he could only have been fired under extremely rare circumstances).

Maybe his long immersion in the literature of the lethal courts of Henry VIII, Bloody Mary, and Elizabeth the Virgin Queen had left him with more of a sense of viperous dark corridors and daggers-to-the-gut than was healthy. When I felt that I knew him well enough to attempt to lure him into a chuckling dispersion of his outlandish fears, he repeated that his own father had died "mad." In fact he often catalogued for me his other close kin, still alive, some of whom he described as mentally disturbed—including his ancient mother who lived in a retirement home just down the block.

I met the old lady several times—she was then in her nineties—and was compelled to agree that, despite considerable charm and the remains of a girlish beauty, she appeared to be advancing into religious mania. Blackburn had told me that, upon learning of his divorce, she'd torn from her New Testament and mailed to him, with no further comment, the page on which Jesus most firmly precludes a broken marriage. (The incidental fact that, in all these pages, I've not yet referred to him as Bill reflects the fact that, after a six-year acquaintanceship, he'd never once asked me to call him by his first name. And the moment when, after three more years, I seized the nettle and addressed him as Bill—on one relaxed evening over drinks— was awesome. I'd weighed the wisdom of such a move well before making it; and now that I'd dared it, the coldest of chills afflicted my spine as I met his all-but-glaring gaze—was it the furious *How dare you?* he implied or a plain sad surprise? I'd never know but *Bill* it remained from that night onward.)

Years after I failed in my attempts to calm his view of a mere English department, Bill's widow—who'd been an ideal second wife in his final years, though he inexplicably refused to see her in his last days in Duke Hospital—told me about finding recent journal notes in which, shortly before his last illness, he recorded crouching to hide in a neighbor's backyard while he was out for an afternoon walk. He'd retired honorably from teaching several years earlier; but now on his walk he'd suddenly caught sight of a department colleague approaching in the middle distance. It was someone he'd long regarded as his supreme vicious enemy. Bill tried to hold his ground and walk on ahead, but finally he couldn't bear the encounter, so a man of his former unshakable dignity ducked aside and hid his tall frame in a painful crouch behind a row of dense shrubs and stinking garbage cans.

Yet when I spent many hours beside him in Duke Hospital in 1972, as his death from cancer bore down hard (the tumor had gone from a salivary gland to his brain), he raised his swollen head off the pillow as I was ending one of my visits and said "I don't see how you stand this." I've still never known what he meant by *this*. Was it the sight of his agony which I visited twice daily, his face contorted by the tumor that by then had wrenched his features almost unrecognizably, the onerous teaching duties which I'd sometimes told him about, my writing; or was it mere life, the long life he'd known by then? He died, soon after, at only seventy-three—a brilliantly generous and almost endlessly tormented life.

In a group of younger friends, Bill could overcome an innate shyness and begin to rouse the joviality which powered his most winning charms. I've known few men more capable than he of entertaining an entire room of assorted friends when he could be persuaded to launch a few of his splendidly narrated comic recollections from sixty years of life in the middle South or his early childhood in Persia. But again, when I spent the frequent evenings alone with him over dinner in my early years of teaching, his disdain for our colleagues—and his patent fear of them—began to prove contagious. John Knowles would say to me years later that "No illness is more contagious than madness." And a fledgling instructor like me, in the first years of his hope to spend at least part of his life in teaching, almost began to suspect that the corridors of a university might be as densely lined with stilettos and poison rings as any Florentine palace in the days of the Medici and their mortal enemies.

Still I maintained our friendship—partly because I had a lot of evenings on my hands, partly because I genuinely liked Bill (even in most of his unpredictable mood swings), partly because he offered paternal affection and wisdom, but above all because he seemed unhurriedly confident that I could become a writer and might fulfill his hope that I'd produce, as Styron and Guy Davenport had, fiction of serious quality. Yet he never made me feel that his friendship depended upon my success as a writer.

It would be years before I discovered that it was my publication of a successful first novel that led Bill Blackburn, most mysteriously, to end our friendship for a number of years. At that painful point, Styron assured me that, when his own first novel was published, he'd undergone an identical rejection from Blackburn. However long Styron and I discussed that shared reality (and we often did), we never understood it. Surely neither of us was aware of having intentionally neglected or

offended so generous, though notoriously sensitive, a man whose early
encouragement we never ceased to acknowledge.

Any attempt to explain the connections between Blackburn's prevailing dread and fear of sudden abandonment by those closest to him
is doomed to textbook psychologizing. In some sense his suspicions
and eventual terrors were among the fuels that powered, first, his comprehension of the poetry and prose he taught incomparably for so
many years and, second, the hunger that preceded the love he invested
in those students in whom he sensed a potential for good writing.

He was by no means the only teacher I've known whose work was
fired by personal qualities that caused him or her great enduring
pain and sometimes undermined his chance of endowing a given student with the very strengths he intended to give—Bill's intensity, for
instance, frightened off several gifted young men. In fact I suspect that
few of my lifelong teaching colleagues, myself included, would claim
to have escaped entirely such painful contradictions. Whether or not
teaching is more conducive to such miseries than, say, a career in law,
medicine, or the priesthood, I can't begin to know. I do know that I've
never been befriended—and in the first decade of our friendship, so
generously helped—by another human being who was as near prone
as William Blackburn to an immovable certainty that the ground
beneath him was as treacherous as any dark marsh and that the thick-
ets on every side were populated with alleged friends plotting his
shame and swift downfall.

3

IN THE OTHER TIME available from my teaching and my
efforts at writing, every week or ten days I'd drive the half-hour to
Raleigh and eat with Mother and my brother Bill and spend an occa-

sional night. The fact that I could now make a monthly contribution to their ongoing welfare was a great relief to me, especially toward the needs of a brother who'd lost his father at so young an age. When I returned to the States, my brother was seventeen and a high-school junior—the same even-keeled and easy kinsman I'd always enjoyed, sharpened now by the maturity required of him when our father died. Bill and I had always loved good books—the Landmark lives of great American boys had been important in his pre-adolescence for instance—and by the time I was home, he'd begun to show a fascination with American history that would ultimately lead to his distinguished career as an essayist, archivist, student and teacher of eighteenth- and nineteenth-century history (for nearly fifteen years he'd direct the North Carolina Department of Archives and History, one of the most respected in the nation).

At that point also, Mother was mainly liking her job at the boys' clothing store. Her natural warmth and curiosity made her welcome all but the most truculent of her customers; and she'd soon built up a sizable core of devoted mothers who'd shop with no one else when their sons needed anything from a Boy Scout uniform (with knife) to a graduation suit, tie, keychain, and shoes. And in my ongoing slender years, even I was able to fit myself out from her older-boys' racks— trousers, shirts, underwear, even suits. The only aspect of her work that began to wear her down after a few years—she was in her mid-fifties—was the need to work till nine two nights each week.

But she liked the man who owned her store, and he well knew he had a gold mine of a saleswoman in Elizabeth Price. Her favorite colleague was a slightly older woman named Vir (to rhyme with *fur*). Vir was a true West Virginian with the classic "ridge runner" accent and unvarnished mountaineer idioms and tales that Mother would store up to tell us at our next dinner. Once we'd laughed our fill, for example, at Vir's saying that she'd just bought some gorgeous water glasses that had "itching" on them (that is, *etching*), Mother would assure us that Vir would do anything on earth for her—a claim that would prove a demonstrable truth a few years later when Mother's eyesight began to fail mysteriously; and Vir quietly saved her from frequent embarrassments as she miscalculated a customer's bill, say, or couldn't read the label on a box of sweaters.

At least one weekend every six or eight weeks, I'd drive the Beetle five hours north to Washington where Michael Jordan shared an apartment with an English engineer whom he'd recently met. The drive itself would be an adventure. Mainly you had to evade the nationally notorious and rapacious Virginia speed patrolmen, and then you had to literally manhandle your steering wheel as gigantic semis roared past and all but swept your tiny German bargain under lethal wheels. But my safe arrival in green Georgetown—Olive Street—rewarded the effort.

Colin, the housemate, was a droll Cambridge graduate our age who had incomparable success in girlfriends; and soon I was enjoying the small parties the two men would throw in their compacted space. By American-youth standards of the time, the evenings were slightly formal. The "chaps" might dress in summer jackets and white trousers, the American girls in summer dresses, the few English girls in summer "frocks"; and the atmosphere would revive my memory of pleasant English evenings, only with better-quality wine and all of us a little more adult in appearance and deportment.

Among other changes, Michael was expanding his own Merton repertoire of charms for the opposite gender, and more than half the pleasure of my weekends on their narrow sofa was a chance to study his and Colin's compatible but highly personal modes of seduction. Soon Colin was squiring Berit, a lovely Swedish girl whom he'd met in Stockholm a year or so earlier and who'd come over mainly to visit him, I assumed. So compatible were the two men, however, that soon—somehow—Berit had decided to stay on in America; and she and Michael were keeping company while Colin, once more—and quite agreeably—went on switching his female tracks.

A more significant change for me was the inevitable evolution of my and Michael's college friendship into something less steadily communicative. I wasn't entirely glad for the change, but I was far from desolate. We went on seeing each other five or six times a year, always with the same mutual trust and frequent laughter. The relation would always mean things to me that it couldn't to Michael, especially as we loaded more years onto our backs and Michael acquired a family (it would be nearly twenty years before I realized that the friendship had meant as much to Michael, though in a very different way, as it always had to me).

Further, I was forging on in my own emotional life. Matyas and I were keeping up a steady transatlantic correspondence in those last days of earnest hard-copy letter writing. And to me at least, there still seemed the possibility of some kind of long-term commitment between us. Even more than love and teaching, however, I'd now launched myself on what I'd so long hoped would be my central sustained work. I'd commenced to write the Rosacoke story that was meant to complete the full volume I'd contracted with Chatto and Random House. With all the pages of notes I'd made since January '57, I still thought I was at work on a novella when I carved out the first sentence of *A Long and Happy Life* in October '58—a sentence that, in eventual reviews and later critical studies, would come to have a life of its own.

When I speak of carving it out, I mean what the metaphor implies. Michelangelo wrote of his own sense that any one of his planned statues lay, pre-existent and awaiting his chisel, within the block of marble he'd chosen. In my own early days of continuous work—and especially in that ambitious beginning—I felt myself literally struggling to see, and then to liberate, an elaborate human action which was pre-existent in my mind, in the lives of imagined (yet quite real) human characters, and finally in the English language, my recalcitrant block of marble.

Just with his body and from inside like a snake, leaning that black motorcycle side to side, cutting in and out of the slow line of cars to get there first, staring due-north through goggles toward Mount Moriah and switching coon tails in everybody's face was Wesley Beavers, and laid against his back like sleep, spraddle-legged on the sheepskin seat behind him was Rosacoke Mustian who was maybe

his girl and who had given up looking into the wind and even trying to nod at every sad car in the line, and when he even speeded
up and passed the truck (lent for the afternoon by Mr. Isaac Alston
and driven by Sammy his man, hauling one pine box and one
black boy dressed in all he could borrow, set up in a ladder-back
chair with flowers banked round him and a foot on the box to
steady it)—when he even passed that, Rosacoke said once into his
back "Don't" and rested in humiliation, not thinking but with her
hands on his hips for dear life and her white blouse blown out
behind her like a banner in defeat.

I'd begun to tell the story less than a month after beginning my
effort to learn the other great skill I'd promised myself—the ability to
teach. The story would take me more than two years to complete, and
by that time I'd begun to feel a good deal more comfortable in the
classroom and the conference office. I kept no journal of my progress
and setbacks in teaching. The three days each week of entire commitment to my students consumed all the energy I felt I could spare
for that large part of my life—even the plentiful energy of a man in his
mid-twenties—but I went on making frequent notes for my writing.
All those notes, and many more, are gathered now in a volume called
Learning a Trade; and they remind me, first, of what a rich pleasure I
took in being back on native ground or very near it.
    I've noted the rural surroundings of my trailer/house, and the
notes remind me of further details. Pastures of beef cattle mooed, bel-
lowed, and mounted one another within a few hundred yards of my
desk (all the cows seemed to be lesbian, frequently mounting one
another in dogged patience, achieving *what?*). Brightleaf tobacco
still grew, regally tall though deadly, on fields within a short walking
distance from the page on which I described it; and the mules that still
plowed the crop on a few small allotments were visible at rest on the
evening hills, side by side in parallel exactitude but never quite touching. At least as welcome was the presence on all sides of woods and
fields quite empty of other human beings.
    And then there were the neighbors. A number of the men and

women I slowly came to know (again, within a quarter-hour of campus) had lived in that corner of Durham and Orange counties for many generations; and they had useful stories to tell me—a gift they offered readily, for the asking, and in an idiom that was virtually indistinguishable from the syntax and rhythm of my story's protagonists. One of them—Claude Bennett—had been born nearby, the son of a farmer whose family had lived in our neighborhood for more than a century. Claude and his wife Betty worked on the production line at American Tobacco Company downtown; and after his retirement Claude would be the man who drove me, with an almost equine patience, to Duke Hospital for the five weeks of daily radiation treatments awarded to my cancer. Even better through the years, the language of his and Betty's family (they have two sons) has kept my ear to the local ground.

Henry May, my agreeable landlord, was from Pennsylvania; but he likewise taught me—almost daily—a great deal I hadn't previously known about the actual land we lived on. He took obvious pleasure in the pond on our west edge, the trees and pastures, all teeming with wildlife. The wildest life I'd seen in Oxford was the occasional bird or feral cat; but soon after moving to Kerley Road, Henry began pointing out the smaller neighbors. Apart from nocturnal prowlers such as possums, raccoons, flying squirrels, and foxes, we had an immense snapping turtle in the pond (who occasionally wrenched a leg off one of Henry's swimming white ducks); and speaking of larger animals, oddly the epidemic of elegant but car-wrecking deer had yet to engulf us. Birds were Henry's mania—the usual tireless and endlessly hungry songbirds and a plentiful overhead supply of red-tailed hawks and wide-winged buzzards—and he could tell me about their habits and even their migratory routes which he knew in detail. A fair amount of his animal lore worked its away into my first four books; and of course I was free to roam his land and the many acres of Duke Forest that bounded him.

On my three no-school days (with Sunday for rest), I'd take my legal pad and climb to a hill above the pond. There I'd chosen a tall

straight shagbark hickory on the edge of a wide-based triangular pas-
ture. I'd sit there, lean back on the tree, then watch and listen closely.
I'd done—and seen and heard—nothing to match this lone silence
since age nine (when Dad sold our country house); and while it was
hardly an exotic experience, I entered in my notes a few first reactions
to what was clearly a rediscovered world.

A distant rifle and a crow flies into a tree that is already bare and
standing white as a nerve. Another shot and every bird is silent, then
the crow signals and everybody starts up again. It took them 10 seconds, though.

Some trees are already bare as though to get it over with as soon
as possible.

One red leaf twisting through the air straight as a plumb line—
with no tree anywhere near.

Air full of shining-new copper wire catching the light from place
to place, seeming to float. And a single strand of silk with the spider
attached working as though he would weave the whole air full of
his shining.

Ducks asleep in the sun, heads under their wings, refusing to
look up when I quack.

Meanwhile I pushed on with my long first scene—Rosacoke and
Wesley's opening motorcycle ride to black Mildred's funeral, then the
service itself. By November 4 I noted that I'd written eighteen hundred words and had Rosacoke entering Mount Moriah Church for
the funeral. By my very slow Oxford standard, I was moving rapidly
enough to feel encouraged, though I noted that I was concerned
that neither Rosa nor Wesley yet had sufficient physical presence.
That was a prime concern of the scenes, especially after I'd read
quantities of D. H. Lawrence in England (Stephen had given me a
three-volume edition of Lawrence's stories; at his best Lawrence's
prose was still so potent I could hardly believe he'd died three years
before my birth). I was determined that my young lovers should affect
the reader almost as profoundly and erotically as they affected one

another—that the reader should be aroused by the reality of the bodies, the odors, the atmospheres of this magnetic young pair. And I labored slowly in that direction as the notes make clear.

A large part of my aim to make the main characters both physically imposing and erotically attractive was a hope that would prove enduring through my whole career (till now at least, fifty-odd years since I started). Two of my early short stories reflect powerful attractions between male characters; but since the characters are pre-adolescent, there's little or no erotic energy in their relations. And only a small number of my later adult characters lead dedicated homosexual lives. I've spent little time exploring the peculiarities of such experience, perhaps because—as I may have shown above—I've observed few such lives.

Few of my queer friends have had the luck to form long-term partnerships; and those who've done so have developed the kinds of relations that are hardly promising as fictional subjects, probably because those relations have not seemed especially subject to the vagaries of chance. So I've been more steadily interested in exploring lives involved in complex families with lengthy histories which are endlessly subject to change and fate, and such lives are generally heterosexual. I've also observed that few readers are interested, over long stretches, in stories of homosexual life; and I've never scorned readers. In short, I've pursued the kinds of lives I've known best since my birth and have slowly worked my way in and out of—happily, sadly, even tragically.

I've said that it would take me a little more than two years to finish the work, and I won't recount the gradual progress in any detail. Two things remain indelible in my memory, though, and can be set down for whatever cheer they may give readers who're in hopes of writing their own fiction. Again it was a long while before I was forced to realize that this narrative was not a long story or a novella but a fullfledged novel. What mattered to me, as I moved ahead, was the realization that I was at regular work on an entirely new thing and that I had no prior experience of making anything remotely like it. Also no one had told me that the single most important rule for successful writing is *Frequency and consistency*. It's an iron rule but its force is virtually inescapable in a form as long as the novel.

Assuming that a would-be writer—of almost any form, prose or verse—has a gift for written expression, then his greatest help is likely to come from compelling himself to sit down, at some predictable time, for X number of days per week and then to stay in place till he's added a respectable piece to his project. From the start of my long story, I aimed for a page a day, some three hundred words. I didn't know that if no words came easily, or at all, I should have stayed in place (with controlled pauses for coffee, peeing, window-gazing) and written something—of whatever nature or quality. I could even have copied out words from a favorite writer—say a superb stretch of prose like Lincoln's Second Inaugural Address or the final few pages of Hemingway's *The Sun Also Rises*, anything to give my hand a real sense of the extent to which any good writing is a *manual* art, a hand-made event. Or I might have speculated further, in my notebook, on the lives of my characters—their looks, their favorite games, foods, films, music, their secret sexual practices and fantasies, their most recent dreams. Above all, what I needed was to train my unconscious mind to deliver its creations to me, on time and in order.

I've often quoted to my students, and myself, another remark from John Knowles. He said "The unconscious mind is like children and dogs. It loves routine and hates surprises." He was assuming, as I now do, that creative work—like almost all expressions of the intellect—arises in areas of the brain that lie beneath our immediate awareness. If we want that work to move toward our daytime recognition, then we must learn reliable ways of luring it upward—usually by some highly personal routines of the sort I've just mentioned. The profound and life-long productive novelist Graham Greene said much the same thing.

In the preface to his collected short stories, Greene noted that if he was troubled by some block in his work, he'd read over the troubled passage just before going to sleep. In the morning he'd almost invariably discover that the problem had been solved by what Greene called the "*negre* in the cellar." When I first read Greene's paragraph,

I thought he was using the French word for black man as perhaps even an equivalent for our N word. Then I learned that *negre*, in French, can also mean "ghostwriter," and I realized that my own experience had duplicated Greene's. Relying on what Greene, or I or anyone else, believes to be the cellar levels of his own brain implies a strong degree of trust in the possession of order-making unconscious chambers of the mind—chambers that can, and will, yield up imaginative results which are original, orderly, and usable. In late '58 then I began to learn that eight hours of sleep, a minimum of physical abuse, and a predictable work schedule would tap into my own such chambers more often than not.

In England, though, and in my first year or so of work on *A Long and Happy Life*, I didn't know that simple fact. It was another vital skill I was carving out in sheer need and persistence, a need to live the life I was all but sure I'd been born to lead. So while I've been lucky enough for all my writing life to be able to work most days of the week, at whatever time I choose, I try to tell my younger friends that—if they can only write twice a week—they should pick the available days and hours, then find a promising place (the quietest possible), then disconnect the phone or any other distraction and sit till the work arrives. Sooner or later, assuming you're a writer, it will. The fact that so very few of the gifted students I've taught—those who say they yearn to *be* writers—prove able to spend their lives in a fruitful writing career is very likely owing to their owning all the needed skills but one.

And the fatal lack of that skill is defined in a daunting minimum of words by Blaise Pascal, the seventeenth-century French mathematician and mystic, in this sentence from his *Pensées*—"All man's troubles come from not knowing how to sit still in one room." For the writing, of fiction and poetry at least, is a solitary business—not as hard as writers often claim (again, if the writer is gifted) but one that's almost invariably conducted in supreme aloneness, sitting still in an otherwise empty room for long days. My initial trouble—for as much as a year, especially in the wake of my ornery Oxford thesis—came in drawing my story out of its corner and finding the language for its transfer from my inner eye to the reader's, a stranger whom I'd never met and who might be as alien to my own tastes and morals as the last man on Pluto. I didn't know my whole story; I was making it up as I wrote, often day by day.

I went on keeping notes but my manuscript is not always dated, so it's no longer possible to be sure when I wrote which pages. I do know that, with few exceptions, I wrote—as I'd always write—in the chronological order of the story itself. I've never felt I can write scene C till I've written the prior A and B. How can I know what foot to put forward till I know where both my feet are now placed; or to quote the famous little girl in the fable—when told to think before she speaks, she says (very sensibly) "How do I know what I think till I see what I say?"

So chronological order was a great help once I'd established a schedule of days and hours, apart from my teaching. The next most powerful aid was the gradual accretion of characters—the detailed human natures of my men and women, major and minor. I've mentioned creating, out of whole cloth (and the memory of a few girls I'd known in my grade-school days), the character of Rosacoke Mustian in "A Chain of Love." That same story had invented the characters of Rosa's two brothers, her younger sister, her widowed mother, her grandfather, and a petulant sister-in-law.

What remained the hardest such challenge was the creation of Rosa's reluctant boyfriend Wesley. His hesitation in honoring, with a marriage offer, an attractive young woman's obvious devotion had to seem at least a credible, nor merely a callous, indifference. And further, he had to have qualities which almost any reader could find magnetic—and magnetic to a woman as intelligent as Rosa. I've already noted then that, almost from the start of the job, I'd realized that my central players would need to exert on the susceptible reader a considerable degree of physical attraction—one that came very near to overcoming any grave dislike a reader might feel for people I wished the reader to like (or at least respond to with careful attention). Such an aim, however, meant that I felt an equally strong need to maintain as much control as possible over the amount of erotic magnetism each character exerted.

I was likely still recalling David Cecil's discussions of Tolstoy's concern with a novelist's need for moral relations with his characters. I was also aware of the extremely thin line which D. H. Lawrence walks, given his damaging lack of a sense of humor, when he makes similar attempts to control his reader's response to his characters. So often he attempts to incorporate his reader's erotic sensibilities into the fiction; and given the extreme difficulty of achieving such an incalculable hope, he succeeds an extraordinary number of times (read his astonishing "The Fox" for instance). But so often he collapses into the absurd, even the sadly comic, in his attempts to manage the reader's intimate relations with his men and women.

In those early days then, Lawrence stood as both a luminous guide and a dire warning. And the remaining pantheon of writers whom I'd chosen in the course of my early reading—Flaubert, Tolstoy, Hardy, and Forster—served me steadily as I wrote onward. In fact an inscribed picture of the wild-eyed, Lear-like elder Tolstoy—which I'd bought from an autograph dealer while I was a sophomore at Duke— hung above my worktable. And with painful slowness, the lines of my story accumulated.

Despite the fact that I was teaching some seventy freshmen and sophomores, hell for leather, three days a week—and greatly enjoying the discovery that those just post-adolescent Americans could be taught the writing of clear and intelligent expository prose—nothing in all my life was now more rousing and rewarding than the realization that I was likewise teaching myself to write a longish, heavily populated, and emotionally intricate stretch of narrative fiction.

In my few short stories, I'd summoned characters who seemed to me alive for intense moments—a few days or hours, a very few minutes of any reader's life. Now I was making a world, with all a world's features—wild nature, houses, cultivated fields, families, solitary creatures seen on all sides, stores, schools, churches, towns. All the powers I'd dreamed of winning as a practicing writer seemed to grow in me now, from week to week; and however many hard days I faced when I wondered where next and how to get there, I can't recall a whole long day when I doubted I'd eventually reach my goal—a substantial account of irresistible human beings who'd hold a wide variety of readers for the time it took to read the words and lodge them in their minds forever after.

4

M<small>Y</small> MEMORY of those working years at home is far less detailed—oddly maybe—than what I've recorded of my three years at Oxford. And I wonder why. The only answer I can offer is that Duke, Durham, and Raleigh were (so far) offering me a considerably less complicated world than I'd known abroad, a world marked chiefly by the writing, the teaching, the few pleasant evenings with colleagues, and occasional drives to Washington. Also when it came to travel, I was all but stone-broke still. My take-home pay each month came to some $300 ($2,100 now). From that sum I began to repay money I'd borrowed from a sympathetic bank manager during my Christmas visit home in '57. Each month I repaid my mother $50 (some $350 now) for her many generosities, and my rent was $45 ($315 now).

Those payments left me with $200 ($1,400 now) for all my other needs and desires—food, rent, heating oil, clothes, a few movies and concerts, gas, and a few dollars saved for an eventual return to Oxford: I was trusting to return at the end of my three-year contract at Duke. Beyond the monthly checks from the university, I had no other income that I can recall, apart from two small checks from *Encounter*—all the more reason then to hunker in the woods and write. Among the few exceptions are the Washington weekends, a single trip to New York in the summer of '60, and a ride with Michael to Princeton to attend Peter Heap's first marriage.

Nonetheless I was far from unhappy. The years in Britain had left me well stocked with memories I continued to process. The final involvement with Matyas had not so much ended, for me at least, as sat merely suspended on what I'd heard as a rising tone—a chord that awaited resolution. Again, no one I knew could afford to telephone England with any regularity. There was no e-mail of course, so letters were the means of communication, and Matyas had the loyal British habit of prompt mail response.

It normally took five days for an airmail letter to cross the Atlantic in either direction. If Matyas got word from me on a Thursday, he was likely to post a reply within forty-eight hours (despite his own heavy teaching load). However welcome Matyas's responses, I was often a little flummoxed at their speed. Still I labored to keep up my end of the correspondence, however placid my news might be in contrast to his. He sent me interesting accounts of his summer return to Eastern Europe and reunions with his family after a nearly fifteen-year hiatus; then regular and lively accounts of his ongoing Oxford life and work. But eventually he wrote—and mailed—a long and unnerving letter of blame.

He didn't cast me as his primary villain—he saw himself as that—yet he certainly saw me as an enthusiastic instigator of a revival, in himself, of queer emotion and practice. In Oxford he'd told me of his fervently Catholic youth, and I knew that his queer energies had brought him essentially no happiness. I thought I'd witnessed a significant amount of proof, however, that our few months together had begun to heal his dread. Once we'd made an initial commitment to intimacy, he'd shown me only generous-hearted affection and a delight in our lovemaking that matched my own (not an easy match). But this bad letter indicated his prior concealment of deep reservations and bitter regret. It certainly suggested that any hope, on my part, of returning to Oxford for a long-term resumption of our affair was gravely misguided. That was hard news to get—and childish, I felt, from a man who by then was near thirty-five. In later letters, however, we each worked to repair his anger and restore at least a postal friendship that was all the stronger for having begun in mutual desire.

Stephen Spender, in California in 1959. Taken by the pioneer American photographer Imogen Cunningham somewhere in the Bay Area while Stephen was teaching at Berkeley, it captures his face better than any other portrait I've seen. He's in the vicinity of fifty years old, with nearly four more decades to go, and is obsessively at work on a book-length poem about his life. His recent poetry has been severely attacked, and he's hoping to rout his critics with something both new and legitimately strange. Whenever he'd visit me in North Carolina in my trailer or eventual house, he tended to sit up, working on the long poem, well after I'd retired to sleep. Now and then he'd let me see a few pages, always in his legible hand; and I always felt he was on a rewarding track, though one that he revised endlessly. He published one or two brief excerpts in literary magazines, but eventually he either abandoned the large project or set it aside for eventual completion. Then he died. If asked for my opinion, I'd urge the keepers of his estate to find a first-class editor and publish the entire poem, if it survives at all, just as he left it. Surely he wrote no better verse.

*   *   *

As for any romance, with sexual union, back home—there was none, barring a very occasional one-night stand with friends. In addition to chaste friendships with my teaching colleagues, I had several visitors from England. The stringent pressures on travel money for British subjects were still in force, and any Briton who managed to reach the States was in need of all the hospitality he could find. In my small quarters I welcomed several Merton friends and Julian Mitchell, whom I noted above—an eventual novelist, playwright, and screenwriter. All these friends were making their first trips to the States as they passed my way, and I mostly enjoyed giving them a brief version of the classic tour of upper Dixie—a drive down to exotic Charleston and Savannah or up to Richmond and Warren County with its village world of tobacco, its sixty-five percent black population, and my undaunted and loquaciously amusing aunts with their superb fried chicken, endless fresh vegetables, biscuits, cornbread, and blackberry cobbler. I even moved into the Mays' house for a few nights and surrendered my trailer bed to John Roberts, my senior Merton friend, and his new (first) wife.

The visits became a little onerous as my writing proceeded, especially since the friends almost always arrived without cars of their own and were dependent on me for local transportation; but I don't recall ever turning one traveler away (Michael was a regular and always welcome guest). Eventually I became bold enough to give most of them breakfast and then a walking stick with directions for exploring the woods and fields on all sides of my desk. I'd also provide semi-knowing instructions on the warding-off of bothersome snakes— the very poisonous copperhead was far from scarce nearby. The likelihood of such surprises was in fact slim; but my visitors seemed to enjoy even the barest possibility of cornering a poisonous snake, given that fact that Britain harbored only a single such creature, the adder which rarely bites a human.

As he'd promised, Stephen Spender often swung through Durham on his frequent lecture tours round America. He plainly relished staying in a *caravan* (the British word for "trailer"). With his love of country quiet and near-solitude, he'd happily absent himself during my writing hours and patrol the woods or set a chair on the hill above the pond and draw the landscape with my colored chalks or read or continue work on the long autobiographical poem which obsessed him for more than twenty years but which, with the exception of only a few impressive excerpts in magazines, he never published. In the evening we'd cook simple meals for one another on my narrow stove, and he'd unreel the often absurd news from his travels.

There'd be full accounts of the inevitable New York visits with Wystan Auden who was rapidly entering the airless tunnel of demanding eccentricity and hard drink that would make his last decades, however hardworking, so merciless on himself and his friends. And he'd have dined with the mentally unsteady but (to Stephen) always kindly and amusing Robert Lowell, not to mention the numerous lectures at small-college English departments of an often mind-boggling naïveté; and more interesting longer stints at Northwestern, say, or the University of Virginia in Charlottesville. He'd even repeat, with laughing approval, Mary McCarthy's remark after attending one of his lectures—"Stephen, that was hopelessly above the heads of three-fourths of your audience and hopelessly beneath the heads of the other fourth": he relished telling such jokes on himself.

Clearly Stephen had a real sense of relieving my own country silence with these dispatches from the Real World; and at first I never tried to stem his flow—the stories were mostly interesting, sometimes even credibly scandalous. But in the later years of our still-frequent American times together, the boredom of Stephen's endless touring round the lecture circuit led him to ceaseless complaints that were finally tiresome to hear, however aware I was of his need to support a London household. The very core of his final travels, and university residences, was boredom; and the word itself—*boring*—became boring to hear from a man who'd exhausted his own profound and enriching early curiosity about most things American. Nonetheless I had dozens of reasons to thank Stephen, and those thanks multiplied right on till his death some four decades after I left England (only the deaths of my parents struck a comparable deep mourning in me).

One of his kindnesses lay in directing me to an extraordinary sophomore student. In the spring of '59, Stephen and I had gone to a reception in the Rare Book Room of the university library; and there in the small crowd I saw Stephen off in a corner, talking intently with—and towering over—a considerably shorter young man who wore thick mad-scientist glasses. Eventually I went over and met Stephen's discovery. He was Wallace Kaufman, an English major who said, at once, that yes, he wrote poems. Initially he seemed suspicious of everything going on around him in this handsomely paneled replication of an eighteenth-century gentleman's library, but he told me of his origins on the north shore of Long Island and of his coming to Duke on a combination of scholarships that made his presence possible.

He left no striking impression, then and there; yet as I drove with Stephen back to the trailer, he lapsed into a silence and then said, in effect, "That young man is the only truly proletarian American I've ever met." I'd not had Stephen's background in such older European class distinctions, so I said "How so?" Stephen said only "Christopher Isherwood would walk across the continent to meet him." Then he laughed. "No, truly. I think you should get to know him. He said he was called Wally, and he seems a true original."

And so Wallace Kaufman turned out to be. I didn't begin to know him till the next academic year, by which time he was a junior. I've noted that he'd then be a member of that group of advanced writing students I met at the Chappells' apartment. And there, almost at once, Wally's rough-edged wit, his initial truculence (which dissolved when his dread of fake sophistication dissolved); and the talent on show in his poems and short stories made him the most interesting of my younger male students—one of the few who, given the nature of student-teacher relations, has proved a lifelong friend.

As the teacher of all those students—so close to my own age—some of whom would soon become friends, I was faced with a complicating reality. I was expected to submit realistic grades on their work and to interact with them in useful ways that didn't violate the never-articulated (in those more innocent days) but implicitly moral expectation of teachers. I didn't have the all-but-impermeable armor of tenure around me, and my three-year nonrenewable contract led me to think I never would, not at Duke. But even we young instructors knew that, like tenured professors, any one of us could be forced to leave the university for an act of "moral turpitude" (I soon learned, through the grapevine, of a male teacher in another department who'd recently been asked to leave for inappropriate behavior with a male student; the teacher was of course married; and apparently the university—as seems to have been standard then—had eased the offender into what proved a lifelong job at a good college elsewhere in the state).

At our small gatherings of instructors, we'd often haul out the "turpitude" phrase and remind ourselves—with nervous laughter—that it surely referred, above all, to sexual intimacy with students. Yet we had more than one senior colleague whose present wife had been his student when they met—had their courtships been turpitude-free? And given our duty as instructors to meet weekly, and privately, with each of our freshmen, we often talked about this or that young woman who seemed clearly to be offering herself for grade improvement, if nothing more committed. There was never talk of a flirtatious male student in those days, though there were surely such young men—as there were several queer instructors.

I vividly recall my first such awkward moment in a conference. An eighteen-year-old female student took the latest assignment—a thousand-word narrative of an interesting experience that had lasted, in the real world, no longer than half an hour of clock time—and produced a thoroughly graphic description of a babysitting experience (a little incredibly, the baby was a just-pubescent boy). My student had written in the first person, and her narrative ended as the babysitter proceeded to undergo her sexual initiation at the hands of the babysat boy—or so her theme claimed; she also claimed it was baldly autobiographical. Remember that this was the late 1950s; Lawrence's *Lady Chatterley's Lover* would become a legal publication in the States only in the early '60s. But here was I in my cubicle.

A plump, bright, and likable girl was seated with her left elbow on my desk as I read her paper, marking occasional errors and questions as my nerves tightened.

What was I going to say when, at last, I had nothing else to do but look up and deliver my response to this better-than-competent piece of work which nonetheless seemed designed to excite the instructor? My memory of her face as I met her eyes at last is of unabashed readiness—*What is this grown man bound to do next?* The office door was shut—a mistake I'd never make again for a student visit in my entire career, unless the student specified that he or she had come with a confidential problem (in which case the door would be slightly ajar). I'd be lying if I didn't say that, for an instant, I welcomed this eighteen-year-old's degree of audacious trust in her teacher's impulses, wherever they led. Well, God alone knows what I said those fifty years ago; but no turpitude of any sort ensued.

And while Wally Kaufman became my best younger friend through the remainder of his undergraduate years, and though my feelings for him were a complex mixture of concern for his lack of a family, respect for his work, and a normal response to his odd magnetism, our friendship grew without the hindrance of a realized intimacy. Wally has only recently shown me a forgotten letter which I wrote him in 1961. I said "I have felt for a long time that one of the things we share, mysteriously, is a deepening relation with our dead fathers."

I was alluding to the fact that my own father had died seven years ago; Wally's had been killed in a car wreck in '57, and my feeling was as honest as it was strong. Young as he was, Wally's work was dealing powerfully and eloquently with that death. His father had been a nonobservant Jew, employed as a machinist at Grumman Aircraft on Long Island, a man who'd had slim apparent interest in his three sons and a turbulent relation with the boys' mother, a gentile of good English family, bedeviled most painfully by bouts of clinical depression that sometimes led to her hospitalization. Though I was only six years Wally's senior, I felt some responsibility for the fact that he was fatherless—as I was. That realization worked eventually to establish between us a relation that had considerably more paternal-filial energy at work than either of us realized in the early years of our acquaintance.

  For three years at Duke then, and later for a year at Oxford, we spent considerable time together. The writing of fiction and poetry, which we shared with one another—and especially the translation of poems from French and German which we worked on together (Wally knew German; I didn't)—was a more important literary bond than I've shared with anyone since. A delight in movies and in laughter for its own sake were likewise strong; and from late in his time at Duke on through our time in England, we traveled together often. Most memorable was a trip we took in the summer of 1960.

I've noted a single trip to New York in my first three teaching years. I went north to visit Stephen for a week at the home of Muriel Gardiner Buttinger. Gardiner was a psychiatrist with whom Stephen had a love affair in Vienna in the 1930s. From a Chicago meatpacking family, and thus wealthy, Gardiner was studying psychiatry in Vienna and had invested a good deal of her money—and the risk of her life—in conveying threatened Jews out of Austria as Hitler loomed. It was the story of Gardiner's career that Lillian Hellman notoriously refused to admit purloining for her own alleged memoir *Pentimento,* a story that became the successful film *Julia* with Vanessa Redgrave and Jane Fonda. Safely returned to the States with her husband Joseph Buttinger, who'd been chairman of the Austrian Socialist Party in exile, Muriel had built one of the last private homes in her uptown neighborhood—at 10 East 87th Street—and the house had become Stephen's perennial lodging during his frequent visits to the northeast. In the summer of 1960 then, I was staying briefly with Stephen there, writing in my own quiet room while he went about his New York appointments.

  Wally was spending the summer before his senior year in his old home ground—Sea Cliff, Long Island—where he had a single room in what he called a flophouse that bore the grander name of the Artists' Colony. Toward the end of my visit, he came into town and joined me and Stephen for several days. It was a time marked by two memorable events. The most striking occurred when Stephen cooked our breakfast and managed to attempt making coffee with a disconnected electric coffeepot that he set on a red-hot eye of the stove. Before Wally or I could rescue the pot, it was promptly ruined, with an accompanying stench of molten Bakelite, a not uncommon Spender debacle. A group debacle occurred that Sunday afternoon when we went with Stephen to call on his London friend the actress Irene Worth.

She'd appeared in Britain, very successfully, in Stephen's translation of Schiller's *Mary Stuart* and was now appearing on Broadway in Hellman's new play, *Toys in the Attic*. She was occupying the handsome apartment of an absent friend, and we had drinks there before going down the block to a restaurant she'd found—a likable unelaborated place. More drinks, then a good deal of lively talk, a good deal of wine with the food. Then somehow Stephen led us far downtown to the apartment—or was it a house?—of a family, one of whom was the brother (or sister) of the very ponderable sculptor Louise Nevelson. By then I, at the very least, was cheerfully sozzled; and the other three in our party were tottering but talkative. Still, I thought a sufficient sobriety prevailed. We discussed the several Nevelson sculptures in the downstairs rooms and her numerous framed drawings; then Wally and I went upstairs with a young daughter and a girlfriend of hers—a thoroughly innocent talk in a bedroom, for maybe half an hour. Then the three of us men—Stephen, Wally, and I—took Irene back to her lodgings: long hugs and kisses all round.

I've mentioned thinking we were sober enough in our call on the family of Nevelson's sibling. But twenty years passed and I went to a party for Nevelson in Durham—she was visiting one of the local institutions. She was eighty but energetic. I relished her famous false eyelashes, long and dense as black fur rugs; and once I'd mentioned my love of her work, I told her that Stephen Spender had taken me and two others to visit her sibling in 1960. Nevelson took a moment to search my face, then raised her laughing voice, pointed, and told me "*You?* It was *you?* They talk about it still—a precious memory!" Then she lowered her voice—"But weren't you all drunk?" When I told her "More or less," her voice rose again—"More, my boy, *more!*" The fact that—on my way to the Nevelson party (alone on my pitch-dark country road)—I had my single lifetime encounter with one immense strange aircraft very near overhead, seems barely strange at all: a hardly deniable UFO as I drove toward Louise Nevelson who'd kept, through her old age, a secondhand memory of me at hardly-my-best in New York long ago but laughing all the same. It felt immensely likely.

An hour or so after Stephen melted Muriel Gardiner's coffeepot, he and Wally and I set off in Wally's 1950 Ford to deliver Stephen to his planned visit with Edmund Wilson. The great critic was staying at his mother's old home, upstate, in the country near Talcottville. It was a long bright day, and we reached Wilson's unpretentious stone house late in the afternoon and went in for a drink and an hour of talk before Wally and I left Stephen there and set off on our own. My chief memories of Wilson include almost nothing he said, beyond a certain almost oblivious kindness to us two young men. I do, though, clearly remember his physical smallness, plumpness, and pallor and the fact that he barely moved from a tall upholstered chair in which, he told us, he often spent whole days and nights—reading. He'd nap upright, then wake to read more until eventually his housekeeper would suggest a wash and a change of clothes (he was then engaged in the reading for his most distinguished book, a study of the literature of the Civil War, called *Patriotic Gore*). He also said that Elena, his fourth wife, spent the summers elsewhere and that he was tended by a local woman who came in for a little cleaning and minimal cooking. At the time, Wilson had just turned sixty-five; but for me he had the almost transparent physical air of an ancient Chinese sage with tiny expressive hands and a tendency to talk straight forward to the air as though none of us was present.

Before dark we left Stephen there and forged off on our own. Wally had long since been a book scout, one who haunted secondhand bookshops, junk shops, Salvation Army stores—anywhere he might find a book of interest to himself or to some other scout or dealer—and we spent the next few days in upstate New York, wan-

Wallace Kaufman was one of the first students I taught after returning from Oxford in '58. A native of New York, he came to Duke on a generous scholarship a year before my return; and his interest in reading—especially poetry—and in writing both poetry and prose caught my interest early on, as did his extraordinary looks: a big-boned, powerfully shaped skull and large unblinking eyes. He was a member of the most rewarding class of writers I ever taught. The Marshall Scholarship took him from Duke to my old college, Merton; and his first year there coincided with my fourth year back in the college. We availed ourselves of joint trips to the entertainments of London; and we shared many friends—including an evening with the ghoulish great painter Francis Bacon. Though later life propelled Wally to the woods of Oregon, we've never lost touch. Here in 1961 he's near the small pond beside which I've lived for more than fifty years.

dering through such places. I'm not sure what Wally found; I only recall that one shopkeeper ordered us to leave his premises when Wally wouldn't say precisely what he was hunting. Maybe Wally looked too knowledgeable in his thick glasses; we might find some treasure the dealer was unaware of—only lately I'd read of some grubby lad who'd just found a first edition of *Walden* in a junk shop and bought it for fifty cents.

In fact not long after Wally returned to Durham in September for his senior year, he phoned me one morning to ask if I'd ever heard of a book called *The Grave* with designs by William Blake, engraved by Schiavonetti. Blake was one of my minor interests (not long before, Stephen had given me a pair of the original Blake illustrations for the Book of Job), and I said I'd indeed heard of the book. Wally said "Well, there's a copy of the first edition downtown at the Book Exchange for five hundred dollars." I didn't have five hundred dollars to spare, but I was devoted to not regretting my economies, and I said I'd meet him back at the store in half an hour. When we met, Wally led me through the spooky corridors of that famed emporium and pointed out the volume.

The book was in excellent shape; and I leafed through the numerous handsome engravings, based on striking watercolors by Blake and, though not among his great achievements, a handsome collection in any case. Then I looked to the inside front cover where the price was penciled in. There was a dollar sign, the numeral five, then two smaller zeroes with a slight line beneath them. I turned to my friend and said "This book costs five dollars, not five hundred." Wally could hardly believe me when I said "In which case, it's yours; you found it." He took another look at the numbers and said "I think you're wrong."

So I said "Then go to the cash register, take out a five-dollar bill, and extend it to the man" (a notorious curmudgeon). Again Wally shook his head but followed my suggestion. A few minutes later we were back on the street with a first edition of Blair's *The Grave* with all Blake's designs as engraved by Schiavonetti—for five dollars plus a few cents tax. And it says a good deal about Wally's good nature that a year later, when he found a broken copy of *The Grave* in some other book midden, he gave me my choice of the engravings. I chose "The Soul hovering over the Body reluctantly parting with Life," and I have it near me still.

5

T HROUGH ALL THAT, my writing and teaching had continued. A year before the New York trip, I'd finished Part One of the story—Rosacoke and Wesley at Mildred's funeral and then on to the picnic at Mason's Lake. Stephen was visiting me in the trailer shortly after I finished that stretch of the story, and I showed it to him. Almost at once he asked to publish it in *Encounter*. I was pleased that he liked the piece but astonished that he felt he could publish such a long stretch of fiction, more than seventy pages of typescript. He managed nonetheless to win the approval of his co-editor, and the pages appeared in the issue of March 1960. That much success seemed encouragement enough; but then I learned that the *Encounter* version of Part One, which I'd called "One Sunday in Late July," had been selected as a prizewinner in the best of the annual short-story anthologies, *The O. Henry Awards*. Thereafter I was only concerned with completing the endless-feeling story and thereby—I thought—at last achieving the volume I'd already contracted for in London and New York. What I couldn't begin to imagine was the effect, not far down the road, of such attention on my future at Duke.

I've mentioned that those last two years of my three-year appointment were so outwardly uneventful that I have few memories which seem either interesting or revealing enough to record. A few other realities were sizable, though, and seem worth recording. I've noted that my sexual life was all but nonexistent (with anyone but myself). For the first time, however, I did begin to acquire a few queer friends of a sort I'd never had before. The first, and most enduring, of them was a graduate student in English named Jim Boatwright. Jim was almost exactly my age. He'd grown up in Augusta, Georgia in a middle-class home that was slightly better-heeled than mine (I once met his father, a kind-seeming insurance agent; but his alcoholic mother never made it to Durham). Jim had attended the University of Georgia, come to Duke on a handsome graduate fellowship, and I met him when he joined several others of us in the warren of freshman-English offices.

He and I were much the same size as to height and weight; and Jim had an intelligent face, already tending to plumpness as the result maybe of his early liking for drink—a liking that had not then begun to affect him otherwise. Despite a pair of pale eyes that tended (in repose) to an inexplicable mournfulness, Jim mainly loved laughter and had a likable tendency to sweeten his gift for well-aimed satire with a steady turning of the gift on himself—he was the ultimate butt of most of his own jokes. In early manhood, he seemed, in the best sense, a fine Southern gentleman—socially adept and graceful, benign and thoughtful, a deeply intelligent student and critic of poetry and drama, and a much-loved teacher. Inexplicably, though, such very real gifts would be increasingly valueless to Jim himself.

Only his very few closest friends—and for years I was glad to be one of those—knew how deeply he deplored himself, how he distrusted each of his own strengths to the point of steady self-sabotage. But that eventual near-suicidal damage had only begun to affect him in his years at Duke. And when we met—first at work, then in my house or in Jim's apartment—we circled one another gingerly in our conversation before we played, on the table between us, the identical face-cards of our sexuality. Each of us was queer and had known it forever, so long in fact that it appeared neither of us was worried about the reality. Jim still had occasional dates with women; I didn't (and hadn't since high school, apart from evenings with Dorothy Roberts). Whether Jim had ever thought of heterosexual marriage, he never said and I never asked. I myself had had no such thought, not for a good while.

Soon after we'd shared that confidence, I began to meet socially with a few other queer graduate students—all of them friends of Jim. They lived in small frame houses near campus, and most of them also taught freshman English. Our evenings consisted of a few drinks—wherever Jim was, a gin and tonic was likely at hand—followed by an often adventurous meal cooked by one of the friends. Since they were even nearer destitution than I, the ingredients were inexpensive and the ingenuity considerable—variations on beef Stroganoff, chicken Tetrazzini, or spaghetti putanesca ("whore's pasta," a hearty Neapolitan dish alleged to fortify the waterfront hookers of that strenuous port).

The talk at those small gatherings—five or six men and a dog or two—included dead-earnest and decidedly opinionated discussions of British and American literature (in the eminently sane and useful framework of the New Criticism of that era), head-knockingly intense arguments about the latest Italian and Swedish films that were then reaching the States, the usual academic gossip, plus a fair amount of queer wit. And though we still called ourselves *queer*, it was at one of those dinners, in about 1960, that I first heard the word *gay* applied to homosexuals.

Gay struck me at once as merely inaccurate if not seriously inappropriate. I saw none of us as especially carefree. I can't recall ever using the word then, to apply to myself and my friends; and it was more than two decades before *gay* would gain an upper hand as the accepted name for male American homosexuals. Through these years I've continued trying to avoid it. The supreme *Oxford English Dictionary* gives the date of its earliest such use as 1935, and the *OED*'s source is a dictionary of underworld and prison slang; the *Oxford American Dictionary* now says "*Gay* meaning 'homosexual,' dating back to the 1930s (if not earlier), became established in the 1960s as the term preferred by homosexual men to describe themselves."

The degree to which it still seems to me a bad misnomer was clarified, above all, when the AIDS plague hit the nation full-stride in the mid- to late 1980s. As more and more thousands of men were vanishing into HIV infection and rapid death, *gay* as a common label for homosexual identity became not only a cruel joke but also a political error at a time when federal money for research and treatment was desperately needed. The enemies of homosexuality were handed, gratis, a name which suited their contention that homosexuals were giddy irresponsibles, negligible creatures; and one of those creatures—a man as gifted and generous as Jim Boatwright—died of the plague in 1988.

Queer may not be the best conceivable other slang name, though it's returning to use as a description of homosexual art and artists; but at least *queer* is exact, in the sense of eccentric (as a final observation on *gay*, a queer acquaintance of mine says "Please don't call me *gay*. If you need an adjective, call me *morose*"). I have no expectation whatever that *gay* will fade from use anytime soon, and who knows what word might replace it, but I'll go on using the word *queer* whenever possible to describe male same-sex attraction and consummation.

Whatever we called ourselves at those small evenings in the late 1950s, our conversation almost invariably wound down, by late evening, into lengthy circlings of queerness—jokes, guesses, warnings, universal rejection of the Freudian theory of excessive mother-attachment, but never (as I recall) an articulate sentence from any of us as to why we were queer and how difficult a fate it might prove to be. What I also have no memory of our discussing was the criminality which the entire nation ascribed to our deepest physical and emotional propensities; and I'm sure that none of us had ever known a man who'd been arrested, not to mention imprisoned, for the crime, though such penalties were far from rare, as any daily paper would reveal (I've noted Jim's death of AIDS in '88; another of our friends would be murdered by a partner-gone-mad).

Succeeding years have shown, thank God, that none of us had the slightest attraction to the very young, a propensity which is surely the most awful of human compulsions. And as for any suggestion of self-obsession in our talk, I'd long ago learned in my undergraduate fraternity years that straight men—in locker rooms, bars, wherever—are equally committed to obsessive concern with sex talk. American men in general appear to think—and talk among themselves—about active sex considerably more often than the majority of women, and the hours devoted to such exercise can grow wearisome fast unless the degree of wit is high and keen and is mostly turned on the men in the room.

* * *

In the summer of 1960, all my Duke friends and I encountered real calamity (the following account comes entirely from my own memory and a single important obituary; one other friend's memory differs from mine only in minor details, so I rely on my own). On the evening of July 20, I went to a picnic in the backyard of a colleague and his wife. With us also were the Quaintances, Jim Boatwright, and one or two other friends. It's my present memory that our hosts had also invited the one older colleague who seemed friendliest to us and the most accessible in his wit and charm. His name was Charles Fenton; he'd joined the English department at the same time as we, and he made a thoroughly likable presence at our parties, despite the fact that he and his wife were inclined toward unnervingly audible wrangling once a few drinks had gone down.

Charlie was forty-one years old—tall, lean, almost handsome—and a widely respected scholar of the works of Ernest Hemingway, a giant who was still alive. For an academic, Charlie's past was complex and interesting. He'd grown up at the Taft School in Connecticut where his father taught; he'd left Yale in 1940, his junior year—and before the United States had entered the war—to join the Royal Canadian Air Force (as an eager young Hemingway had joined the American Red Cross Ambulance Service). Charlie served honorably for three years as an aerial gunner, hardly a secure job. Then he worked for several years as a journalist before returning to Yale. By 1949 he was a member of the faculty there.

He came to Duke with two solid books behind him—a life of Stephen Vincent Benét and *The Apprenticeship of Ernest Hemingway*, two very different writers. Charlie's subsequently published correspondence with Hemingway about the study of his literary apprenticeship is fascinating in what it shows of the younger man's pugnacity in defense of his work-in-progress and the famous author's part-ferocious, part-sympathetic defense of his own privacy. Charlie was hardly installed in Durham before he won the special admiration of us doomed younger colleagues—doomed to brief terms at Duke. From his position of tenured security, he was perfectly prepared to express his opinions of our more pompous colleagues in the full professoriate (the department was then entirely run by the "fulls"; no younger members had any power whatever in such decisions as hiring and firing).

Of course we relative youngsters relished such opinions as Charlie's; they were much like what we heard simultaneously from Bill Blackburn, though shorn of Blackburn's spooky air of omen. So on that July night in 1960, we ate our grilled chicken in the pleasant dark of our friends' yard and waited for the long-delayed guest. When he hadn't appeared by nine, our host phoned Charlie's house to check on his coming but got no reply. Next morning I drove to campus to get my mail; and as I entered the postal station, my colleague Grover Smith — a noted T. S. Eliot scholar — met me head-on and asked if I'd heard the news. Well, what news? Grover rushed on to say "Charlie Fenton has killed himself. A few hours ago he jumped off the top of the Washington Duke Hotel" (the old Washington Duke, before its implosion).

I took my mail and walked across campus to the main library. At once I saw Jim Boatwright huddled in the lobby with two or three other graduate students. I must have felt too stunned to join them, so I gave Jim a wave and started upstairs toward the card catalogue. Before I'd climbed far, Jim beckoned me back; and when we met I could see how sad he looked — was he that hungover from last night's picnic, or had he heard the news?

My mind has retained the next image — Jim standing two steps below me, looking up, very pale. By then his eyes were full.

Needing confirmation maybe, I had to say "What?"

"Charlie Fenton is dead."

It was still past belief. But I said "How?"

"He killed himself at dawn."

I remember thinking how Hemingwayesque those five words sounded — though it would be almost exactly a year before Hemingway himself died, another dawn suicide.

Jim and I sat on the wide stone steps, sandbagged by the news yet partly aware that, along with a powerful grief, we'd also acquired — in our own eyes — the fresh adult dignity that was rare enough in our shielded generation. We were now participants, however sidelined, in something truly large in the great world—our world, at least. We well knew that Charlie had hardly died to lend us that much. In time, however, I'd see that maybe his final unknowing act as a teacher was to set an example for his younger colleagues of the solemn duties of learning and teaching, the awful temptations of the job.

Jim and I both knew at least part of the story; but what we'd learn in the numb days to come amounted to this—and a good deal of it came to me from an hour's talk I'd had with Charlie early that summer, the two of us seated on those same library steps. In the spring the notoriously evil-tongued widow of a Duke English professor—a woman named Hessie Baum (the very name is a serpent hiss)—had phoned Charlie's wife to say that she had seen, out her window more than once, Charlie entering the woods with a young woman. Soon thereafter Charlie came home from campus to find his house empty—while he was teaching one day, his wife had ordered a moving van, emptied the house, and departed with the children. "She didn't even leave me a goddamned washcloth," he told me. He also said that, though he'd begun to love the other woman (a graduate student), there'd still been no sexual intimacy between them.

That relationship obviously intensified as spring moved into summer. By then Charlie and the young woman, whom I'll call Nancy, were walking openly on campus together to the tune of busy gossip. I even saw them sitting together on the grass of the crowded quad in bright sunlight for an afternoon concert (an all-but-unheard-of gesture of openness for a senior professor in those days). I didn't know Nancy especially well, but I liked her—she and Jim were good friends. Still, Charlie's single episode of confiding in me had left me with the feelings of a well-wishing co-conspirator in their romance. Charlie went on with his plan to teach in summer school, after which he'd depart for a year's research in Spain—he was planning a book on the Spanish Civil War. I think Nancy returned to her family home where she had a summer job. But Charlie went north to see her, and soon they were engaged to marry once Charlie's divorce became final. Nancy would join him in Spain for at least part of the next year.

Meanwhile we younger colleagues saw him as often as possible during the summer session; and he seemed the same jocular man, if sometimes a little abstracted. What we didn't know, however, at the picnic was that, when summer school ended that day, Charlie stopped by the English office to leave his grades and tell a secretary that he was driving to Mexico the next day for his divorce. Later, the secretary said that, when she told him he needed to cheer up soon—he seemed depressed—he thanked her for the sympathy but added that he'd just taken his German shepherd to the vet to have him put down. I at least knew that I'd passed him that final afternoon in the swinging doors of the library stacks and exchanged a few words—no more than a brief summer farewell, I thought. So much for a young writer's insight into terminal pain.

A later investigation would indicate that, for whatever reason, at about eight that evening he'd checked into the old Washington Duke Hotel in the midst of downtown Durham and been given a room on the eighth floor (had he turned his house over to temporary renters, or was he already contemplating death, as the killing of his dog might suggest?). The police would discover that he'd spent a good part of the night covering numerous pieces of paper with words to this effect, typed on his portable—

> Charles Fenton is fearless
> charming
> likable
> stalwart
> magnanimous . . .

All the pages had been discarded in the room's wastebasket. Then before dawn he'd gone downstairs and checked out of the hotel, only to return a few minutes later and ask the desk clerk if he could have his key back—the parking lot wouldn't open till six (other accounts said that his car wouldn't start). The clerk gave him the key, Charlie went upstairs, entered the eighth-floor room to stash his luggage but soon went up to the twelfth-floor hallway, removed a screen from a window, climbed out onto a narrow ledge with no protective rail, and managed to work his safe way round the building to a point at which he could fall straight into the street without the interruption of a nearby building.

In a last act of flawless bravado, he swan-dived down—or so said the two construction workers who were heading to their job in the dawn light and saw his unblocked descent into Chapel Hill Street. Also, behind in his room, was a plane ticket to New York. Apparently he'd called his estranged wife the previous day and asked her to meet him at the airport. When she inquired about his fiancée, she said that he told her those plans were off. He'd plainly been a man in agonized confusion till—maybe—a clear summer sunrise clarified his purpose. Apart from two distraught women and the children, he left a campus already stunned by the damp summer heat and silence of vacation time when no one's at work but the minimal students of summer session and a few devoted scholars rapt in the stacks.

Some of them were older colleagues who'd found his shoot-from-the-hip candor and his public affair with a student distinctly unacceptable, and one or two Yale colleagues who said that (once he'd accepted a chance to leave Yale) some such ending seemed inevitable. He also left his friends among the younger colleagues, some six or eight of us— casual friends who'd provided no help at all in his final pain.

I never claimed to know him well, though we bantered for two years—with occasional glances in more serious directions. Dr. Charles A. Fenton's obituary in *The New York Times* of July 22, 1960 says that he won the Twentieth-Century-Fox-Doubleday Award for a war novel entitled *You'll Get No Promotion*. If I knew that before he died, I don't know how much he achieved on the project. I do know however that, with no coaching from me, he'd tracked down my first story in *Encounter* and volunteered how much he liked it (which was more than a vast majority of my senior colleagues had done; I was learning that academics are at least as afflicted by professional jealousy as any other humans).

This belatedly I realize that I might have, at the least, asked him out for a drink at my place and some supper in town (I'd even begun experimenting, on my tiny stove, with one or two of my own favorites— chicken cacciatore, for instance). But my English social training had

expired apparently; and despite his opening up to me that evening on
the library steps, I never considered that this man—some fourteen years
older and enveloped in what seemed an effortlessly generated air of
male glamour, glamour devoid of macho swagger—might have been
in need of a friendly gesture from another male colleague who shared
some of his interests, though I have no illusion I might have saved him.

He died in desperate solitude; and for what it's worth now, I can say
that the circles spreading out from his ending surely darkened my fictional story as the pages came from me in the year and a half I'd still
need to finish my account of the early adulthood of Rosa and Wesley.
Even my very last pages darkened; and I'd known of their shape since
the winter afternoon I conceived the whole so quickly—not entirely
perceiving, that early, a final darkening tone—in my sitting room on
Sandfield Road, Oxford, with a kerosene stove steadily choosing not to
kill me, though five feet away from my sleeping lungs.

I've mentioned my essential solitude in those years back home, the
first years in which I thought of myself as a full-grown man. I was
strengthened in my sense of maturity by the fact that Mother and Bill
were half an hour away in Raleigh. My nearness allowed them to call
on me for various kinds of filial or fraternal help; and I was after all
contributing a monthly sum to their support. It was the largest single
item in my budget, larger than my rent; and it helped me realize that
(in my own mind at least) I was not only the head of a household—
which my dying father had asked me to be—it was also, far more than
I realized, a vital investment in an anchorage.

Though such financial specifications may stink of grudge and
regret that I had needy kinsmen, I can only add that the contrary was
true. What I'm trying to convey is the after-all-familiar realities of a
young man or woman with a first real job and fewer dollars than his
needs require (and those demands included the wavering pressures of
sexual need and a drive for steady company). The chance of my discovering a partner to share my own life, and any house larger than a
trailer (on my present income), seemed highly unlikely. I knew of no
all-male partnerships in the Duke faculty of those days and none in

the middle-class circles of Durham, Raleigh, and Chapel Hill (there must have been many). Further, I can't recall feeling especially burdened by the solitude. Like a great many men of that age, then and now, I was driven by the powerful furnace of sexual hunger but hardly by any immediate need for a permanent domestic surrounding.

In fact looking back at my life from the age of eleven on—and comparing my feelings with those of others whom I've observed closely—I can say truthfully that my sexual nature was as powerful as any I've encountered at close range, whatever the direction of that man's desires. I mention the fact, not in pride—far from it—but only to describe an emotional reality. And the strength of those desires was by no means easy to manage. Way more than once I wrestled with the galvanizing truth of Racine's description of sexual obsession in *Phèdre*, his greatest tragedy—

> C'est Venus tout entière à sa proie attachée.
> *(It is Venus wholly attached to her prey.)*

Yet again, my coals were as effectively banked as they'd been for long stretches of my Oxford years. I developed one or two brief crushes, one or two old loves exerted intermittent force—the distant homes of the lovers contributed to my control—and the ceaseless demands of my work kept me mostly content.

That stability was old and familiar, sometimes so familiar as to be annoying in itself. More than once I longed to be the kind of man who could howl at the sky or pound a fist through a Sheetrock wall, but I couldn't—I'd learned otherwise. I've mentioned how, as an only child till I was eight, I adjusted to a life devoid of playmates. The pursuits that made a lone boyish life possible were also prophetic of my adult life. As soon as I'd learned how, I read voraciously—everything from comic books and Bible stories to *Robinson Crusoe*, *Gone With the Wind*, and *The Boy's King Arthur*. At least once a day, I played with a set of first-class building blocks sent to me by our one wealthy cousin, who lived in Chicago.

I don't think I knew there was any such profession as architecture;

if I had, I might be building houses now, not writing this page. And atop all my other childhood work, I drew and painted endless pictures. The greatest gift to my childhood, however, came when my parents moved us into a wooded suburb where we stayed from the time I was five till I was nine. I've noted above that those long hours of roaming alone in silence, and in the sudden company of occasional wild animals, fed all my prior dreams and aroused new ones. As much as Wordsworth or Thoreau, I was a child who heard nature speaking to him—or so he thought (and still thinks).

So there in my mid-twenties, in another set of woods and by a real pond, I managed my two strands of work with the addition of my Duke friendships, my occasional weekends in Raleigh, and the drives to Washington. It would be a few years—from thirty onward, say— before I felt myself staring with any sustained degree of longing at the hope of enduring love and company. Meanwhile *A Long and Happy Life* grew darker and longer and emotionally more prophetic in the intricate groundwork of the dance that Rosa and Wesley traced as they neared and parted and at last chose one another. The novel's forecast pertained to the hungers I'd feel more powerfully a little down my own road, the normal hungers of human creatures—a reliable partnership each evening and night, if nothing more.

For me, as I was coming to understand in the act of writing about people very different from myself, those hungers would be endlessly complicated by the fact that my magnet was set for men in a world where such an innate draw was punishable—in the state and the nation where I had every hope of living the rest of my life—by an assortment of the severest punishments, short of death, that the law could dole out. And if that reflection sounds self-pitying to a younger reader, born in a less-stringent era, I'd ask the reader to consider this (and to check it in reference works if necessary)—it's merely, and appallingly, true to the facts of the time and place. And the fact that I can read in this morning's *New York Times* of homosexual repressions in sub-Saharan Africa, and in the huge Anglican Christian membership of those same countries, makes me wonder how enduring the present-day change to mildness in certain American and European laws may ultimately prove to be. Yet strangely perhaps, I doubt I felt truly endangered in the mid-1950s.

Fairly often in the local papers, I could read accounts of men convicted of what was called "the crime against nature"—acts subsumed, apparently, under the single old word *sodomy*. But despite all my queer grad-student friends' stories of pickups in local bars, truck stops, or bus stations—the traditional meeting places of the time—again I'd never known a man charged with the crime of sodomy, much less convicted (in London, Gielgud had been convicted of something less than a crime). I'd even met a man who was having an affair with a married highway patrolman. And given my longtime aversion to smoke-filled saloons, I was hardly likely to find myself in trouble for a public assignation.

Once I went with friends to the one queer bar in Chapel Hill. It was on the main street down a dark flight of stairs, and the room was soaked in dense blue light. Cans of beer or Coke were available—no stronger liquids in a mostly dry state—and the clientele (no women were visible) were either clumped in the center of the small space or arranged one-by-one along the four walls. There was no dancing, only dim songs from a corner jukebox that required frequent feeding. My friends at once joined the central clump; but soon I found myself in what seemed my natural habitat—the periphery, with the one-by-one set, propping up the walls in chosen isolation. What was I meant to do next, though?

Attempting to look as magnetic as possible, in a blue light that might well have proved slowly fatal, I dared quick glimpses of the nearest faces and imagined that I might fall in love with several (I'm truly not joking—they were mostly attractive). But an unaccustomed shyness had already swamped me and forbade my advancing on anyone. And surely no one advanced on me. Was I truly that lacking in magnetism, were my face and body all wrong for the game, was I too old? (again, I'm not kidding—through all my adult life, I've hardly been a draw, for men or women). A good many men in the central clump were even older than I, but most of the one-on-ones seemed as much as two years younger and were either even shyer or were only there for scenery (either *becoming* the scenery or *studying* it in awed silence seemed the only two options). In the course of twenty agonized minutes, I'd drunk my beer and said not a word. Hell, I didn't even smoke. So with a fake smile, I said a quick goodbye to Jim Boatwright (who'd been laughing loudly from the start in the midst of the clump as if that were home). Then I climbed to the street and drove myself back quickly to the trailer. End of local queer-bar life. Never again, quite literally (and almost never elsewhere).

6

WHILE MY TEACHING DUTIES were heavy, they were hardly as onerous as, say, the work of a high-school teacher of English or math. I continued to be able to confine my classes and conferences to three days a week, however long the days; and often they ran from eight to five, sometimes later. Nonetheless three years at any job so demanding can require a vast amount from the worker and yield perhaps as large a return as any public-school teacher yields. I've mentioned the sheer fatigue induced in even a teacher as young as I; likewise I've noted that, when I started, I was close to my students' age.

In my first year back, for instance, I taught two students who'd been freshman friends when I left for England (they'd had to be privately asked not to call me "Reynolds" in the presence of the class). But at the end of three years, I seemed a light-year older than eighteen or twenty-one. By then I no longer felt like a fraud when students addressed me as Professor Price, despite the fact that I wasn't yet a professor. And any interest I'd retained in their private lives or social activities had drastically faded. Even an invitation to my old fraternity's annual homecoming barbecue was easily declinable. If I went I'd stand awkwardly at the edge of the jollifications, knowing almost no one and addressed as "sir" by any student who felt a well-bred responsibility to involve me in the fun. And the fun at Duke, even as late as the early 1960s, was dry—the slightest drop of alcohol on campus could result in expulsion from the university and was thus nowhere near the student obsession it is now in the sodden years of the early third millennium when we graduate numerous firmly established alcoholics each year.

Late in those first years, I'd begun to feel increasingly like a teacher of the sort who'd meant something to me in my own student years; and some of the skills involved proved invisible but urgent—a sane awareness of how much energy to devote to an average lecture or conference, an understanding of which students were eager to toy with my office hours and which were genuinely interested in learning. Finally I began to establish which departmental duties—committees and meetings—could be briskly dispatched and which were truly useful, to the department's necessary work, to the health of my own teaching life, and to my growing comprehension of the degree to which an academic department in a fine university is often no more benign or intellectually respectable than, say, a division of Chrysler Motors (a few years ago, I asked a president of Duke who was then a close friend to tell me the difference between presiding over Duke or over Ford Motor Company; he said "At Ford, you can fire someone").

Lest any of that seem excessively cool and careerist, I should add how thoroughly I enjoyed the demands of those early classes, how I loved exploring poems and novels I'd long admired with students to whom they were as foreign as Tibetan sacred texts, and what a sense of reward I got from struggling to guide a number of my students into the writing of clear and accurate American English prose (though I'll have to confess that the teaching of writing became increasingly unlikable as the years passed, and students came to us from widely spread American high schools that had essentially abandoned any such instruction).

It would still be difficult for me to imagine a literate adult who couldn't be excited by the challenge of working with a roomful of post-adolescents as they first encounter Shakespeare's *King Lear* (the classic study of a dilemma so many of them will encounter when their own parents age into dementia) or Conrad's *Heart of Darkness* (the great fictional study of the ravages of Western colonialism and the perhaps endless hatred we've earned as nations who lied and murdered our way to the natural riches belonging to other people). Almost from the first week, I began to see how the teaching of a good text could quickly become a new and especially rewarding means of reading it. To this day, I think I've never quite plumbed the depths of many novels, plays, and poems more deeply than those I studied, hard, to feel fit to teach in those early years.

Further, my colleagues and I—and a few enthusiastic students—organized something I can hardly imagine my Critical Theory–obsessed colleagues considering now: we rehearsed and performed, one night, a book-in-hand reading of *King Lear*. Blackburn, with his rumbling bishop's voice, was our Lear; I was Gloucester. And all the roles were well-enough cast to detain a full-house audience of students and faculty for the nearly four hours a complete reading took. I can still resummon the excitement I felt, driving home alone near midnight. Writing was still very much my chief vocation, but teaching was surely my love.

And by the time I reached my own late twenties, I'd begun to be aware of the degree to which my own love of teaching was a legacy of my love of almost all my own past teachers, from the first grade through three years of graduate study. For me, most of those women and men worked before and among us students in an unparalleled aura of serious virtue. I never had an athletic coach; but I'm sure that no whistling mentor could have mattered more to me than devoted women like Jennie Alston and Crichton Davis in grade school, the dizzy but profoundly gifted Phyllis Peacock in high school, the monkish Harold Parker at Duke, or the worldly yet entirely committed David Cecil, Nevill Coghill, and Helen Gardner at Oxford.

As I moved more deeply into teaching, I became aware of another pleasure of the job and its most solemn duty. From the time I was six or seven, I'd been an intensely—but independently—religious boy and man. I had brief stretches, in adolescence and early manhood, of commitment to organized Christianity—to churchgoing as a chief means of worshiping the God I perceived in nature and daily life. But as I've noted above, that formal commitment had disappeared by the time I left home for England.

My teaching, however, slowly became my primary means of attempting to practice the life of a good man, a responsible child of God. My fiction has never concerned itself outright with religious realities, and I'm not aware of passages in that fiction which have conscious designs on a reader's religious sensibilities, though a few of my poems may. But since the curriculum assigned to me in my first years at Duke offered an entire semester each year in which I was to expound the work of four of the supreme religious poets of the English (or any other) language—Chaucer, Shakespeare, Donne, and Milton—I could hardly avoid hinting at my own convictions.

Not that I did so overtly, far from it. I've never detected a missionary gene in my biochemical battery, but a work like Chaucer's *Pardoner's Tale* or Shakespeare's *The Tempest* or Milton's "Lycidas" aroused in me degrees of enthusiasm that might well not have surfaced had the writers themselves not invested profound religious thought in their work. They were each thinking steadily about not only the official expressions of belief available in the time we have, but also the literal mysteries of faith and doubt—who or what made us, for what purpose, and what does it propose to do with us in response to the choices we make in our few decades of conscious life? Most central of all, I'd try to raise Leibniz's troubling question—"Why is there something and not nothing?"

I'd been a student recently enough to know that few questions interest young readers more than those. Once a teacher has familiarized himself with the content of a poem, his next problem as the guide of class discussion is how to involve students in noting the physical structure of a work—its form of language, the strategy of its storytelling, and its ultimate design upon an audience. Third, he needs an aptitude for whatever forms of honest yet entertaining footwork he can devise to beckon the class into an exhilarating, and finally instructive, look at a sizable subject—a subject as large as, say, Shakespeare's assertion (in the mouth of Edgar toward the end of *King Lear*) that "ripeness is all" or Milton's declared effort, near the start of *Paradise Lost*, to "justify the ways of God to men."

So while I acknowledge that those mysteries have propelled my work most potently in my years of teaching, it's worth adding that I've never thought of myself as any sort of priest in hiding; and I've seldom been free of grave human error. Even when I've taught a seminar in the Gospels of Mark and John, I've resisted the attempt by a few Christian class-members to enlist my admission of brotherhood. In the seminar room my aim is to guide them through as clear an understanding as possible of the career of a man called Jesus of Nazareth who lived in an obscure corner of the Roman empire in the first century A.D. and whose acts and teachings are most reliably preserved in those two narratives—Mark being, almost surely, the oldest of the canonical four gospels and John being the one which seems most certainly to enclose the memories (no doubt highly edited and expanded) of a man who witnessed the life of Jesus at close hand and who describes himself as "the man whom Jesus loved." Should a student decide to worship Jesus as the incarnation of God, that decision is an act in which I don't participate. In discussions of *Paradise Lost* and the long career of John Milton—which includes total blindness at about age forty-three—I feel freer to come down on one side or the other in those theological debates which arise in the poet's retelling of the story of Adam and Eve; and that freedom derives from the fact that Milton makes no specific demand for the reader's faith or even his agreement, only his focused attention and a ruthlessly honed intelligence.

Those descriptions of my early teaching are true, not only to my own feelings at the time but also to a certain 1950s spiritual fervor that many young men (and a relative few career-seeking women) invested in their careers and, in return, seemed to derive from them. Almost a decade before I'd taught my first class, I joined in a panel discussion of English teaching at Meredith College in Raleigh. My teacher

Mrs. Peacock had asked me to be there; and my brief remarks—published in *The North Carolina English Teacher*—are an accurate forecast of a strain of feeling that would fortify me through my apprentice years. The peroration from my little speech may sound at least mildly absurd now but I'll own up.

> Dryden said, "By education most have been misled" . . . The effectiveness of English teaching is in direct ratio to the teacher's ability to bring students to the realization that English is life. The teacher must take his subject out of the classroom and into the world, for English is not a subject. It is life. So long as we remain heirs of the English heritage, whether we speak, think, act, see, or hear, we must use the English language—and we must employ it with accuracy, intelligence, and understanding. Socrates said, "The soul takes nothing with her to the other world but her education and culture; and these, it is said, are of the greatest injury to the dead man at the very beginning of his journey thither." . . . And you have souls in your hands.

I was seventeen years old, and my audience consisted of teachers from nearby high schools and junior colleges. If one of them snickered, she had the kindness to conceal her amusement—*What can this boy know of the endless drain of a job as demanding as the job of a celibate priest? And all for wages that are often less than the pay of a yard man, a janitor, or the coach of a middle-school football team.*

In my three weekly days of writing, the ability to sit at home and work steadily also improved. My first published story after returning was "Troubled Sleep," an imagined narrative suggested by Nevill Coghill's inaugural lecture as Merton professor. It appeared in *Encounter* in April '59; and the sight of it in print—and a story in print feels very different from one in typescript or what we now call hard copy—further strengthened my sense of possibility. Not only might I become a professional writer, now I was one—paid for my work in an internationally respected magazine, read by strangers with extraordinary standards of judgment (standards which they'd begun revealing to me in frequent letters).

That appearance came a little more than a year before my three-year contract with Duke was set to expire, and by then I'd begun planning a yearlong return to Oxford. With a small monthly contribution to my savings, I figured I'd have $3,000 ($21,000 now) to fund a year's work on a D.Phil. I've noted that David Cecil had agreed to resume direction of the degree; and Nevill, among a few other friends, was ready to welcome me. Better still, on the evidence of frequent letters, my expectation of resuming some form of close relation with Matyas was pitched high. Meanwhile I pressed on with my teaching as *A Long and Happy Life* neared the ending I'd foreseen as long ago as January '57. The manuscript of that one story was nearing two hundred pages; yet because, from the start, I'd thought of the narrative as the final piece in a volume of stories, I continued to think that what I'd soon be submitting for publication would be a volume of five short stories and a concluding novella.

My notes for the long story give no indication of when I thought I'd be done with *A Long and Happy Life*; but I know I shipped off the manuscript with excited pride late in '60, a little more than two years after the start. And I have a note of receipt from Diarmuid, dated December 20, 1960. He said that he'd forward the manuscript immediately to Jason Epstein at Random House (Hiram Haydn, who'd given me the original contract for a book of stories, had by then become one of the three founders of a first-rate publishing house called Atheneum). When Diarmuid had read the whole ms., he sent me a longer message on December 27.

> I read the long story, and I must say I think it's very good. The only fault that occurs to me is that [it] is long enough to be a novel, and it does rather unbalance the other stories, and it might be better to consider offering the long story as a novel and waiting for more short stories to come along to round out a story collection? Will you let me know how you feel about this?

*   *   *

On the thirtieth I responded at length, objecting strenuously.

> *. . . the five stories and the novel are a* book, *not a miscellany. After the first story, they were written quite consciously as a whole book. Their themes are intimately connected, over-lapping, mutually enriching, I think; and they are arranged in an antiphonal way—one story raises questions which another considers and sometimes answers. I hope you won't think all this is narcissistic mystification. I could outline what I mean in considerable detail if you asked me to . . . but I'll stop with saying that* A Long and Happy Life *is the title of the whole book—there are two stories about young children, one about adolescence, two about youth, two about great age.* [I was confused then as to the number of stories.]

Matters moved far more rapidly thereafter than they might today. On January 13 Diarmuid had a letter from Jason Epstein that said, in part . . . *neither Bob Loomis nor I liked the Reynolds Price. We thought it lost itself in its language: that the characters never emerged from the sea of words.*

When he forwarded the news, Diarmuid trimmed off the remainder of Epstein's letter (it discussed the work of other writers whom Diarmuid represented). When I got the portion pertaining to me, I went straight to Bill Blackburn's office to share it with him (Bob Loomis had been a student of Bill's only a few years before me, though I'd never met him).

I was disappointed. Random House was a well-stocked publisher in midcentury America, far more so than now—though Jason Epstein was hardly the Grand Panjandrum he'd become for a while before retiring (I'd never heard of him till I received his message to Diarmuid)—and I was a fledgling who'd swanked it coolly among his friends for the past three years, claiming he had a contract with Random House. But maybe because Hiram had continued to express an interest in bringing me to his new house, Atheneum, I was hardly devastated. I honestly believed—hell, I knew—that Loomis and Epstein were flat wrong about my prose and the characters it projected. And Blackburn confirmed me in my hope that Haydn, whom I'd never met, would bail me and my stories out.

So he did. Little more than two weeks later, Diarmuid wrote again, in his winning but often barely readable script. *Hiram just called to say wonderful—but he and his other allies are going to raise the question of doing the long item as a novel first—so pending this discussion the contract can wait. As you know, I'm very strongly for this move, for I think it will aid your reputation more.*

As compared with Loomis and Epstein at the time, Hiram and one of his allies—Simon Michael Bessie—were decidedly tall senior figures in American publishing; and to cut short a longish discussion (all blessedly conducted by letter, no telephone pressure), I eventually saw the wisdom of culling out the long story, publishing it as the novel I'd been so slow to recognize, and then saving my short stories for a second book. Chatto and Windus had also worried about the combination of stories and novel and were relieved when I agreed to the separation.

With spring, there were rapidly gathering encouragements. The fact that Atheneum was a young house with relatively few authors on its roster meant that I received extraordinarily close attention from their superb staff. Hermann Ziegner presided over the preparation of the manuscript and wrote me whenever he, or any other in-house reader, questioned my merest comma—no high-handed copyediting whatever (I'd heard nightmarish tales of such treatment at some other houses and at least one famous magazine, *The New Yorker*). And Harry Ford, who'd come from Alfred Knopf and was already a much-admired book designer, enveloped me from the start in his plans for the book's typography, the full-cloth binding, the jacket drawing, and a good deal else. Though I'd yet to meet anyone in the firm, almost all of them had gone to considerable early lengths to express their enthusiasm for the novel.

And Hiram Haydn—who was incidentally a Ph.D. in literature, the ongoing editor of *The American Scholar*, and himself the author of more than one admirable novel—stayed in steady touch, with each piece of news on the manuscript's progress. Some three years ahead, he'd prove a more paternal editor than I was comfortable with; but he literally never forced any of his suggestions upon me. And when it came to editing, I can recall only a single question from him. Early in the process, he wrote to say that on a certain page it seemed to him that, for a moment, I'd altered my third-person point of view—was the change intentional? I replied that it was, and I tried to tell him why; he was satisfied. Otherwise in the entire prepublication process, there was only one real crisis. All these years later I've still never met another serious young writer who'd gone to a good house, large or small, and met with such a warm and patient yet discriminating welcome. I suspected I was lucky—Diarmuid, who was hardly given to flattery in any direction, told me I was—and I tried to show my awareness of the great good fortune lavished on me.

The one hitch in a phenomenally smooth voyage came when I heard in 1961 from Atheneum's lawyer, the then-young but eventually noted Alan U. Schwartz. Hiram had asked him to vet the manuscript for possible libel or privacy problems. Only a first-time author's naïveté had kept me from telling Atheneum at once that I'd unconsciously adopted, for the name of my central male character, the name of a well-known citizen of Durham. Even I was made aware of the problem only when Bill Blackburn eventually said to me "I trust you've got Mr. Wesley Beavers's permission to use his name." Well, of course I hadn't. Who *was* Mr. Beavers?—and incidentally the word *beaver* had not then acquired widespread meaning in the South as the female genital. It soon appeared that the living Mr. Beavers was a realtor at the prime real-estate agency in town. I must have subliminally acquired his name from the local paper, maybe from an ad. And Alan Schwartz carefully and sympathetically outlined for me the legal problems that might arise from using the name (he was exactly my age and very much a junior man in a famous literary-law firm, but he's gone on to be an enormous success).

New York state had a statute covering invasions of privacy; and since the book would be published in New York, it was likely that any suit against me for the use of a real person's name would probably be filed in New York (is it possible to invent a credible name that someone doesn't possess?). The fact that Mr. Beavers had not already sued for his name's appearance in *Encounter* for instance or in the O. Henry volume was no indication of what he might do in the future. Schwartz went on to explain that if I could find several other men of the same name in the area of my story "your position would be improved" but no more than that. I'd previously suggested the possibility of getting Mr. Beavers's consent for the use of his name.

But Schwartz said "an attempt to procure his consent is risky because it certainly will draw his attention to the book." At that point, my lawyer had reached his expected lawyerly conclusion—"I, for one, would be much happier if you could change his name to some name not as indigenous to the locale of this book. This may seem like a harsh conclusion but experience has demonstrated that in this field at least prevention is much less costly than the cure." Fairly aghast by then, on Schwartz's sympathetic suggestion I spent hours searching the Duke Library's vast collection of phone directories. If there was another Wesley Beavers in the United States, he seemed to have no listed number.

But as I thought more intensely about my lawyer's "harsh conclusion," it seemed impossible to accept. My character had been named Wesley Beavers since he first appeared in "A Chain of Love" which I'd written in 1955. To change his name now, six years later, would be like changing my own name at my advanced age (the fact that so many Hollywood stars had accepted name changes from their employers had always seemed unimaginable—Lucille LeSueur becoming Joan Crawford, Marion Morrison becoming John Wayne).

No one at Atheneum, nor Diarmuid Russell, brought any pressure on me for a solution. So at last I asked Alan Schwartz to send me an uncomplicated permission form; I'd beard Mr. Beavers in his den at the realty company and throw myself on his mercy. I should have known of course that no responsible lawyer is capable of writing a simple form; but at least Schwartz sent me a several-page form in which Mr. Beavers sold me the use of his name, forever, for the sum of one dollar.

I phoned Mr. Beavers for an appointment and—very edgily—went to his office. Since I hadn't specified my business, he was likely expecting to meet a young Duke faculty member in the market for a house. At first sight I knew two things—Mr. Beavers was some thirty years older than I, and almost surely never read a novel. I accepted the chair he offered, in a courtly old-school manner, and proceeded to explain myself. I'd written a novel in which I named one of my main characters Wesley Beavers—somehow I'd acquired his name unconsciously (which was true). My character was a man in his early twenties from Warren County, N.C.; and my story involved his love relation with, and eventual commitment to, a girlfriend named Rosacoke Mustian.

Alan Schwartz had warned me against any temptation to offer Mr. Beavers a copy of my manuscript; and in fact I didn't mention Rosacoke's illegitimate pregnancy, a service offered to her by Wesley. That far, Mr. Beavers had listened patiently; so next I smiled nervously and asked him to sign a permission form which I happened to have with me—"You know how these New York lawyers are . . ." Mr. Beavers had spent his life selling houses and land, so it was highly likely he'd had a good deal to do with lawyers well before I was born.

He took the form and leafed through it slowly. At last he looked up and said "Mr. Price, I'm not a famous man. My name is not going to do your book a bit of good." Again, I tried to explain my dilemma as simply as possible—I'd been using his name for years, benignly; it would be very hard now for me to change it. He read the last page of the form again, where he sells me the use of his name forever for the sum of one dollar. Then he looked up and said "Call me in a few days, hear?—and I'll let you know what I can do with this."

My heart sank of course but I rose, thanked him, and asked when I should phone. He said "Let's see—today's Wednesday. We've got a lawyer here in the office; I'll ask him to look this over. Call me next Wednesday." A whole week, God! My heart plunged through the floorboards. Yet I could hardly ask him to hurry.

After a week's hard waiting, though, I phoned again; and the real Wesley Beavers said "Sure, I'll sign your paper. Come on down here this afternoon." Quickly I phoned Alan Schwartz in New York. With inevitable caution, he said "Fine—we *hope*. Go down but take a witness, and be *sure* he accepts the dollar specified in the agreement. If he refuses it—and he may try, being the wily old trader you say he is—the permission is void. And before you go down, record the serial number of the dollar you'll give him." I co-opted one of the English department secretaries—a woman named Barbara Skipper; her beautiful young face would surely be a help—and down we went in my still-trusty Beetle.

Mr. Beavers greeted us almost cheerfully and proceeded to sign the form which Barbara witnessed with her signature just below his. Then I tried to hand the man his dollar. He waved it off—"Oh keep your dollar, boy. *Keep* it." I'm sure he knew what he was attempting to do; but I persisted and, while he stood frozen with his hands at his sides, I actually reached forward to deposit the dollar in his shirt pocket. He didn't stop me. The right to my Wesley's name was now assured; and the relief was enormous (I'd still had no luck whatever in finding a substitute name; and not so long ago, I found my record of the serial number of that crucial dollar among some ancient papers in the depths of a drawer).

The remainder of that spring and early summer were busy with a good many concerns that lay beyond the novel. My teaching continued. In the freshman course we were now reading modern poems, poets who ranged from Gerard Manley Hopkins to Frost and Auden. And in the sophomore survey, I was guiding the class through long stretches of British and Irish poetry that ranged from the work of Pope and Wordsworth on through Keats and finally Yeats. Almost none of the poems was new to me but the chance to discuss them with a class of some thirty upperclassmen—a good many of whom were more than intelligent and ready to talk—was again illuminating.

Among other revelations came the understanding that, not yet but a little later, I myself would very much need to return to the writing of poems—poems that could absorb and clarify elations and mysteries in my own daily life, emotions that could not be imported directly into my fiction. For all my love of prose narrative, and my thanks for the good it's done in my life, I've never once doubted that the higher art, just behind music, is poetry; and the help it's given me—in the reading and writing—has seldom been less than enormous.

Among my concerns were the ongoing arrangements of a forthcoming year in England. And as my hopes for returning to Oxford solidified, I wrote to the Principal of the Postmasters at Merton and asked if there was a chance I could spend the summer in my old rooms in Mob Quad. He replied at once to say that my request presented no apparent problem and that, further, I'd be made a member of the high table for the summer and Michaelmas term. Such a generosity was surprising, even for those gentler times—the savings on food and drink would be large; and the pittance I'd be charged for the two rooms was negligible. Further—and lo!—showers had been installed in Bill Jackson's old scout's pantry on the ground floor of Mob, though the bogs remained in their old position—against the south side of the chapel.

7

T HE SOLUTION to another very serious concern remains mysterious to me, and my files don't offer a full explanation nor does my memory. I've mentioned, more than once, that I and my colleagues had been hired on three-year nonrenewable contracts. Yet at some point in our third year, Arlin Turner—our new chairman who was hard at work on his Hawthorne biography—let the instructors know that all eight or nine of us would be offered a fourth year to search out another job for ourselves when our Duke appointment ended. That dispensation, standard enough in academia, didn't appear to affect me since I'd be in England for that extra year. So I went to Professor Turner to inquire as to whether I'd be given one more year's employment on my return from England. I specified that I'd be spending that year in Oxford, hard at work on the D.Phil. which I'd already commenced.

Turner was a shy and secretive man but courteous. Once I'd explained myself, he looked across his desk at me slowly and then said "Why do you think you need a doctorate?"

It was a little as though God had said "Why do you think you'll need oxygen from this moment onward?" I replied that I'd hoped, for more than ten years, to spend a great part of my life teaching in a university and that I assumed a doctorate was the indispensable union card for such an intent.

Turner thought for another long moment and then said "Reynolds, if you go on writing fiction of the quality you've produced in recent years; and if it goes on meeting with such critical welcome, I can't see why a doctorate would be required for you to continue a teaching life at Duke."

The newness of such a thought was again overwhelming; yet Turner was a highly respected member of the scholarly guild and chairman of a large department at what was then considered the prime university in the American South—one with increasingly warm ambitions to stand even higher in the list of American universities. So he plainly wasn't lying.

We talked another few minutes (a ten-minute professional talk with Turner was a relative eternity). And by the time I was on the way back to my office, I was seeing how I could—that very day, if I chose—abandon my plans for an Oxford doctorate, though I'd go on planning to revisit my old rooms in Merton, reigniting a strong relation with Matyas while I wrote however many more stories I'd need to complete a volume—my second book. One way or another, I thought I had enough ideas to keep me busy; and I'd need to be occupied steadily enough to combat the Thames Valley blues.

A further encouragement lay in the fact that my friend Wally Kaufman had recently won a generous Marshall Fellowship for two years of study in Britain. He'd applied to Merton, been accepted, and should be arriving a few weeks after me for a B.Litt. thesis on

Wordsworth. I've generally been a slow responder to titanic psychic events in my life, so the elation attendant on the actual discovery that I was now liberated from a doctoral degree only dawned on me over the weeks it took to get me back onto the surface of the North Atlantic.

My third year of courses—with all the last rounds of freshman themes, upper-class term papers, and final exams from them all—would end in early June 1961. I'd booked my passage to England long ago—the old *Queen Mary* again, sailing from New York on July 13—and had only some five weeks left for preparations. Given the uncertainty of my plans at the end of the forthcoming year, I felt I had no choice but to vacate my much-loved trailer beside its pond (Mr. May had never raised my original forty-five-dollar rent). So once again I turned to the packing—would I ever settle in a single place and live there forever?

I was lucky that Mother's basement could easily absorb my dozen-odd cartons of books, records, pictures, and clothes. By early July then I'd slowly moved almost all my boxes to Raleigh; and not at all incidentally, I'd spent as much time as possible with her and Bill. By then my brother had just completed his sophomore year at Duke, and Mother was continuing her job in the boys' clothing store. While her salary was still small for the hours she invested (always upright), the chance to see her old friends as they visited the store was patently good for her spirits, as she readily acknowledged. When I'd mention the hope that, should my novel succeed, I might be able to retire her, she'd always laugh and fend off the notion—"But son, what would I do with the time?" Well, I had no serious alternate life to offer anyone who savored independence, on however slim a budget, as intensely as Elizabeth Price.

After I'd accumulated more than four years of astonishingly reliable service from my Volkswagen Beetle, I was planning to leave it for Bill. When I was back I could either reclaim it or, money permitting, buy something new. Meanwhile I made several trips to Warren County for meetings with Aunt Ida in Macon and my three Price aunts in Warrenton. By then Ida was in her early seventies and was living alone since Uncle Marvin's death. In the same Rodwell house in which she'd by now spent most of her life, she seemed as at-home as any deer in the woods; and the house itself was the world's most welcoming to my heart and mind. I'd always sleep in the far bedroom, in the space and on the iron bed in which I'd been born twenty-eight years before.

After a modest supper Ida and I would sit in our accustomed swing on the front porch, and the evening would slowly darken around us in its indigo way. The apparently immortal whippoorwill would commence its maddeningly repetitive call across the road—maddening but indispensable. The house just behind us was quiet as the earth that would one day enfold it, with all its freight of love and tragedy— the deaths of both my maternal grandparents at early ages, of one of their children in infancy, the orphaned sadness of my mother's girl-hood and who knew what other broken hearts among a houseload of children, my own hard birth, and Ida's ten-year suicidal depression (she jumped from a rapidly moving car, took a hard head wound, but survived and very slowly recovered).

And as Ida answered my latest question about our history, I'd occasionally take my—for now—maybe final glances at her face. Was this our last meeting? Who or what or where might she be a year from now, assuming I returned to this spot in safety? In any case, here we affirmed our unquestioned devotion in words about others (all of them kinfolk), in chuckles that eventually silenced themselves while sleep advanced from beyond the oaks we could no longer see at the edge of the yard when darkness at last perfected itself.

On July 2, less than two weeks before my departure from Raleigh, the radio announced that Ernest Hemingway had just killed himself by gunshot in Ketchum, Idaho. He was only three weeks from the age of sixty-two and had been not only far the most famous writer of my life-time but one whose work—since I began to read it in high school—had been of central importance to my own. A decade after his death, I'd write a long essay called "For Ernest Hemingway." It was both an attempt to describe what was supreme in the work of a writer who, in the shadow of his death, had begun to be picked at by the sharks whom he'd long foreseen in *The Old Man and the Sea* and also an effort to understand his meaning to me, both my life and my work. After a visit to the handsome old house in Key West, which he'd abandoned after his second divorce, I realized that what had moved me most—from my early adolescence till now—was the often concealed voice of a badly wounded man. All Hemingway's much-publicized swagger, at the edges of Spanish bullrings or in the midst of the world's saloons, could not entirely conceal that pain and its outcry. And my early discovery of its presence in words—the words he'd taught so many other readers and writers to use as if it were the speech of our tribe—had strengthened me to know what language itself could do for a private pain.

Michael Bessie at Atheneum had told me, some weeks before Hemingway's death, that he'd managed to get a copy of the proofs of *A Long and Happy Life* to the great man; perhaps he might read it and say a word to help us. I well understood that the likelihood was hardly existent. What man of my own generation, though, would not have been roused at the thought that a story of his own might have gone past the eyes of such a master—one who might just speak up? Is it too absurd to recall, here nearly fifty years later, that one of my first thoughts at the news of Hemingway's awful death was the realization that, if my novel had ever reached him, it hadn't saved his life? He'd valued good work after all, at whatever honest trade, more highly than anything else in his life—indeed in the world. Still, like so many other members of his immediate tormented family, he'd chosen to end the pain in violent refusal. His last wife Mary would later say that, for long months afterward, she'd picked bits of skull out of the wall behind his last shot.

On the grand old overnight Silver Meteor, on the Seaboard Air Line Railroad from Raleigh to the imperiled glories of Penn Station, I got myself to New York a few days before my sailing date; and after a good night's sleep at the Taft, I had my first experience of what was then politely called (though never by Eudora Welty) the drunch with Diarmuid. *Drunch* of course meant "drunken lunch," and so it was for me—Diarmuid maintained the self-possession of Achilles on the plains of Troy. We each drank three virtually pint-sized martinis, talked of my excellent luck so far, and said a good deal about our mutual friend Eudora. We were worried about her, pinned down at home by a mother who'd been ill now for at least five years (the woman whom Diarmuid and I didn't know, but suspected of being a termagant, was nonetheless loved to the furthest point by Eudora). As I've said, Diarmuid was the son of the Irish mystic poet Æ, a lifelong intimate friend of Yeats and numerous others from the Celtic revival's flowering of poetry and drama in the early years of the twentieth century. And with no air whatever of showing off, Diarmuid had good stories of the famous modern Celts. The great Lady Gregory for instance had given the young boy Diarmuid a gold watch for his birthday but concealed it on her person. It was up to the child to frisk her thoroughly and find the gift, which he did, though (as he told me) "There was rather a lot of Aunt Augusta to search."

My favorite—and a chillier tale—was his story of approaching William Butler Yeats about Diarmuid's father's funeral. George Russell had died in England but been brought to Dublin for burial. Mrs. Russell simply said to my eventual agent "Diarmuid, step round to Willie's and ask him to give the eulogy at your father's funeral." When Diarmuid got to Uncle Willie's, the poet was still in bed, reading proof. Russell and Yeats had been friends since early manhood and were close companions in much of their work. So Diarmuid delivered his mother's message; Yeats read another line of proof, looked up, and said "Oh Diarmuid, tell your mother I'm afraid I won't have time to do meself justice." Æ was buried then without words from Willie; and it was not long after that Diarmuid chose to come to the States for the rest of his life.

One of his many Irish stories—generally elicited by questions from me, who'd taught Yeats's poems for the past three years—would be told with a kind of stony glee from Diarmuid, by then on his second or third martini (and I recount them here strictly from memory, with no earlier notes to support my confidence). Diarmuid's tales of chicanery or foolery in contemporary publishing were offered with similar level-headed emotion, though God knows how. When his and Eudora's correspondence was eventually published, it became clear that she'd been a writer-and-client of special (though noncommercial) value to him and the agency in its earliest days. But when he and I spoke of her through the drunches of the next long decade, his concern for Eudora and the fact that he felt she was overburdened at her mother's querulous bedside was apparent; yet what he never showed in our conversations was any clear degree of affection for Eudora—or any other client.

Though thoroughly Irish, Diarmuid's emotional reserve in conversation was unbroken. Perhaps it was merely reserve; perhaps he was incapable of displaying the sort of feeling that might have been expected of one who'd done Eudora, and others, such loyal service—Eudora's gratitude and affection, for instance, was literally boundless; and she never entirely recovered from his death as she showed quite plainly in our own frequent talks so long as her memory could express itself (several years after his death, when I was well past forty, she suddenly rebuked me for not attending his funeral in Bedford, New York during Christmas week of 1973).

Despite their long closeness—and Eudora's many visits to Diarmuid and Rosie Russell's home near Katonah, New York (I accompanied her there for one happily uproarious overnight stay)—Diarmuid never visited Eudora in her home till well after he knew he was dying of lung cancer. Then he flew down with Rosie for a typically over-the-top Mississippi celebration of Eudora's work. I was there too and quickly saw that he'd gone beyond any desire to converse. But my awareness of the care that Eudora took of his fragile state, in the midst of so much ballyhoo, was silently touching.

The sight of a much-reduced Diarmuid attending the social events of that weekend was more than poignant—the cancer had sculpted his hawk head to the literal bone, like an object washed for years by a harsh sea. It was still capable, though, of meeting my gaze across a crowded and twittering room of club ladies with a very slow and narrow-eyed but closed-lip smile. By then he'd after all guided my career for nearly twenty years with seamless wisdom and—rarest of all, then and now—a same-day-received response to all letters and a courteously fierce will to defend me at any time he felt my interests needed such attention. And through it all I never heard an impatient word from him; nor (once I'd accepted his assurance that *A Long and Happy Life* was truly a novel) did I have another moment's resistance to his proffered, but never insisted upon, advice. Such literary agents were rare enough in his lifetime; now they are all but nonexistent.

On one of my few pre-embarkation afternoons, I went to meet Hiram Haydn at the first home of Atheneum in the '30s on the East Side; and he took me up and down the central staircase of the small converted residence and introduced me to virtually the entire staff—from his two partners down through the copyediting, design, and publicity departments. They all seemed likable human beings, as they'd already proved to be in correspondence; and their loyalty would continue for years to come (Hiram fell out with his partners in only a few years; and on Diarmuid's recommendation, I stayed at Atheneum when Hiram left for an unsatisfying stint at Harcourt Brace).

Later that afternoon Hiram, Harry Ford, and I walked to Grand Central where we boarded a train for Westport, Connecticut and were met at the station by Hiram's wife Mary—I'd be spending the night.

Mary was younger than Hiram and was a fellow North Carolinian; in fact I'd known one of her sisters since my childhood. In their likable home I had a half-hour to wash up, meet their teenaged son Michael, then head downstairs for outdoor drinks before dinner. Almost none of my present friends drinks the way a great many of us did, quite casually, in the 1960s; and there on a green-edged patio, Mary and Hiram and Harry and I drank a good deal and laughed till past summer-dark before going in for excellent food.

It was then that I had the first chance to begin really knowing Harry Ford who'd already designed my novel so elegantly. A small-scaled man, fifty-two years old, he was given in those days to a large-scaled enjoyment of his usual surroundings (his wife had stayed in New York). And in the course of the evening, I learned that Harry and I shared even more interests than I did with Hiram—poetry, music, and laughter above all. After his death in 1999 at the age of eighty, a knowledgeable mutual friend told me that Harry was born a bastard child and never knew a father. I'm unable to guarantee the assertion (and the mutual friend—the poet Anthony Hecht—has subsequently died); but if true, it could explain a number of the increasing difficulties Harry displayed in dealing with several of his male novelists and poets, me included eventually.

Yet it would be Harry with whom I continued my publishing career for twenty-six years more, till a much-changed Atheneum requested his departure; and he returned to Knopf. With all the warmth and thanks I feel for Harry's help—above all in our first twenty years when he and his second wife Kathleen, whom I really loved, would pay me an annual visit in Durham—I still have enduring gratitude for all that Hiram Haydn gave me and my work at the start. When I left him on Forty-second Street that July morning of '61, back in New York, Hiram assured me that, during my absence in England, he'd move Heaven and Hell for Rosacoke and Wesley; and with his tall frame and his huge beetle-browed head, he very nearly did.

On the day before sailing, I went alone to the first American showing of Luchino Visconti's masterpiece, the long film *Rocco and His Brothers*. It was not the first Visconti film I'd seen; but my own thoughts for the next long fiction were beginning to circle relentlessly round the idea of a multigenerational family novel, one which leaned on my own family's history. And while *Rocco* concerned itself with the tragedies confronting a family who come from southern Italy to crowded Milan, the film's complexities of love, loyalty, violence, and hate excited my ideas further (because they were so much like problems in my own extended family). It likewise introduced me to the work of a young actor—Alain Delon—who'd soon be the prime male star of Franco-Italian film. What was most surprising about Delon's work in *Rocco* was the fact that, through nearly three hours, he managed to portray a young man who is not only (of all things) a serenely beautiful prizefighter but also a kind of secular saint—and a thoroughly credible one at that.

With such a bold and ultimately productive memory, I boarded the *Queen Mary*. Nearly all I remember from my third eastward crossing is the nearly unbearable heat of my cabin, buried deep as it was in the hold, for the first two days at sea—it took that long for the New York swelter to be flushed out by cooler ocean air—the old ship was not air-conditioned. Five days of shipboard life—which must have included talks in the lounge with at least a few others, surely the immense heavy English meals and frequent naps—have failed to register in my memory. I recall a farewell glance back toward the Statue of Liberty and a renewed love of the ocean itself (the half-asleep monster that barely tolerated our passage and whom I felt I might have spent my whole life risking as some form of professional sailor), then a landing five days later at nine in the morning on a pier in Southampton—July 18, 1961, almost three years exactly since I'd last seen England.

Since I'd have no further worries involving graduate work—and would have no car and very little money—I was looking forward to unhurried meetings with my old friends (mainly David, Nevill, Tony Nuttall, and Win Kirkby in Oxford; Stephen and John Craxton in London, Anne Jordan in Brighton, and whatever new friends I'd meet wherever). The theatres of Stratford, London, and Oxford would be nearby—plus the better restaurants when I had the cash. And since Merton had generously said I could live in college for the whole year, I'd hope to spend a great deal of time on the short stories I'd begun to plan, to round out the volume that would be my second book. I even had dim ideas for a second novel.

In very few weeks, I'd be getting the first sets of proof on *A Long and Happy Life* from New York and London—the elegant slender galley proofs that we got in those years and then the smaller corrected page proofs that gave a young writer the last rousing sense of writing his book almost from scratch, though massive corrections could cost him a packet. I was already hoping to enlist Tony Nuttall with proof-reading help. He was married now, living in north Oxford, and starting work on his own D.Phil., supervised by Iris Murdoch after being refused by Helen Gardner.

With any luck, I'd hope to have the finished book in hand by early spring, some ten months before I was thirty years old. That hope, and the false expectation of frequent warm meetings with Matyas, were the strong cords that (through a bright day) literally drew my train on to Oxford, the only city in which I'd actually lived with all but unbroken pleasure for a bold stretch of years—and would do so again.

RP on the balcony of the Merton College boathouse, winter 1961, taken by Wallace Kaufman. I'm back in Oxford for a fourth year—a year that I thought would consist largely of writing a doctoral thesis or fiction of my own. The thesis proved unnecessary and was abandoned before I reached England, and very little fiction proved ready to be written so soon after my completion of *A Long and Happy Life*. I spent a good deal of time, then, with old friends like David Cecil, Nevill Coghill, Stephen Spender, and Tony Nuttall. My former student and friend Wally Kaufman was a student at Merton by then; and on one of our frequent walks round Christ Church Meadow—neither of us owned a car—Wally took this picture. The river is the Isis which ran past the Meadow, and I look unusually serious. Well, it's plainly a gray day.

REYNOLDS PRICE

In the summer after he published *A Long and Happy Life* in 1962, and won the William Faulkner Award, Reynolds Price returned to North Carolina where he's continued to teach and write. He's now published thirty-eight full-length volumes of fiction, poetry, plays, essays, and translations; and at last glance he still appeared to be at work. In 1963 his heroic mother rapidly began to lose her eyesight, the result of two cerebral aneurysms; and despite surgery to repair the condition, one of the aneurysms ruptured. She died suddenly in the spring of 1965. Soon after that, Price's brother Bill served in the navy for three years, with a year's duty in Vietnam aboard an LST landing craft which had already served in the invasion of Normandy in 1944 (it was also the ship in which Bill had sailed from Virginia to Vietnam).

With the profit from a never-produced screenplay, Price bought a sizable dwelling near the trailer/house where he'd completed his first books. He continued to work alone in the new house, surrounded by the same trees and animals. He was likewise visited by many friends and occasional loves, none of whom proved residential. In 1984 a large malignant tumor was discovered in his spinal cord; and after radiation and four surgeries at the hands of the miraculous Dr. Allan Friedman, he settled into full-time wheelchair life. The demands of a disabled existence made it necessary to add accessible quarters to his house; so ever since, he's continued life there with the steady help of a generally benign series of live-in assistants.

Kate Vaiden, the novel he was writing when his cancer manifested itself, was published in 1986 and won the National Book Critics Circle Award. Ensuing years have seen him publish—among numerous other books—*A Perfect Friend*, his first novel for children and adults; large collections of his short stories and poems; and a gathering of fifty-odd commentaries which he'd broadcast on National Public Radio. His time since the early 1980s has included national productions of his six plays—including *Private Contentment*, a script commissioned for PBS's first season of *American Playhouse*. His dramatic trilogy *New Music*, the forty-year history of a family, premiered at the Cleveland Playhouse in a production that permitted audiences to see all three plays in a single long afternoon and evening or on three consecutive evenings. And his *Full Moon*, originally commissioned by Duke Drama, appeared at San Francisco's American Conservatory Theater.

In 1988 he was inducted into the American Academy of Arts and Letters, his work has been translated into seventeen languages; and in the fall of 2008, he marked the fiftieth anniversary of his ongoing teaching at Duke.

INDEX